Sports Mania

Essays on Fandom and the Media in the 21st Century

Edited by
Lawrence W. Hugenberg,
Paul M. Haridakis,
and Adam C. Earnheardt

McFarland & Company, Inc., Publishers
Jefferson, North Carolina, and London

LIBRARY OF CONGRESS CATALOGUING-IN-PUBLICATION DATA

Sports mania: essays on fandom and the media in the 21st century
/ edited by Lawrence W. Hugenberg, Paul M. Haridakis and
Adam C. Earnheardt.
    p.   cm.
    Includes bibliographical references and index.

    ISBN 978-0-7864-3726-9
    softcover : 50# alkaline paper ∞

    1. Mass media and sports.   2. Sports spectators— Social aspects.
3. Sports spectators— Psychology.   I. Hugenberg, Lawrence W.
II. Haridakis, Paul M., 1957–   III. Earnheardt, Adam C., 1970–
GV742.S673   2008
306.4'83 — dc22   2008023091

British Library cataloguing data are available

Cover Images: ©2008 Shutterstock

Manufactured in the United States of America

*McFarland & Company, Inc., Publishers
    Box 611, Jefferson, North Carolina 28640
    www.mcfarlandpub.com*

Table of Contents

FAN IDENTIFICATION

FAN MOTIVES

FAN-PRODUCED CONTENT

Preface

Undoubtedly like those of you reading this preface, the editors of this anthology like sports. In fact, we are fans of sports, athletes, and teams. We watch sports on television, access sports news and information online, and talk to our friends and family about sports. Because of our fascination with sports and our own levels of fandom, we have an intense interest in research related to sports fandom and sports media. Conducting sports fandom and media research for us is an engaging experience, almost as much as watching football on Sunday afternoons or staying up late to catch the most recent sports news on ESPN's SportsCenter.

The basic purpose of this book is to be one of the first "out of the gate" to cater to this intense interest and to offer state-of-knowledge research pertaining to an array of issues centering on sports fandom and the media. Accordingly, we recruited some of the preeminent scholars in sports communication research to write chapters pertaining to their respective areas of expertise. Our hope is that this book stimulates further exploration into one of the most salient cultural products of the 21st century: sports fandom.

What initially attracted us to this topic were the various classifications for and definitions of fandom. Even among the three coeditors, there was some discussion (and a few disagreements) about how to best classify fans. We know, for example, that the term "sports fandom" creates different meanings for people. What we wanted to explore with this anthology was how sports fandom symbolizes more than fascination or fanaticism. If people classify themselves into different groups, it is just as likely that people classify themselves based on levels of fanship.

This book is important because it examines the various manifestations of sports fandom as well as the effect of fandom on sports media use and discussion about sports. This examination takes place through a variety of lenses. From the use of television to mediate the sports experience to the use of the Internet in cultivating fan-athlete relationships, this book offers a glimpse into the role media play in nurturing the sports fan.

Although some recent scholarship in the form of journal articles has explored the impact of sports fandom and the media, few books exist that examine the role of sports in society and even fewer have touched on the concept of sports fandom. When sports fandom is examined within these texts, it is usually done so with limited scope and relegated to a chapter in the back of the book. For example, not since Lisa Lewis's (1992) edited book *The adoring audience: Fan culture and popular media* have scholars explored, at length, the nature of fandom.

We realized early in this process that there is a great need for an anthology that explores sports fandom and the media. This need is evidenced by the groundswell of support for this type of research in the major communication associations. For example, there is growing support for the inclusion of a sports communication division in the National Communication Association (NCA). Dozens of panels during the recent NCA conventions were devoted to sports related themes, several of which focused primarily on sports fandom. Likewise, the International Communication Association welcomed several papers related to sports and fandom during recent conventions. The Broadcast Education Association recently approved a sports communication division. Regional communication associations as well as associations in other disciplines (e.g., psychology, sociology, popular culture) often entertain sports fandom research during annual conferences. The interest in sports fandom and media studies continues to grow and attract new scholars. Our hope is that this book will contribute to this exploding research tradition.

The growth in communication technologies has expanded sports media environments and created new options for fans. This has altered the way sports are consumed, expanded fans' opportunities for discussing sports, and led to more research on fandom, behavior, and sports media use and effects. We note in the Introduction that this line of research has no disciplinary boundaries. As you read the following chapters you will be introduced to scholars and cutting-edge research from a variety of disciplines including communication, psychology, and sociology. You will be introduced to the new approaches taken to understand sports fandom and the media.

The genesis of this volume was the editors' realization of their shared interest in sports communication. The response from scholars in many disciplines wanting to participate in this project was overwhelming. Throughout the process, it has been our pleasure to work with each of the authors in getting manuscripts ready for publication. To each of our contributors, it has been an honor to work with you. Each editor would like to thank his wife for her patience and understanding. We would also like to thank Rekha Sharma, a doctoral student at Kent State, who worked as our editorial assistant on many of the chapters.

We are looking forward to working together on our next volume on sports communication, sports media, and sports fanship.

Larry Hugenberg • Paul Haridakis • Adam Earnheardt

Introduction

Fan. Fanatic. Enthusiast. Spectator. Many terms have been used to describe the varying degrees of fandom. These same terms often are used to describe the sports fan. The picture of the sports fan typically is captured by the media in throngs of rowdy crowds as face-painted fanatics clad in the colors of favorite teams. For many, however, sports fandom symbolizes more than fanaticism. Whereas critics have, at times, classified sports fans as deviants, fans have classified themselves into different groups often based on sport, region, team, or athlete. Other fans may define their level of interest on a continuum that ranges from mere spectators to the statelier "aficionados."

The chapters in this volume explore those varying degrees of fandom and the role of the media in fan cultivation from a variety of perspectives. They reflect the eclectic nature of sports fandom and contemporary sports media research. Some focus on the influence of various forms of sports content and various media. Others take a more audience-centered approach, emphasizing what fans do with sports content as opposed to what the mediated content does to them. While varying in focus, each chapter represents solid systematic social science research from an array of perspectives.

The authors have approached fandom studies from diverse theoretical perspectives applying varying qualitative and quantitative methodologies to the study of sports. The chapters represent a cross section of studies and topics that reflect the rich cross disciplinary nature of sports studies and scholarship. They also telegraph a bright and exciting future of sports scholarship that emphasizes the centrality of human communication in how fans are embracing new media environments in which to enjoy, study, understand, and share with each other sports and mediated sports.

Clearly, no single collection of studies can encompass the role of sports in human communication, the role of human communication in sports fandom, or the importance of media and mediated messages to sports fandom. But, the chapters in this volume reflect the centrality of human communication in the individual–sports exposure–effects relationship by focusing on representative important variables at each level of that relationship. Here, we summarize briefly some of those variables under the headings of (a) sports media content, (b) the sports fan, (c) fan identification, (d) fan motives, and (e) fan-produced content.

Sports Media Content

Sports provide the context for the communication phenomena studied. In most cases, this includes the effects of sports on the consumers and/or the way people use sports. Important to this effects process is the consumption of certain sports media content. Although fan background characteristics and media use activities are important precursors to effects of exposure to and consumption of sports fare, it is important to know what content fans are consuming. Of course, this is not to suggest that all content is media-driven and media-produced. Our discussion of sports content comes full circle in the final section of this book when we move from media-produced content to fan-produced content.

To begin our examination of media-produced content, Wenner provides an application of a critical approach to commercialized narratives in the mediated sport setting. Considered are the workings of sports dirt, the reading of sports fans and their interpretive communities, and the necessity of ethical assessment in evaluating strategies used in television commercials featuring sports fans. Illustrations are drawn from a variety of product categories to show how "sports dirt" is spread widely, and often problematically, into the broader cultural environment. This chapter sets the tone for the remaining chapters by encompassing the issues of ethics, fan engagement, and sport.

Next, Martin and Breitenfeldt examine two case studies that seem to suggest that, at least in times of crisis and confusion, sports serve a therapeutic function. Professional football helped a nation heal following the terrorist attacks of September 11, 2001, and Hurricane Katrina in 2005, by uniting players, fans, victims, and crisis volunteers. Teams from New York and the New England area not only directly helped victims of the 9/11 attacks, but also symbolically helped return the United States to a sense of normalcy following the confusion and chaos of the attacks. Likewise, the New Orleans Saints, specifically their physical return to the Superdome in New Orleans, provided hope to a city following an event that left many homeless and without hope.

Lastly, McGuire and Armfield provide a glimpse into the unique research dichotomy through which we can better understand how announcers create sports narratives and evolve over the course of an athletic contest. Their examination advances the study of narratives created by sports announcers and provides additional insight into how the same event, in this case the Mexico–United States World Cup soccer match, is presented on English and Spanish language television programs.

The Sports Fan

The sports fan today is an integral part of the sports communication process—not only a viewer, but a disseminator of information as the fan interacts with other fans in face-to-face and online contexts. Several chapters deal with background characteristics of sports fans that impact the viewing of sports and what people do with that experience as they interact with each other and use media (particularly online media) to extend their viewing and involvement with sports.

Clearly, the extent to which someone is a fan of a sport, team, or player, as well as other background characteristics, influences use of sports. Therefore it is important to understand the psychological and social circumstances (e.g., individual differences) fans bring with them to the sports consumption experience. These factors influence what is selected and what is done with it. Background affects expectations, motives, perceptions, involvement, sports communication activities, identification, interpretation, social connection with other fans, and numerous other effects of sports exposure.

To begin our study of the sports fan, Gantz, Wilson, Lee, and Fingerhut examine a fundamental issue associated with sports fandom that relatively few studies have tackled: "Why is it that some people become passionate about sports while others couldn't care less?" They examine this question by exploring the factors that cause people to be more or less susceptible to the lure of athletes, teams, leagues, and the competition associated with all types of sporting events. Specifically, this chapter offers an exploratory study of the origins of sports fandom.

Next, Wann and Grieve explore proactive pessimism, a coping strategy in which individuals become increasingly pessimistic, and less optimistic, about their teams' chances at an upcoming contest as the event draws near. Their discussion centers on the importance of team success leading up to the contest and the coping strategies fans sometimes employ.

To conclude this section, Turman, Stein, and Barton explore the functions of "sports apologia" and note that fans play an important role in the way sports are consumed and interpreted. Because fans hold athletes in such high regard, athletes are expected to account for their actions when their on field behavior directly influences a team's success or failure. The authors use the Zidane World Cup incident as an example of the global implications that result from fan response to on-field behavior that requires image repair.

Fan Identification

Several studies in this anthology examine the development and functions of fan identification. This includes an exploration of how fandom influences identification with athletes, teams, and other fans. But, fandom is only one background factor considered in the study of identification. Other personality traits examined or referenced in identification articles include self-esteem, sensation-seeking, competitiveness, and particular felt needs (e.g., need for group affiliation). In addition, social/environmental factors also are addressed, such as cultural and ethnic background, arousal level, moods/emotions, and the influence of friends, family, and other fans.

For example, some sports fans identify particularly strongly with a team, and this psychological connection to a team can have many consequences. Dietz-Uhler and Lanter review the affective, cognitive, and behavioral consequences of identifying as a sports fan. They explore the more extreme emotions sports fans experience when they identify strongly with a sports team as opposed to those who identify weakly with a team.

In the next chapter, Lavelle notes that there has been a lively discussion about fan culture in sports scholarship, along with a growing interest in how the Internet and other forms of interactive media have become vehicles for fans to express their opinions. Using discussion from Internet fan sites, Lavelle explores the range of Internet discussion about Chinese NBA All-star Yao Ming, the complexities of fan identifications, and the nuances of psychic involvement with Ming.

Fan Motives

For decades scholars have suggested that audience activity can at times enhance and at other times mitigate the effects of exposure to particular media fare. Never before, however, have we had as many media from which to choose as we do in the 21st century. The varying activities in which sports fans participate, many of which are examined by the authors of the chapters in this volume, provide rich opportunities for scholars to test the important role of audience activity on the uses and effects of sports fare. The activities associated with viewing sports may be very different than the activities associated with sharing sports content with others more socially or interpersonally.

For example, the motives for watching sports online may be very different than the motives for watching them in person or on television. Motives for sharing and discussing sports may be very different than the reasons for viewing sports. The characteristics of fans most likely to occupy traditional roles of spectators of sports and of those likely to share that content with others also may be quite different.

To begin our exploration of motives in this volume, Sloan and Van Camp summarize the major theories used to explain sports spectatorship along with the contemporary empirical research associated with those theories. They present data from a longitudinal study of sports spectators, their motives, and how these motives mediate the affective experience of watching a game, and of winning or losing a game.

An axiom of uses-and-gratifications theory suggests people are purposive, goal-directed, and motivated in their media use. In this study, Earnheardt and Haridakis identify more clearly sports fans' motives for watching televised sports and explore relationships among fandom and motives for viewing televised sports. Using the Television Viewing Motives Scale (TVMS) and some specific sports-viewing motives identified in prior research, they test a new, comprehensive typology.

In the next chapter, Hugenberg and Hugenberg investigate human motives revealed through communicative acts, specifically motives of young NASCAR fans. The narratives of young NASCAR fans explain how they developed their interest in NASCAR and why they continue to be fans. Fandom motives identified in the study include, in part, family influences, being with others, the thrill of racing, and enjoyment and escape.

Lastly, Spinda and Haridakis examine the rapidly growing activity of fantasy sports. They examine online fantasy sports from a uses-and-gratifications perspective using open-ended essays to generate motive items relevant to fantasy sports, culminating in an index of fantasy sports motives based on three studies. Motives for playing fantasy sports are explored in relation to a number of audience variables, such as involvement, creativity, and media exposure relevant to fantasy sports.

Fan-Produced Content

Articles in this volume represent cutting-edge research. The breadth of the content and literature upon which the authors draw provides much information of what we now know about sports viewing, online connection, and content differences. Perhaps most importantly, they provide fodder on which to build as we seek to advance our understanding of the uses and effects of sports consumption in environments in which fans are using media not only for viewing sports, but also to create sports media content and for social/interpersonal interaction relating to sports.

This latter point cannot be overstated. Chapters in this volume demonstrate that people are no longer just viewers of sports content provided to them by media organizations. With enhanced communication technologies, sports fans also occupy independent roles of creators and disseminators of sports media content themselves, via avenues such as fantasy sports, websites, and online social networking. Sports are being used by fans in newer media environments to enrich their sports consumption experience, to enhance social interaction with friends and family, and perhaps to widen social circles by connecting with other fans to discuss, debate, enhance involvement, and to learn.

For example, through direct observation and analysis of messages posted to CSTV.com during the NCAA Men's Basketball Tournament, Berg and Harthcock examine how participants construct and express individual and social identity as fans. The results reinforce prior findings for offline fandom and add new dimensions to that research by showing how identification with teams and the sport itself is demonstrated through screen names, avatars, and signature lines.

Next, Baerg's contribution broadens our understanding of the ways in which video game players interact with the medium. Baerg explores the kinds of research being performed in this burgeoning field. Although social science research on violent video games has received much attention, little has been done to understand the ways in which players use the media. In short, Baerg identifies and explicates one of the ways in which a specific group of *Madden Football* fans understand their engagement with this highly popular digital sports game.

Serazio notes in his chapter that, in recent years, fantasy sports gaming has blossomed into a multibillion dollar industry. He explores the meanings and experiences of fantasy gaming and "virtual" sports consumption through a qualitative analysis of responses to open-ended questions and interviews with fantasy gamers. The study highlights how consuming sports and directing sports content through a lens of fantasy gaming ultimately changes the dynamics of the sports fan experience. Serazio argues these developments could possibly change the future of the real games themselves.

Finally, fan forums and message boards on sites such as gatorbait.com and gatorcountry.com, and fan-created sites such as fireronzook.com, have allowed Gators fans to become active participants in the game — rather than passive spectators on the sidelines — of collegiate athletics. Using a case study of the Florida Gator Nation online, Watts illustrates how sports fans, through their participation online, have the opportunity to build community with one another as well as report and even create news about their team. She argues that this activity empowers fans to gain agency and a sense of involvement in regards to their chosen team.

Summary and Onward

The content studied herein is quite varied, including advertisements during televised sports; particular sports events or tournaments; commentary by sportscasters and other fans; comments and behavior of athletes; and various content related to video games, fantasy sports, sports rivalries, online discussions/posts pertaining to sports, incidents and events. At times the researchers focus on the direct effects of sports on fan perceptions, behaviors, coping with results of sports contests and/or events surrounding the contests (e.g., 9/11). At other times, the chapters deal with more secondary effects such as the use of sports content on fan discussion, and the like.

Together the studies demonstrate that exposure to sports, while having effects on fans, does not have such effects in a vacuum. Sports also provide the context within which they are consumed (in person, via television, online). The effects depend on the complex relationship among exposure, fans' social and psychological characteristics through which the content is filtered, and what is becoming more important in newer media environments, what fans are doing with that sports content subsequent to their initial exposure to it. This latter point suggests the increasingly important role of fans in the societal implications of sports.

In short, fans are no longer simply spectators in the sports consumption process. They are also active participants in the sports production/dissemination process. But, they are doing more than just sharing and discussing sports. They are building community and social capital. Sports bring people together. And fans in the early 21st century are using all avenues available, including media, to assist them in doing that.

Sports are the glue that ties the studies together. Together these studies evidence how sports are one of the many contexts in which to understand broader social implication of the uses and effects of sports media. These studies reflect the intersection of important variables in the entire sports communication experience, from audience background characteristics, to motives for watching and sharing sports fare, to exposure to it, to what fans are doing with the content.

SPORTS MEDIA
CONTENT

———⟋⟋⟋———

Playing Dirty

On Reading Media Texts and Studying Sports Fans in Commercialized Settings

LAWRENCE A. WENNER

In contemporary culture, the notion of the fan is both iconic and destabilized. At once, we recognize the fan as an omnipresent feature of living an increasingly commodified existence amidst the forces of popular culture. From perpetual spectatorship rises fanship. Yet it is not that simple. One may make the converse case that fanship breeds spectatorship. Of course, both claims are true. It is also true that defining the fan has been elusive (Hills, 2002; Sandvoss, 2005). Mirroring Justice Potter Stewart's definitional dance over pornography, we may think we know fanship "when we see it." Indeed, fans are all around us. We see star-struck followers of celebrity, those awestruck by skill or artistry, and others who live (and die) by their team.

When we think about fans and fanship, we often look "out there." As Jenson (1992) observed, this has enabled a less than flattering characterization of the fan as obsessive or hysterical or engaging in psychological compensation. Yet, when we focus our glance, as Walt Kelly's Pogo did, on the enemy, we see the fan, and "it is us." With this realization comes a more fawning view of fanship imbued with cultural capital stemming from, as Fiske (1992) argued, a richness centered in engagement, creativity, and resistance. With characterizations of the fan running the gamut from cultural dope to empowered, Grossberg (1992) has suggested that there is much complexity and ambiguity in studying the "affective sensibility" of (and about) the fan. Nowhere is this more the case than with the sports fan.

Approaching Sports Fanship

In both sports sociology and media studies, the sports fan has come under scrutiny. A main path of inquiry, advanced by Wann and his colleagues (Wann, Melnick, Russell, & Pease, 2001), has done considerable sorting out of key contours and dynamics. Here, there have been efforts to validate sports fanship scales, distinguish fan from spectator, direct from indirect sports consumers, and lowly from highly identified sports fans as well as systematic stocktaking of motives, rewards, and dynamics of sports fanship. Throughout much research, there has been worry over the sports fan. We express concern over the fan's psychological health (generally it's fine) and the strategies of some to BIRG (bask in reflected glory) or CORF (cut off responsibility for failure) to maintain it. We worry, too, about fan violence, yet this important but fortunately uncommon phenomenon has told us little about the range and texture of sports fanship. In mediated settings, my colleagues and I (Wenner & Gantz, 1998) have even worried (often needlessly it seems) over the sports fan as couch potato or on a path for trouble in marital or relationship life. (They do no worse than the rest of us.)

In all this (and a much wider body of) research, getting a handle on the sports fan has often seemed a convoluted exercise. How can the term pertain all at once to supporters of a team, others drawn to the abilities or celebrity of an athlete, and others who passionately, but more broadly, follow a type or class of sport? To complicate matters, such orientations to fanship are not mutually exclusive and can be characterized by disparate levels of salience, knowledge, passion, and other forms of personal involvement and reward. Just whom do we put in the sports fan basket? Do we count only "real" fans, and does their existence negate those less committed from being counted? Such complexities beg the question of where the commonality of fan experience lies. One answer is that at the base of fanship is consumption.

Consuming Sports Fanship

Recently, Crawford (2004) has made a compelling case for the necessity of studying sports fanship in the context of consumption. He builds on arguments by Giulianotti (2002) that the everyday state of contemporary sports is characterized by "hypercommodification" that has, as Kellner (2001) noted, anchored a norm for sports in "spectacle that sells the values of products, celebrities, and institutions of the media and consumer society" (p. 38). This has been part of a broader sea change to, as Bauman (1998) has put it, a "primacy of consumption in social relations" where one "needs to be a consumer first, before one can think of becoming anything in particular" (p. 26). In the sporting context, Crawford (2004) concluded that so much relates "directly or indirectly to acts of consumption" that "being a fan is primarily a consumer act and hence fans can be seen first and foremost as consumers" (p. 4). Amplifying Crawford, Horne (2005) built a broader case for the "consumerization" of the fan being driven by media logics that have naturalized the necessity of sponsorship and advertising in the purview of sports.

Indeed, the commodified sports fan is a ubiquitous feature of contemporary life. Through the media, not only are we are both cast into this role, but moreover the role is performed before us in the hopes that we will carry it into the marketplace. This is at the heart of what Abercrombie and Longhurst (1998) called the spectacle/performance paradigm of the audience. Nowhere is this more evident than in televised sports. Here sport must be consumed with all of its "spectacularized" entailments. In the course of the experience, fans not only perform their roles by consuming sport, but are subject to an array of idealized fanship assertions in the commercialized context. In viewing games, there are carefully chosen camera shots that focus the limits of fanship performance suitable for consumption. Television game announcers speak not only about action but characterize reaction and related expectations of the idealized fan. Most importantly, in relation to the game broadcast itself, the mediated sports fan is often represented as consumer in the imagination of adjacent television commercials.

Representing Sports Fanship

Anderson (1983) makes a strong case that fanship shares much with nationalism in that both are anchored in an "imagined" sense of community where there need only be "perceptions" of shared identity. Crawford (2004) has argued that this is particularly true in constructing the notion of sports fanship in a hypercommodified era: "Sport fan communities, to a large degree, have always constituted an 'imagined community,' but changes in the nature of community within wider society, the (re)development of sport venues and the proliferation of mass media resources and consumer goods have increasingly commodified the sense of belonging offered by contemporary sport, which is packaged and sold to fans" (p. 60). The television commercial in companion to sports programming has particular self–interest in shaping constructions of an "imagined community" of fans. Indeed, fans as consumers garner considerable interest from advertisers as the audience for sports programming tilts towards an elusive and desirable younger male demographic.

Most importantly, by having a dominant voice in casting the sports fan in consumer roles, advertisers can naturalize how sports relate to the consumption of other things. Thus, by examining commercial narratives, we learn not only how the fan's role is imagined but more importantly how it is used as conduit. Constructions of the fan in commercials, then, are key to understanding how the power of sports is dispersed into other consumption settings. Yet the narrative construction and employ of the fan has been little examined. Most inquiry focuses on "real" fans and their behaviors, affect, and culture. Those studies focused on social construction in commodity settings have often had other priorities, related to, but not centered on sports fanship. For example, Messner and Montez de Orca (2005) and Wenner (2008) have focused on the characterization of men, often not portrayed as fans, in commercials that run in sports programming. The research here attempts to redress such shortcomings in focus and offers an avenue to critically center interrogations on the social construction of the sports fan in consumer culture.

Approaching Sports Fanship in Commercialized Media Settings

It was noted earlier that much worry (often needless) has been evident in research on sports fans. From this, one might conclude as well that there would be little need to worry about the social construction of the fan. However, there are more reasons to be suspicious, and this drives critical inquiry in certain directions. Collectively, we remain uneasy that ubiquitous and ever resourceful advertising may be working us over. After all, it is difficult to escape the logic that advertising would not be paid for if it were ineffective. Certainly it is difficult to believe that mere exposure does the advertising trick. As a result, the sense that fallacious connections are being made to enlist our sympathies is inescapable. It is this sense that likely spurs us on as active readers in pushing back at the logics unwound in commercial messages.

In realizing the necessity for resistance we recognize that our transactions with commercial messages are ethically problematic. These issues are the focus of this inquiry into the social construction and use of the sports fan in commercial messages. The approach applies a dirt theory of narrative ethics tailored to deconstruct commercial narratives and their reading and interrogate the ethical nature of that transaction (Wenner, 2007). The three prongs of the approach and questions raised for considering the sports fan constructed in commercial messages are discussed in the next sections.

The Dirtied Sports Fan   The notion of communicative dirt, incipient in work by Douglas (1966) and Leach (1976), has been more fully developed in critical media theory by Enzenberger (1972) and Hartley (1984). Conceptualized as "matter out of place," the movement of dirt has special resonance in understanding the cultural reach of hypercommodified media sports (Hilliard & Hendley, 2004; Wenner, 1991, 1994, 2004, 2007, 2008). As it does in other settings, dirt facilitates the transfer of power and logic from one context to another. Thus, when we speak of "sports' appeal" or build a case that "sports provide a special setting for marketing products," this recognizes the power of sport dirt. Through manufactured connections, dirt helps make the sell. This is recognized when advertisers use constructions of sports and fashionings of the fan to advance consumption in disparate spheres. Although the dirt, a real or imagined attribute of sports or the fan, may in itself be benign, the contagion that results from its strategic use may be ethically problematic.

In focusing dirt theory analysis on the sports fan in commercials, one keys on "following the dirt." What is the character of the sports dirt imported into the commercial? Where does it come from and where does it go? What other cultural dirt is appended to sports and the fan and how is this transformed and used? How is sports dirt used in shaping the narrative? How are the logics of sports dirt and fanship appended to the logic of the sell? What distortions, fallacies, or deceptions are facilitated as dirt moves from one setting to another? Questions such as these begin the messy enterprise of dirt analysis and underlie the next set of considerations. These focus on how reading and the characterization of the reader, and hence sports fan and the sell, relate to dirt.

The Constructed Sports Fan   Set firmly in the tradition of reader-oriented criticism, the second component of dirt theory organizes core concerns over what readers bring to the text. From this position, it is inescapable for readers not to soil new texts with old dirt, as it is the familiarity of dirt that allows us to make sense of new things. Although there are many variants of reader-oriented criticism and reception theory (Machor & Goldstein, 2001; Tompkins, 1980), Iser's (1974, 1976, 2006) three overlapping concerns provide a good structure to interrogate dirt, the working of sports, and the construction of the sports fan in commercials.

Iser focuses first on the contextualization of implied reader. On one hand, we need to understand how marketers as authors have reached to readers through contextual understandings of fanship and assumptions about sporting "interpretive communities" (Fish, 1980). On the other hand, we need to look at the roles that sports and sports fanship play in contextualizing the broader interpretive community for the ads themselves. Second comes the focus on how readers are drawn in and by the text. We need to examine how fans and other readers characterized in portrayals in on-screen textual surrogates and by off-screen clues are pushed towards preferred reading positions through such things as direct address and camera position. This characterization in and by the text aims at understanding how dirt may aid in coaxing a preferred reading position. A third concern of Iser is in interrogating the reading act itself. We need to consider what the text implies about the reader's standpoint and abilities to negotiate redundancies and gaps in texts. In doing so, we focus on the roles that sports dirt and cultural understandings of the fan play in influencing how redundancies will be received and which gaps need filling. Through these overlapping concerns, much can be learned. Foremost, liberties taken in characterizing sports, the sports fan, and the reader of commercial messages are crystallized. In this course, we also may more clearly see improprieties taken in the attempt to control reading to strategic advantage. Thus, the next step in dirt theory interrogates the tenor of such realizations.

The Deconstructed Sports Fan The final layer of analysis in dirt theory concerns ethical assessment of the transaction between dirt and its reading. While resisted by some as presumptuous in literary, aesthetic, and cultural criticism (Carroll, 2000), ethical criticism has come to be viewed as inescapable in narrative analysis (Booth, 1998; Gregory, 1998). The more recent ethical turn in cultural critique (Eaglestone, 2004; Eagleton, 2003; Kellner, 2000; Zylinska, 2005) has been driven by the need to address the free-floating relativism inherent in postmodernism and the realization that ethical interrogation need not require prudish moral prescription. Most importantly, the approach can complement other critical concerns, such as the one here with dirt, to focus stocktaking on the ethical dynamics of the text and reading. In assessing matters of greater good, minimization of harm, truth telling, exercising other respecting care, and being balanced, fair, just, and a host of other issues, ethical criticism can illuminate moral flaws in media products as both aesthetically defective and culturally problematic. As such, the approach is particularly appropriate in interrogating the propriety of dirt imported into commercial narratives and the dirtiness encouraged through characterizations both of the reader and reading (Wenner, 2007).

In focusing on what dirt does in television commercials featuring sports and the fan, some overarching issues need consideration. A dirt-versus-impact equation needs to be assessed. After all, a little dirt, like dust, may be organic, doing little harm. On the other hand, too much dirt can cover or clog things. And just a bit of dirt, like water in a gas tank, can have dire consequences. Further, we need to look carefully at what the "matter out of place" actually is. It might well be that assumptions concerning sports or the fan brought to service were ethically flawed prior to importation.

In moving forward in ethical assessment, we need to assess the workings, movement, landing, build-up, and interaction of sport and fan dirt with other matter. Has this dirt taken liberties in characterizing interpretive communities or pushed improperly to control reading? Have logics concerning sports and fanship been used to devalue the greater good, obfuscate inequities or truth, mask injustice or diminish other respecting care? At the end of the day, these are big questions to put on the shoulders of sports and the sports fan. Still, they are answered every day when dirt from sports and carefully "imagined" constructions of the sports fan are used in popular culture and, more particularly, in advertisements.

The Milieux of the Commodified Sports Fan To examine a range of answers about how dirt from sports and fanship may be routinely used in commercial narratives, a convenience sample was drawn from a larger exploration of commercials featuring sports fans from the large proprietary video database at adforum.com.[1] The video collection of television commercials at adforum.com, with approximately 75,000 spots, is the largest available online. The site features primitive search capacities by product category and theme. Through iterative searches of keywords such as sports, sports fan, and fan as well as systematic scanning by individual sports, leagues, and product categories (beer, automobiles, credit cards, etc.), a universe of approximately 100 commercials featuring sports fans was identified.

To structure analysis, these spots were distributed into six categories. Five of the six analytical categories hover around sports in cohesive ways. The *reflecting sports* category promoted products offered by "institutions of sports" such as leagues or sports programming networks, thus "reflecting" their brand of sports and fanship back at consumers. The *accessing sports* cluster moved away from this more specific mirror to a class of products such as cable/satellite operators, phone service providers, and fantasy league organizers/developers that provide linkages to sports. The *wearing sports* group features the sports fan in relation to the quintessential behavior of buying sports clothing from megamerchandisers such as Nike and through league and retail stores. The *drinking sports* category shows the fan in pursuit of quenching thirst through beer and soda. The *paying sports* set showcase how the fan's tab may be paid by using services and products from one of sports' major underwriters, the credit card industry. A catchall sixth category, *all-consuming sports*, places the fan relative to a diverse collection of products ranging from breakfast cereals to insurance to big-box retailers.

Interrogating Sport Fanship in Commercialized Media Narratives

With its multi–layered approach, dirt theory requires a "thick" reading (Geertz, 1973) aimed at capturing the interplay of dirt, textual dynamics, and ethical problematics. Thus, in the sections that follow, there is brief consideration of the range of characterizations of the fan offered within each of the five distinct categories. These are used to contextualize more focused analysis on one spot in each grouping that poses overarching assertions about "how sports fans are." To this point, each of the commercials singled out for more extensive analysis features the word "fan" or "fans" in its title.

Reflecting Sports   This large category of ads showcases sports' institutional "imagination" of its own fans. Here, sports and media institutions draw on cultural archetypes of fans and their relationship to sports to build their brands. An exemplar series from Major League Baseball reminds dejected fans holed up (under the sink, in a tree or bathroom) after their team has lost that they are baseball fans and to watch the next playoff round. France Football shows two fans engaged in discussion so passionate that they do not note falling down a cliff. Fox Sport Network shows the sports addict ruining his life through such dedicated imbalance. ESPN and Fox Sports Network both show the passion of fans for their team at odds with passion with (or even attention to) one's significant other. ESPN shows fans as engaged in characterizing them as "coach" and loyal in pining for "next" year. Throughout these and other ads, the die-hard passion of fans is showcased.

Most archetypal and all-encompassing was the NFL's "Nation of Football Fans" spot. A piano anthem drives a diverse montage of fans facing the camera with solemn narration telling viewers: "We're a nation of football fans. A nation of believers, dreamers, and rugged individuals. United in the belief that while all fans are created equally, we each love the game in our own way. The Super Bowl, as American as America gets. It could be your 40th, it could be your first. You might just watch for the commercials. With our families, and friends. Tonight, we're all connected by the game. So, on this, our Super Sunday, we just want to say thanks. We're proud to be part of the family." From start to finish, we see individual and groups of fans gazing at the camera in different settings. We see the diehard Chicago Bear fan braving the cold, a father and grown son wearing identical jerseys, a diverse group of blue collar workers, bar room toughs (the "rugged individuals"), teens on the beach (we see one's hand go across a jersey-covered heart), a young Hispanic boy signaling his team as number one, a 20-ish Washington Redskin sweatshirt–clad fan nursing a hot coffee, an enthusiastic pairing of older woman fans, a young woman fan, a young girl (with a t-shirt opposing the Dallas Cowboys), and a host of others— young, old, white and not — gathered at the hearth of football, often in Norman Rockwell–inspired living room tableaux. Significantly, the spot closes with disparate scenes of football bringing people of all ages together consuming and cheering the spectacle. Amongst the final shots are archetypes of idyllic Americana: a beaming father (wearing a New England Patriot sweatshirt) and his young boys (wearing jerseys) dashing from church in the snow, a jubilant interracial family with African-American husband surrounded by jersey-clad Asian-American wife and children in front of their upper middle class home, and closing on an enthusiastic youth football team and their cheerleaders waving pom-poms surrounded by their coaches in front of yellow school buses.

What we have here is a classic case of football meets nationalism married to "the way we were" meets "the way we are." Of course, nationalistic dirt has often driven sensibilities about sports (Wenner, 1994). Further, as Anderson (1983) has observed, nationalism is often reliant on an "imagined" sense of community fueled by nostalgia. Thus, this marriage is a particularly dirty and potent one. This is abetted by the dirty naturalization of "we" throughout. The dirty equation of the citizen's right to equality to a predilection to consume sports masks an oxymoronic pallor. Yet there is no denying that there is an uncomfortable power and truth to the posing of the Super Bowl "as American as America gets." With this comes not only the dirty linking of sports fanship to the melting pot but also realization and celebration of the consumerist logic that pervades contemporary culture. All of this is cemented in the dirty constancy of consumers wearing their fanship in the form of jerseys, sweatshirts, and caps. This "signing" of fanship in the necessities of consumption brings implications for reading.

In this, the interpretive community has been transformed along a continuum of spectator to patriot to consumer. This pathway comes to define the sports fan as a consumer and implies that not to do so would be not only unnatural but unpatriotic as well. Thus, to read against the grain requires an unaligned and implicitly alien position, something the text does little to encourage through its myth of inclusiveness with portrayals of idealized characterized readers as young/old, white/nonwhite, male/female, and ultimately in the middle class where most see themselves. As well, the "family" thread in narration and in pictures reinforces the power of this reading position as a "homecoming" holiday with all the traditional fixings. Indeed, in its course the characterized reader's "going to church" has enabled permission to "go to football" with all of fanship's consumer entailments. Not only are readers characterized to rejoice in this, but the assertion that "we're all connected by the game" begs the question of whether we could be connected without it.

The transaction of dirt with reading raises a number of ethical concerns. Foremost is the problematic juxtaposition of nationalism and NFL fanship. Certainly, one is not a litmus test for the other. Further, this kind of soppy, jingo-infused analogizing takes liberties with critical citizenship, and thus a more righteous nationalism that might keep nations from the pitfalls of "true-believerism" that will inevitably land them in trouble. Thus a deception about the role of the citizen has been logically imposed on the characterized role of the sports fan. A second, not unrelated, ethical concern has to do with the naturalized painting of inclusion and diversity. Like any consumer space, sport is open for business for dollars and any color, gender, or age. It is in its best interests to naturalize sports fanship with the lifecycle of all of those breathing. Thus, it is not surprising that the narrative works to "integrate" difference with idyllic multicultural tableaux. Even with putting the suspect nature of this manufactured warmth aside, what remains is a false inclusiveness with the pointed implication that if you cannot find a place in what is represented as the ultimate inclusive consumer space, then you are suspect. Implicit in the construction and its reading is that one who is not a football fan, and more egregiously one who does not embrace its consumerist entailments, is the "other," a devalued alien who does not belong.

Accessing Sports Moving away from core sports and media institutions, commercials in the accessing sports group feature sponsors that seek to build a structural link to sports. This grouping includes cable/satellite operators, phone service providers, fantasy league organizers, computer game or console companies, and others. Thematically, these are more geared to what could charitably be called the "sports nut." Some of these advertisers, programmers of "big buckets" such as cable/satellite providers and phone companies, necessarily draw a picture of a generically enthused "all-sports" fan. Others that organize fantasy sports involvement or are selling gaming hardware or software show-case fans in more specific terms, such as followers of NFL football or Major League baseball. In either case, what is being sold is "living for sports." Thus, we find "Johnny Bandwagon" bubbling with enthusiasm for Optimum's vast sports programming, Adelphia customers waxing poetic over their DVR football package, ESPN fantasy league players deliriously engaged in strategizing while distracted from their office work, Obox customers (in Israel) excitedly enacting a football game in the streets, and a Verizon customer inappropriately stumbling into a restaurant for a date carrying an oversized NCAA basketball bracket. Although this cluster of products concerns access that is predicated on "riding the fumes" of sports, the consumption myth stresses activity.

This emphasis on activity meshes with Crawford's (2004) arguments that much fanship activity in a consumption economy concerns performance of the fan role. This is clearly seen in Cingular's "Super Fan" spot, which structures its sell in a debate about the right way to perform the role of the fan in the age of pervasive personal media technology. In the debate, two forms of dirt clash with the common goal of perfecting the role of the avid fan during the NCAA basketball tournament. Set in a busy airport, the commercial shows a young Asian-American man, dressed in stylishly casual attire that would not be out of place in Silicon Valley, checking his cell phone. He is approached by an enthusiastic, white, paunchy, and balding super fan in his late 20s. In contrast to the cell phone sophisticate, the gushing super fan seems a bit of a slob, a matter compounded by his wearing of green team colors and carrying a pom-pom. Half of his face is painted in green, and his head is fitted with a gold lamé paper crown topped with tinsel and a wagging set of cartoonish antennae. Calling for attention, the super fan commands: "Check it out, I've got March Madness!" This elicits the cool retort, "You don't have March Madness." Dumbfounded, the super fan exclaims: "What? Look at me!" as we see a green painted W on his fleshy chest. In response comes the cell phone user's techno-offensive. Drilled with a series of questions about his ability to follow his team with "only two clicks" or to "constantly update" his bracket, the deflated super fan can only murmur "no." Our suave techno-fan salts the wound by asserting, "Then you don't have March Madness, you have March sadness," a strategy that marginalizes our super fan's strategy as "old school" and a bit pathetic. At this point the narrative breaks for an announcer to tell of the benefits of Cingular Media Net. A coda to the narrative returns as the super fan poses to his technologically superior counterpart, "You want to see what else I painted?" A firm, swift "no" to the improper implications of this, and a Cingular tag line from the announcer, close the commercial.

Dueling dirt is a key feature of this spot. Here traditional, and stereotyped, sports dirt in the form of the team-color-painted super fan faces off against the techno-dirt of one characterized as the new and improved model. But the "dirt war" is really not one of sports versus technology. As a matter of fact, such characterization misses the point of how a dirt war is won. This war is about the attributes of technology, cell phone technology in this case, appending itself to sports in a way that forms a new compound that both undermines and extends earlier social constructions. Here, techno-dirt, long posed as a panacea for problematics little realized, refashions what it means to be a super fan. The appendages to this transformation are flattering as well. The "old school" sports fan is a bit of a loser (Messner & Montez de Oca, 2005), while his techno-infused update is savvy in a world of globalization.

This reliance on a stereotyped drawing of the loser sports fan has structural implications for reading processes. Foremost, it influences reading position and the characterization of the interpretive community. Presented with such a buffoon, readers have little choice but to align with the savvy techno-sophisticate. By their doing so, the familiar myth of technology and progress are further advanced. Camera position enhances this throughout. We take in the fleshy absurdities of the painted super fan from the cool stance of his counterpart who knows far better. Further, not only are we reminded, using redundancy, of the limitations of old school fanship, but the familiarity of the myth of technology provides the ready filling of gaps towards preferred sense-making.

There is a moral argument as well. Implicit in the naturalization of the technology myth is the concept that sports fanship thus enhanced is better than that which is not. Unfortunately, in this argument, the characterization of "better" necessarily hinges on the logic of efficiency and access to data as demonstrative of superiority. For the dedicated sports fan, it is difficult to see how efficiency and data will advance the depths of affective involvement. Rather, it easier to argue that an efficient sports fan is more likely to be a casual one. Indeed, it may be anathema to the true fan to get in, get out, and get it over with; rather, the draw may be to revel in nuance, texture, and conjecture. Seen as such, an apparition is posed as truth in this ad to fashion a deception that will advance its own self-interests. Understandably perhaps in an ad seeking to advance adoption of technology, there is still a bias in the characterization of what is desirable in fanship. The marginalizing of a carefully drawn super fan as a buffoon may have further dangers as it deflates a new-techno fanship of the authenticity, fun, and enthusiasm that have come to be associated with sports fanship.

Wearing Sports The sign of the sports fan is spread no more widely through culture than by the ubiquitous wearing of branded merchandise and sports fashion. The sale of jerseys featuring the name and number of notable athletes contributes mightily to the ancillaries that enhance the bottom line of leagues and teams. On the heels of celebrity athletes, sporting goods companies such as Nike, Adidas, Reebok, and Puma have grown from shoe companies to global conglomerates that set the standard for sports-centered fashion and casual wear. Indeed, the mix of sports-centered products that might be worn as walking billboards is seemingly endless. Jerseys, t-shirts, sweatshirts, caps, shoes and the like all form the communicative basis for contemporary consumer sports culture. In buying these, sports fans essentially sign themselves on as fans. In this course, not only have they invested in a drawing of their fanship identity, they have practiced its purchase through consumption.

Encouraging this practiced consumption is important to many parties. For the sports teams and their stars it is a remarkable marketing engine; their branding message is communicated, and the disseminators of the message pay for the privilege of doing so. The whole notion is almost a Catch-22 of marketing, and if the endeavor weren't so pointedly voluntary, it would smack many as an ethical affront. The phenomenon is of course about belonging. Here, consumption not only purchases membership, but advertises it. Through this, sports fanship identities anchor forays into broader social space, bringing sports dirt in announcing one's identity, and facilitating the likelihood that others in the fanship community may be found. There is a necessary symbolism to plunking down good money to sign one's fanship. The act signifies commitment, both to one's performance of the role as fan and to the consumer logic that is anchored to it.

Thus, it is not surprising that commitment is a key feature of television commercials that promote both the brands and products of sporting garb. On the retail front, Dick's Sporting Goods targets those fans heading for the weekend game with its promotion of "Fan Friday" where all "official team merchandise" is on sale. Internet storefronts, such as NFLShop.com, also preach to those already committed with the "opportunity" to have such team merchandise "delivered to their door." The travails of the "overcommitted" are lampooned in a series of commercials by Adidas that characterize those afflicted with "footballitis." In these brand building ads, we see top scientists at Adidas observing and dutifully measuring the cartoonish gyrations of those plagued by iterative acting-out of kicking or cheering in support for their team while wearing Adidas and team-branded merchandise. This notion of the sports fan's commitment as a malady of sorts is also hinted at in a characterization of "Boston Red Sox Fans" in a commercial by Nike.

Following a major stylistic of Nike's "Just Do It" campaign, "Red Sox Fans" unfolds without dialogue and Nike is not revealed as sponsor until the tagline provides the reminder to "Just Do It" and we see the Nike "swoosh." A set camera positions viewers on the field at Boston's Fenway Park, looking at a desirable set of front row box seats. What unfolds is a montage of the fans sitting in that box, beginning in 1919, the year after the Red Sox won the World Series, until 2004, when the Red Sox next won the World Series. Much meaning in the montage is driven by the soundtrack. Over the course of the commercial, a sad "old-timey" violin-led minuet tugs at heartstrings, evolves into interplay between more hopeful and lingering wistful full orchestration, and closes to a pleasant coda marking the end of a very long dance in 2004. Mirroring the musical soundtrack, a quasi-synched sound effects track plays a similar tune. We hear bats cracking, cheering, and clapping mark the downs and eventually ups of this fan saga.

These sounds are anchored in visuals that are chronicled by an odometer-like spinning of the years being ticked off below a smaller letterbox screen. Here, we see the family and friends in the field-side box change. We see the original group age, new family members including those from new generations join the mix, and the signs of fanship evolve. Throughout, significantly and certainly not benignly, we see a thread of consumption. This moves in seemingly simple ways, from early appearances of ice-cream cones and popcorn, to the bringing of mitts, to the ubiquity of cups for beer and soft drinks, to the wearing of Red Sox caps, sweatshirts, and warm-up jackets. Over time, the naturalization of "dressing for the game" is emphasized and changes. In early years, men, women, and children are all attired in fine dress clothes—stylish suits, ties, dresses and formal overcoats and hats to match. Over the years this formality gives way to an increasing pervasiveness of logoed baseball caps, sweatshirts, jackets, and, importantly, the wearing of team colors, in this instance red, white, and blue.

The thematic evolution of consumption in this ad mixes with the commitment archetype of the die-hard fan to brew the dirt that drives this ad. The naturalization of both in parallel is important. For their commitment through thick and thin, the sports fans are shown as both noble and loyal. In their front row seats, these fans are nobility, handing down both the privilege and experience through generations much like those in a royal box at the opera. The beauty of being a television fan, of course, is that one shares those front row seats and one can be just as loyal from that position. Through this, the notion of privilege can be extended and with it the naturalization of consumption of (in this instance Nike) branded sporting attire. This builds on a savvy logic. Those thusly privileged are "entitled" to be rewarded for their loyalty by consumption of (manufactured) signs of that loyalty. The seemingly unmoving reading position of this ad facilitates this myth. What we appear to be watching is an untainted history of the plight of the Red Sox fan. However, the set reading position can easily work to mask the nuanced change in the characterization of the fan shown to evolve over the years. This "masking" naturalizes the increasing consumption that characterizes being a sports fan.

At its essence, this story is a morality tale, telling us that loyalty will be rewarded. Here, good deeds, in the form of loyal consumption, foster just deserts. Indeed, it is a dubious equation, but far more marketable than "misery loves company." The notion also builds on the "myth of hard work," where the work of one generation contributes to a bettered life for those that follow. Here, being a Red Sox fan is frustrating work. One's ancestors must toil and die before their progeny can reap the benefits of their loyalty. Thus, the misery of the sports fan can be cast as a badge of honor, a sign of nobility. The nobility notion also interplays with the ethics of meaning. Here, race rears its head through what Barthes (1973) has called "ex-nomination." Perhaps it is too much to ask for in terms of the veracity of a tale where a coveted Fenway box seat is handed down through the generations, but in its course, Nike has shown all of the fans occupying those seats from 1919 until 2004 as white. The naturalization of "entitlement" for those who can hand down desirable box seats helps mask that fanship is often not democratized in the way that it is often used to sell sports to the masses.

Drinking Sports   Over the years, wetting one's whistle while watching sports has become a naturalized artifact of fanship. Beer, in particular, has a longstanding cultural association to those enmeshed in sports (Collins & Vamplew, 2002). Consuming beer has, of course, always been consumption. Yet, as Collins & Vamplew (2002) point out, this act has come over the years to become a special sign of male camaraderie when placed in the context of sports. Traceable to working class pub behavior after local contests, downing a brew has become an integral archetype of male sports fanship. As sports fanship began to mirror the "civilizing influence" of sports in the industrial age, the sports stadium made accommodations to spectatorship as a family experience and soft drinks broadened the consumption ritual (Elias & Dunning, 1986).

The sample group of beverage commercials draws on sports dirt to fuel goodwill in diverse narratives. Catering to a narrower young male demographic, the beer group on average draws on quirky humor to garner attention. Here Bud Light shows plotting young male fans who hide a "secret fridge" from game day guzzlers being foiled by knowing neighbors. Budweiser draws on male-female stereotypes to show a young man at a candlelit dinner with his lover fantasizing about replacing the woman's relational talk with play-by-play commentary of a game. Holsten beer (in Hungary) shows the die-hard fan crawling on the ground, re–enacting the cheer of "Goal!" On a more serious note, Coors Light characterizes fans in a stadium as "those about to rock" by getting a beer in front of them at their seats. Drawing itself as just as integral to sports as beer, soft drinks mix themselves in amongst universal attributes of fans. An ad for Fanta in the European market shows the soda as that which bridges the gap "between us" in a dueling set of fans heading home from a game on the subway. In a parody of the seriousness over football contests, Pepsi idealizes "bold warriors" who "meet for glory" in the "game of tailgating." Dirt from the implied global universalism of sports fanship is painted no more clearly than in Coca-Cola's "World Cup of Fans" spot. Aimed at the developing world market, the ad aims to expand football's ability to "integrate" a wide diversity of fans to include Coca-Cola as similarly integral and natural to the spectator experience. In this quest, football fanship and Coca-Cola consumption are posed throughout as inescapably entangled. Yet, there is no mistaking that Coca-Cola seeks to build on the dirt of sports. The ad is predicated on an if-then construction: if football, then Coca-Cola.

Opening to driving world-beat Euro pop music, we see a young African man with his face painted. At first glance, the paint may be misconstrued as tribal face paint, but a closer look confirms that this along with cap and shirt are a display of team (most likely national) colors. The next shot brings a jersey-clad young boy standing in front of a high brick wall painted with a worn Coca-Cola sign. This is followed by a series of shots emphasizing the scale and importance of the football competition. Here we see shots of large crowds and trophies. Superimposed over this in two parts comes the question, "If there was a World Cup of fans, would you qualify?" This is followed by an idealized fanship montage. We see hordes of fans, the wearing of team colors, painted bodies, the sipping of Coca-Cola in a stadium, action at an important contest, cheering, an intermix of football being played on a poor playground, much waving of national flags, fans hugging each other, and a celebratory parade. Accompanying the montage and beat come lyrics commanding: "Tonight make it magnificent, tonight make it your own!" To this broader goal, the end of the montage poses three behaviors that are consecutively superimposed over the exciting visuals. These reveal the ad's if-then strategy. We see the additive equation "Eat football. Sleep Football. Drink Coca-Cola." The ad closes with the Coca-Cola logo set inside a globe-like red and black soccer ball.

In none of the earlier ads that have been considered has the interweaving of sports dirt to consumption of the product been so bold. Quite simply, one cannot qualify as a football fan without making the eating and sleeping of football "magnificent" by drinking Coca-Cola. To not do so would imply that one does not belong. Importantly, there is an explicit reach to include those who have little in their lives. In this effort, Coca-Cola joins sports in positioning itself as a broader answer to the question of how the poor might garner a little joy and gain the ability to share in a larger cultural spectacle.

A number of clues in the visual text signal that the interpretive community for reading aims at the masses; this ad does not only speak to those who are already sports fans but seeks to recruit those on the sidelines into the excitement of what is posed as a "world" community. The poor, seen in withered neighborhoods and playing football on shabby dirt fields, are featured as characterized readers. While the white and more privileged are shown, they are drawn more stoically as faces in the crowd or functionaries in a parade. The action figures shown exuding joy from sports, as spectators and on the field as players, are overwhelmingly people of color drawn from all across the developing world.

In essential ways, Coca-Cola's call to fanship, and its employ of sports dirt, is ethically problematic. Here, both sports and Coca-Cola are offered as a placebo masquerading as the real thing. Being given an opportunity to participate in the cultural spectacle of sports and to pay to imbibe in the associated ritual of consuming Coca-Cola does not redress the social inequities facing the poor in developing nations. Certainly, neither World Cup nor Coca-Cola would be likely to make such a claim. Still, dirt mixtures such as the one offered here in this commercial mask the question of how the poor participate in and shape dominant culture and social priorities. These masking processes show that answers posed in terms of consumption are inherently flawed. Further, the dynamic perpetuates the infantilization of the poor with the lure of the shiny materialism that comes in consuming the excesses of sports spectacle and in a drink that offers little nutritional value in portions of the world where this is most needed. The critique here is not so much an indictment of Coca-Cola or sports for that matter. It may be too much to ask them to temper their promotional logics as they are so ingrained in consumer culture. More importantly, one cannot argue against the poor having a little bit of fun. The argument here only points to the dangers of sports dirt in serving wants and masking needs. The potential for its employ here is considerable and deserving of attention.

Paying Sports   The economic life of sports dirt is featured further in the *paying sports* cluster of commercials. Showcasing the closeness of that connection, ESPN characterizes fans using their "total access" affinity Visa card. The promise that "you get closer to sports with every purchase" is accentuated by sporting action appearing out of nowhere every time the card is whipped out and by the hook that "you spend, you score" and "earn" team jerseys, autographed "collectables," game tickets and the like. Visa's "Day After" features a series of excited fans in various settings—a corporate washroom, a mailroom, a locker room, a gym, a police car, on the back of a trash truck, mid-procedure in a medical operating room — telling others about the game and that they "shoulda been there." In that comes the dig and the reminder that Visa's sports dirt is primary because "if you want to be there, bring your Visa card" because tickets can't be purchased with American Express. The purchase of fanship status and the opportunity to consume sports is similarly featured in MasterCard's "Red Sox" spot. Part of the brand's "there are some things money can't buy, for everything else there's MasterCard" series, we hear what a diverse group of fans, all wearing some team-logoed attire, would give for Red Sox World Series tickets. Running the gamut from "500 bucks," "four grand," "two months' salary," "my entire savings account" to "my truck," "my car," "my computer," "my dog," "my girlfriend," "my first born kid" to "anything," an announcer concludes that seeing the Red Sox in the World Series is "priceless," but reminds, while the camera keys in on a World Series t-shirt, that MasterCard is accepted "wherever they are sold."

The proxemic dirtiness of bringing the fan's money to sports in credit card commercials speaks to the centrality of consumption in fashioning fan identity and performance. In strategic ways, consumption is shown to enhance performance. The consumption-performance link is stressed in Capital One's "No Hassle Rewards" card "Fans" spot that features three "wild and crazy" Arizona Diamondback fans following star pitcher Randy Johnson from city to city. The spot opens with Johnson on the mound throwing a third strike to close an inning; in the outfield Capital One signage is seen. As Johnson heads to the dugout, he nods with a smile to the three cheering super fans dressed not only in attire accentuated by Diamondback purple, but sporting purple fright wigs, face paint, and a clownish multi-pronged crown. Superimposed titling tells us this is Cincinnati as Johnson comes off the field to the threesome's animated chant of "Randy, Randy, Randy!" As the experience repeats itself in the tunnel to the field in Houston and again on the field in Pittsburgh, Johnson complains to a coach, "They come to every game, every city!" The coach, whipping out a credit card, conjectures that "they must have Capital One No Hassle Rewards" as an unseen announcer interjects that "free flights start at any time, any airline, anytime ... so you can fly free faster, and more often." Closing the commercial on an extension of the narrative theme, we see the three zanily attired fans continue their "Randy, Randy, Randy!" chant as they approach him lounging by a pool in Miami. They apologetically back off as they see him in the company of a pretty woman. In the last scene, Johnson, still poolside with the fans dancing and chanting in the background, laughs and asks the viewer "What's in your wallet?"

Dirt from fanship drives this commercial while consumption is shown to drive fanship. Throughout the necessity and nuisance of fans is shown. Throughout, as well, the necessity of consumption in fanship is shown. The narrative works to cement these two notions. Fanship dirt also comes with other implications. With the fan's consumption comes the right to "own" part of the object of fanship, in this case Randy Johnson's attention and ultimately privacy. While the line is carefully drawn here as the zany fans retreat in recognization of Johnson's private moment with a woman, one is left wondering if the boundary would have been crossed had that perceived social barrier not been in place. Indeed, the ad's "self-reflexiveness" plays with dangerous sports dirt, the stalker fan who has become too much obsessed with sports and now moves to consume the object of desire, the targeted athlete. The stalker model, after all, is about coming to take the object of desire as one's own.

To its credit, reading position in this ad does not side with the stalking group of fans. Rather, the interpretive community's point of view is very much aligned with Johnson, who gains the reader's sympathy for enduring the harassing behavior and appreciation for being good-humored about it. Yet in Johnson's tale comes a lesson for less sociopathic fanship. Readers consuming sports are complimented for being smart in "earning" through their fanship. Thus, the reading position further encourages sports fans to see themselves as consumers. Fans are spoken to in direct address as Johnson queries them about the card they have in their wallets. This sports to consumer appeal directly relies on sports fanship as a conduit.

The major ethical problem here has to do with the proper boundaries of sports fanship and the question of what one is entitled to when one makes a fanship "purchase." In humorously characterizing the super fan while at the same time dancing with the discomfort of the stalker, this commercial recognizes the "blurred genre" (Geertz, 1973) of sports fanship. In its increasing commodification, the bounds of fanship are necessarily pushed by the notion of reciprocity in exchange. Here sports dirt stimulates enthusiastic affect while pushing the line of expectation that comes with consumption towards one of entitlement. In doing so, fans' demand for "value" gains legitimacy, and in doing so, fanship may be transformed. Certainly, in sports fanship, it has always been the case that one hopes that one's team or favorite does well. But fanship historically has had little to do with what Marx (1990) called "use value," a matter that Baudrillard (2000) characterized more clearly in a bifurcation of pragmatic concerns distinguished as "functional" or "exchange" value. Indeed, fanship withers on such vines of instrumentality and economic value, even though fanship often drives an economic exchange for a key vantage point. Rather, the "symbolic" and "sign" values, to use Baudrillard's schema, have been the constituent features and draw of fanship. To say that fanship in any sense is pure is, of course, naïve. But it is fair to recognize that its character changes when a consumerist evaluative logic pervades. It is also fair to recognize that the commercials in the *paying sports* category do much to advance this logic, and in doing so, incrementally change cultural sensibilities about sports fanship.

Discussion

In all of the commercials considered, dirt from sports and the sports fan have been used to both soil and seal the sell. Invoking the logic of dirt theory, soiled goods fuel sold goods. In each of the five categories, the mediation of the sports fan works to commodify the experience. This is true whether the product is or *reflects* sports, provides *access* to sports, is *worn* as a sign of sports fanship, is consumed as in *drinking* a beverage while at the same time consuming sports, or facilitates *paying* for the fanship experience. These product categories are, of course, only the tip of a much larger commodified iceberg that seeks to build on the dirt of sports and the characterization and sympathies of the sports fan.

There is no doubt that this study is, in many regards, limited. Here, brief consideration was given to only five categories of television commercials that featured the sports fan in the sell. Further, more focused analysis was limited to only one commercial in each category. Still, the thick approach of dirt theory mined a set of important themes deserving of further exploration. In commercials, narratives must necessarily transform the sports fan into consumer. As these fanship narratives are perhaps the most common and visible in contemporary space, they have come to anchor contemporary definition of the sports fan. In this context, we do not see the casual fan. The *reflecting sports* category, in particular, reminds us that "diehard passion" is to be expected and failure to exhibit this level of passion is suspect and alien. Reinforcing fanship as active performance, the *accessing sports* group characterizes the desirability of fans to "live for sports." With this comes a call for redefining activity in the context of "die-hard" fanship; here a "new and improved" model is enmeshed in an unrelenting "techno-myth." As a result, the activities of fanship come to be defined by the instrumentalities of technology and dominate the "affective sensibilities" of the fan (Grossberg, 1992). Consideration of the *wearing sports* category of commercials magnifies one of the conundrums of contemporary promotional culture, where the "billboard" pays the sponsor for the privilege of displaying the branding message. Here, sports fanship is shown as active performance, so active that it is characterized as "hard work" for the "privileged" and "committed." As both reward for and sign of this, active sports fanship entails wearing sports fan-coded attire. The *drinking sports* category aims to align the universality of beverage consumption with the consumption of sports. Coca-Cola's progression to "eat football, sleep football, drink Coca-Cola" leaves little symbolic intent masked. Through their "World Cup of Fans" spot, we see clearly how sports and inclusion into its fanship community are integral to both recruiting and providing a "sense of place" for those who often do not have much of one in consumer culture. The *paying sports* category cements the "buy" with the "sell" of sports. Here, buying gets better when one is buying sports or even buying "through sports." Yet, with this comes a transformation of fanship, a structural shift away from "symbolic" and "sign" value to a focus on the nature of the "exchange" and "use" that may be made of the purchase. This characterizes an important shift. With increasingly pragmatic goals, the instrumentality of fanship is heightened.

In matters like these, the moral consequences of the social construction of the sports fan as consumer can be seen as far-reaching. Embedded in key strategies is the reliance on complementary false notions of citizenship and inclusiveness. With this comes a self-interested shift to characterizing fanship by "techno-activity," a preoccupation that stresses instrumentalities over the texture, and hence meaning, of the experience. Most importantly, perhaps more than any other place in contemporary culture, media constructions of the sports fan have come to naturalize fans as walking commodity signs. Casting aside the larger question over the impacts to human expression that come with aligning its routine practice with corporate vocalizations, such characterizations of the sports fan contribute to a sense of "false democratization" that comes with mistaking consumer power for citizen power, a sleight of hand that Coca-Cola, in particular, relied on in cementing its product to the dirt of sports in the developing world. To the extent that all of these matters characterize a shift to an "exchange value" model of sports fanship, they also mark a structural alteration of the contours of one part of cultural life. It is inescapable that in this comes a stated moral imperative, seen here in the limited but very visible domain of sports, about "how to live."

Even with its limited scope, this study opens the door for others on the social construction of the sports fan in commodity culture, an area that has not been explored in depth. In offering a dirt theory approach to commercialized narratives, a posture has been taken that the sports fan is neither cultural dope nor often engaged in imaginative resistance to the larger commodity culture that surrounds the routine spectacle of contemporary sports. A chief advantage of dirt theory is that it recognizes that there necessarily is dirt and that dirt necessarily works. Dirt's workings are compounded with sports dirt because the sports fan is particularly prone to enjoy "rolling around in the dirt of the advertiser" (Wenner, 1991, p. 392). Because of this tendency, the appeals to reading sensibilities and the characterization of fans in media texts often provide a window through which ethical breaches may be seen. As future studies of the mediated sports fan explore the complexities of the fanship experience, the moral consequences of fanship influenced by the logic of commodification need to be considered. To take fans at their own word that they are hardly impacted by such sensibilities would miss the air that contemporary fans breathe. In looking ahead at the sports fan, it is hard not to see a consumer, even if that is not the reflection seen in the mirror.

Notes

1. The proprietary video collections at adforum.com primarily service the advertising industry in campaign development. A chief benefit of the adforum.com collection is that it is devoid of "user-generated content" or "viral videos," such as those that are key features of youtube.com or ifilm.com and have even infiltrated advertising industry-centered collections at adcritic.com.

Patriots and Saints

How the NFL Helped America Cope with Terrorists and Natural Disasters

STEVEN E. MARTIN AND AMANDA BREITENFELDT

As the Roman gladiator takes his place in the arena, the crowd of mixed gender, social class, and race erupts with energy. Although the gladiatorial games brought people together in unity, the events also acted as a diversion from Rome's poverty and the impending downfall of the Empire (Coakley, 1986, p. 47). Divided viewpoints surrounding the positive and negative aspects of sports have, indeed, been evident since the Roman Empire. While one side rallies around the opportunities that sports offer, the other side condemns the seemingly mindless violence. With the popularity and variety of professional sports ever-increasing as a source of entertainment, our understanding of how sports both reflect and create our culture is essential.

Whether one views sports as advantageous or problematic to society often determines one's critical stance. Noam Chomsky, for instance, has argued that sports are distractions from serious and very real social problems: "opinion makers such as the *Times* and *Nightline* address only one-fifth of the public, those who are college-educated and in the habit of voting. For everybody else, the mass media provide distractions, which are meant to keep people stupid and passive." Chomsky's favorite example of keeping people "passive and stupid" is the sports industry, in particular professional football (quoted in "Manufacturing Consent," 1994).

Yet, there also exists a more positive take on sports. Curry and Jiobu (1984) argued that sports help to erase divisions between races, classes, and genders. In addition, they concluded that sports allow the "validating [of one's] dreams" (pp. 78–81). For these authors, sports function as an agent for positive social change in our world.

33

Still other critics of sports have offered a middle-ground approach. Eitzen (1999) wrote a careful and balanced consideration of sports' influences in society, including whether sports unite or divide a community, whether they are healthy or destructive, and whether or not sports can lead to success in one's personal life (p. v). Finally, Coakley (1986) has argued that answers to such questions depend entirely upon context and each individual circumstance. He considered whether sports are primarily "an inspiration or an opiate?" (p. 22). In answering his own question, Coakley claimed that since sports are "the creations of people interacting with one another" the answer will change depending on the various economic climates and shifting social values (pp. 34–35). Coakley also emphasized that examining sports with a critical lens helps us discover "(1) what sport[s] could be in society, (2) how the opportunities and choices related to sport[s] vary from one group to another, (3) how sport[s] could be changed to reflect the interests of all those involved, and (4) when and how sport[s] could become a catalyst for change in society" (p. 34). Coakley concluded, then, that sports' roles in society are entirely context-dependent, a premise upon which this essay rests.

Building upon this discussion, this chapter exhibits how sports served as a unifying force during crisis situations. We argue that sporting events can serve as a rallying point for a community through the process of identification by honoring the victims of a given crisis. Additionally, sporting events can provide fans with a therapeutic function. Sports can function as relief from the overwhelming inundation of information from the media, but do not necessarily detract from the gravity of the actual social crisis or material problems. Especially during extreme times, we demonstrate that sporting events can actually work to unite and promote a stronger sense of community in the United States.

In order to support our contention, we examine two case studies to illustrate how sports function to bring communities closer together in times of crisis rather than acting merely as mindless entertainment. The first case study examines the New York Jets, the New York Giants, and the New England Patriots' embodiment of patriotism after the terrorist attacks of September 11, 2001. The second considers how, after Hurricane Katrina hit the Gulf Coast, victims looked to the New Orleans Saints, and the rebuilding of the Superdome in the city of New Orleans, as a sign of hope and support for the future.

Each case study examines how various elements work together to create a sense of community that revolves around a sports team. Therefore, sports can foster a sense of identification between the sports organization and its fan-base (which seems to grow exponentially in times of crisis), possess the potential to resolve a perceived crisis, construct a symbolic hero to rally behind, and use ideographs, or terms which embody prevalent cultural values, to create camaraderie. These elements demonstrate how the discourse surrounding professional sporting events works to unite a community in crisis situations. Although some critics still consider professional football (along with hockey, boxing, and martial arts, as just a few examples) as legalized violence that takes attention away from important issues in favor of focusing solely on victory (Margolis, 1999), sports can also function therapeutically by offering fans a sense of optimism that promotes hope, unity, and community in the United States.

Sports and September 11, 2001

The terrorist attacks on 9/11 stopped the nation. Thousands of people were killed, millions of people were mourning the victims, and the FAA declared the United States a no-fly zone. As rescue crews worked to recover bodies from the wreckage, many wondered how life could go on following such a tragedy. Some found resolve in attending church, others by reaching out to loved ones. Messages of hope from the government and support from other countries calmed some minds. Yet, people still wondered how daily life could ever again be "normal." The simple answer, it seemed, was by returning to the routine of ordinary, everyday activities. For football players, it was returning to work. For football fans, in New York in particular but also across the nation, it was attending or watching on television the customary Sunday football game.

After the National Football League postponed the games immediately following the terrorist attacks, all teams resumed play on September 23, 2001 (Elfin, 2001). Because of the events of 9/11, the media that weekend focused on the New York Jets, the New York Giants, and the New England Patriots. Both the Jets' and Giants' players had worked at Ground Zero during their week off, helping to bring cases of bottled water to rescue workers to thank the volunteers for their hard work (Goldberg, 2001; Kimball, 2001). New England Patriots' offensive guard Joe Andruzzi was especially affected by the attacks. All three of his brothers were New York City firefighters, and one "was inside the World Trade Center just minutes before it came down" ("Rhode Island Businessman's Bracelets," 2002). That weekend both the New York Giants and the New York Jets won their respective games, bringing something positive back to New York. The Jets defeated the Patriots that weekend, but the Patriots would go on to win the biggest of the battles, both literally and metaphorically, for the nation: the Super Bowl.

Unity through Identification

Following the terrorist attacks, the NFL's controversial decision (some critics believed large gatherings of people in tightly packed stadiums made nice targets for subsequent attacks) to resume normal play served as a means to unite fans and America. The NFL's decision, we argue, can be viewed as symbolic action. Kenneth Burke (1989a) distinguishes between action and mere motion (p. 53). Burke defines "motion" as all things objective and natural, and "action" as something done with a purpose; it is symbolic. To Burke, all *action* is rhetorical. Thus, action possesses potential to unite or divide communities. As Wander (2005) explained, "the significance of rhetoric, folklore, and myth lay in their potential for securing an intuitive sense of community among all Americans" (p. 99). Burke's theory of identification explains how actions, though perhaps not "persuasive" in the traditional sense, may function to create this shared sense of purpose, or a sense of "community." Identification, as opposed to persuasion, results when the audience perceives themselves to be like the speaker (Burke, 1950, p. 20). The symbolic *action* fosters a sense of community through its ability to create such identifications.

The identification between football fans, football players, and victims of 9/11 grew as people were able to connect to the events by watching football on Sunday. Many fans could sympathize with the Jets, the Giants, or any New Yorker. Some fans empathized with the feelings of Joe Andruzzi, because they, too, had loved ones in harm's way. Additionally, those sports fans who were not from New York could feel more connected to the rest of the country and the horrible events of 9/11 through the teams and players. As Herman Edwards, head coach of the Jets, observed, "there are a lot of people on this football team who are associated with people who've been involved in this thing [9/11], and as the days go on, the stories keep coming in" (quoted in Kimball, 2001, p. B23). Fans, thus, took part in the healing process both by viewing sporting events and also by communicating directly with their favorite players or coaches in the NFL.

The televised games alone that first weekend after the attacks allowed the fans in attendance, the players, and viewers across the country to connect to each other. Players and coaches paid homage to victims and made statements of national unity by wearing United States flag decals on their helmets and caps, and fans followed suit by dropping their particular team affiliation to wear red, white, and blue ("Drill," 2001; Elfin, 2001). Similarly, before all games, the NFL honored the lives lost on 9/11, and all the heroes working in dangerous conditions, with a "moment of silence, a 1-minute film about last week's events, a special rendition of 'America the Beautiful' by Bon Jovi, Lionel Richie and Mary J. Blige and performances of the 'Star-Spangled Banner'" (Elfin, 2001). During the "Star-Spangled Banner," volunteers presented a flag the size of the football field.

The uniting through identification as citizens of the United States, or more specifically as victims of the attack on 9/11, can also be seen in the (overly) sportsmanlike conduct amongst teams and fans throughout the NFL in the week, and even in the entire season, following the attacks. Aside from spectators changing out of their normal team's apparel to wear red, white, and blue, many fans forsook their customary "booing" of the opponent and instead cheered for them. This happened especially with the New York Giants and the New York Jets. The Giants, for example, "took the field Sunday to a standing ovation from [Kansas City] Chiefs' fans, who normally rain down derision on visiting teams" (Goldberg, 2001, B1). Likewise, "New England fans set aside their partisanship and gave the Jets a warm greeting, high-fiving players as they ran on the field" (Goldberg, 2001, B1). Both the Jets and Giants won their games on September 23, 2001, and, following the game, the Jets dedicated the game ball to New York City. The support of the opposing fans, and the wins by both New York teams, brought the nation together in support of New York. The fans united through watching football and communicating with its players and coaches.

Terrorist attacks were particularly troubling to our nation's psyche. New York Jets head coach Herman Edwards captured this effect eloquently, "That's what terrorism is about, getting you out of whack so that all of a sudden everything you do is fearful to you. We don't live that way in America, and we shouldn't accept it. We have to get back to what we do" (quoted in Kimball, 2001, p. B23). For sports fans, the NFL's decision to play the games as scheduled helped create a return to normalcy. Yet, importantly, spectatorship became not so much about victory over one's rival as about simply playing the game. Fearful of more attacks, the NFL justifiably could have canceled games for several more weeks, or even the rest of the season, but instead the decision to play the games gave fans a way to get back to normal — to heal. Skeptics of the NFL's true motives would have argued that the NFL's decision was about money as much as any other reason, and may be accurate in that assessment, but the *perception* by players and fans was that the NFL helped return the U.S. to its normal Sunday routine. Advertising dollars and ticket sales profits likely were not in the forefront of players' and fans' minds when the NFL made the decision, but returning to normal was on their minds, as players' and fans' remarks indicated.

Through their words and other symbolic representations, players and coaches prescribed a good dose of therapy for how to overcome the chaos brought about by terrorism with a return to daily routines. Bill Belichick, head coach of the Patriots, said, "We're all very respectful of what happened and to the people it happened to. We'll have Joe's [Andruzzi's] family here and nobody was more in it than they were" (quoted in Mannix, 2001, p. B19). After winning his game, Giants' quarterback Kerry Collins stated, "We wanted to win this game for a lot of different reasons. One of them was to brighten people's days back in New York" (quoted in Goldberg, 2001, p. B1). Further exemplifying this sentiment, Jets running back Curtis Martin said, "Every man in his heart felt he was representing New York. We just felt it was something we had to do. People would've been even more sad than usual if we had lost this game. We were determined not to let it happen" (quoted in Lange, 2001, p. S1). Vinny Testaverde, quarterback for the Jets, seemed to summarize what many players were thinking when he remarked that, "Football is about life. People were looking for some enjoyment today, some relief from the last two weeks. Maybe we were able to help them out" (quoted in "It's Unanimous," 2001, p. C3). These remarks demonstrated the football players' determination to be a part of many sports fans', and especially New Yorkers', healing process, showing them that positive things could still happen.

The NFL's return served as a catalyst for other people as well. One spectator of a Broncos–Cardinals game remarked, "It's a very good outlet of a lot of things you've got pent up inside" (quoted in Goldberg, 2001, p. B1). Atlanta Falcons' fan Ginny Wehunt, sporting her team's logo on one cheek and a "USA" logo on the other, said simply, "You have to have a life" (quoted in "Drill," 2001, D9). The football games on September 23, 2001, functioned for many fans as a way to honor, respect, and pay tribute to the victims and the rescue workers, while moving on and beginning the healing process.

The Super Bowl and Patriotism

MacCambridge (2004) argued that football has long surpassed baseball as the national pastime. Thus, it is not surprising that "Super Sunday," also known as the day of the Super Bowl, has become the most watched television event of the year, even attaining "the status of unofficial holiday in the nation's civic culture" (p. xiv). Although the Super Bowl attained such status before 9/11, the Super Bowl that followed the terrorist attacks served as an even greater symbol of unity in the nation.

The Super Bowl has often adopted a "Mardi Gras" theme when New Orleans hosts the event. The 2002 Super Bowl, however, emphasized a theme of patriotism. For example, the symbol for Super Bowl XXXVI contained the Roman numerals sprawled across a map of the United States, which was colored to look strikingly similar to the U.S. flag. Rather than emphasizing New Orleans, as the symbols for Super Bowl XXXI and Super Bowl XII did by adding Mardi Gras colors (purple, green, and gold) and "ribbons," the symbol represented the entire nation. Moreover, on the Superdome in New Orleans, the location of the Super Bowl, the league displayed a copy of the Declaration of Independence and a banner reading: "United We Stand." In addition to these patriotic symbols, Mariah Carey sang the only national anthem she said she would ever sing, former NFL players recited the Bill of Rights, and four former presidents, along with former first lady Nancy Reagan, read excerpts from Abraham Lincoln's speeches during the pre-game ceremonies (Foster, 2002). These images, along with images of United States troops overseas, were watched by over 130 million viewers (Slater, 2002). Adding to the patriotic theme was President George Bush's declaration of the Super Bowl as a "national security event," at which the FBI and FEMA were present (MacCambridge, 2004, p. 425). All of these symbols and representations celebratory of United States civic culture and pride served to enhance the "unbridled patriotism" of the Super Bowl (Shapiro, 2002, A1).

A second element that allowed football to unite the audience was the literal and metaphorical uses of the word "patriot." Interestingly, and conveniently, one of the teams that advanced to the Super Bowl was, indeed, the New England Patriots. For many, their battle through the season, and then in the Super Bowl, symbolized the nation's healing process from terrorism and the actual military battles that would take place in the Middle East. The Patriots were 14-point underdogs, and their eventual upset win solidified the symbolic triumph of patriotism, and by extension the United States, over evil and terrorism. Newspaper stories about the Super Bowl's outcome frequently linked the Patriots' victory over the St. Louis Rams to the larger sense of patriotism fans felt. Although the players themselves downplayed any sense of "destiny" surrounding their victory, journalists and fans alike nonetheless deemed the win as "preordained" (Berkrot, 2002). Many fans even remarked that a Patriots victory was their "destiny" or "fate" (Weiss, 2002). Other articles created links between patriotism and the "aptly named" Patriots, and stated that the Patriots' victory provided the perfect "Hollywood ending" (Shapiro, 2002, p. A1). The double-meaning of "patriot" seemed a common theme surrounding the Super Bowl; as New England Patriots owner Robert Kraft said, "We're all Patriots, and tonight, the Patriots are world champions" (quoted in Pells, 2002). When journalists, fans, players, coaches, and owners played up the double meaning of the word "patriot" they symbolically extended the meaning beyond a football team's victory in a game and implied that all football fans had in some way triumphed as "world champions."

The NFL, its players, and its coaches honored victims and volunteers after 9/11 and began the healing process by returning to a normal routine. The games during that first weekend after the attack, and on the road to the Super Bowl for the Patriots, represented more than just entertainment. They illustrated some of the major beliefs of the fans through their actions and their use of the patriotism motif. Based on player, coach, and fan comments, football was instrumental in revealing one possible path to healing and a return to something "normal."

Katrina and New Orleans: Saints March and the Nation Follows

Unfortunately, the site that held the Patriots' Super Bowl in 2002, the Superdome in New Orleans, became the location of the next crisis examined. Hurricane Katrina hit New Orleans on August 29, 2005. After the levees broke, water flooded 80 percent of the city ("Summary box," 2006). For the 25,000 to 30,000 people who had not evacuated, the New Orleans Superdome became their only shelter. The Superdome's structure remained intact during Hurricane Katrina, but, with the winds and rain that followed, over 70 percent of the roof was compromised, allowing the rain to damage the interior of the dome ("Saints Will Return," 2006).

Although many people equate New Orleans with Mardi Gras and a generally festive atmosphere, the city has a second claim to fame: sports. New Orleans has hosted six Super Bowls, Final Fours for both men's and women's college basketball, the Olympic trials, and the Sugar Bowl every New Year's Day for college football (Brennan, 2005, p. C12). The city is also home to the NFL's New Orleans Saints and the NBA's New Orleans Hornets (Steele, 2005). For New Orleans and the sports world, the rebuilding of sports in the city was also the beginning of the rebuilding of hope for the city.

Identification between the City and the Nation

As a crisis, Hurricane Katrina differed from 9/11 because the hurricane came and went in Louisiana and Mississippi, whereas terrorism was an ongoing threat to the entire nation. Still, the need to unite as a country in order to support the victims was necessary. Some people did so through various charities, others through newscasts and celebrity appearances, but once again sports prevailed as a rallying point for the city, the state, and, ultimately, the entire nation. Three main groups in coordination with the Saints helped the rest of the nation identify with the crisis: the players of the Saints, the state government of Louisiana, and the NFL.

The players on the Saints used the national media coverage they received as a catalyst to fulfill their perceived responsibility to give hope to the citizens. In many ways the Saints playing football was a reminder to fans of what New Orleans once was and hopefully would be again. Saints' wide-receiver Joe Horn visited the Houston Astrodome, where Katrina survivors were displaced. After his visit, Horn said, "I thought football would be irrelevant to them [victims of Hurricane Katrina] right now, but it's not. I thought I would cry once I stepped into that dome, but seeing people smile, and having kids ask for autographs uplifted me. They went through this catastrophe, and they still want us to play football" (quoted in Halling, 2005, p. 62). Being visited personally by football players gave fans something to be excited about in a time of crisis. It also united fans and players. As Horn's fellow teammate, running back Fred McAfee, said, "I want to go and play my heart out for these people. Football is something to hold on to. Right now, *it is their connection to what is real*, because what they are experiencing is surreal" (emphasis ours; quoted in Halling, 2005, p. 62). Sports fans from New Orleans and throughout the nation could especially empathize and/or sympathize with McAfee, "whose connection to the disaster was made real when he saw television footage of his 5-year-old niece being winched to safety from a rooftop" (Halling, 2005, p. 62).

In addition to the players' desire and commitment to win for New Orleans, the support of the Saints' return to the Superdome by the NFL and the state government allowed sports fans to bridge the gap between what sports were to

New Orleans in the past and what they would be in the future. A little more than 6 months after Katrina, NFL commissioner Paul Tagliabue announced that the Saints would play their first home game since Katrina on September 24, 2006, in the Superdome (Hyman, 2006, p. D10). That support, along with the league's pledge of $20 million to repair the Superdome, brought the NFL closer to the fans of the Saints and also sports fans in general who were donating to help victims ("Summary Box," 2006). Likewise, Louisiana's Governor Kathleen Babineaux Blanco's response to the Saints' return to New Orleans allowed for identification of the nation with the state's feelings. She said, "The return of the New Orleans Saints to Louisiana for the 2006 season is welcome news. While I join the team in its gratitude for San Antonio's hospitality during a very difficult and challenging season, we know in our hearts that the Saints belong in Louisiana. Like so many citizens of our state, I'm eager to welcome the Saints as they go marching into Louisiana for good" ("Governor Responds," 2005). "The Saints" as a rallying cry started with players' connection to the fans, continued with the NFL's concern for the Saints, and culminated with the Governor's excitement about the Saints' return. All of these aspects allowed sports fans and people throughout the United States to unite around the cause, whether they identified with Saints fans, the football players, Tagliabue, or the governor. As economics professor Dennis Coates pointed out, "the Saints have been great ambassadors of goodwill and morale builders. No one can deny that. People can rally around them" (quoted in Steele, 2005, p. D1).

The Superdome: A Symbol of Hope

In contrast to the way sports united New York after the terrorist attacks on 9/11, sports became the unifier in New Orleans because it had been a great hub of sporting events for the nation *before* the crisis occurred. The Saints were identified as the team that unified the city and state, because, in a sports city, the largest structure and location for many events was the Superdome, the Saints' home. In fact, the Superdome became *the* symbol of hope for the rebuilding of all of New Orleans.

The discourse surrounding the Superdome is full of inspiring metaphors. New Orleans resident and pre-game show director of the Super Bowl, Lesslee Fitzmorris, described the Superdome as "the greeting card for New Orleans" (quoted in Brennan, 2005, p. C12). Pre-Katrina the Superdome was thought of as the "entrance into the city ... big and strong and invincible. The way it looms on the horizon, it just might be the closest thing U.S. sports has to the Emerald City" (Brennan, 2005, C12). This idea of the Superdome as "invincible" and "beckoning all to come inside" came true just before Katrina hit. It housed some of the people displaced, and, although the roof was damaged, the building remained structurally intact. The Superdome survived.

Before Hurricane Katrina, the Superdome served as a symbol of strength. After Katrina, the Superdome was transformed into a symbol of hope. Although critics wondered aloud about why the Superdome was being rebuilt while many people were still homeless and other main venues were still closed, the Superdome had become both a local and a national focal point. There were allegations about crime and other horrible events that took place in the Superdome in the days immediately following the hurricane (Ward, 2006), but those events came to symbolize an "opposing team" rather than the structure itself. Maintaining its claim as one of the three largest domed structures in the world (the Georgia Dome and London's Millennium Dome have surpassed it since its completion in 1975), the Saints' home survived the hurricane and its aftermath (Halling, 2005). More than just a greeting card, the rebuilt Superdome demonstrated progress and conveyed hope for the future. The Saints' owner had pledged to stay in the city and the team received additional funding from the NFL. Aside from the Superdome's symbolism as the landmark of New Orleans, its connection to so many teams and sports throughout the years had created a united backing from sports fans and the nation. That a part of the city's identity was restored increased the hope that the sports world in New Orleans would result in a trickledown effect benefiting other avenues of life. Journalist Lewis (2005) justified this idea: "We're not saying that sports are more important than education or the other things that we need for recovery. But using the power of sports to create economic impact gives us all something to shoot for" (p. 9).

The hope and unity the New Orleans Saints represent took on an epideictic role at Super Bowl XL. Again at one of the most televised events in history, the victims of the crisis were honored by the NFL. The NFL chose New Orleans natives Aaron Neville and Dr. John to sing the national anthem. During the pre-game, the NFL acknowledged the devastation that had taken place through a video montage of the damage ("Summary Box," 2006). This notion refreshed the issue in the minds of many Americans. In addition to remembering the devastation left in the aftermath of Hurricane Katrina, Super Bowl XL also shed light on the future of New Orleans. News circulated that the Saints would play September 24, 2006, in the Superdome. The day before the Super Bowl in Detroit, a mural on the Superdome depicting the helmets of the Atlanta Falcons and the New Orleans Saints, the date of the game, and the slogan "Go Saints" was finished. Tagliabue commented that, "We are pleased that this historic reopening will feature the annual renewal of the traditional Falcons–Saints rivalry" (quoted in "Saints Will Return," 2006).

Whether or not the Saints would rebound and be able to compete in the NFL after the chaos and devastation of Katrina remained to be seen. The players, however, seemed keenly aware that their burden to play well would be particularly high in the following season. As New Orleans native and football receiver Michael Lewis summed it up, "We are holding an entire state on our back right now. We have to represent the state and the city, and give them everything we have" (quoted in Halling, 2005, p. 62). And, to the shock of many sports commentators, the New Orleans Saints, homeless a year previous, reached the playoffs in 2006. Indeed, the Saints became one of their conference's best two teams, losing to the Chicago Bears in the National Football Conference's championship game, despite a history of mediocrity and a long playoff drought. In 2007, some sports commentators picked the Saints to go to the Super Bowl (Saraceno, 2006). The Saints had never been favored to reach the Super Bowl. Sports could have been viewed as a failure for the city of New Orleans following Katrina, but the (unexpected) success of the Saints inspired not only New Orleans but the entire nation.

Combining the United

Although linked geographically by the Superdome, each case study—the Super Bowl following the 9/11 terrorist attacks and Hurricane Katrina—was analyzed separately. Between the two crises many differences exist. For example, people in New York City had no warning before the attack occurred. In New Orleans, news of Hurricane Katrina was available, but, as a natural disaster, it could not be stopped or fully predicted. Naturally, then, due to the radically dissimilar nature of each event, different emotions also prevailed. In New York City, and throughout the nation, people were fearful that another attack could and would occur, while in New Orleans the sentiment was of surreal devastation. The storm had passed, but the destruction was overwhelming.

Even though the crises differed as far as the scenery and actions, after both 9/11 and Hurricane Katrina, sports functioned rhetorically to re-unite the nation. In each case, subsequent events fostered a sense of identification among the victims, the sports teams, and the larger population. Regardless of previous team identification, sports fans, and even those not previously interested in sports, were able to relate to either of the New York teams, the New England Patriots, or the New Orleans Saints. Many football players' comments in both situations showed the sense of responsibility to the fans and all the people of the city to continue to play. The second criterion for rallying the community after the crises was the display of hope for the future. For New York, one of the biggest displays of hope for the future was the NFL's decision to play football only one week after 9/11. In doing so, the NFL began the process of returning to everyday activities to overcome the fear many Americans faced, ushering a return to normalcy in the United States. Regardless of the NFL's true motives (it could have easily been a financial decision more than for any other reason), the decision nevertheless symbolized to others that fear would not stop a United States tradition. Another symbol of hope for the nation following 9/11 was the Patriots' overcoming their underdog status to become Super Bowl champions. The win, and the Patriots' path through the season, was a positive element that the community and the nation could turn to for inspiration as the United States recovered. In New Orleans, the symbol of hope became the Superdome. It had been damaged, but, as support came in to rebuild the stadium, hope of the rebuilding of all New Orleans began to spread. These similarities illustrate how sports were able to unite a city or a nation during a crisis.

Finally, it is possible to provide at least several positive examples of "what sport[s] could be in society" and "when and how sport[s] could become a catalyst for change in society" (Coakley, 1986, p. 34). In the weeks and months following 9/11, "what sport[s] could be" was the answer to the question: "how can a person go on?" Likewise, football and the NFL became "a catalyst for change in society" by helping the community start the healing process. Football served as a form of public therapy, which suggests it was more than a mere distraction. "Real" issues are not forgotten or overlooked by attending a football game. They are, perhaps, suspended for a short time, but they are not replaced. As football fan Noelene Kennedy phrased it, "It's [football] a very good outlet of a lot of things you've got pent up inside. I've been looking forward to coming and yelling my head off" (quoted in Goldberg, 2001, p. B1).

For New Orleans, sports seemed to play an important role in the city's return to normalcy. Like sports' role as a catalyst after 9/11, the role of sports after Hurricane Katrina was to help change the perception of New Orleans from a devastated city to an area important enough to rebuild. The Saints and the NFL did this by starting to rebuild the Superdome and scheduling its completion for the Saints' first home game after Katrina on September 24, 2006. Not only did football return to the city that has hosted many Super Bowls, but the Saints finished with one of their best records in franchise history. They even reached the conference championship game, a first for New Orleans professional football.

Throughout this analysis, sports' ability to unite a community and to honor victims in a crisis situation was illustrated. Sports' role, in this case the NFL's role, was more than a negative distraction from issues in the world. In fact, in both crises, the issue, whether it was terrorism or a natural disaster, was not ignored. Instead, the issue was brought to the forefront of many football games, where the NFL honored victims and volunteers. Then, five years later, Super Bowl XL, the one following Hurricane Katrina, paid tribute to the evacuees, victims, and rescue workers involved in the natural disaster. Sports, whether loved or hated, truly became therapeutic symbols of optimism for fans and the nation.

Two Nations, Two Networks, One Game

An Analysis of the ESPN and Univision Telecasts of the 2002 Mexico–United States World Cup Match

JOHN P. MCGUIRE AND GREG G. ARMFIELD

Few sporting events generate the worldwide interest and passion of World Cup soccer. In 2002, this quadrennial event occurred in the nations of Japan and South Korea, capped off by Brazil's victory over Germany in the Cup final. Interest in the World Cup was found in every corner of the globe, with an estimated one billion people in 213 countries watching the Brazilian victory on television (Tudor, 2006).

The tournament was filled with memorable matches, including a meeting between Mexico and the United States (U.S.) in the Round of 16. The June 17, 2002, game marked the first time Mexico was playing the U.S. in a World Cup game, despite the long history of international matches between the two nations. In mainstream U.S. sports media, the game was accorded no more attention than other major sporting events occurring at the time, including the U.S. Open golf championship and the ongoing Major League Baseball season. What pre-match media coverage there was of the game in the U.S. sought to play up the vast cultural differences between the two countries with regard to the importance of the World Cup.

For Mexican fans, the match represented a landmark moment. Mexican novelist and social commentator Carlos Monsiváis believed a victory was important with regard to Mexico's self-image compared with the U.S. (Iliff & Case, 2002). Some press reports previewing the game also played up the idea of the game's being much more than a match to determine which team advanced to the World Cup's quarter-finals. These journalists used political tensions between the two countries (e.g., disagreements over immigration and water rights) to build up the rivalry aspect of this match (Garofoli, 2002; Iliff & Case, 2002). When the U.S. defeated Mexico 2–0, press reports included bitter reactions from some Mexican team fans. "We could have lost to anyone," one Mexico City cab driver told the IPS news agency, "but against the United States it is a sad and shameful outcome" (Cevallos, 2002). This sort of sentiment was common in subsequent Mexican and Latino news reports.

Telecasts of the Mexico–U.S. match also pointed to cultural differences in game coverage. Two U.S.–based networks held broadcast rights for the 2002 World Cup. The Entertainment and Sports Programming Network (ESPN) aired English-language broadcasts of Cup games, and Spanish-language broadcasts of the World Cup could be seen in the United States on the Univision television network. Univision broadcasts had all of their announcers on site at the tournament whereas ESPN had only one broadcast team in Japan and South Korea. Other ESPN broadcast teams did their play-by-play in the network's studios located in Bristol, Connecticut, describing video feeds of games off a monitor (Ahrens & Farhi, 2002). Attention also centered on the announcing styles in the broadcasts. ESPN broadcasts were seen as conventional in terms of the announcer's performance (except when the U.S. was playing), whereas Univision announcers would stand out for their screaming (GOOOAAALL!) when a team scored (Ahrens & Farhi, 2002). Media reports also documented that Univision continually out-performed ESPN in television ratings. This was especially true in the match between Mexico and the U.S., where Univision had 42 percent more viewers than ESPN ("Univision Broadcast," 2002).

The Hispanic population constituted more than 11.5 million television households in the U.S. in 2007 (Nielsen Company, 2007). As the number of Spanish-language media outlets grows to meet this audience demand, it would be useful to gain additional insight into how the same event is presented on English- and Spanish-language programs. Through content analysis and critical analysis in this paper, we will contrast commentary heard during the two broadcasts of the Mexico–U.S. soccer match from the 2002 World Cup. It is anticipated that this research will build upon existing literature examining effects that sports commentary has on its audience as well as contribute to research examining English- and Spanish-language broadcasts of similar events.

The remainder of this chapter is divided into four sections. First, we will offer a brief literature review with an emphasis on past research about (a) English- and Spanish-language television content, (b) international soccer, and (c) sports commentary. Special attention will be given to Morris and Nydahl's (1983) typology of commentary used by announcers during live sports broadcasts. Second, our content analysis methods will be discussed. Third, we will present the results of our content analysis for the ESPN and Univision broadcasts of the U.S.–Mexico 2002 World Cup match. Finally, we will present a discussion of the findings from our research as well as ramifications and limitations of this study.

Literature Review

The focus of this study (a match in the 2002 World Cup) represents the collision of sports, media, and nationalism. Significant research has been done in all of these areas. However, this research will focus specifically on (a) contrasting English- and Spanish-language broadcast content, (b) the use of international soccer as the focus of academic research, and (c) the impact of television sports commentary.

Contrasting English- and Spanish-Language News Content

Although there has been a lack of research contrasting English- and Spanish-language broadcasts of sporting events, there have been studies contrasting English- and Spanish-language news content. One study explored the impact of agenda setting on residents living in a Texas city with a large Hispanic population. Ghanem and Wanta (2001) contrasted the nightly news programs of three networks (CBS, ABC, and Univision) and found an agenda setting effect with the Univision broadcasts. No other significant agenda setting effect involving the English-language networks could be detected. Ghanem and Wanta posited that survey participants watched only one network (Univision) for news. Therefore, it would be logical that the Spanish-language network (Univision) could influence news viewers in this manner.

Rodriguez (1996) examined the idea of a created nationalism within the presentation of Univision's primary news broadcast, *Noticiero Univision*. In analyzing the content of Univision's primary newscast versus the primary newscast seen on ABC television (*World News Tonight*), Rodriguez found similarities between the structures of the news stories. News reports on Univision and ABC were visually structured in the same manner, with reporters applying basic tenets of American journalism, such as objectivity and fairness. The major difference was found in the cultural personalization used within each story. This was exemplified by a report indicating that cases of measles were on the rise. Whereas ABC personalized the story by interviewing people of European-American descent near Chicago, Univision's reporter interviewed Latino families in San Francisco. Rodriguez (1996) concluded that Univision's newscast envisioned a mass audience of Latinos in the U.S. interested in getting news reported from a specific cultural perspective. While the Latino population in the U.S. is made up of people of different nationalities, these different nationalities still share some common geographic, political, and cultural interests.

Soccer as a Research Focus

Perhaps no team sport has received greater scrutiny from an international research perspective than soccer (known as football in other nations). Tudor (2006) identified more than 30 academic works on sports and the media that used international soccer as the focus of research. Tudor's survey broke down the inventory of soccer studies into five major areas of research: linguistic discourses, audiovisual, expertise, narrative, and national identity (p. 220). The majority of research regarding international soccer has focused primarily on narratives or national identities constructed in broadcasts.

Several researchers examining international soccer have focused upon a single game between rivals to examine how nationalism is portrayed. Tudor (1992) critically analyzed the 1990 World Cup coverage in England and found such broadcasts often ended up offering two distinct narratives about competing teams. Opponents of England, like Cameroon, were often framed in broad stereotypes, reflecting the nation's status in the world (seen in this case as a third world country). Tudor described the narrative involving the English team as being far more nuanced. In the Cameroon match, England avoided an upset by winning in extra time (an additional period played after the traditional 90-minute match). Tudor found the broadcast concentrated not only on the English performance on the pitch, but also on building narratives that were congruent with the nation's image of its national team and, reflexively, the nation's national identity.

Tudor (1992) also discussed the evolution of narratives within English soccer matches, even minute-by-minute revisions shaped by the events of the game. As the researcher suggested, one role of narratives is shaping the eventual end of the story. Tudor suggested athletic contests (such as soccer matches) run counter to the idea of the pre-determined narrative, as players and misplays often make a contest's outcome anything but certain. Therefore, game events (unknown until they happen) could radically alter the broadcast narrative. In the case of the 1990 England–Cameroon match, announcers offered explanations for events that ran counter to the English team narrative (expectations of an easy victory over the Cameroon side).

Alabarces, Tomlinson, and Young (2001) examined the 1998 World Cup match in France between Argentina and England. The two nations had a history of conflict, on and off the soccer pitch. The political conflicts included Juan Peron's nationalizing of British business interests in Argentina in the 1940s and the British successfully repelling an Argentine invasion of the Falkland Islands in 1982 (Alabarces, Tomlinson, & Young, 2001). The two countries have also had conflicts on the soccer field. Argentina scored historical victories over English sides on British soil earlier in the 20th century that were still being brought up in the media coverage leading up to the 1998 match. The game itself was a closely fought battle, with Argentina coming out on top as a result of penalty kicks. While Argentina celebrated its new "national heroes" in the victory, British media accounts praised the English team for its spirit and courage in forcing the game to penalty kicks (even after one of their star players was sent off the field for committing a serious foul) (Alabarces et al., 2001).

At that same World Cup, the U.S. was matched against Iran in a qualifying game. It was one of the first head-to-head confrontations between the two nations in a sporting event since the Iranian hostage crisis. Delgado (2003) examined print coverage by U.S. newspapers in the days leading up to the match and found that, although the hostage crisis had occurred nearly two decades before, journalists still couched articles previewing the game as a clash of nations that were enemies over the hostage incident.

As noted above, many issues had helped create tension in Mexico–U.S. relations at the time of the 2002 match (e.g., immigration). Past research by Tudor (1992) and Delgado (2003), among others, suggested that these off-field issues would have an impact on the sporting commentary delivered during sporting matches.

Television Sports Commentary and Audience Impact

A significant body of research exists regarding television sports commentary. While some research has considered how the audience evaluates sports announcers on their performance (see McGuire, 2002), most sports broadcast commentary research has focused on televised sporting events and its effect on the audience (Sullivan, 2006).

The announcer's framing of televised sporting events can impact the emotional effect on viewers. Comisky, Bryant, & Zillman (1977) found that announcers who intentionally dramatized athletic contests (in this case, a hockey match) had the ability to make such events more enjoyable for the audience. Another study that manipulated the commentary of a tennis match between two competitors (Bryant, Brown, Comisky, & Zillman, 1982) found similar effects. Three groups witnessed the same match, but one group heard commentary that suggested the players got along, a second group heard commentary that suggested the players were heated rivals, while the control group heard an unbiased account. Researchers found the group watching the commentary that suggested a heated rivalry found the match more exciting, interesting, and enjoyable than the other two groups (Bryant et al., 1982). Bryant (1989) later suggested that televised sports involving a great deal of physical contact (e.g., football and hockey) were most appealing to viewers when announcers emphasized the conflict between the teams and players. Sullivan (1991) also found that viewers could tolerate the amount of violence seen in a sporting event (e.g., players exchanging punches during a basketball game) if commentators framed such behavior as being acceptable. This and other research in the area of commentary suggested that sports announcers have the ability to frame contests to create a high level of conflict, thereby increasing the level of enjoyment for viewers.

Morris and Nydahl (1983) delineated the different types of commentary used by sports announcers to create drama and to inform the audience during a live sports broadcast. The researchers examined utterances made by CBS announcers Gary Bender and Billy Packer during the 1982 NCAA men's basketball championship game. Two major categories of television sports commentary were identified: basic and elaborative. Commentary identified as basic was seen as being objective, interpretive, or historical. Commentary identified as elaborative was classified as motivational, speculative, foreshadowing, critical, metaphoric, empathetic, and subjective. Morris and Nydahl's typology (Appendix A) of sports broadcast commentary points to announcers' varying their call of a game to allow for description of the basic events of a contest as well as the framing of events they described for their audience.

Sports commentary is also used as a way of providing understanding and explanation to events that happen either in favor of or against a fan's favorite team. McGuire (2002) found that sports announcers engaged in selective perception in their commentary when explaining positive or negative events impacting the team for which they were announcing. In the study, subjects listened to separate broadcast segments involving the school's basketball team. In one segment, the school's team was pulling off an upset win. The other segment had the school's team losing to a team it was expected to beat. Subjects rated the attributes of announcer excitement and overall announcer performance significantly higher on the "winning" segment compared to the "losing" segment. McGuire concluded that the flow of games (and whether the team was winning or losing) could significantly impact the commentary of the announcer. As our study suggests, the Mexico–U.S. match had two distinct broadcasts with two distinct audiences. Events within this particular contest may have impacted the type of announcer commentary found on the ESPN and Univision broadcasts.

Hypothesis and Research Questions

As suggested by this brief literature review, there has been research examining the contrasts between English- and Spanish-language news content, international sports commentary, and the impact of sports commentary on the audience. As this study is particularly interested in contrasting the broadcast commentary from ESPN (English) and Univision (Spanish) of the Mexico–U.S. World Cup match, Morris and Nydahl's (1983) typology of sports commentary provides the means for analyzing the two broadcasts. The first research question explored the number of utterances classified as basic commentary:

RQ1: *Which broadcast (ESPN or Univision) had a greater number of basic commentary utterances?*

In addition to examining the amount of basic commentary, it would be useful to break down usage in the three sub-categories of basic commentary as identified by Morris and Nydahl (1983):

RQ2: *What types of basic commentary utterances (objective, interpretive, and historical) were used by the ESPN and Univision broadcasts?*

The next two research questions consider the usage of elaborative commentary used on the ESPN and Univision broadcasts as well as the number of utterances in each of the seven elaborative commentary sub-categories:

RQ3: *Which broadcast (ESPN or Univision) had a greater number of elaborative commentary utterances?*

RQ4: *What types of elaborative commentary utterances (motivational, speculative, foreshadowing, critical, metaphoric, empathetic, and subjective) were used on the ESPN and Univision broadcasts?*

In addition to evaluating the type of commentary used on the two broadcasts, it is useful to examine the influence of events during the game on the nature of the ESPN and Univision broadcasts. Tudor (1992) has suggested that the narrative of sports commentary can change depending on what is happening in a particular contest. McGuire (2002) has also suggested that positive or negative events unfolding in a game could influence the commentary of announcers representing one particular team's perspective. As the Univision broadcast was presented from the perspective of the Mexican team (and for the Mexican team fan base in the U.S.), it would be expected that the failures of the Mexican team in the match would impact the Univision announcers and cause them to be more critical of the Mexican team's performance. As a result, it is expected that critical commentary would be used more than other types of elaborative commentary in the Univision broadcast:

H1: *Critical elaborative commentary will be used significantly more frequently on the Univision broadcast than other types of elaborative commentary.*

Method

Content analytic methods (Riffe, Lacy, & Fico, 1998) were employed to analyze the live broadcast commentary of the 2002 World Cup match between the United Sates and Mexico.

Procedures

Live broadcasts of the 2002 World Cup match between the U.S. and Mexico were videotaped from the ESPN (English) and Univision (Spanish) networks. A word-for-word transcript of the English-language broadcast was produced by one of the authors and verified, while a bilingual undergraduate student, whose first language is Spanish, produced a word-for-word transcript of the Spanish-language broadcast. A second bilingual undergraduate student then verified that transcript. Transcriptions of both broadcasts consisted of literal transcription of the discourse employed among both the play-by-play announcers and the color commentators. The 95-minute, commercial-free game (including five stoppage minutes) consisted of 12,539 words from the ESPN broadcast and 17,041 words from the Univision broadcast. All non-game commentary (i.e., promotional and sponsorship spots) was excluded from the transcripts as the focus of this research was on the live, unplanned, natural interactions between play-by-play announcer and color commentator.

Coding Procedures

The authors served as coders for the study. A training session was conducted, providing coders with a codebook and instructions to clarify subsequent coding responsibilities. Upon completion of the training session, a trial coding process was conducted on the first 10 percent of the transcribed English (ESPN) broadcast. Each coder independently analyzed the transcript, and intercoder reliability was assessed (Riffe et al., 1998). Reliability was calculated using Scott's Pi. Overall, reliability was .90.

Broadcast commentary transcripts were analyzed following Morris and Nydahl's (1983) content analysis scheme. Broadcast commentary was first coded as basic or elaborative. If the coding unit was determined to be basic, the second level of coding was objective, interpretive, or historical. If the coding was determined to be elaborative, the second level of coding was motivational, speculative, foreshadowing, critical, metaphoric, empathetic, or subjective. Appendix A provides illustrations of each form of basic and elaborative play-by-play and color commentator game calls.

Results

The results are grouped by topic and discussed in order. Altogether, 1,058 basic and 343 elaborative comments were made. Content analysis found the frequency of basic descriptions significantly exceeded the frequency of elaborative sentences [$\chi^2(1) = 7.02, p < .01$]. This supports the notion that contemporary sports broadcasting is more than just the play-by-play, as 24.5 percent of the comments from the ESPN and Univision broadcasts were elaborative.

Differences were also observed in the overall number of basic and elaborative comments used by ESPN and Univision. These differences are discussed below.

The first research question asked whether ESPN or Univision had a greater number of basic commentary utterances. As Table 1 shows, the commentators for Univision used significantly more basic comments ($n = 599$) than ESPN ($n = 459$), [$\chi^2(1) = 42.07$, $p < .001$]. This trend was further explored with research questions two and three, which explored the specific difference revealed in the basic commentary utterances between the ESPN and Univision broadcasts.

Table 1. Theme Frequencies by Network

Network	Basic	Elaborative	Total
ESPN	459 (79%)	121 (21%)	580
Univision	599 (73%)	222 (27%)	821
Total	1058 (75.5%)	343 (24.5%)	1401

Note. $\chi^2(1) = 7.02$, $p < .01$

The second research question asked about the type of basic utterances used by ESPN and Univision commentators. To answer this question it was necessary to break down the number of basic utterances for the two halves of the match (see Table 2). During the first half of play, the ESPN and Univision commentators did not significantly differ on overall basic commentary utterances [$\chi^2(1) = 3.41$, $p > .05$]. However, as the match progressed, and the chances of the U.S. pulling off this historic upset became more apparent, Univision commentators used significantly more basic utterances [$\chi^2(1) = 54.63$, $p < .001$] than ESPN commentators. Specifically, the Univision commentators used significantly more interpretive comments during the second half ($n = 124$) compared to the first half ($n = 52$). ESPN commentators, on the other hand, began referencing the historical significance of the potential U.S. upset during the

Table 2. Basic Theme Frequencies by Network

Network	Objective	Historical	Interpretive	Total	$\chi^2(df = 1)$
First Half					
ESPN	139 (66.5%)	17 (8%)	53 (25.5%)	209	
Univision	192 (64%)	15 (5%)	93 (31%)	300	
Total	331 (65%)	32 (6%)	146 (29%)	509	3.41, $p > .05$
Second Half					
ESPN	169 (67.5%)	29 (11.5%)	52 (21%)	250	
Univision	175 (58.5%)	0	124 (41.5%)	299	
Total	344 (63%)	29 (5%)	176 (32%)	549	54.62, $p < .001$
Game					
ESPN	308 (67%)	46 (10%)	105 (23%)	459	
Univision	367 (61%)	15 (2.5%)	217 (36.5%)	599	
Grand Total	675 (64%)	61 (6%)	322 (30%)	1058	42.08, $p < .001$

Table 3. Elaborative Theme Frequencies by Network

	Motivation	Speculative	Critical	Subjective	Empathetic	Foreshadow	Metaphor	Total	$\chi^2 (df = 1)$
First Half									
ESPN	0	11 (20.5%)	9 (16.5%)	23 (42.5%)	0	7 (13%)	4 (7.5%)	54	
Univision	26 (25%)	30 (29%)	16 (15.5%)	14 (13.5%)	2 (2%)	6 (5.5%)	10 (9.5%)	104	
Total	26 (16.5%)	41 (26%)	25 (16%)	37 (23.5%)	2 (1%)	13 (8%)	14 (9%)	158	30.87, $p < .001$
Second Half									
ESPN	2 (3%)	14 (21%)	8 (12%)	27 (40%)	3 (4.5%)	11 (16.5%)	2 (3%)	67	
Univision	29 (24.5%)	23 (19.5%)	26 (22%)	17 (14.5%)	2 (1.5%)	14 (12%)	7 (6%)	118	
Total	31 (17%)	37 (20%)	34 (18.5%)	44 (23.5%)	5 (2.5%)	25 (13.5%)	9 (5%)	185	28.99, $p < .001$
Game									
ESPN	2 (1.5%)	25 (20.5%)	17 (14%)	50 (41.5%)	3 (2.5%)	18 (15%)	6 (5%)	121	
Univision	55 (25%)	53 (24%)	42 (19%)	31 (14%)	4 (2%)	20 (9%)	17 (7%)	222	
Grand Total	57 (16.5%)	78 (23%)	59 (17%)	81 (23.5%)	7 (2%)	38 (11%)	23 (7%)	343	54.91, $p < .001$

second half of the game ($n = 29$) compared to no historical references used during the game's first half ($n = 0$). Overall, Univision commentators used more interpretive utterances ($n = 217$ compared to $n = 105$) and the ESPN commentators used more historical references ($n = 43$ compared to $n = 15$) to frame the outcome of the match.

The last two research questions explored the elaborative utterances used by ESPN and Univision commentators. Research question three explored the number of elaborative utterances used by the ESPN and Univision commentators. Univision had a greater number of overall elaborative comments ($n = 222$) than ESPN ($n = 121$), [$\chi^2(1) = 54.91, p < .001$].

Research question four investigated the difference between the ESPN and Univision commentators' use of elaborative commentary utterances. To answer this question, it was necessary to break down the number of elaborative utterances for the two halves of the match (see Table 3). The Univision commentators used significantly more elaborative utterances during the first half [$\chi^2(1) = 30.87, p < .001$] and second half [$\chi^2(1) = 28.99, p < .001$] of the match. As the match progressed, the elaborative comments increased. Specifically, the Univision commentators used more critical comments (first half $n = 16$, second half $n = 26$), and more foreshadowing comments (first half $n = 6$, second half $n = 14$). Conversely, ESPN commentators used more empathetic (first half $n = 0$, second half $n = 3$) and motivational comments (first half $n = 0$, second half $n = 2$).

Finally, the hypothesis predicted that critical comments would be significantly more frequent on the Univision broadcast than other types of elaborative commentary. This hypothesis was not supported, as the frequency of critical comments ranked third for the first half of play, second for the second half of play, and third overall for total elaborative comments from the Univision broadcast. Although this hypothesis was not supported, it is interesting to note the increase of critical comments in the Univision broadcast from 16 in the first half to 26 in the second half, an increase of 48 percent. This and other elaborative observations will be discussed in the next section.

Discussion

The research goal of this study was to contrast the ESPN and Univision broadcasts of the 2002 Mexico–U.S. World Cup match based on Morris and Nydahl's (1983) content analysis scheme. A significant difference was found between the use of basic and elaborative utterances used by the Univision and ESPN commentators. Univision commentators used a greater number of both basic and elaborative utterances when compared to the ESPN commentators. Furthermore, Univision commentators used 4,500 more words in their broadcast than did the ESPN commentators. This may simply represent a function of broadcast style (talking more or less during a television sports broadcast) between the announcing teams involved in the broadcast.

In breaking down the types of basic commentary used in the broadcast, it is important to analyze the changes in commentary styles as the game flowed from a 1–0 surprise lead for the U.S., to a 2–0 lead that was proving insurmountable no matter what the Mexican team tried. A review of basic commentary utterances from the first half of the match found no significant difference between the ESPN and Univision broadcasts. This changed in the second half as the Univision commentators began using significantly more interpretive comments than did the ESPN commentators.

As Tudor (1992) suggested, the events of a sports contest will ebb and flow, as will the narrative being constructed by those covering the event. We suggest that as the U.S. victory was becoming more evident in the latter stages of the match, the Univision commentators commenced offering more interpretation within their commentary to explain why the Mexican side was trailing in a game they expected to win. Univision commentators employed 124 interpretive comments in the second half compared to 52 coded in the ESPN broadcast. An example from the second half is when the Mexican team had a scoring chance go awry, and one commentator explained, "Louis Hernandez can't reach it, but his intention was that Borgetti could head it in the first try." This utterance suggests that while the Mexican team was capable of creating scoring chances against the U.S. side, it was some combination of misplays, miscommunication, or just bad luck that was keeping the Mexican team from registering a goal.

As McGuire (2002) found in his study of announcer evaluations, the fact that his or her particular team was failing would impact the announcer's commentary. As the Univision crew presented the game from a Mexican (or Hispanic) perspective, the commentators may have reflected the same frustration those Mexican team supporters were feeling at that point of the match.

Meanwhile, the ESPN broadcast crew employed a greater number of historical comments (29 vs. none for Univision's crew) during the second half. ESPN commentator Jack Edwards tried to connect the historical importance of what was happening in Asia with the actions of fanatical U.S. soccer supporters back home: "Well it may be four o'clock in the morning eastern time, but I guarantee you they're going wild at Columbus Crew stadium right now, where thousands have been gathering in the middle of the night to watch these games." Edwards made this comment as a way of emphasizing that interest in soccer in the U.S. was growing as a result of the national team's play in the World Cup.

The analysis of data from the ESPN and Univision broadcasts also revealed a significant difference in the number of elaborative commentary utterances between the networks (222 on Univision to 121 on ESPN). The study found a significant difference in the use of elaborative commentary in both the first and second halves of the match. As with the interpretive comments used in basic commentary, the data suggested that the flow of the match (with Mexico trailing for nearly the entire game) impacted the type of elaborative commentary employed on the two networks. The ESPN broadcast did employ more instances of empathetic ("Unbelievable disappointment for Mexico") and motivational ("Blanco does that out of frustration") utterances in the second half after using none in the first. The Univision broadcast also had more utterances (14) that foreshadowed the outcome of the match during the second half when compared with the first half. When the referee decided against awarding a yellow card for a hard foul by a Mexican player late in the second half, the commentator noted none was given because "the game is almost over and there is no need to make things harder." This announcer's comment could be seen as a concession that defeat was inevitable, as if to prepare Mexican team fans for disappointment that was to come.

The analysis failed to support the hypothesis that a specific type of elaborative commentary (critical) would be used significantly more often on the Univision broadcast than other types of elaborative comments. It should be noted that the number of critical comments did increase over the course of the Univision broadcast (26 in the second half to only 16 in the first half) compared to a total of 17 critical comments in the ESPN broadcast. Some critical comments dealt with the officials assigned to the match. At a critical point of the second half, the Mexican announcers believed U.S. player John O'Brien had touched the ball in the penalty box, an infraction for which the player should have been sent off the field and the Mexican team given a penalty shot at goal. When no call was made, one Univision commentator declared, "It's strange that neither the referee nor the assistant saw it, because everyone is shouting for it and that makes you react and get everything under control." The other commentator joined in the criticism, lamenting that "they excused the handball, the card and the penalty kick [against] the American team." Most of the critical comments were directed at the Mexican team for its poor play and the actions of one Mexican player, Rafa Márquez, which resulted in a red card and an automatic ejection from the match. One of the Univision commentators bemoaned the fact that Márquez had been sent off for a flagrant foul against a U.S. player before the game ended: "Márquez leaves, and this shouldn't be the image the Mexican team leaves in the field." In this example, the commentator is not only criticizing the player for earning the red card, but is also trying to protect a national narrative that the Mexican squad, even in defeat, engaged in fair play. As other soccer research regarding sports commentary narratives have demonstrated (Tomlinson & Young, 2006), the image of the national team is as important within the broadcast as the narrative about the match.

While the 2002 Mexico–U.S. World Cup match is one of many international matches played between the two nations over the years, this particular game had especially important implications for the two soccer nations, thereby making this match commentary especially relevant for research. When evaluating the sheer number of utterances used by the commentators on the two networks, it can be suggested that, while the usage of basic versus elaborative commentary on the ESPN and Univision broadcasts is generally the same (73 percent basic, 27 percent elaborative on ESPN; and 79 percent basic, 21 percent elaborative on Univision), the actual sub-types of basic and elaborative are used differently. As Rodriguez (1996) suggested in his study of Univision's *Noticiero Univision* program, the Spanish-language news broadcast looks visually similar to its English-language counterpart. The difference is in the presentation and perspective used in covering the Latino viewpoint of the story contrasted with the use of Caucasians on the English-language newscasts. We suggest that the same can be said when contrasting the ESPN and Univision broadcasts of the 2002 Mexico–U.S. World Cup match. While the two broadcasts were generally the same in some ways, the method and commentary used by the separate announcing crews reflected a contrast in styles, and, most likely, in passion for the sport.

While the ability to generalize findings about sports commentary from this one event is limited, we suggest the unique nature of this particular event (two U.S. television networks presenting the same sporting event in separate languages and from unique perspectives) advances our knowledge regarding narrative construction employed in sports commentary. More importantly, this study demonstrates a need for future research to explore how major cultural and societal events are presented to and viewed by a diversified U.S. television audience. As non–Caucasian television households (e.g., Latino and Asian) grow in number, it will become increasingly important for those in media research to grasp how non–English-speaking networks in the United States are presenting televised events to their target audience and how these broadcasts differ from English-speaking networks.

Appendix A

Codebook for Typologies of Television Sports Commentator Utterances

Typology	*Example*
Basic: Objective (OBJ) An objective observation of either action or fact during game.	"Pope punches it forward to Donavan, but it goes over the top to Blanco."
Basic: Interpretive (INTER) An expert interpretation of execution or flow of play.	"Eddie Lewis is dropping so far back he is essentially the left back."

Basic: Historical (HIST) A placing of individuals or events in historical or statistical meta-perspective.	"Well it may be four o'clock in the morning eastern time, but I guarantee you they're going wild at Columbus Crew stadium right now, where thousands have been gathering in the middle of the night to watch these games."
Interpretive: Motivational (MOT) An attribution of motive for behavior.	"Blanco does that out of frustration."
Interpretive: Speculative (SPEC) An educated guess about game as it is in progress.	"I would imagine we're going to see monster stoppage time added to this second half."
Interpretive: Foreshadowing (FORE) An intuition or insight suggesting a possible or probable impact on outcome of entire game.	"Bruce Arena has one more sub and he hesitates to use that last sub because if suddenly this game would turn around and you go into overtime and then you had an injury, you'd be like Spain was in their last game where they ended up playing the entire overtime a man down."
Interpretive: Critical (CRIT) A general assessment of blame.	"Borgetti can't lay it off cleanly."
Interpretive: Metaphoric (MET) An implied or direct comparison.	"Hey, it's backyard wrestling right now, 8 yellow cards in this match, 4 each way."
Interpretive: Empathetic (EMP) An attempt to make viewers feel what another feels.	"Unbelievable disappointment for Mexico."
Interpretive: Subjective (SUBJ) Subjective comment charactering behavior.	"And, that's a cheap shot by Márquez; it's a shame because he's a classy player in every other facet of his game."

Note. Typologies from, "Toward Analyses of Live Television Broadcasts," by B. S. Morris and J. Nydahl, 1983, *Central States Speech Journal, 34,* 195–202.

THE SPORTS FAN

Exploring the Roots
of Sports Fanship

WALTER GANTZ, BRIAN WILSON,
HYANGSUN LEE AND DAVID FINGERHUT

Introduction

Sports spectating is a predominant form of leisure behavior in today's world (James, 2001), particularly in the United States where enthusiasm for following sports abounds. The number of people attending sporting events continues to grow. For example, in 1999 the combined attendance at National Football League (NFL), Major League Baseball (MLB), National Basketball Association (NBA), and National Hockey League (NHL) regular season games exceeded 116 million (Frank, 2000). This was a 16 percent increase from 1984 when the attendance reached 100 million (Madrigal, 1995, p. 205). An increase in attendance also has been seen at college sporting events during the same time period (U.S. Census Bureau, 2000, cited in Capella, 2002).

Another indicator of the substantial growth in spectator sports and sports fanship is the dramatic increase in media time allotted to sports programming. Between 1960 and 1988 the total number of hours allotted to sports programming on the three major networks (ABC, CBS, NBC) increased by 600 percent from 300 hours to over 1800 hours (Wenner, 1989). Since the introduction of ESPN in 1979, sports-only channels have garnered increased viewership — and revenues. In 2000, ESPN ranked fifth among television networks in terms of revenue (McAvoy, 2000). In the 2007 Up Front Opinion Study conducted by TV Guide Network, sports programming emerged as the most sought-after genre, surpassing serialized drama, reality competition, and comedy in terms of the upfront demand. Figures related to sports spending also suggest the ongoing expansion of the sports business in the United States.

Total sports ticket sales were about $15 billion in 2005, an increase of more than 30 percent from 2000. Annual spending on sports advertising increased by 40.4 percent between 2000 and 2005, topping $8 billion in 2005 (Horrow,

2006). It is predicted that in 2010 total sports spending in the United States will rise more than 40 percent from that of 2005, reaching $61.6 billion (Horrow, 2006).

In the United States, a growing number of people think of themselves as sports fans (James, 2001). Between 1960 and 1975, self-identification as a sports fan jumped from 30 percent to 45 percent. In 1990, 73 percent of a national sample of adults indicated they were either "very interested" or "fairly interested" in sports (Lieberman, 1991). Another national survey, done in 2000 by ESPN, found an increase in the fan base of all twelve major sports measured (Frank, 2000; James & Ridinger, 2002).

Taking notice of the pervasiveness of sports spectatorship and the increase in the fan base for spectator sports, Lieberman (1991) argued that sports fanship represents a quintessential part of American culture. Sports certainly have had a great influence on the lives of many people in America (Capella, 2002). In spite of this, only a smattering of social science research was conducted on sports fans prior to the 1990s (Jones, 1997; Wann & Hamlet, 1995). Since then, though, there has been a significant increase in the amount of research on sports fans (Capella, 2002; James & Ridinger, 2002).

Contemporary explorations of sports fans address a wide array of topics: socio-demographic characteristics and differences in sports-watching behaviors of sports fans (Anderson & Stone, 1981; Gantz & Wenner, 1991; Dietz-Uhler, Harrick, End, & Jacquemotte, 2000; James & Ridinger, 2002; Wann, Saddil & Dunham, 2004; White & Wilson, 1999; Wilson, 2002); motivational factors for being a sports fan, attending a sports event, and the attachment to a team (Bernthal & Graham, 2003; Funk & Ridinger, 2004; Mahony, Nakazawa, Funk, James, & Gladden, 2002; Trail, Robinson, Dick, & Gillentine, 2003; Wann, Schrader, & Wilson, 1999); measurement of motivations (Funk, Ridinger, & Moorman, 2003; Trail & James, 2001; Wann, 1995); the causes and consequences of fan identification (Branscombe & Wann, 1991; Dietz-Uhler & Murrell, 1999; Fisher & Wakefield, 1998; Gladden & Funk, 2002; Heere & James, 2007; Hillman, Cuthbert, Cauraugh, Schupp, & Bradley, 2000; James, Kolbe, & Trail, 2002; Jones, 1997a; Laverie & Arnett, 2000; Leonard & Schmidt, 1987; Wann, 2006b; Wann, Tucker, & Schrader, 1996); self-esteem and team identification (Bernhardt, Dobbs, Fielden, & Lutter, 1998; Cialdini, Borden, Thorpe, Walter, Freeman, & Sloan, 1976; End, Dietz-Uhler, Harrick, & Jacquemotte, 2002; Gibson, Willming, & Holdnak, 2002; Hirt, Zillman, & Erickson, 1992; Wann, 1994; Wann & Branscombe, 1990a; Wann & Dolan, 1994); factors associated with specific behavioral responses such as aggression (Branscombe & Wann, 1992b; DeNeui & Sachau, 1996; Wann, 1993; Wann, 1994; Wann, Hunter, Ryan, & Wright, 2001); and fan involvement in a sports and a sports team (Funk, Haugtvedt, & Howard, 2000; Funk & James, 2001; Funk & James, 2004; Funk & Ridinger, 2004; Hill & Greene, 2000; Shank & Beasley, 1998).

Relatively few studies have tackled a fundamental issue associated with sports fanship: Why is it that some people become passionate about sports while others couldn't care less? What are the factors that cause people to be more or less susceptible to the lure of athletes, teams, leagues, and the competition associated with all sporting events? The purpose of this exploratory study is to investigate the origins of sports fanship.

Sports Fanship

Fanship extends beyond sports and appears to represent a "common feature of popular culture in industrial societies" (Fiske, 1992, p. 30). In popular culture, fanship is loosely defined, with many self-identifying as fans of a program or a star. Across popular culture domains, the connotation of fanship is largely negative. Fans of popular culture are most often regarded as obsessed, deviant, and deficient; fanship is generally associated with a pathology caused from unfulfilled fantasies and desires (Jenkins, 1992; Jenson, 1992). Sports fans are also stigmatized largely due to hooliganism, riotous victory celebrations, and passiveness or laziness as "couch potatoes" (e.g., Nash, 1938; Sloan, 1989; Smith, Patterson, Williams, & Hogg 1981; Zillmann, Byant, & Sapolsky, 1989). However, in general, sports fanship has been portrayed in a relatively positive light, pointing to an active, participatory audience benefiting from the role of the sports fan as a means of escape, self-fulfillment, and social integration (Gantz & Wenner, 1995; Smith et al., 1981). Fanship for sports also appears to be qualitatively different than fanship for other genres of programming. Gantz, Wang, Paul, & Potter (2006) compared the exposure experience among fans of sports, situation comedies, reality programs, dramas, adult-oriented animation, and night time talk shows and found that sports fans were more involved, more active, more strongly motivated, and more likely to extend the viewing experience (before and afterward) than fans for other programming genres.

Some studies of fanship use the terms "fans" and "spectators" interchangeably. This is problematic because spectators may not be fans (Shank & Beasley, 1998)—and fans may not have the resources to regularly attend games. Pooley (1978) suggested that the two terms needed to be differentiated on the basis of the degree of engrossment and passion about a team or the sports itself (Jones, 1997b). As Pooley (1978) noted, "Whereas a spectator of sport will observe a spectacle and forget it very quickly, the fan continues his interest until the intensity of feeling toward the team becomes so great that parts of every day are devoted to either his team or in some instances, to the broad realm of the sport itself" (p. 14).

Anderson (1979) pointed out the Latin origin of the term "fan" meaning "fanatic," and suggests that a fan should be defined as an ardent devotee of sport or an individual with excessive enthusiasm for sport (cited in Jacobson, 2003). Spinrad (1981) defined a fan as an individual who thinks, talks about and is oriented towards sports even when he/she is not actually doing anything related to sports. Madrigal's definition (1995) suggests that, for fans, sports have a great deal of emotional and value significance. From a slightly different perspective, Guttman (1986) felt that the term fan referred to "the emotionally committed 'consumer' of sports events" (p. 6). In a similar sense, Hunt, Bristol, & Bashaw (1999) defined a sports fan as "an enthusiastic devotee of some particular sports consumptive object," thus a consumer of organized sports (p. 440). In a more practical sense, Gantz & Wenner (1995) considered fans as those who "know about the techniques, guidelines, and rules associated with the sport they follow; many are walking compendiums of the current status of particular players and teams. Wild applause, cheers, catcalls, groans, and shouted epithets seem reasonable manifestations of affective involvement" (p. 59).

Conceptualizations such as these point to the wide range of ways in which the term sports fan has been defined (Jacobson, 2003). They also suggest that most of the definitions revolve around the concept of the individual's perceived interest in — and importance of — sports (Shank & Beasley, 1998). These conceptualizations also suggest that sports fanship is a multidimensional concept, with cognitive, affective, and behavioral domains. As Gantz and Wenner (1995) noted, multidimensional operational definitions of sports fanship help us look "beyond emotional involvement or identification, carving the concept along a continuum that is made up of cognitive, affective, and behavioral components ... as a composite of knowledge, affect, and viewership" (p. 59).

Sports fanship is more likely to be a continuous rather than a dichotomous concept. Nonetheless, the literature is replete with (often dichotomous) typologies: spectators versus fans (Pooley, 1978; Wann et al., 2001); serious and normal sports fans (Smith, 1988); die-hard and fair-weather fans (Wann & Branscombe, 1990a); temporary, local, devoted, fanatical, and dysfunctional fans (Hunt, Bristol, & Bashaw, 1999); and hot or cool supporters (Giulianotti, 2002). While typologies such as these often make their own points in a succinct manner, they may gloss over important differences among fans, as fan motives and behaviors are more rich and complex than suggested by such typologies (Wann & Branscombe, 1990a).

Yet, the dichotomous split of fans and non-fans is relevant to the current study in that it will help us investigate the roots of sports fanship based on distinguishing characteristics of sports fans. A small number of studies have documented differences between sports fans and those who don't care for sports. Gantz & Wenner (1995) found that fanship made a difference in the sports viewing experience. While fans were highly invested in, involved in, and responsive to the viewing experience, non-fans viewed televised sports without much interest, concern, involvement, or responsiveness. Overall, fans had "a qualitatively different, deeper, and more textured set of expectations and responses than nonfans" (p. 57). In his study of personality differences between fans and non-fans of European football (soccer), Russell (1995) found that fans were more impulsive, exhibited weak behavioral controls, and also actively sought excitement and action as a means of avoiding boring activities.

Likely Precursors of Sports Fanship

The preceding discussion on sports fanship indicates that individual, personality-based attributes, and environmental/social factors, are likely to determine if an individual becomes a sports fan or stays on the sidelines as a disinterested party (Sloan, 1979b). Wann (2006b) provided important insights here in his assessment of the precursors of identification with sports teams. According to Wann (2006b), three broad sets of factors lead to team identification: personality factors such as competitiveness and the need for belonging and affiliation; environmental factors such as parental interest in sports and geographic proximity to sports teams; and team-specific factors such as a team's tradition and level of success. In all likelihood, then, fanship will be the result of a mix of internal and environmental forces.[1]

Environmental Factors

It seems obvious that family interest in sports will play a role in the development of sports fanship. Parental interest — as well as the opportunity to share important activities with parents (siblings, too)— represents a very attractive lure for youngsters. The same is likely to be the case with sibling interest in sports and, as children age, friends. Encouraging others to participate in sporting events as well as to become imbued with strong feelings about sports is a part of the socialization process (Weiller & Higgs, 1997). Such encouragement may begin during infancy, with the toys and clothing given to infants (Edwards, 1973, cited in Sloan, 1979b). Sports socialization during childhood plays a role, as does playing sports as a child (Dietz-Uhler et al., 2000; Jacobson, 2003).

Much as parents serve as a critical socialization agent in instilling values and engaging in everyday behaviors, their encouragement may stimulate a passion for sports that lasts well beyond childhood. Yet, not all children of sports fans become fans, much as a parent's political beliefs are not always shared by their offspring. Other opportunity factors such as sibling and peer interest in sports as well as personality factors enter into the equation.

Personality Factors

A number of scholars have demonstrated that personality traits influence the ways in which individuals use and respond to mass communication (e.g., Weaver, 2000). Four personality traits seem likely to play a role in the development of sports fanship: competitiveness, sensation-seeking, risk-taking, need for group affiliation.

Competitiveness. With respect to the potential contribution of competitiveness in the development of sports fanship, achievement-seeking theory provides a useful perspective. Achievement-seeking theory suggests that individuals have competitive needs for achievement and self-esteem. Sports fanship can satisfy these needs by enabling individuals to vicariously experience competition and overcome obstacles (Maslow, 1970; McClelland, Atkinson, Clark, & Lowell, 1953; Murray, 1938). It has also been shown that individuals with higher levels of competitiveness are more likely to attend sporting events (Shoham & Kahle, 1996). Competitiveness also was found to be a significant predictor of sports interest (Mowen, 2004; Puri, 1996).

Sensation-seeking. Sensation-seeking is described as a tendency to seek out "varied, novel, and intense sensations and experiences and the willingness to take physical, social, legal, and financial risks for the sake of the experience" (Zuckerman, 1994, p. 27). Individual differences exist in optimal levels of stimulation and arousal experiences sought (Zuckerman, 1994). That is, individuals have varying threshold levels for arousal and stress/stimulation (Kane, 1971; Petrie, Holland, & Wolk, 1963; Ryan, 1969). Individuals who do not experience enough tension, arousal, risk, or stress in their normal lives seek to experience them through other means (Elias & Dunning, 1970). When stress/stimulation falls below threshold levels, stress/stimulation-seeking increases (Sloan, 1979b).

Sports are exciting because of the inherent drama, tension, and risk involved; the outcomes are unknown and much is riding on those outcomes (i.e., the salaries and careers of players and team officials; pride and status of individuals and cities; personal finances among those who wager). From a sensation-seeking perspective, sports are attractive for those who have a strong drive or need for stimulation, stress, or arousal (Sloan, 1979b; Zuckerman, 1994). Indeed, sports provide a socially acceptable way of creating and experiencing such risk or stress/stimulation (Klausner, 1968).

Sensation-seeking is a multidimensional trait. Three dimensions appear relevant here: impulsivity, risk-taking, and disdain for boredom. Each merits discussion and measurement.

In Zuckerman et al.'s sensation-seeking approach (1993), impulsivity appears to be an important moderating variable in sports viewing habits. Kremer and Green (1999) found that adolescents with higher levels of impulsivity were more likely to watch aggressive sports such as football and hockey. McDaniel (2003) found this relationship held true for both genders and violent combat sports.

Zuckerman (1994) sees risk-taking behavior as a component of sensation-seeking, arguing that "the sensation seeker underestimates or accepts risk as the price for the reward provided by the sensation or experience itself" (p. 27). According to Rosenthal (1968), "more extreme risk in sports provides more stress, but ... only those who learn to control their fear and allow appropriate, self-testing risks experience the full euphoria that follows the dangerous situation" (cited in Sloan, 1979b, p. 228). Some scholars have conceptualized risk taken through sports as a vertigo or disequilibrium that also may be experienced with controlled doses of arousing drugs (Caillios, 1961; Kenyon, 1968; Trippert, 1969). Arousal experienced in the process of risk-taking facilitates the expenditure of excess energy (Bouet, 1969; Weiss, 1969); it also provides the satisfaction sought in the process of taking risks, not the outcomes of those risks (Sloan, 1979b).

Disdain for boredom is also linked to sensation-seeking. Diversion theory addresses the mechanism through which people deal with the tedious dimensions of everyday life. According to this perspective, people can escape from work or other tedious tasks through play. Play can bring a very general change of pace to life, which can lead to the individual's physical and mental well being (Sloan, 1979b). Sports spectating is considered one of the best forms of play in that the fan's own physical environment as a spectator produces pleasurable, empathetic, kinesthetic understanding and stimulation, with which the fan can more readily escape from the boredom of his or her life (Harris, 1973).

Need for group affiliation. Finally, sports fanship also may satisfy an individual's need for group affiliation. According to Mullin, Hardy, & Sutton (2000), less than 2 percent of sports spectators attend sporting events alone. Wann (1995) argued that people have "the desire to maintain group contacts and seek refuge from feelings of alienation," thus group affiliation needs is a primary reason for being a fan (p. 378, cited in Cunningham & Kwon, 2003, p. 130). Sports fanship also allows an individual to acquire an identity as a part of a collective unit. Collective identities provide individuals with a sense of belonging and solidarity (Jacobson, 2003).

Because so little has been written about the origins of sports fanship, this exploratory study was guided by the following research question rather than a set of hypotheses:

RQ: *To what extent do personality factors (competitiveness, sensation-seeking, and need for group affiliation) and environmental/social factors (parental, sibling, and friend encouragement to follow sports) predict sports fanship?*

Method

Sample

This study was conducted at a large Midwestern university. The sample was drawn from students enrolled in a small number of introductory, undergraduate telecommunications classes. A total of 194 students participated. There were 102 (52.6 percent) females, 86 (44.3 percent) males, and 6 (3.1 percent) who did not report their gender. The mean age of the sample was 20.74 years ($SD = 1.57$; *range* = 18 to 32). Those who participated received extra credit in their courses.

Procedure

Participants filled out self-administered questionnaires in class. Before the questionnaires were distributed, one of the authors read a script containing information about the study and informed the participants that participation was optional. Because the questionnaire was administered toward the end of that day's class, participants were told they could leave when they completed the questionnaire. Data collection in each classroom took approximately 25 minutes. Participants did not appear to rush through the questionnaire in order to leave.

Questionnaire

The questionnaire consisted of a series of questions that measured sports fanship; personal involvement with exercise and sports; parental, sibling, and peer interest in following sports and encouragement to watch sports; attendance at sporting events; and personality attributes.

Sports fanship was measured in three different ways. First, from Gantz & Wenner's (1995) multidimensional assessment of fanship, a total of 41 items measured interest in following sports, perceived knowledge of sports, the amount of time spent following sports and sports news on television, newspapers, the Internet, the phone, and radio; and the amount of time spent talking about sports with friends. Interest and perceived knowledge were assessed using an 11-point scale (0 = "not interested [knowledgeable] at all," 10 = "extremely interested [knowledgeable]"). Interest and perceived knowledge were assessed for 16 sports (major league and college baseball, college and NFL football, college and NBA basketball, soccer, hockey, golf, tennis, track and field, swimming, NASCAR, Indy racing, downhill skiing, and X-games type of sports) (Interest $M = 61.42$; $SD = 26.19$; alpha = .86; Perceived knowledge $M = 54.77$; $SD = 30.61$; alpha = .89). Exposure items asked respondents to note how many minutes or hours they spent following sports; hours spent watching sports on weekdays; hours spent watching sports on weekends; minutes per day watching sports news on cable networks; minutes per day spent reading about sports on the Internet; minutes per day spent following sports using one's phone; minutes per day spent following sports news and talk on the radio; and minutes per day spent talking about sports with friends ($M = 2,321.71$ [minutes/week]; $SD = 2,481.81$; alpha = .71). Responses were converted to z-scores and summed to form the index ($M = -.0087$; $SD = 2.54$; alpha = .65).

The second measure of sports fanship relied on work conducted by Wann and his colleagues (Wann & Branscombe, 1993; Wann, 1995). The items in this measure, which overall focuses one's passion, commitment, and enjoyment of sports, were: I consider myself a sports fan; my friends see me as a sports fan; I believe following sports is the most enjoyable form of entertainment; my life would be less enjoyable if I were not able to follow sports; being a sports fan is very important to me; closely following my favorite team is very important to me; I care a great deal about how my favorite team does; I really dislike my favorite team's greatest rivals; and I like to display my favorite team's name or insignia at school, at work, where I live, or on my clothes. An 11-point agreement scale (0 = "don't agree at all" and 10 = "completely agree") was used for each of those items (M = 54.55; SD = 30.22; alpha = .97).

The third measure of sports fanship consisted of three items that assessed the degree to which each respondent cared about sports (any of the local college's teams, any other college teams, and any professional teams) using, again, a zero to 10 scale anchored by "don't care at all" and "care a great deal." (M = 19.45; SD = 8.22; alpha = .84)

A small number of items measured activity levels linked with sports and exercise. Respondents were asked if they played organized sports (such as Little League baseball, high school sports, soccer leagues, gymnastics) as a child/youngster. Almost all (91.1 percent) said they had. They also were asked if they still played on organized sports teams (including intramurals at school). Half (50.6 percent) said they did. Respondents were asked how many days a week they strenuously exercised such as jogging, lifting weights, swimming, aerobics, or participating in pick-up sports games (M = 2.63 days per week; SD = 2.22).

The next portion of the questionnaire tapped the environmental and social influence factors. Parental, sibling, and peer encouragement were measured with three sets of similarly worded and structured items. For parental influence, respondents were asked how much they agreed with the following four statements: my mother or father are sports fans; when I was younger, my mother or father encouraged me to participate in sports; when I was younger, my mother or father encouraged me to watch sports on TV; when I was younger, I watched a lot of sports on TV with my mother or father. An 11-point scale (0 = "no agreement at all," 10 = "very strong agreement") was used. (M = 21.28; SD = 7.59; alpha = .89).

For sibling influence, the items were: my siblings are sports fans; when I was younger, I played sports with my siblings; when I was younger, my siblings encouraged me to watch sports on TV; when I was younger, I watched TV sports with my siblings (M = 21.27; SD = 12; alpha = .90).

Three items were used for friends: When I was younger, my close friends were sports fans; when I was younger, my close friends encouraged me to watch sports on TV; when I was younger, I watched a lot of sports with my friends (M = 17.52; SD = 8.98; alpha = .95).

The last portion of the questionnaire consisted of multi-item measures of the five personality attributes under consideration. Participants responded to each of the items here with a zero to 10 scale, where zero meant the item was "not at all like me" and 10 meant the item was "exactly like me."

Competitiveness was assessed with 15 items based on work conducted by Heggestad and Kanfer (2000). The items were: I perform best when I compete with others; I am not a competitive person; I try to avoid competitive situations; I would rather cooperate than compete; I like to turn things into a competition; even in non-competitive situations, I find ways to compete with others; when it comes to a game, it really matters to me who wins or loses; winning is the only thing that matters; I always try to be better than everyone else; I focus hard on the goal of succeeding; I am a perfectionist; games where there are no winners or losers are boring to me; I enjoy challenging tasks over easy tasks; no task is too difficult to complete; I work hard at being the best; I enjoy betting on sports ($M = 82.31$; $SD = 20.46$; alpha = .73).

Sensation-seeking was measured with three sets of items. Zuckerman, Kuhlman, Joirema, Teta, and Kraft's 19-item Impulsive Sensation Seeking Scale (1993) was used for impulsivity. The items used were: I tend to begin a new job without much advance planning on how I will do it; I usually think about what I am going to do before doing it; I often do things on impulse; I very seldom spend much time on the details of planning ahead; I like to have new and exciting experiences and sensations even if they are a little frightening; before I begin a complicated job, I make careful plans; I would like to take off on a trip with no preplanned or definite routes or timetable; I enjoy getting into new situations where you can't predict how things will turn out; I like doing things just for the thrill of it; I tend to change interests frequently; I sometimes like to do things that are a little frightening; I'll try anything once; I would like the kind of life where one is on the move and traveling a lot, with lots of change and excitement; I sometimes do "crazy" things just for fun; I like to explore a strange city or section of town by myself, even if it means getting lost; I prefer friends who are excitingly unpredictable; I often get so carried away by new and exciting things and ideas that I never think of possible complications; I am an impulsive person; I like "wild" uninhibited parties ($M = 108.47$; $SD = 32.52$; alpha = .88).

Three items measured how much the individual is likely to take risks. The items were: I am drawn to experiences with an element of danger; I seek an adrenaline rush; I enjoy taking risks more than others ($M = 17.77$; $SD = 8.02$; alpha = .94).

Seven items from Zuckerman's Susceptibility to Boredom Scale (1971) were used to assess how likely an individual is to become bored. The items were: I can't stand watching a movie that I have seen before; I get bored seeing the same old faces; when you can predict almost everything a person will do and say, he or she must be a bore; I usually don't enjoy a movie or play where I can predict what will happen in advance; I get very restless if I have to stay around home for any length of time; the worst social sin is to be a bore; I have no patience with dull or boring persons ($M = 26.49$; $SD = 13.01$; alpha = .80).

Four items measured an individual's need for group affiliation: I'd rather work in groups than by myself; I feel more alive when I am part of a cohesive group; group membership is rewarding to me; I tend to enjoy being part of groups ($M = 27.11$; $SD = 8.22$; alpha = .85).

Results

Sports Fanship

The three sports fanship indices were strongly correlated with one another. The weakest correlation was between the passion/commitment/enjoyment measure and the interest/knowledge/exposure index, $r(191) = .74$, $p < .01$, while the strongest correlation was between the passion/commitment/enjoyment index and the caring about sports index, $r(191) = .86$, $p < .01$. These strong, positive correlations point to the use of just one of the indices in the regression analyses assessing the relationship between fanship and the environmental and personality variables under consideration. Because of the internal consistency of its items, the passion/commitment/enjoyment index was chosen for those analyses.[2]

Fanship and Sports Activity

Bivariate correlations were run between fanship and playing organized sports as a youngster and between fanship and currently engaging in strenuous exercise. The relationships were significant, but comparatively modest. The correlation between fanship and playing organized sports was $r(190) = .30$, $p < .01$. The correlation between fanship and exercise was $r(190) = .22$, $p < .05$.

Fanship and Personality Traits

Bivariate correlations also were run between fanship and all personality traits. All personality traits were positively correlated with sports fanship (Table 1). Fanship was related most strongly to competitiveness, $r(190) = .58$, $p < .01$, and least with boredom, $r(191) = .17$, $p < .05$. Moderately strong correlations also were recorded with sensation-seeking and need for affiliation, both $r(190) = .31$, $p < .01$.

For a different look at relationships between fanship and personality traits, an independent-samples t-test was run with the outer-quartiles of fanship ($M_{low\ fanship} = 1.00$, $SD = 1.10$; $M_{high\ fanship} = 9.62$, $SD = .36$) as the grouping variable (Table 2). Results indicate that the mean scores for each personality trait significantly differed between quartiles. Specifically, individuals with high fanship levels were more likely to be competitive as well as higher on the disdain for boredom, need for stimulation, sensation-seeking, and need for affiliation

Table 1. Correlation between Fanship and Personality Traits

	Fanship	Competitiveness	Boredom	Need for Stimulation	Sensation-Seeking	Need for Affiliation
Fanship	—	.584**	.172*	.182*	.312**	.306**
Competitiveness		—	.263**	.339**	.502**	.303**
Boredom			—	.345**	.355**	.237**
Risk-taking				—	.689**	.192**
Impulsivity					—	.337**
Need for Affiliation						—

Note. ** $p < 0.01$, 2-tailed. * $p < 0.05$, 2-tailed.

indices than their non-fan counterparts. This analysis suggests that all five personality traits are likely to play a role in determining whether or not an individual is a sports fan.

Table 2: T-Tests of Mean Difference in Personality Traits between Respondents in the Outer Quartiles of Sports Fanship

	Low Fanship	High Fanship	Std. Error Difference	t	df	Sig. (2-tailed)
Competitiveness	4.02	7.07	.30	-10.20	94	.000
Boredom	3.24	4.13	.40	-2.22	94	.029
Risk-taking	5.04	5.76	.34	-2.11	93	.038
Impulsivity	4.69	7.04	.57	-4.15	93	.000
Need for Affiliation	5.79	7.20	.45	-3.13	93	.002

Regression analysis was used to examine the extent to which each of these personality traits predicted levels of sports fanship. Boredom, need for stimulation, sensation-seeking, and gender were not significant predictors of fanship and were removed from the analysis. Another regression was run using only competitiveness and need for affiliation as independent variables. Both of these personality traits significantly predicted fanship ($\beta_{competitiveness}$ = .536, $t(186)$ = 8.67, $p < .001$; $\beta_{need\ for\ affiliation}$ = .144, $t(186)$ = 2.326, $p = .02$). This model also predicted a significant amount of the variance in fanship scores, $R^2 = .355$, $F(2, 186) = 51.13$, $p < .001$.

Fanship and Environmental Encouragement

Correlations were run for the sports fanship measure and the three environmental encouragement variables (parental, sibling, and peers). Sports fanship was positively correlated with all encouragement variables (Table 3). Fanship related strongest to peer encouragement, $r(191) = .75$, $p < .01$, and the least to sibling encouragement, $r(173) = .44$, $p < .01$. Fanship was strongly correlated with parental encouragement, $r(190) = .69$, $p < .01$. Differences between sibling encouragement and the other two encouragement variables might be a product of the gender, relative age, and number of siblings. Unfortunately these variables were not measured.

Table 3: Correlations between Sports Fanship and Environmental Encouragement Measurements

	Fanship	Parental Encouragement	Sibling Encouragement	Peer Encouragement
Fanship	—	.687**	.435**	.745**
Parental Encouragement		—	.507**	.642**
Sibling Encouragement			—	.375**
Peer Encouragement				—

** $p < 0.01$, 2-tailed.   * $p < 0.05$, 2-tailed.

An independent-samples t-test was run with the outer-quartiles of sports fanship as the grouping variable (Table 4). All environmental encouragement variables showed a sizable and statistically significant difference in means on the fanship measure. In each case, the environmental encouragement variable's mean was greater for sports fans than for non-sports fans.

Table 4: T-Tests of Mean Differences in Environmental Encouragement Measures between Respondents in the Outer Quartiles of Sports Fanship

	Low Fanship	High Fanship	St. Error Difference	t	df	Sig. (2-tailed)
Parental Encouragement	3.96	8.57	.43	-10.77	94	.000
Sibling Encouragement	3.33	6.84	.64	-5.50	84	.000
Peer Encouragement	1.88	8.00	.41	-14.92	94	.000

To test the predictive strength of each encouragement variable, a linear regression analysis was run with fanship as the dependent variable. Sibling encouragement was not a significant predictor so it was removed from analysis and another regression was run. Both parental ($\beta_{parental} = .355$, $t(188) = 6.13$, $p < .001$) and peer ($\beta_{peer} = .517$, $t(188) = 8.92$, $p < .001$) encouragement were significant factors in predicting fanship. In all, the model accounted for a significant amount of the variance in fanship: $R^2 = .629$, $F(2, 188) = 159.38$, $p < .001$.

Personality Traits and Environmental Encouragement

A linear regression analysis was conducted to test the relative contributions of personality traits and environmental encouragement factors to predicting fanship. The four factors in this model were competitiveness, need for affiliation, parental encouragement, and peer encouragement. Need for affiliation was not a significant predictor and was removed from analysis. The remaining three factors significantly predicted fanship at the $p < .01$ level (Table 5). Peer encouragement was the strongest predictor ($\beta_{peer} = .445$, $t(186) = 7.34$, $p < .001$), followed by parental encouragement ($\beta_{parental} = .309$, $t(186) = 5.28$, $p < .001$), leaving competitiveness as the weakest factor in the model ($\beta_{competitiveness} = .182$, $t(186) = 3.41$, $p < .01$). This model predicted a significant amount of the variance in sports fanship $R^2 = .651$, $F(3, 186) = 115.55$, $p < .001$.

Table 5: Linear Regression Analysis for Factors Predicting Sports Fanship

	B	SE B	B	Sig.
Competitiveness	.326	.096	.182	.001
Parental Encouragement	.390	.074	.309	.000
Peer Encouragement	.472	.064	.445	.000

Discussion

This exploratory study was designed to enhance our understanding of the origins of sports fanship. The authors anticipated — and found — that a mix of environmental and personality factors contributed to sports fanship. It is clear that a good number of variables, on their own, are linked with levels of sports fanship. These variables include gender; parental, sibling, and peer encouragement; participating in sports as a youngster; frequency of engaging in intense exercise; and each of the three personality attributes assessed — competitiveness, sensation-seeking, and need for group affiliation. When examined collectively, the list of significant predictors of sports fanship shrinks. In all likelihood, this is because the predictors account for the same variance. In our case, the strongest predictors of sports fanship were peer encouragement, parental encouragement, and competitiveness. In short, the best predictors featured a mix of environmental and personality attributes. In all likelihood, fanship is the result of encouragement and personality.

Because this study represents a retrospective look at the origins of sports fanship — that is, respondents were asked to recall their childhood experiences — we can not, with full certainty, argue that each of the variables determined to be a predictor of fanship actually is a causal agent or merely a correlate or byproduct of fanship. It is easiest to demonstrate this with encouragement from peers. For the most part, friendships are chosen. It is possible that children interested in following sports become friends with similar interests (i.e., in sports). In such a case, sports fanship might precede encouragement from friends.

We also could not determine if fanship might result solely from environmental encouragement of personality factors. For example, can a strongly competitive person who likes risk taking, likes sensation-seeking, and disdains boredom become a fan if the person was not in any way encouraged to participate in — or follow — sports while growing up? Alternatively, can strong encouragement at home and from friends overcome a person's disinterest in competition, risk taking, and sensation-seeking?

Finally, this study did not exhaust the list of variables that might contribute to sports fanship. Instead, we deliberately selected variables that, through linkages in the literature — or intuitively — seemed to be related to the origins of sports fanship. This study, then, represents a starting point. While a short list of factors accounted for a sizeable portion of the variance, other environmental and personality variables may add to our understanding of the origins of sports fanship and merit further study.

Notes

1. Demographic attributes such as gender may come into play here, too, as males are more likely to become sports fans than females (James & Ridinger, 2002). Yet, gender is less likely to be a factor than environmental and personality attributes, and sports fanship among females is rising (Dietz-Uhler et al., 2000; James and Ridinger, 2002). Studies also have shown that female and male sports fans respond in similar ways to mediated sports (Gantz & Wenner, 1995). It is just that, compared with males, a small proportion of females are sports fans.

2. This study was not designed to examine differences between males and females, as a number of other studies have documented that males are more likely to be sports fans than are females. Yet, that relationship was tested, as a measure of predictive validity, with each of the fanship indices. Across indices, females recorded lower sports fanship levels than males. Wann's fanship scale showed that females ($M_{females} = 5.29$, $SD = 3.34$) reported lower sports fanship levels than males ($M_{males} = 7.00$, $SD = 3.20$). A two-tailed t-test revealed that this difference was significant, $t(186) = -3.568$, $p < .001$. The new 3-item fanship scale measuring how much individuals care about different levels of sports displayed similar significant results, ($M_{females} = 6.05$, $SD = 2.80$; $M_{males} = 7.04$, $SD = 2.60$), $t(186) = -2.518$, $p = .013$. Lastly, Gantz and Wenner's interest/knowledge fanship scale showed males ($M_{males} = .27$, $SD = .89$) averaging higher fanship levels than females ($M_{females} = -.23$, $SD = .93$), $t(186) = -3.762$, $p < .001$.

The Coping Strategies of Highly Identified Sports Fans

The Importance of Team Success on Tendencies to Utilize Proactive Pessimism

DANIEL L. WANN AND FREDERICK G. GRIEVE

According to the Team Identification–Social Psychological Health Model (TI–SPH; Wann, 2006), high levels of team identification can facilitate social well-being by assisting in the development and maintenance of two types of social connections with others: enduring connections and temporary connections. Enduring connections result from residing in an environment in which connections to other fans of the team are readily available, such as when one lives in the city represented by a team (e.g., New York Yankees fans who live in New York City). Temporary connections occur when one does not reside in the community represented by a team but finds him- or herself temporarily in the company of other fans of the team (e.g., a New York Yankees fan who lives in Boston, home of the rival Red Sox, who watches Red Sox games with several other similarly displaced fans).

Research is highly supportive of the model. For instance, team identification has been found to be correlated with several measures of social well-being, including lower levels of loneliness and alienation, higher frequencies of positive emotions, and high levels of social life satisfaction and self-esteem (Branscombe & Wann, 1991; Wann, Dimmock, & Grove, 2003; Wann, Inman, Ensor, Gates, & Caldwell, 1999; Wann & Pierce, 2005; see Wann, 2006, for a complete review of this literature). Further, research indicates a causal pattern in which identification predicts psychological health (Wann, 2006) and is not limited to a specific setting, such as at an athletic event (Wann, Walker, Cygan, Kawase, & Ryan, 2005).

Another important component of the TI–SPH model involves the coping strategies utilized by highly identified fans to assist in the maintenance of their well-being. Many fans, and particularly highly identified fans, experience a threat to their identity when their favorite team performs poorly. In fact, research indicates that the threat can be so great as to lead these fans to experience strong negative affect (Hirt, Zillmann, Erickson, & Kennedy, 1992; Schwarz, Strack, Kommer, & Wagner, 1987; Wann, Dolan, McGeorge, & Allison, 1994; Wann, Friedman, McHale, & Jaffe, 2003). Consequently, highly identified sports fans have developed a large number of strategies designed to help them cope with the threat. For instance, fans can adopt biased attributions of team performance (Wann & Dolan, 1994; Wann & Schrader, 2000), biased perceptions of the team and its fans (Dietz-Uhler & Murrell, 1999; Markman & Hirt, 2002; Wann & Grieve, 2005), and belief in curses (Wann, Zaichkowsky, & Mattigod, 2005).

Another common coping strategy used by highly identified fans involves pessimistic beliefs about their teams' past and future performances. With respect to pessimism about previous contests, fans may choose to employ retroactive pessimism, adopting the belief that their team lost a contest because it never really had a chance from the start. By retrospectively becoming pessimistic about their team's initial chances, fans are better able to cope with the team's loss. Support for this strategy among sports fans was documented by Tykocinski, Pick, and Kedmi (2002) in their research on fans of a losing soccer team who lowered their post-game estimates of success relative to their pre-game estimates. Wann, Grieve, and Martin (2006) extended Tykocinski et al.'s work by demonstrating that use of the strategy was prominent only among highly identified fans.

A second form of pessimism is proactive (i.e., defensive) pessimism. Proactive pessimism is found among persons who become more pessimistic about an upcoming event as the event draws closer (Sheppard, Ouellette, & Fernandez, 1996). Proactive pessimism was recently documented among sports fans by Wann and Grieve (in press). In this research, individuals were asked to complete a questionnaire packet four weeks prior to the start of a Major League Baseball season. Participants completed the packet again three weeks later (i.e., one week prior to the start of the season). The packet assessed the subjects' level of identification with their favorite baseball team as well as their expectations for and excitement about the upcoming baseball season. Consistent with predictions, and indicative of proactive pessimism, the highly identified fans reported lowered expectations at Time 2 relative to Time 1 (that is, they became proactively pessimistic). No such pattern was reported among those low in identification.

The current investigation was designed to replicate the work by Wann and Grieve (in press). Because it was only the initial test of proactive pessimism among fans, such a replication was warranted. That is, additional work is needed that examines proactive pessimism among other fans of different sports. In the present study, we investigated the use of proactive pessimism among college basketball fans. However, rather than assess evaluations of an upcoming season, as was the case with the Wann and Grieve study, we attempted to extend that work by acquiring evaluations of a specific game. Highly identified fans view the role of team follower as a central component of their overall social identity (Wann, Royalty, & Roberts, 2000). Consequently, the team's performance is highly relevant and poor performances can serve as a threat to this valued identity (e.g., Hirt et al., 1992). Research in social identity theory suggests that it is the combination of high levels of group identification (e.g., sports team identification) and identity threat (e.g., the possibility of performing poorly in an upcoming game) that leads to the use of coping strategies (Doosje, Ellemers, & Spears, 1999; Ouwerkerk, Ellemers, & de Gilder, 1999). Further, recent efforts suggest that the need to cope with threat is a key reason individuals engage in pessimistic coping strategies (Blank & Nestler, 2006). Therefore, the specific hypotheses of this study were:

H1: *Participants would report less positive (i.e., more pessimistic) evaluations of their team's chances at winning a target contest as the game approached.*

H2: *The pessimistic evaluations of a team's chances would be most prominent among highly identified fans (thus, we hypothesized a two-way interaction involving team identification and time).*

Method

Participants and Design

The current research involved fans' reactions to an upcoming college sporting event. The participants were students of the visiting team's university. Thus, their team was playing an away game. The original sample consisted of 79 college student participants. However, 34 participants failed to successfully complete either the Time 1 questionnaire or the Time 2 questionnaire. Thus, these individuals were removed from the data set, resulting in a final sample of 19 men and 26 women participating in exchange for college course credit (M age = 22.2 yr., SD = 5.0). The design for the study was a 2 (Level of Team Identification: High or Low) × 2 (Testing Session: Time 1 and Time 2) mixed factorial design. The first variable was a grouping variable and the second variable was a repeated measures within-subjects variable.

Materials and Procedure

Time 1 session. The Time 1 session occurred approximately two weeks prior to the start of the NCAA Division I college basketball season and approximately six weeks prior to the target basketball contest (a contest involving the home university's men's team and a regional rival). Upon entering the Time 1 session and providing their consent, participants (tested in groups) were handed a questionnaire packet containing three sections. The first section asked participants to provide three demographic items: age, gender, and the last four digits of the participant's Social Security number (this information was used to match the Time 1 and Time 2 questionnaires). The second section asked participants to complete the Sport Spectator Identification Scale (SSIS; Wann & Branscombe, 1993) with their university's men's basketball team as the target. The SSIS contains seven Likert-scale items with response options ranging from 1 (*low identification*) to 8 (*high identification*). Thus, higher numbers represent greater levels of identification. The SSIS has been used in a number of studies involving sports fans and has strong reliability and validity (see Wann & Branscombe, 1993; Wann, Melnick, Russell, & Pease, 2001).

In the third section, participants were asked to answer two questions designed to assess their expectations of success for their university's team in an upcoming game against a regional rival. This section was used to assess participants' pessimism. First, participants read that the researchers were interested in their opinions about an upcoming game between their university's men's team and the regional rival. Next, they were asked "Who do you feel will win the game?" to which they responded by circling either the name of their university's team or that of the rival team. Second, the participants were asked to estimate the number of points they expected their university's team to score in the target contest. After completing the questionnaire packet (approximately 10 minutes), participants were debriefed, reminded that there would be a post-test session in the coming weeks, and excused from the testing session.

Time 2 session. The Time 2 session occurred approximately 5 weeks after the Time 1 session and 1 week prior to the target basketball contest. Upon entering the session and providing their consent, participants (tested in groups) were handed a questionnaire packet nearly identical to that used in Time 1. The only differences were that the gender and age items were omitted from the post-test protocol, as was the SSIS. Thus, respondents were again asked to provide the last four digits of their Social Security number (for matching purposes) and to complete the items assessing their expectations of success for their university's team in the target game. After completing the Time 2 questionnaire (approximately 5 minutes), participants were debriefed and excused from the testing session.

Target Contest

The target contest involved a men's college basketball game between two regional rivals (the campuses are less than 150 miles apart). The teams had a long history of basketball competition, having played one another over 140 times spanning more than 70 years. Both teams played at the NCAA Division I level. Prior to the target contest, the participants' team had been performing extremely well and currently held a perfect record of five wins and no losses. In fact, two of their wins had come against schools from top conferences and their margin of victory was 24 points. The home team (rival team to participants in the current study) entered the target contest with a record of no wins and four losses. By combining the success of the visiting team (i.e., participants' team) with the lack of success for the home team, it is clear that expectations for the visiting team were quite high heading into the target contest.

Results

The seven items comprising the SSIS (Cronbach alpha = .93) were combined to form a single index of identification. A median split procedure was performed on the Time 1 identification scores to establish a low identification group (n = 21, M = 11.33, SD = 3.59, range = 7 to 18) and a high identification group (n = 24, M = 29.92, SD = 7.93, range = 19 to 44). A one-way analysis of variance (ANOVA) indicated that the two groups were significantly different in their levels of identification with their university's men's basketball team, $F(1, 43)$ = 97.58, $p < .001$. Seen in Table 1, males and females did not report significant differences on any measure, with the exception of estimates of points scored at Time 2. However, gender was not involved in a significant interaction in analyses involving this dependent variable, and thus all subsequent analyses were conducted across gender.

Table 1. Means and Standard Deviations for the Measures by Gender.

Measure	Males	Females	F(1, 43)	p =
Team identification	22.37	20.42	0.32	.57
	(10.55)	(11.88)		
Time 1 Expectations for team success	1.63	1.42	1.91	.18
	(0.50)	(0.50)		
Time 2 Expectations for team success	1.21	1.15	0.23	.63
	(0.42)	(0.37)		
Time 1 points for team	75.26	68.54	3.32	.08
	(8.67)	(14.27)		
Time 2 points for team	81.16	74.42	4.94	.03
	(7.65)	(11.47)		

Note: Standard deviations appear in parentheses below each mean.

It was hypothesized that highly identified fans would deal with the potential threat of the team's defeat by proactively becoming more pessimistic about the team's chances of success in the target contest against their regional rival as the game approached. To test this prediction, two sets of analyses were conducted: examinations of the team that was expected to win the target game and examinations of the participants' predictions of the number of points their team would score in the target game. Thus, we expected that highly identified fans would report lower expectations for a win and lower numbers of predicted points at Time 2 (i.e., closer to the contest), relative to Time 1. With respect to estimates of the contest winner, proportions of participants predicting a victory for their university's team appear in Table 2. As seen in the table, the pattern of proportions was in direct opposition of the expected pattern of effects. That is, rather than reporting a decrease in expectations for success of their team at Time 2, the respondents reported greater expectations for success at Time 2, and this pattern was particularly true for highly identified individuals. In terms of statistical tests, tests of proportions revealed that the Time 1 (.49) to Time 2 (.82) increase in proportions for the entire sample was statistically significant, $z = 3.29$, $p < .01$. With respect to the identification groups, the Time 1 (.52) to Time 2 (.71) increase in proportions for low identified participants was not statistically significant, $z = 1.26$, $p > .20$. However, for highly identified fans, the Time 1 (.46) to Time 2 (.92) increase in proportions was significant, $z = 3.45$, $p < .01$. Additionally, the Time 1 proportions for low identified individuals (.52) and highly identified fans (.46) was not statistically significant, $z = 0.40$, $p > .50$. The Time 2 proportions for low identified fans (.71) and highly identified individuals (.92) was marginally significant, $z = 1.84$, $p < .10$.

**Table 2. Time 1 and Time 2 Proportions of Participants
Predicting a Victory for Their University's Team
for All Participants and Separately for
High and Low Identified Individuals**

Time	All Participants	Low Identification	High Identification
Time 1	.49	.52	.46
Time 2	.82	.71	.92

The second series of analyses was conducted on predictions of the number of points scored by their team in the target game. To test the hypothesized pattern of effects, subjects' Time 1 and Time 2 estimates were examined using a 2 (Level of Team Identification: High or Low) × 2 (Testing Session: Time 1 and Time 2) mixed factorial analysis of variance (ANOVA). Means and standard deviations for this analysis appear in Table 3. The ANOVA revealed a significant time main effect, $F(1, 43) = 11.71$, $p < .01$. As revealed in Table 3, across both identification groups, the participants estimated higher numbers of points scored for Time 2 relative to Time 1. There was no main effect for identification group, $F(1, 43) = 2.61, p = .11$. The two-way interaction was significant, $F(1, 43) = 4.05, p < .05$. However, in contrast to the hypothesized pattern of effects (but consistent with the proportion data described above), highly identified fans were particularly likely to report increased point estimates. Post hoc comparisons (t-tests) revealed that the Time 1 to Time 2 change for highly identified persons was statistically significant, $t(23) = 4.11, p < .001$. The Time 1 to Time 2 change for low identified persons was not significant, $t(20) = 0.93$, $p > .30$.

Table 3. Time 1 and Time 2 Means and Standard Deviations for Estimations of Points to Be Scored by Their Team for All Participants and Separately for High and Low Identified Individuals

Time	All Participants	Low Identification	High Identification
Time 1	71.38	70.62	72.04
(12.56)	(13.43)	(11.99)	
Time 2	77.27	72.95	81.04
(10.49)	(9.62)	(9.90)	

Note: Standard deviations appear in parentheses below each mean.

Discussion

Proactive pessimism, or the tendency to become more pessimistic as a self-relevant event draws near, has been found to be used by sports fans as they attempt to cope with the threat of a potentially poor performance by their team (Wann & Grieve, in press). The current research was designed to extend past efforts which had focused on the pre-season predictions of baseball fans by examining evaluations of a specific basketball game against a regional rival. Specifically, it was hypothesized that highly identified fans would become more pessimistic (i.e., report lower chances of success and estimate fewer points scored for one's team) as a rival game approached.

However, contrary to expectations, highly identified fans became more optimistic (i.e., less pessimistic) as the game approached. This fact was indicated by a greater proportion of these persons predicting that their team would win the target game and in their increased estimates of the number of points to be scored by their team. Given that past research had verified the use of proactive pessimism among fans (Wann & Grieve, in press), these patterns of effects were intriguing. To understand these results, one should consider the team's performances prior to the target contest. Recall that participants in this study were students of the visiting team's university and that the team had been playing extremely well leading up to this game. In fact, it had yet to lose that season (it had a perfect 5–0 record). It seems that the team's successes rendered the use of proactive pessimism illogical. That is, because the participants' team had been playing so well, the threat of poor team performance may have seemed unlikely (or at least less likely). Rather, as the game approached and the team continued to win, highly identified fans most likely gained confidence in their team, culminating in their expressions of optimism exhibited at Time 2. As a consequence, the highly identified participants chose to boost their identity as a fan by BIRGing — basking in the reflected glory of their team's recent successes (Cialdini et al., 1976) — and by increasing their perceptions of the team's abilities (and, hence, perceived likelihood of success in the target contest). As noted, several studies have indicated that highly identified fans often report overly positive evaluations of their team including ratings of current performance (Dietz-Uhler & Murrell, 1999) and ratings of future performance (Funk & James, 2001; Wann & Branscombe, 1993), and they expect greater success for individual team members (Murrell & Dietz, 1992).

It is likely that proactive pessimism is employed only in cases where fans' expectations of success are not high or cases in which the fans have a great deal of anxiety over the game. Thus, proactive pessimism could be an important coping mechanism prior to more important games, such as between two heated and closely matched rivals, a playoff game, or championship game. Since fans have a great deal of self-esteem invested in such games and their anxiety tends to be higher prior to such contests (Wann, Schrader, & Adamson, 1998), their use of proactive pessimism increases.

Thus, the fans in the current sample appear to have elected to enhance their fan identity rather than protect it through proactive pessimism. This suggests that fans can be selective in choosing which coping strategy they wish to employ. Certainly, fans have many strategies at their disposal (see Wann, 2006). Further, recent research does indicate that fans selectively choose certain strategies to fit specific situations (End, Birchmeier, & Mueller, 2004). For instance, Wann, Morris-Shirkey, Peters, and Suggs (2002) found that highly identified fans tend to report biased interpretations of performance-relevant team information (e.g., the number of championships a team has won) but a high degree of accuracy when discussing performance-irrelevant team information (e.g., the name of the team's mascot).

The enhancement of fan identity found in the present study meshes with the findings of Wann and Grieve (2005), where fans of winning teams, more so than fans of losing teams, were more likely to denigrate fans of the other team. Both sets of findings relate to enhancement of self-esteem; one set (Wann & Grieve, 2005) deals with enhancement after the game out come, while one set (the present study) deals with enhancement before the game. In both cases, though, it is the fans of the winning team who feel secure enough to promote themselves through their estimates of the team or other fans.

Understanding the Voice of the Fan

Apologia, Antapologia, *and the 2006 World Cup Controversy*

PAUL D. TURMAN, KEVIN A. STEIN
AND MATTHEW H. BARTON

Sports fans are recognized for their fanatical devotion to their beloved sports teams as they develop what is perceived to be an unhealthy sense of personal identification (Wann, 1994; Wann, Brewer & Royalty, 1999) with teams at all levels (secondary, collegiate, and professional). No other sport in the world draws more attention and fanaticism on a global level than the FIFA World Cup tournament that occurs every four years. In 2006, worldwide viewership topped 30 billion for the three-week event that ended in the final match between France and Italy (Sandomir, 2006). Often scrutinized for their violent behavior in the stands, soccer fans were appalled by a head butt to the chest of Italian center Marco Materazzi by World Cup outstanding player Zinedine Zidane during the closing minutes of the contest. The resulting penalty was deemed to be instrumental in allowing Italy to overtake a superior French team to win the World Cup in a 5–3 sudden death shootout. Afterwards, Zidane refused to apologize for his actions, alleging that Materazzi provoked him by insulting both his mother and sister.[1] Many fans continued to criticize Zidane's on-field behavior, but debate ensued as a result of the justifications he made during his response to the criticism.

Zidane's defense of his behavior to the media and his fans represents an important feature of sports fandom within today's society. Such self-defense discourse involves what Ryan (1982) described as the speech set of *kategoria* and *apologia* (attack and defense), whereby any critical focus on the apology should also examine the attack preceding it. Zidane's on-field behavior clearly necessitated the need to defend his actions, especially when considering that weeks before the World Cup began, Zidane officially announced his retirement from soccer at tournament's end. Many felt that his actions during this final game scarred a world renowned athlete's otherwise illustrious career. However, we argue in this chapter that focusing exclusively on athlete *apologia* ignores a third component which Stein (2006) referred to as *antapologia* (response to *apologia*). *Antapologia* is an important feature of the apologetic situation because the rhetor may choose to construct the initial image repair based on what he or she perceives to be the likely response by the offended person(s). When the discourse addresses the account of the act, it constitutes an instance of *antapologia*. Thus, the purpose of this chapter is to examine the theoretical implications of sports *antapologia* that results from fan reaction to athlete apology by using the World Cup soccer head butt incident as an illustration of *antapologia* rhetoric.

Online Avenues for Fan Response and Commentary

By allowing sports spectators a vehicle for providing commentary on sports of all kinds, Internet blogs have become an increasingly common technique for fans to further identify with their sport. Web blogs are a form of website that allows authors to provide commentary or news on a wide range of subjects (e.g., food, politics, local news), or serves as a form of online diary for its users. As the relevance of web blogs continues to grow, numerous news outlets have devoted segments in their daily newscasts to reporters who track and comment on popular websites. This practice has aided in establishing the web blog as a credible source of information, although much of the discussion that flows from these sources represents simple assertions, opinions, and conjecture with limited journalistic quality. In the past, news coverage was reported almost exclusively by seasoned journalists who served as the voice of record. "In this digital age, however, we can all be real-time observers, and opinion often trumps fact. Which is to say, for those uninterested in actual reporting, the print media have almost become an afterthought" (Ballard, 2006, p. 58). Some have used the term "reclinerporting" to describe the quality of the growing number of blogs that allow commentary with little to no direct contact to the individuals involved, and are written to an audience with a desire for bias toward their favorite teams.

A number of sports organizations (e.g., National Basketball Association, Major League Baseball, etc.) have expanded into this growing media outlet. For instance, professional teams have gone as far as allowing fans the opportunity to set up fan profiles on their website, write web blogs, and interact with other fans (Elliot, 2007). Blogs have become an increasingly relevant feature of the sports landscape, so much so that a number of outlets, including the *Sporting*

News, have devoted a section of their weekly magazine to tracking the most memorable quotes from numerous sports blogs. There is little doubt among seasoned reporters and legitimate news outlets that fan websites are increasingly making and breaking news in a way that is transforming the relationship between fans, athletes, coaches, and organizations (Layden, 2003). One important area of considerable interest related to these new media outlets (e.g., organization websites, chat rooms, blogs, online polls, etc.) is how athletes and teams engage in the function of image repair related to on- and off-field events. The nature of sports apology has expanded so much in the past decade that today's athletes have developed a wide range of arguments to perform image repair, and a fan's ability to react to an apology for an inappropriate behavior often requires that one further respond to the initial apology. The Zidane World Cup incident represents an example of the global implications that result from fan response to on-field behavior that requires image repair.

Making Sense of Apologia *Studies*

Communication scholars have defined *apologia* as a particular type of discourse that focuses on the "self defense" needed to combat external personal attacks on one's character (Ware & Linkugel, 1973). Studying *apologia* as a particular genre was solidified by Ware and Linkugel (1973), who argued that accusations and subsequent apologies are so common that naming them was a useful way to understand this particular communication phenomenon. "In life, an attack upon a person's character, upon his [her] worth as a human being, does seem to demand a direct response. The questioning of a man's [woman's] *moral nature, motives,* or *reputation* is qualitatively different from the challenging of his [her] policies" (p. 274, italics in original). Their goal was to establish factors that define the apologetic form and then look for working subgenres of self-defense discourse. These efforts produced the recognizable strategies of denial, bolstering, differentiation, and transcendence.

Early studies in *apologia* were limited to politics (e.g., Benoit, Gullifor, & Panici, 1991; Ling, 1970), as scholars attempted to identify which strategies were used and to some extent why these particular strategies were chosen, and these studies are most common in the literature. As work continued in this area, other scholars, particularly in public relations, began using Ware and Linkugel's categories to explain corporate responses to crisis (e.g., Hearit, 1999; Hearit & Brown, 2004), while others attempted to expand the boundaries by focusing on culture and race (Hatch, 2006).

However, the most prominent extension to *apologia* stems from Benoit's (1995) work on image repair. Benoit sought to create a more complete theory of accounts, apologies, and image repair strategies. He argued that human beings inevitably face situations of real or alleged wrong-doing, and these situations are recurring and damaging to reputations for four reasons. First, because people live in a world of limited and essential resources, they compete over their distribution. Second, "circumstances beyond our control sometimes prevent us from meeting our obligations" and this negatively impacts others (p. 1). Third, human beings are imperfect, meaning they are prone to make both "honest" mistakes as well as those motivated by self-interests. Finally, the individual nature of human beings creates different sets of goals that conflict with others. Underlying Benoit's theory is the claim that "maintaining a positive reputation is one of the central goals of communication" (p. 63). Consequently, when one's actions are considered "reprehensible" to a "salient audience," that individual's image is damaged and must be repaired.

Despite discussions about the importance of focusing on the speaker's motives (Kruse, 1977) and the situational and structural features of an apologetic situation (Kruse, 1981b), little work has been done to broaden the theoretical focus on *apologia* especially in terms of sports. In her examination of sports apologia, Kruse (1981a) identified a number of situations requiring apologia on the part of the athletes and successful strategies which resolved ethical violations. These included: (a) suggesting that the team would be unaffected by the ethical violation, (b) shifting responsibility to the sports organization, (c) stressing a desire to be a team player, and/or (d) placing the blame on the emotion of the situation.

Nelson's (1984) study of sports apology examined tennis legend Billie Jean King's comments surrounding her disclosure of an extramarital, lesbian affair with her secretary. Relying primarily on the defense created by King's pro tennis peers, Nelson concluded that, when an individual or supporters of the individual use transcendence as a strategy, it is possible to shift the situation into another context viewed favorably by the audience. In King's case this was privacy and personal autonomy. The other sports study of note is that surrounding Olympic figure skaters Tonya Harding and Nancy Kerrigan (Benoit & Hanczor, 1994). During an interview with CBS reporter Connie Chung, Harding attempted to deny the allegation that she had helped plan an attack on Kerrigan at a practice facility in Detroit. Although Harding's husband was the actual perpetrator, Benoit and Hanczor (1994) concluded that Harding's use of bolstering, denial, and attacking the accuser were "clearly appropriate" because the past had shown them to be effective in situations where an individual has been "accused of heinous acts" (p. 425).

A theoretical and practical extension of Ryan's (1982) speech set of *kategoria* and *apologia* comes from understanding how the target audience(s) responded to the image repair attempt. Claims of effectiveness can not be established by examining the text of the apology alone. Although new scholarship on *antapologia*, the typology of discursive responses to *apologia*, shows promise in completing Ryan's speech set, few studies are currently available. This makes drawing definitive conclusions difficult at this time. However, Stein has developed and applied this typology in an analysis of the discursive responses to the Soviet U2 spy plane incident (Stein, in press), to Mel Gibson's explanation for comments made after his DUI arrest (Stein, 2007), and to newspaper responses to Bush's *apologia* following Hurricane Katrina (Stein, Larson, & Grady, 2007). Examination of these studies reveals that responses to *apologia* reinforce the two functions of *antapologia*— to strengthen the attack and to weaken the *apologia*. This tactic often emerged as an incomplete *apologia* wherein the agent failed to capture the gravity of his/her actions.

We argue that this potentially emerging genre of study is particularly important for understanding contemporary sports because of the changing influence of technology. The ability to blog and post online responses directly to articles means that athletes and other prominent figures are not simply dealing with a handful of editorials and the mainstream press, they are also dealing directly with fan response.

Sports and professional athletes have gained increasing prominence in the U.S. and around the world over the past two decades, yet, ironically, this influence is at best underestimated and at worst understudied by academic investigations. One notable omission from these studies is the voice of the fan as it relates to *antapologia* (Stein, in press). With the powerful and common presence of the Internet, fans are able to not only post comments, but rally together to boycott athletes and their product lines. We believe that although *apologia* studies are illuminating in terms of strategies that various rhetors use, the actual effect their statements have on audiences is too often omitted from these studies. Even when analysis of audience reaction is provided, it is usually in the form of public opinion polls, offering little critical examination of the discursive response to the *apologia*. Focusing on the fan response is not only a powerful way to test the impact of apologies on salient audiences, it is also a direct avenue for advancing a deeper theoretical understanding of the way the response discourse impacts an athlete's ability to repair his/her image.

Method

In order to systematically examine the discourse provided by sports fans in response to Zidane's account, we utilize Stein's (in press) typology of *antapologia* strategies. This typology was initially developed to examine Soviet discourse in response to U.S. *apologia* following the 1960 U-2 spy plane incident and has since been applied in a variety of unique contexts, including Bush's post–Katrina *apologia* (Stein et al., 2007) and Mel Gibson's account of his anti–Semitic drunken tirade (Stein, 2007). According to Stein (in press), there are two primary functions of *antapologic* discourse — one strengthens the initial attack (including two specific strategies) and the other weakens the *apologia* offered by the accused (with eight identified strategies). We regret that we cannot provide a detailed illustration for each of these strategies because of space constraints, but a typology and description of these strategies are summarized in Table 1.

Table 1. Typology of *Antapologia* Strategies

Strategy	*Key Characteristic*	*Examples*
Strengthening the *Apologia*		
1. Identifying concessions in the *apologia*	Shows what the *apologia* admits to	The man admitted the gun used in the robbery was his
2. Refining the attack based on the *apologia*	Modify the initial attack in order to strengthen it	You didn't just damage my windshield, as I initially said, but also the headlights
Weakening the *Apologia*		
1. Portions of the *apologia* are false	Part of the account is untrue	He denied that he was in the room at the time, but video surveillance proves otherwise
2. Contradicted previous *apologia* strategies	Current strategies are not consistent with previous strategies	He denied that he punched the man, but later argued he was provoked
3. *Apologia* does not take adequate responsibility	*Apologia* does not meet the accuser's demands or is incomplete	We will accept nothing short of an apology, yet they continue to evade responsibility
4. *Apologia* reflects character flaws of the accused	*Apologia* highlights negative personal traits of the accused	Only a man devoid of morals would try to blame the victim's family
5. Defense against attacks made in the *apologia*	Accuser responds to attacks made in the *apologia* (attack the accuser)	She says the attack is motivated by greed, but I'm simply looking for justice
6. Harm will come from *apologia* itself	The discourse itself causes harm in addition to the initial act	His insincere apology sets a bad example to the junior senators
7. Attributing motive to the *apologia*	Accuser argues that there are negative motivations behind the *apologia*	You are admitting responsibility only because your staff told you to say this
8. Arguing that the *apologia* mirrors earlier speeches and/or events	The accuser says that the *apologia* is comparable to earlier accounts	You always say you're on a trip whenever you plan to meet up with your girlfriend

Despite the simplicity of the typology depicted in Table 1, we want to be clear that our intention is not to merely deductively apply this typology of *antapologia* strategies in a way that would make the discourse fit neatly into the prescribed categories. Edwin Black (1980) described a rather idealistic method of rhetorical criticism where one approaches a text "without conscious expectations drawn from any sources other than the rhetorical transaction itself" (p. 331). For this analysis, we do not support a strictly atheoretical approach to studying the texts; however, we do recognize the inherent limitations of generic criticism. Because fan responses to Zidane's *apologia* carry the potential to be unique, in addressing these responses we seek an approach that begins with a theoretical framework, but allows for some discursive strategies to emerge inductively. While sports fans may use many of the same strategies used in other contexts, new strategies will likely surface. These new strategies, if any, will be integrated into the typology, thereby making it a more comprehensive list of options available to rhetors seeking to respond to instances of *apologia*.

The texts used in the analysis include a variety of fan blogs and comment sections in response to articles written by professional journalists. There was a tremendous amount of fan commentary in regard to the World Cup and Zidane's effectiveness as a player. However, there was much less commentary focused exclusively on Zidane's *apologia*. Therefore, we feel confident that we were able to garner most fan statements in response to the account of the head butting incident. Obviously, with the vastness of the World Wide Web, we may have inadvertently omitted some fan discourse. Yet, we believe we have a sufficient number of texts to determine the primary strategies used by fans in response to the incident. The main sites accessed for fan statements include *Fox Sports Blogs*, *SFGATE Blog*, *The Guardian*, *Topix.com*, and *Reuters*. We were not selective in which texts were used for the analysis because we examined the entire population of texts available.

Fan Antapologia *in Response to Zidane's Account*

Several of the *antapologia* strategies used by fans in response to Zidane's account were consistent with other contexts, yet much of the discourse was unique. For one, the polarizing nature of the debate between fans created a situation where some fans offered criticisms of the *apologia*, while others acted as surrogate apologizers in their efforts to defend the *apologia*. In previous cases where *antapologia* has been examined, the individuals levying the initial attacks were most likely the ones responding to the *apologia*. During the World Cup incident, however, no official attack was made, but the media frenzy created conditions that necessitated a formal explanation from Zidane. The fans were not impacted directly by the events that transpired on the soccer field, but they felt connected to the situation because of their emotional involvement in both the sport and the 2006 tournament. This involvement was manifested in blogs and other chats as fans utilized a variety of *antapologia* strategies to strengthen and weaken Zidane's *apologia*. Those fans responding to the account with criticism used the following strategies: (a) arguing that the *apologia* reflected character flaws of the accused, (b) attributing motive to the *apologia*, (c) Arguing the *apologia* was incomplete or insufficient, and (d) arguing the account was simply untrue. The fans who chose to defend Zidane's *apologia* utilized the following strategies: (a) arguing that the *apologia* was complete or sufficient, and (b) arguing that the *apologia* reflected positive characteristics of the accused. The remaining part of the analysis provides specific examples to illustrate each of these strategies.

Apologia Reflects the Character Flaws of the Accused

In several blogs, fans argued that Zidane's non-apology for his actions was reflective of his poor character. For example, in a *Reuters* (2006) blog, a fan argued: "Whatever Materazzi said, ZZ [Zidane] should not have reacted like that and deserves to be punished. And what value does his apology have when he then says he doesn't regret what he did. I think it's disgusting and he should not be held up as a role model unless he apologizes properly." In this instance, the fan argued that Zidane should not be a role model because he did not apologize properly. It is interesting to note that the lack of apology became a greater reason for revoking Zidane's status as a role model than his actual on-field behavior. In the SFGate blog (2006), a fan offered a similar remark: "Zidane's non-apology says as much about him as his act. There are parallels between him and one of America's character-challenged athletes. Zinedine Zidane might as well be French for Pete Rose." In each of these examples, fans provided the blog readers with an additional attack on Zidane's image, one that exists independent of the original harmful act. In doing so, they created more difficult rhetorical constraints for Zidane, who is already required to account for his head butt of Materazzi.

Attributing Motive to the *Apologia*

In some cases, fans would call into question the overall sincerity of Zidane's *apologia* by identifying potential motives behind the discourse. The primary motive provided by fans was that Zidane was coached to say the things he did. For example a *Guardian* (2006) blog read: "The interview on TV by Zidane was coached for sure. It was not his face but the face of France that he had to save." Another comment from the same blog read: "In fact, it is pathetic — to my mind at least — that someone who, in principle, is so keen on his immaculate (aren't we all) reputation should have taken part in a French media high-audience spoon feeding/milking operation. [Zidane] sat on his high chair, the player had the press man (spoon feeder) say things for him ('is it true,' etc.), leaving him the honourable task of aying and naying." In both examples, the fans implied that Zidane's words were provided to him by other people and that the media may have played a role in allowing Zidane to account for his behavior more easily. Another *Guardian* (2006) blog is even more explicit in accusing the media of doing Zidane's work: "In order for Zidane to justify his headbutt, he has to cite extreme provocation. Before he took the chance to say anything, the press and the public had already taken that step for him. So determined were a large part of the media to defend Zidane and maintain his status as a sporting icon that they were very quick to accuse Materazzi of racial abuse." Here, the fan argued that the press had decided on an appropriate defense for Zidane and had already begun to implement that defense before Zidane could select his own strategy.

Arguing That the *Apologia* Is Incomplete

Another frequent strategy used by fans was to argue that Zidane's *apologia* was in some way deficient. The most common position articulated was that Zidane only expressed regret and, therefore, did not offer a full mortification for his behavior. A fan in the *Washington Post* (2006) blog wrote: "I am really disappointed that he [Zidane] claims to have no regret for his physical attack. In essence, that he is sorry we all had to witness his violent outburst but that he would do it again without hesitation. This really makes the case for forgiving and forgetting a lot more difficult."

Another *Fox Sports* (2006) blogger said: "Personally, I think that when the concept of apology is separate from that of regret, the man in question is indeed not sorry for his actions, but rather he is sorry for what has resulted (if that makes sense). I don't think Zidane is sorry at all about the simple act of the headbutt, or more specifically that he inflicted physical pain on another man or that he lost his cool. I think that he is sorry that his team was put at a disadvantage, that he may have put a tarnish on French football, and that the kids had to see it ... that kind of thing."

Both blogs illustrate that fans recognized the distinction between apologizing (or even regretting) harmful behavior and feeling sorry that consequences result from the act.

Other fans argued that Zidane's *apologia* was incomplete because his strategy of claiming provocation was not sufficient to justify the violent response. A fan wrote in the *Washington Post* blog: "Ok, so Materazzi insulted his mother and sister. So what? Take it like a man. After all, it's not like you're playing an individual sport. You've got a whole team — and a nation — depending on you. What a lame apology?" Another fan argued in the *SFGate* blog: "Zidane claims Materazzi insulted his mother and sister.... Zidane must have been in fights constantly in school. Those sorts of insults are just not that rare and people over the age of 10 usually know how to brush them off. Only the deranged or the most colossally spoiled of athletes could possibly reach adulthood thinking that it's O.K. to punch or headbutt somebody just because he says something about your mother."

These examples show that fans were critically evaluating the logic present in Zidane's strategy of provocation, thereby drawing the conclusion that his explanation was inadequate.

The *Apologia* Is Untrue

Another strategy used by fans in responding to Zidane's account was to argue that portions of the *apologia* were patently false, lacking in credibility, or devoid of evidentiary support. For example, a *Fox Sports* (2006) blogger wrote: "He [Zidane] claims that Materazzi repeated his statement three times, but from the replay, I can't see where much of anything could have been repeated three times." Here, the fan dismissed the idea that Materazzi may have insulted Zidane during the course of the entire match, arguing that Materazzi did not have sufficient time during the match to provoke Zidane with three offensive remarks.

Fans also argued that Zidane himself lacked credibility, thus casting doubt on his defense: "Ok, so he knows he messed up and now he is trying to redeem himself by saying that his sister and mother was insulted. Yeah right! I don't believe him. The whole time he looked like he was about to lose his temper. Not a team player" (*Fox Sports* blog, 2006).

Another blog also cast doubts on the credibility of the account: "Not a single player has come forward saying that Materazzi has insulted them in the way Zizou alleges previously. Not Thuram and Trezeguet who have played against him for years, not old foes from the EPL, not opponents in Europe, not an opponent from this World Cup. Nobody" (*Fox Sports* blog, 2006). This fan claimed that Zidane's account lacked credibility because Materazzi had a history of clean play — one devoid of antagonism toward other players. Another fan simply claimed there was no evidence to support Zidane's statement: "So, we come back to what we anticipated would be the outcome from the get go. Zidane says one thing and Materazzi says another. Zidane should keep the award [Golden Ball] because we can't prove that he is lying or telling the truth" (*Fox Sports* blog, 2006). Here, the fan did not overtly claim that Zidane's account was false, but just that there was no evidence to support the truth of it. The strategy weakens the overall *apologia* by questioning whether we should believe Zidane's claims of provocation.

Although several fans who used *antapologia* strategies offered criticism in response to the *apologia*, many fan comments functioned to defend the *apologia*. This type of discursive response is unique to this context. In other case studies, the *antapologia* was designed to either strengthen the initial attack against the accused or to weaken the *apologia* of the accused. During the World Cup incident, fans took on the role of surrogate apologizers in an effort to strengthen Zidane's defense.

The *Apologia* Is Sufficient/Complete

While many fans argued that Zidane failed to offer a complete *apologia* for his behavior, several fans were more than satisfied with his defense. Some fans felt that he showed true remorse for his behavior, whereas other fans acknowledged the fact that Zidane only "regretted" elements of the incident, yet they were still satisfied with this response. One blogger wrote: "ZZ [Zidane] has apologized and moved on and so should the football world" (*Fox Sports* blog, 2006). Another fan wrote: "Zidane has apologized to his young fans and has admitted his moment of madness, something that can happen to anyone" (*SFGate* blog, 2006). The statements of these two fans illustrate that many fans did not attempt to make a distinction between true mortification and merely regretting certain negative outcomes from the incident. They merely accepted Zidane's statement as an acknowledgment of wrongdoing. Other fans, however, sought to defend the statements of "regret" as a sufficient form of apology. For example, one blogger wrote: "Anyone who has a pair would understand. There is such a thing as fighting words [fan then provides citation for Wikipedia]. It's right to apologize, but Zinedine is saying he's not Jesus, and he does not regret it. I don't see any inconsistency. I respect him" (*SFGate* blog, 2006). Another fan reiterated this idea: "It's really quite easy to explain. Zidane is sorry that it happened. In his mind, the event was caused by Materazzi. Zidane is really saying he is sorry that Materazzi said that, because it forced him to respond. Zidane said something about, I am only a man, I would rather be knocked to the ground than to have heard those words. So, he is sorry that the event transpired. However, since Materazzi did say that, he does not regret his response. Zidane feels that his response was, in a way, warranted" (*SFGate* blog, 2006).

In these examples, both fans argued that it was sufficient for Zidane to be sorry that the event happened, even if he continued to claim that the event was provoked by Materazzi.

Apologia Reflects Positive
Characteristics of the Accused

The final strategy used by fans in defense of Zidane's *apologia* is similar to the image repair strategy of bolstering. When rhetors use the strategy of bolstering, they attempt to offset the damage done to their image through the harmful act by emphasizing their positive characteristics. Fans could potentially counteract the negative effects of the head butt by emphasizing other aspects of Zidane's character. For example, one blogger argued: "Zidane was very coura-geous and very clear last night on French TV channel Canal Plus. He said what he had to say. He regrets the inappropriate moment chosen for retaliation after Materazzi gravely insulted his mother and his sister.... All I have to say is bravo!" (*Guardian* blog, 2006). Another fan praised Zidane's reputation: "Even every-body is sure that among the Italian football team everybody knows Zidane very well, respect him a lot, believe what he said tonight and know that their team-mate Materazzi is a liar" (*Fox Sports* blog, 2006). For both fans, Zidane's char-acter is a critical issue in determining the acceptability of the *apologia*. For one fan, character was directly related to the believability of the account. For the other fan, the *apologia* itself reflects a high level of character. What distinguishes this *antapologia* strategy from bolstering is that the emphasis on character is always connected with the *apologia*. With bolstering, this is not always the case. Bolstering is a means of improving one's image, but it is often isolated from other strategies designed to directly account for the harmful act. These final two forms of antapologia served to defend Zidane's apology while also fram-ing the response and his behavior positively for the reader. Overall, fan involve-ment manifested in blogs and other chats both strengthened and weakened Zidane's apologia, producing a number of unique implications for our under-standing of antapologia in sports.

Conclusion

By applying Stein's (in press) typology to the Zidane head butt incident, a number of implications can be drawn regarding (a) the role of sports in the everyday lives of sports fans, (b) the unique features of sports *apologia* and *antapologia,* and (c) the significance of blogs for extending the apologetic dis-course. First, a number of interesting implications emerge from fan responses (both negative and positive) to Zidane's apology for his on-field behavior dur-ing the 2006 World Cup Championship. In her seminal work on sports *apolo-gia,* Kruse (1981a) identified a range of situations that required self-defense discourse on the part of athletes, contending that successful image repair strate-gies depended upon the violator's adherence to the "team ethic of sport." Suc-cessful sports *apologia* was dependent upon one's ability to convince fans through the media that the team would not be negatively affected by the inap-propriate behavior. Many could conclude that Zidane's behavior was connected directly to his team's World Cup loss, by removing his team's best player from participating in the sudden death shoot out that ultimately decided the game's outcome. For instance, research (Branscombe & Wann, 1991; Wann, 1994; Wann, 2006c; Wann, Allen, & Rochelle, 2004; Wann, Brewer, & Royalty, 1999; Wann & Waddill, 2007) shows that when individual team identification is high, these fans are likely to experience stronger post-game affect (both positive and negative depending on the team's performance). Yet, fan responses seemed to overlook the fact that Zidane's behavior was associated with the team's chance for a World Cup victory. It is interesting to discern whether his lack of regret/remorse over his behavior and focus upon Materazzi's provocation helped focus fan attention on the apologetic act rather than the game's final outcome. Potentially, Kruse's (1981a) research on sports *apologia* reflects a simpler time in sports when fan reaction to the apology was difficult to measure.

In addition to this implication toward sports and fandom in our society, it seems relevant to ask "Are the media easier on athletes than on other public figures which violate expected/appropriate behavior?" In her examination of L.A. Dodger great Don Sutton's comments about (and brawl with) fellow Dodger Steve Garvey, Kruse (1981a) suggested that despite a need to expand the context of *apologia* studies, sports apologies "do not differ strategically from the character defenses offered by those in the sociopolitical world" (p. 280). However, this analysis suggests that in many cases the standards applied to athletes are different. In the case of politicians, who are elected to make choices about appropriate behavior for individuals in society, part of this challenge is being able to speak well and maintain an impeccable track record of public service and behavior. Sports figures are in a position, among other things, of entertaining people, acting as a diversion from the stress of work and family responsibilities. As such, athletes' primary responsibilities are to perform well in their respective sports and, by extension, satisfy the public's need to be competitive, be involved, and be labeled winners. These latter needs are all important, but they are not the primary responsibility for athletes. This leads to our final observation. Although athletes may be apologizing for on- or off-field conduct and people hope they constantly make good choices, the expectations for their apologies are shallower because athletes are expected to be good at their sports, not at creating policies in life to live by the way political figures are.

Second, in many instances the discourse generated by fans during the 2006 World Cup was different from the *antapologia* strategies used in other case studies. In previous analyses, the individuals or organizations levying the initial attack were likely the same parties responding to the *apologia*. This was certainly the case with newspaper editorials during Hurricane Katrina, members of the Soviet government during the U-2 incident, and Jewish organizations responding to Mel Gibson's remarks. However, fan criticism of Zidane was not the impetus for his subsequent *apologia*, but rather the overwhelming and often negative media coverage of the head butt. Despite the disparity between this and previous contexts, fans still utilized several of the most common *antapologia* strategies in their responses to Zidane's account. A critical distinction, though, is that many fans chose to defend rather than criticize the *apologia*. This type of *antapologia* is a new addition to the theoretical framework and may emerge only in cases where those offering the *antapologia* were not involved in issuing the initial attack.

Another unique element of 2006 World Cup discourse is that the fans intelligently established an important distinction between mortification for one's actions and mere "regret" for the incident that occurred. Simons (2000) noted *apologia* as a genre of criticism is guilty of the "tendency to substitute classification for clarification" and that Benoit's approach in particular lacks a critical edge by concluding that "a given strategy works some of the time" (also implying that the converse is true) (p. 440). The semantic difference between mortification and regret is something that should be pursued further, whether researchers choose to focus on the *apologia* or the *antapologia* during an image repair scenario. As Simons suggested, a deeper focus on analyzing the rhetorical situation is necessary to spur *apologia* scholarship forward.

Third, analysis of this incident suggests that sports blogs shape apologetic discourse in new ways and should continue to be studied. Lee and Barton (2003) argued in their study of Clinton's response to the Monica Lewinsky affair that *apologia* studies failed to account for the use of ordinary language terms as well as the complexity of the apologetic context because the rhetorical situation is defined too narrowly. If communication is a goal-driven activity and communication instruction is designed to increase the probability of achieving those goals, then studying *antapologia* is the next logical step to understanding which strategies work, and why. In the case of Zidane, it is illuminating to see that any given *apologia* can have a wide range of responses and because of the immediacy of fan blogs athletes now have a more clear idea of the step(s) they need to pursue to repair their image. Studying this case also expands Ryan's initial work on the speech set showing the rational progression of attack–*apologia*–*antapologia*.

Note

1. Days after the head butt incident, Zidane appeared on French TV station Canal Plus to explain his actions. During the interview he stated, "He grabbed my shirt and I told him to stop. I told him if he wanted I'd swap it with him at the end of the match. That is when he said some very hard words, which were harder than gestures. He repeated them several times. It all happened very quickly and he spoke about things which hurt me deep down." When further probed about the exact statement made by Materazzi, Zidane noted "They were very hard words. You hear them once and you try to move away. But then you hear them twice, and then a third time.... I am a man and some words are harder to hear than actions. I would rather have taken a blow to the face than hear that.... I reacted and of course it is not a gesture you should do. I must say that strongly. It was seen by two or three billion people watching on television and millions and millions of children. It was an inexcusable gesture and to them, and the people in education whose job it is to show children what they should and shouldn't do, I want to apologise." The interview further inquired whether he regretted his actions, at which he stated, "I can't regret it because if I do it would be like admitting that he was right to say all that. And above all, it was not right. We always talk about the reaction, and

inevitably it must be punished. But if there is no provocation, there is no reaction. First of all you have to say there is provocation, and the guilty one is the one who does the provoking. The response is to always punish the reaction, but if I react, something has happened. Do you imagine that in a World Cup final like that, with just 10 minutes to go to the end of my career, I am going to do something like that because it gives me pleasure? ... There was provocation, and it was very serious, that is all. My action was inexcusable but you have to punish the real culprit, and the real culprit is the one who provoked it." A complete text of the interview is available at <http://news.bbc.co.uk/ sport2/hi/football/world_cup_2006/teams/france/5174758.stm>.

FAN IDENTIFICATION

The Consequences of
Sports Fan Identification

BETH DIETZ-UHLER AND JASON R. LANTER

One of the most interesting aspects of sports fans is their degree of involvement and affiliation with their favorite sports team. Indeed, perusal of the popular press suggests that sports fans reveal their connection to a favorite team in interesting ways, including wearing team apparel, displaying bumper stickers on their cars, and engaging in celebratory behaviors that range from fairly passive (e.g., cheering) to utterly destructive (e.g., tearing down goalposts). For some fans of sports, their level of involvement is relatively low key, whereas for other sports fans, they seem to live and breathe for their favorite team. What accounts for the differences in these fans? The answer likely lies in their level of sports fan identification, or their psychological attachment to a sport or a team. Some sports fans identify particularly strongly with a team, and this psychological connection can have many consequences. The purpose of this chapter is to review the affective, cognitive, and behavioral consequences of identifying as a sports fan. However, before reviewing these consequences of sports fan identification, we review the definition of a group as well as social identity theory, which provides the basis for the study of sports fan identification. We also discuss the various conceptualizations of sports fan identity, how it is measured, as well as why fans identify with a team.

It is important to be clear about the distinction between fans and spectators. Sports fans are those who actively follow a sports team or sport, while sports spectators are those who physically witness a sporting event (i.e., attend a sporting event, watch one on television, listen to one on a radio; Wann, 1995, 1997). Sports fans establish a psychological connection with the team, whereas spectators merely observe a sporting event. Most sports fans are also sports spectators. Clearly, both fans and spectators are equally important for a variety of reasons. However, the focus of this chapter is on sports fans.

Group Identification

To understand group identification, it is necessary to discuss what is meant by a group. In fact, there is little consensus about what characteristics of a collective make a group. Although most social psychologists would agree that a group is a collection of people who are perceived to belong together and are dependent on one another, there are other ways to conceptualize groups. For example, Moreland (1987) discussed "groupiness" or social integration as a quality that every collection of individuals possesses to some degree. As the level of social integration increases, people start to think and act more like a group than a collection of individuals. Other social psychologists (Dasgupta, Banaji, & Abelson, 1999; Lickel et al., 2000) maintained that the perception of a collection of people as being bonded is important. This perception, named entitativity, refers to the extent to which a collection of people is perceived as a coherent entity. Some groups, such as people in line at a bank, are perceived as being low in entitativity. Other groups, such as members of a family or members of a professional sports team, are perceived as being high in entitativity.

As discussed previously, some sports fans possess a stronger connection to a team or sport than others, presumably due to their degree of group or social identification with a sport or team. Social identity is defined as "that part of an individual's self-concept which derives from his [her] knowledge of his [her] membership in a social group (groups) together with the value and emotional significance attached to that membership" (Tajfel, 1978, p. 63). Tajfel and Turner (1979) summarized this theory with three theoretical principles. First, group members strive to maintain a sense of positive social identity. Second, group members base this social identity on favorable comparisons that can be made between members of their own group and members of another group. Third, members will attempt to leave their group or join a more positively valued group when their social identity is not satisfactory to them. Applied to the study of sports fans, social identity theory suggests that some fans identify with a team or sport more strongly than others, presumably to feel good about themselves (at least to the extent that their perceptions of the team or sport allow such feelings).

Sports Fan Identification

Most fans of sports can easily name their favorite team or teams. They are equally likely to be able to readily report the strength of their connection to a team, or their level of sports fan identification. Generally, sports fan identification refers to the degree to which a fan feels a psychological connection to a team or sport (Murrell & Dietz, 1992). More complex conceptualizations of sports fan identification exist. For example, Dimmock, Grove, and Eklund (2005) provided evidence to suggest that sports team identification can best be conceptualized by including cognitive (e.g., knowledge of group membership) and evaluative (e.g., value of group membership) aspects of identification. Recently, Jacobson (2003) advised sports-fan researchers to consider the interpersonal (e.g., the network of fans) and symbolic (e.g., attachments to successful others) factors that comprise a fan's identification with a team, arguing that both types of factors contribute equally to sports fan identity. Regardless of how sports fan identification is defined, there is a wealth of evidence to suggest that it exerts a strong influence on sports fans' affective, cognitive, and behavioral reactions to sports, which is the focus of this chapter.

Sports fan identification can be measured both directly and indirectly. Direct measures typically include instruments constructed specifically to measure sports fan identification. The most widely and extensively used tool for measuring sports fan identification is the seven-item Sport Spectator Identification Scale (SSIS; Wann & Branscombe, 1993). Other, less-frequently used measures of sports fan identification include the Connection to a Team Scale (CTS; Trail & James, 2001), and the Psychological Commitment to a Team Scale (PCT; Mahony, Madrigal, & Howard, 2000). These latter two measures have been mostly used to predict the marketing behavior of sports fans. Recently, Wann and Pierce (2003) compared the SSIS with the PCT and found both measures to be highly correlated and predictive of a number of sports fan behaviors.

Indirect measures of sports fan identification also exist. For example, measuring the frequency of attendance at sporting events or number of sporting events viewed on television can provide information about a fan's level of identification (Murrell & Dietz, 1992). Similarly, marketing behavior such as the amount of money spent on sports fan apparel and paraphernalia can serve as a proxy measure for sports fan or team identification. Of course, indirect measures of the sort described here are often used as indicators of the consequences of sports fan identification.

Finally, it is worth asking how fans come to identify with a particular sport or team. One of the most interesting investigations about the origins of team identification was conducted by Wann, Tucker, and Schrader (1996). The results of their study showed a variety of reasons for original interest in a team, including (in order of importance) parental interest in a team, talent of the team players, geography and the influence of friends, and the success of the team. Other investigations (e.g., Jones, 1997a) find similar reasons for identifying with a particular team, although not necessarily in the same order as Wann, Tucker, and Schrader. For example, Jones (1997a) found that geographical location was the predominant reason given for being a fan of a team. End, Dietz-Uhler, Harrick, and Jacquemotte (2002) found that the success of a team was the primary reason for team identification.

There are clearly a number of reasons why fans decide to become attached to a particular team or sport. Despite the differences in their reasons for involvement with a particular team, it seems that some fans have a stronger psychological attachment to a team than do other fans. In fact, the level of identification with a team or sport can range from quite weak to extremely strong. A wealth of research on the consequences of sports fan identification suggests that this psychological attachment can exert powerful influences on affective, cognitive, and behavioral aspects. In the remainder of this chapter, we review the research on these consequences of sports fan identification, paying particular attention to the positive and not-so-positive consequences of sports fan identification.

Affective Consequences of Sports Fan Identification

When sports fans identify strongly with a team, they tend to experience more extreme feelings than those who identify weakly with a team. Among the affective consequences of sports fan identification that have been investigated are level of arousal, sympathy, post-game affect, and enjoyment. Research shows that fans who report being strongly identified with a specific team or sports display more heightened levels of arousal than fans who weakly identify with a team or sport. For example, Branscombe and Wann (1992a) found that strongly identified American fans had higher blood pressure readings after watching a boxing match between a U.S. and a Russian boxer than before the match, while those weak in identification showed no changes in blood pressure. Similarly, Wann, Schrader, and Adamson (1998) found, among other things, that strongly identified fans of a team were more likely than weakly identified fans to report increases in anxiety as an important competition approached.

An interesting and timely investigation about the sympathy expressed by sports fans was recently conducted by Wann and Waddill (2007). Following the fatal crash of Dale Earnhardt, Sr., NASCAR fans reported their level of identification with their favorite driver and attitudes toward Earnhardt's crash. They found that evaluations made by fans of Dale Earnhardt reflected greater sympathy than fans of other drivers, although the pain expressed by strongly identified Earnhardt fans was only a bit higher than weakly identified Earnhardt fans.

One of the most widely examined affective reactions of sports fans are the emotions they express following a sporting event. In an early investigation of the emotions experienced by strongly identified fans, Hirt, Zillmann, Erickson, and Kennedy (1992) found that following a win by their favorite basketball team, strongly identified fans reported more severe emotions (i.e., higher levels of elation and depression following a win and a loss, respectively) than weakly identified fans. Wann, Royalty, and Rochelle (2002) found that team identification was positively correlated with positive affect (e.g., happy, pleased, satisfied) expressed by fans of a basketball team following a win by the team.

Most recently, Crisp, Heuston, Farr, and Turner (2007) examined the emotions felt by fans of soccer following a loss. They found that strongly identified fans reported feeling angry, but not sad, whereas those weakly identified fans reported sadness but not anger.

Finally, research in this area has investigated the level of enjoyment reported by strongly and weakly identified fans. For example, Madrigal (1995) found that team identification was positively correlated with enjoyment while attending a women's basketball game. Similarly, Wann and Schrader (1997) found that strongly identified fans reported greater enjoyment while watching their team win than those who identified less strongly.

In sum, this brief review of the effects of sports fan identification on affective responses suggests that sports play a powerful role in the emotional reactions of sports fans, especially those who identify most strongly. For those with a deep psychological attachment to a team, emotions such as enjoyment, happiness, satisfaction, and anxiety can fluctuate dramatically depending on the success or failure of the highly-valued team.

Cognitive Consequences of Sports Fan Identification

Like affective reactions, there are a variety of cognitive consequences of identifying with a sports team. Some of the cognitive consequences studied to date include team knowledge, perceptions of teams and fans, and attributions. In an investigation of the knowledge of a team in a particular sport and sports in general, Wann and Branscombe (1995) found that strongly identified fans of a men's basketball team reported more knowledge of the team and of the sport than those weakly identified. In a highly interesting study of the language of sports fans, Wann et al. (1997) reported a strong, positive correlation between strength of sports fandom and understanding of sports terminology. Strongly identified sports fans, not surprisingly, appear to possess greater knowledge of sports in general and of their favorite teams in particular than those weakly identified.

It is also not surprising that strongly identified fans appear to be biased in their perceptions of their favorite teams as well as in their perceptions of the fans of their own and opposing teams (e.g., Hastorf & Cantril, 1954), perhaps as a self-esteem maintenance strategy. In an investigation of the evaluations of past, present, and future performance of a team, Wann and Dolan (1994) reported that strongly identified fans made more "team-serving" evaluations of their favorite team than did weakly identified fans. Sports fans also have been shown to be biased in their evaluations of fellow and rival fans. For example, after reading a fictional scenario about a fellow and a rival fan, strongly identified fans reported more positive evaluations of the fellow fan than the rival fan (Wann & Dolan, 1994). With regard to overall evaluations of a team, strongly identified fans of both football and basketball were more likely than weakly identified fans to report positive evaluations (e.g., based on how much they liked the team, how successful they thought the team would be, and how good the team was relative to other teams) of the teams (Murrell & Dietz, 1992). Of course, all of these consequences can be predicted from social identity theory, which argues that to maintain a positive view of our own group, our evaluations of our own group and its members will be more favorable than evaluations of another group and its members, and this generally holds true even when there is evidence to the contrary.

Likewise, social identity theory would predict that the attributions made by strongly identified group members would be biased in a manner that supports the ingroup and its members. Briefly, attributions refer to the explanations made for behavior. Sometimes, the perceived causes of behavior are internal, such as personality traits or ability. At other times, the perceived causes of behavior are external, such as the weather or other people's actions. In the case of sports fans, one would expect that strongly identified fans would make more internal attributions (e.g., "We really played well") following a victory, but more external attributions (e.g., "The referees were clearly against us") following a loss. Wann and Dolan (1994) found that following a college men's basketball game, strongly identified fans expressed more internal attributions about the team's performance after a win, but more external attributions about the team's performance after a loss. Strongly identified fans of college football report similar attributions. Dietz-Uhler and Murrell (1999) found that strongly identified fans were more likely than weakly identified fans to evaluate a football team more favorably after wins than losses, after game outcomes that were expected rather than unexpected, and after games receiving more positive than negative media coverage.

Behavioral Consequences of Sports Fan Identification

Perhaps the most widely investigated and certainly the most easily observable consequences of sports fan identification are behavioral. In this section, we review research on such behavioral consequences as self-presentational strategies, loyalty, aggression, prosocial behavior, and psychological well-being. In one of the earliest investigations of sports fans, Cialdini et al. (1976) identified an interesting self-presentational strategy, which they termed Basking in Reflected Glory (BIRGing). They found that university students were more likely to wear university apparel following a victory (rather than a loss) by the school's football team. Students were also more likely to use collective pronouns when describing a team victory than a team loss. Subsequent research has shown that, indeed, sports fans have a tendency to identify more strongly with winning rather than losing teams (End et al., 2002; Wann & Branscombe,

1990a). In a recent investigation of this self-presentational strategy on the World Wide Web, End (2001) found that fans did not BIRG by providing more links to successful than unsuccessful teams from their home pages. However, they did BIRG when using the team's electronic message board by praising winning teams and derogating losing teams. There have, of course, been other self-presentational strategies identified in the behavior of sports fans, all of which appear to serve the role of protecting a valued sports fan identity and maintaining positive self-esteem. For example, CORFing is when a sports fan Cuts off Reflected Failure by disassociating with a losing team (Wann & Branscombe, 1990a; Wann, 1993). COFFing, Cutting off Future Failure, occurs when someone dissociates from a person or team that they believe is likely to lose in the future (Wann, Hamlet, Wilson, & Hodges, 1995).

All of the literature on strongly identified sports fans suggests that they are loyal to their team, to its players, and to a sport. In a study examining the depth and breadth of that loyalty, Dietz-Uhler, End, Demakakos, Dickirson, & Grantz (2002) asked participants to read a hypothetical scenario of a player from their favorite team who had engaged in criminal activity. Results showed that strongly identified fans reported more favorable evaluations of the athlete and the team than did less strongly identified fans. When a social identity is threatened, such as when a player from one's favorite team engages in illegal behavior, those who identify most strongly with a group often feel the strongest need to defend it. In a similar line of research, Wann and his colleagues have examined the relationship between team identification and willingness to assist a team in illegal behavior. Their results show that strongly identified fans are more likely than weakly identified fans to express a willingness to engage in illegal activities for their favorite team (Wann, Hunter, Ryan, & Wright, 2001), to consider anonymous acts of violence (Wann, Haynes, McLean, & Pullen, 2003), and to be more willing to engage in violent acts after a team loss than a team victory (Wann et al., 2005). These studies report on sports fans' willingness to support illegal behavior and willingness to consider engaging in illegal activity. A question to consider is whether or not strongly identified fans would actually engage in negative behavior.

Some research on aggression among sports fans suggests that strongly identified sports fans are no more likely to be aggressive than fans who are less strongly identified. For example, Wann, Fahl, Erdmann, & Littleton (1999) found no relationship between fan identification (e.g., the psychological importance of being a sports fan in general) and trait aggression. Wann, Peterson, Cothran, & Dykes (1999) did find a positive relationship between team identification (e.g., the psychological importance of being a fan of a particular team) and aggression. Strongly identified fans reported a willingness to anonymously injure a star player or coach of a rival team, although there were no effects of team identification on willingness to anonymously murder someone. Other research suggests that there is a relationship between team identification and aggression. Wann, Shelton, Smith, & Walker (2002) found that sports fandom and trait aggression were positively related, although only among male participants.

In the popular media, sports fans are often depicted as being highly aggressive, particularly when their team is losing, or — most surprisingly —following an especially important win. In fact, picture and video footage abound of fans tearing out goalposts, setting garbage cans and cars on fire, and even overturning police cars. Work by Lanter (2000) on celebratory violence suggested that team identification may play a role in expressions of aggressive behavior. Strongly identified fans of a college basketball team reported engaging in more celebratory violence following an important team victory than those less identified with the team.

Painting an equally ambiguous picture of the positive and negative aspects of sports fan identification is work on the role of team identification in prosocial behavior. Platow, Durante, Williams, Garrett, Walshe, Cincotta, Lianos, & Barutchu (1999) examined the impact of a variety of factors on contributions of money to charity workers before and after football games. Fans contributed more money to charity workers who identified themselves as supporters of the fans' favorite team than of the opposing team.

Recently, Wann, Dimmock, & Grove (2003) examined the role of sports fan identification on social connections and psychological well-being. In a study of fans of Australian Rules Football, team identification was found to be positively related to social, but not personal, well-being (Wann, Dimmock, & Grove, 2003). Additional support for the Team Identification–Social Psychological Health Model is found in a study showing that team identification was positively related to social well-being (Wann & Pierce, 2005). Most recently, Wann (2006a) advanced this model to suggest that both enduring and temporary forms of social connections are enhanced by sports team identification. Indeed, the social connection to a university, as well as to the identification with the team, increased after the university's men's basketball team won the national championship (Lanter & Blackburn, 2004). The effects of team identification on social well-being clearly support one of the more positive consequences of strongly identifying as a sports fan.

Conclusion

This review, although not exhaustive, of the role of identification on affective, cognitive, and behavioral aspects of sports fans suggests, at the least, that this type of identity is worthy of investigation. Not only does this research highlight the importance of groups to people's lives, it also helps to explain the importance that so many people place on their teams. Starting with social identity theory, it is clear that groups serve an important purpose for most people. In addition to providing people with a sense of belonging and a sense of self, identifying with a group can serve an important psychological function. According to Tajfel and Turner (1979), that psychological function is self-esteem. Put simply, to the extent that one's group compares favorably with another, relevant group, people feel good about themselves. The research reviewed here certainly supports this perspective; sports fans accrue more positive benefits following team wins than losses, including more favorable moods (e.g., Wann, Royalty, & Rochelle, 2002), higher self-esteem (e.g., Hirt, Zillmann, Erickson, & Kennedy, 1992), and more confidence (e.g., Murrell & Dietz, 1992).

At the same time, there is evidence for the stability of team identification (e.g., Wann, 2006b). The strength of sports fan identification tends not to wane following a team loss. Again, this outcome can be explained by social identity theory. When an important social identity is threatened, as in the case of a team loss, group members adapt and adjust to the threat by engaging in a variety of behaviors that still allow them to maintain a positive view of their group and, as a consequence, of themselves. Again, the research reviewed here suggests that sports fans engage in a host of behaviors that allow them to maintain a positive view of their team, including holding positive evaluations of their team, making team-serving attributions for their team's performances, engaging in more favorable behavior and holding more positive attitudes towards fellow than rival fans, and displaying fierce loyalty to their team.

In short, to fully understand sports fans, it is essential to view their affective, cognitive, and behavioral reactions from the perspective of the group. Of course, one can call into question the exact nature of the sports fans' group membership. In other words, do sports fans accrue typical group benefits as a result of identifying as a sports fan, or as a member of the team? Research on self-presentational strategies, most notably BIRGing, suggests that sports fans seem to perceive themselves as actual members of the team (e.g., "We played really well yesterday"; "I like how we held them off in the ninth inning"). Obviously, sports fans did not "play well" nor did they "hold them off in the ninth inning." It could be argued that sports fans benefit from two types of group membership; one as an actual group member of the group of sports fans, the other as a virtual group member of the sports team.

It would be interesting to examine the levels of identification with the actual group of fans and the virtual team. An examination of the most typical sports fan identification measure, the SSIS, reveals that team identification is construed as a psychological connection to the team, not as a connection to the group of fellow fans, nor as a virtual member of the team. Perhaps the differences in the levels of sports fan identification that have been observed, which consequently influence affect, cognition, and behavior, can be explained by these different, yet unmeasured, types of identification. That is, perhaps those who score highest on the SSIS, and thus experience the strongest affective, cognitive, and behavioral consequences, identify strongly with sports fans as well as with the team.

Of course, identification of various dimensions of group identity is not novel. For example, Hinkle & Brown (1990) proposed that social identity consisted of two dimensions or components, (a) individualistic versus collective and (b) relational versus non-relational. Optimal Distinctiveness Theory (e.g., Brewer, 1991) suggests that social identity can be construed along two dimensions, the need for assimilation (to be like others) and the need for differentiation (the need to be different from others). Among sports fan researchers, Dimmock et al. (2005) suggested that sports team identification can best be conceptualized by including both cognitive and evaluative dimensions, while Jacobson (2003) encouraged sports fan researchers to consider the public and private dimensions of sports fan identity. Perhaps a consideration of these or other dimensions of sports fan identity would allow for a richer, more predictive understanding of the differences in levels or types of sports fan identification.

A potentially more relevant consideration than the dimensions of group identity is research on types of groups. Deaux, Reid, Mizrahi, & Ethier (1995) identified five types of social identities, including personal relationships, vocations/avocations, political affiliations, ethnic/religious groups, and stigmatized groups. These five types of identities were derived from analyses of the perceived similarities of various social identities. Prentice, Miller, & Lightdale (1994) distinguished between common-bond and common-identity groups. In common-bond groups, the bonds and levels of attraction are primarily between group members. In common-identity groups, the attachment and attraction is to the group. Groups based on friendships are categorized as common-bond groups, while those organized around a common interest or activity are categorized as common-identity groups.

Similarly, Gardner & Gabriel (2004) discussed collective (i.e., group bonds) and relational (i.e., interpersonal bonds) interdependence in groups, and found gender differences in these types of interdependence. Females reported higher levels of relational interdependence, whereas males reported greater collective interdependence. Taking these results into consideration may help to further explain discrepancies between the reasons males and females considered themselves sports fans (Dietz-Uhler, Harrick, End, & Jacquemotte, 2000). Females reported being a fan of sports for social reasons such as watching or attending a sporting event to spend time with family or friends. For males, sports fandom seems to serve a less-relational function. They reported being a fan because they enjoy the excitement of following sports and seeking information about sports.

It would be interesting to consider viewing sports fans using the common-bond/relational interdependence and common-identity/collective interdependence group typology. It may be the case that sports fan identity serves a common-bond/relational function for some group members. If so, then one would expect this group to be more interested in their relationships with other sports fans. Fans whose sports fan identity serves a common-identity/collective function would be expected to be more concerned with the team and the sport. This investigation could also provide more information about gender issues in sports fans.

Another interesting group typology to consider is the functions of various types of groups. For example, Johnson et al. (2006) recently investigated the various social motivation functions of a variety of different types of groups. Their research focused specifically on three types of groups. Intimacy groups, such as families and friends, have high levels of interaction, similarity, and importance to their members. Task groups, such as study groups and juries, have a high degree of interaction and are typically characterized as sharing common goals and working toward specific outcomes. Social categories, such as women and Hispanics, usually have low levels of interaction and similarity. Focusing on the motivational principles identified by Mackie & Smith (1998), they found that intimacy groups were most associated with affiliation needs, task groups with achievement needs, and social categories with identity needs. Applied to sports fans, it would be interesting to investigate the various needs served by being a sports fan. Perhaps sports fan identification serves different needs for different types of fans, which might account for the different affective, cognitive, and behavioral reactions to sports.

There is also research on gender differences in sports fans (discussed above) which shows that sports fandom serves different functions for male and female fans (Dietz-Uhler, Harrick, End, & Jacquemotte, 2000). Interestingly, these gender differences exist even though males and females report similar levels of identification with a team and similar levels of perceiving themselves as sports fans (Dietz-Uhler, End, Jacquemotte, Bentley, & Hurlbut, 2000).

Future research might consider focusing on various dimensions and typologies of sports fan identity, as well as the various needs served by those dimensions or types. It would be interesting to gain a better understanding of why some fans identify more strongly with a team than do others, as well as why the affective, cognitive, and behavioral consequences differ. For example, why do some fans engage in celebratory violence while other, but equally identified, fans refrain from such activity? Why do some fans report greater despair following a team loss than other, but equally identified, fans? The answer might lie in the manner in which sports fan identification is measured and conceptualized (i.e., identification with sports fans and virtual identification as a team member), or it may lie in a host of other potential mediators, such as the functions that sports fandom serves. This is an issue that might be fruitful for sports fan scholars to explore.

I Am Yao Ming

Identification and Internet Fan Discussion

KATHERINE L. LAVELLE

"The Chinese have never had [a professional] athlete succeed on the world stage.... They've been waiting for someone like Yao" (McCallum, 2003, p. 39). This statement, made by Eric Zhang (McCallum, 2003), Yao Ming's Chinese-American advisor, indicates the significance of Yao Ming for Asian and Chinese people. In 2002, the 7'6" Shanghai native was drafted number one overall by the Houston Rockets, making him the first foreign born player drafted into the National Basketball Association (NBA). He was a sensation, making the All-Star team his rookie year, and receiving several high profile American commercial endorsements from Apple, VISA, and Gatorade (McCallum, 2003). He is the most recognizable Chinese athlete in the Western world. Part of the reason that Yao received so much attention was the support of his Asian fan base. Asians and Asian-Americans identified with him because he shared their ethnic and/or national heritage. One of their ways of expressing their solidarity and support of him was by posting on *ClubYao*, a fan website devoted to news and discussion about Yao. Using Kenneth Burke's discussion of identification, and scholarly research on fan culture, I examined how Yao's Asian-American fan base identifies with him by examining discussion threads on his official website. In order to analyze these writings, I examined identification and popular culture scholarship, the representation of Asian-Americans in sports, and international basketball players, as well as a thematic analysis of selected discussion posts.

Identification & Popular Culture

Identification is a term that has been used by Kenneth Burke to describe how persuasion can be observed in human communication. Burke (1950) was concerned with how language expresses the motives of a person. Usually, iden-tification occurs when a speaker uses specific language or common themes to relate to the audience (Burke, 1950). For example, if a speaker were talking to a group of Cleveland sports fans, s(he) might start by talking about how much s(he) likes the Cleveland Browns football team. Identification is a way speak-ers eliminate distance between themselves and their audience, or create "con-substantiality" (Burke, 1950). Burke (1937) argued that a need for people to identify always exists because they are separate; they have different motives that they express through language, and in order to eliminate division, the speaker needs to find common motives or ways of talking about issues that bring people together.

Burke (1937) argued that identification can be expressed in several ways. Initially, identification can occur with regard to property. Burke (1950) out-lined several things that can be termed "property," most notably economic goods, but it can also refer to a common position, reputation, or citizenship of the speaker and the audience. These characteristics may be emphasized differ-ently depending on their context. Burke (1969/1989c) provided the example of students in a class to explain how this component of identification works. "Two students, sitting side by side in a classroom where the principles of a special-ized subject are being taught, can be expected to identify the subject differently, so far as its place in a total context is concerned" (p. 186). One student might use that classroom knowledge immediately, whereas the other might not draw upon it for years to come. For instance, if it were a French history class, and one student traveled to France the next semester, that knowledge would be applicable immediately. However, if the other student did not go to France until she was 50, only then might she identify with that knowledge.

Because identification cannot be measured like a science experiment, "belonging is rhetorical" (Burke, 1969/1989c, p. 186). It has to be talked about in order to exist. Consequently, this understanding of rhetoric and persuasion is applicable in many fields, including anthropology, which examines how peo-ple within specific cultures interact with each other. Rhetoric "is rooted in an essential function of language itself, a function that is wholly realistic, and is continually born anew; the use of language as a symbolic means of inducing cooperation in beings that by nature respond to symbols" (p. 188). Understand-ing how language functions in this sense is critical to evaluating how identifi-cation works as persuasion.

Another manner of expressing identification is through popular culture. The relationship between popular culture and an audience was examined exten-sively by John Fiske (1989) in his study of the interaction of popular culture and its fan bases. Fiske asserted, "There can be no popular dominant culture, for popular culture is formed always in reaction to, and never as part of, the forces of domination" (p. 43). He argued that popular culture, whether it be art, music, or anything else, must be "relevant to the immediate social situa-

tion of the people" (p. 25). The audience needs to find some way that a popular cultural artifact is connected to their own experience. "The meanings of popular culture exist only in their circulation, not in their texts; the texts, which
are crucial in this process, need to be understood not for and by themselves,
but in their interrelationships with other texts and with social life, for that is
how their circulation is ensured" (p. 4).

Burke (1931) discussed this phenomenon in his book *Counterstatement*,
arguing that a text gains meaning depending on how the general public reacts
to it. The originators of the popular culture artifacts do not decide what they
mean to the audience. Instead, "meanings can be produced, reproduced, and
circulated only in that constant process that we call culture" (Fiske, 1989, p.
27). Looking at how a text is circulated and what the audience does with it helps
explain the impact of popular culture.

One of the best ways to understand how popular culture affects its audience is through fan culture scholarship. Recent work has examined how fans
not only consume cultural artifacts, but change them to fit their own interpretation (Consalvo, 2003; Jenkins, 2000). For instance, Consalvo studied "fan
poaching," which is a practice often used by online communities to change
popular culture texts. Consalvo examined fan groups of the television horror-
drama *Buffy the Vampire Slayer*. These fans wrote short stories that were used
to produce original texts using the television show as an inspiration for their
work. For example, a story line evolved creating relationships between two
straight male characters, something that would only be tangentially suggested
by the way that the characters were presented on television (Consalvo, 2003).
Brown (1997) explained this practice: "Fandom is a means of expressing one's
sense of self and one's communal relation with others within our complex society" (p. 13). When fans take ownership of a text, it means that they care enough
about it to go beyond it. They do not just view it, they relate to it. Brown's article deals with comic book fans, who are often ridiculed by mainstream society but find belonging in this common interest. Similarly, Kendall (2000)
studied how an online community used their outsider status within mainstream society to find togetherness online. Kendall was concerned with how
hegemonic masculinity was articulated within a cyber community: "U.S. cultural expectations regarding technology usage converge with stereotypes concerning race and gender, resulting in a white nerd masculine identity congruent
with related forms of masculinity found in computing and engineering fields.
In enacting this form of masculinity, BlueSky participants demonstrate both
its divergence from and convergence with hegemonic masculinity" (p. 271).
Although Kendall's research suggests that these communities reinforce dominant notions of race and power in American society, might there be other communities that embrace their ethnic and/or national identity online? I want to
examine this phenomenon.

Asians and Asian-Americans in Sports

Previous research on Asians and Asian-Americans in sports focuses gener-ically on fans, especially on why they like particular teams or types of sports. But what about fandom based on ethnic and/or national identity? Asian iden-tity is difficult to define because the term "Asian" refers to billions of people in Asia, from countries as diverse as China and India, and all of the different groups of people who reside in, or have ancestral roots from, that area of the world. Cultural studies scholars have explored comprehensively this question (Ang, 1998; Chow, 1998). I recognize that "Asian" and "Chinese" are unstable terms that refer to almost contradictory identities and characteristics. How-ever, given the classification of Yao as an Asian and/or Chinese athlete, this paper focuses on examining the articulation of Asian identity.

One of the identifying traits of Asian identity is the model minority myth. Wong, Nagasawa, and Lin (1998) defined the myth by stating "Asian-Ameri-cans are believed to enjoy extraordinary achievements in education, occupa-tional upward mobility, rising income, and are problem-free in mental health and crime" (pp. 95–96). In other words, they do not fit into the negative stereo-types attributed to blacks and Latinos in the U.S. Asians are supposed to be what immigrant groups aspire to achieve in the U.S.

The model minority myth is considered positive by many, especially non–Asian people (Ancheta, 1998). This stereotype is far different from such stereotypes as black athletes are more likely to be guilty of an accused crime than are their white counterparts (Berry & Smith, 2000), or that all Latino/as are illegal immigrants who commit criminal behavior in the U.S. (Dixon & Linz, 2002). However, the model minority myth can be problematic for Asian people. First, it turns them into a silent minority (Ancheta, 1998). Wong et al. (1998) explained, "The model minority is also used by the white majority to neutralize social unrest by dissident minority groups in society. The 'success' of the minority is offered as proof that the American dream of equal opportu-nity is valid for those who conform and who are willing to work hard" (p. 100). It ignores the struggles faced by new immigrants, especially poor ones from countries where they did not learn English, or gain the education or skills nec-essary to make the transition into living in America (Ancheta, 1998; Wong et al., 1998). For example, in an ethnography of Asian high school students in Chicago, Lee (1996) found that administrators used this myth to place students into class sections. Through her interviews and assessments of how students were placed in classes, she found that students, especially those who were recent immigrants and not ready for the advanced American coursework because of the language barrier, were often in classes that did not match their proficiency level. As a result, these students were unsuccessful because they were unable to meet the high standards established by members of more affluent and Amer-icanized groups from China, Japan, and Korea (Lee, 1996).

Second, there is an expectation that if a person looks Asian, he or she is part of some pan–Asian culture — a culture that does not really exist (Wu, 2002). For instance, Tuan's (1998) ethnographic study of Asians from a variety of citizenship statuses found that third-generation Japanese-Americans were expected to speak a dialect of Chinese. This phenomenon is often present when Asians are depicted in films (Chan, 2002). Even today, there are few realistic and varied depictions of Asian people in U.S. cinema. Moreover, Asian religious values and culture are often presented in a simplistic way that ignores differences and years of definition that cannot be isolated to a couple of simple phrases.

In sports, there are scholarly articles and books that analyze the problems faced by African American athletes (Berry & Smith, 2000; Hoberman, 1997) and female athletes (Billings, Halone & Denham, 2002). There is little coverage about the unique situation faced by Asian athletes. Mayeda (1999) made an important scholarly contribution to this work when he examined the representation of two Japanese pitchers in American Major League Baseball. The beginning of his article reviewed some of the previous negative depictions of Asian athletes in American media texts. Mayeda's article includes a long quote from a journalist in a 1992 edition of *Runner's World*; Amby Burfoot provided this explanation for Japanese runners' inability to succeed: "Japanese are passionate about sports and surely rank among the world's most disciplined, hardest-working and highest-achieving peoples. These qualities have brought them great success in many areas and should produce the same in sports. Yet the Japanese rarely succeed at sports. They fall short because, on average, they are short. Most big-time sports require size, speed, and strength. A racial group lacking these qualities must struggle against great odds to excel" (quoted in Mayeda, 1999, p. 208). This appalling comment is not made in isolation. Mayeda mentions several other references in American popular press articles that discuss the physical limitations of Asians that prevent them from succeeding in sports. These comments contradict the strong athletic traditions in many Asian countries, including the success of Japanese baseball. Instead of relying on these stereotypes, Mayeda encouraged his audience to combat them. "For Asian national and Asian-Americans (both male and female) who are so often categorized as resigned and athletically inferior, finding athletic heroes could be very useful not only in dissolving racial stereotypes, but also in promoting ethnic pride" (pp. 214–215). Mayeda pushed for the presence of Asian sports role models that are positive. Perhaps Yao Ming is that presence?

Yao Ming

In the past 20 years, the NBA has become increasingly internationalized. With the success of Eastern European and Russian players, such as Vlade Divac and Aryanas Sabonis, the 21st century saw not only the increase in the number of players, but the successful assimilation of these players (Araton, 2005). The 2003 playoffs (which coincided with the end of Yao's first year in the league), were a breakthrough for international players. In the Western Conference finals, the Dallas Mavericks were led by the fundamental play of Canadian (and future two-time league MVP) Steve Nash and German Dirk Nowitzki (the MVP of the 2006-07 season). They were defeated by that season's champions, the San Antonio Spurs, which boasted two international players as critical to their championship success: France's Tony Parker and Argentina's Manu Ginobli. With the exception of Nash, who received only one Division I scholarship offer, these players by-passed stints in American colleges, and instead opted to play on international clubs as teenagers. Their model for success has been increasingly common for international players. Unlike previous players, these players trained exclusively abroad (like Yao Ming). There has been much discussion about the success of this model in comparison to the success of American-bred players.

What is not in question is the on-court success of this group of players (Araton, 2005). These four men (along with other international players such as Andrei Kirilenko and Pau Gasol) are bright, personable, speak fluent English (as well as other languages), yet in the United States they have little press exposure as personalities off the court. Parker recently married *Desperate Housewives'* Eva Longoria, but she seems to attract most of the media attention. These players do not have major U.S. television commercial endorsements. They have not had documentaries made about them, such as Yao's *The Year of the Yao* (2005). They are not greeted like the Beatles on press stops. Instead, the Yao Ming phenomenon appears to be unique to Yao Ming.

Yao Ming was a phenomenon when he was drafted. Terence Chea (2004), in an April 3, 2004, edition of the *Associated Press*, described him as follows: "The 23-year-old Shanghai native has become a cultural icon in Chinese communities throughout the United States, offering the perfect vehicle to market basketball to Asian-Americans—a fast-growing market coveted by advertisers because of its relatively high income level." In another article that discusses the significance of Yao's entry into the NBA, Oates and Polumbaum (2004) explain: "Driving what the U.S. media has come to call 'Yaomania' is a global juggernaut that includes the league and intertwined corporate interests seeking to capitalize on Yao's high profile and popularity, which so far include Nike, Apple, Visa, interactive game developer Sorrent, Gatorade (owned by Pepsi) and, recently added, McDonald's" (p. 193).

Yao's popularity had been building. Unlike some players who might receive some attention in the months building up to their draft, there was speculation about his entry into the NBA for nearly two years before he was drafted (Fatsis, Wonacott, & Tkacik, 2002). Yao is groundbreaking because he is from China, a country not revered for its basketball stars or well understood by many Americans. Houston Rockets' President George Postolos was quoted by Jonathan

Feigen (2004) describing Yao's marketing power: "This is the next logical step in the sequence. There is no telling where it's going to lead. We're very interested in having a continuous presence in China and doing whatever we can to develop our relationship. We know we have literally hundreds of millions of fans of Yao Ming and the Rockets. We're looking to address them any way we can" (p. 1). One Chinese immigrant described the connection felt to Yao; he is "one player representing the whole country" (Blinebury, 2002, p. 14).

The Asian fan base supported Yao in a number of ways. Jack McCallum's February 10, 2003, profile of Yao provides two explanations of his popularity with Asian fans. First, group ticket sales at the Toyota Center, the Houston Rockets' arena, skyrocketed among Asian groups, rising from .5 percent in 2001 to 11–12 percent in 2002 (McCallum, 2003). Second, over 200 million Chinese fans watched Yao's first game (McCallum, 2003). The NBA has a long regular season, 82 games, but Yao's first game was extremely popular, unlike a regular season NBA game in the U.S. A regular season game might draw a few million viewers at most. These fans visibly showed their support even though Asian-Americans constitute only 4 percent of the U.S. population. Yao's popularity could be attributed to what he represents to his Asian fan base. China's largest sports magazine, *China Sports Weekly*, assessed Yao's popularity in the February 7, 2003, issue. "Yao has given a new Chinese image. People thought of Chinese people as short and skinny, not fierce, unable to play competitive sports. Yao has shown they are wrong. But he's also stayed kind and friendly and warm" (McCallum, 2003, p. 62). Yao represents to many a good balance of an ideal Asian, he is able to compete against non–Asian athletes and still maintain his individuality.

Leonard (2003) discussed some of the potential problems presented by characterizations of Yao when he entered the NBA. It was thought that he would become the face of Asia for the league in the sense that he would represent some collective identity not previously seen in the NBA: "He embodies both ideological usefulness as a model minority in the world of basketball (among the "gangstas" of the league) and economic importance in a global sports market — at the same time being a symbol of pan–Asian pride through his successful presence as an Asian man in the hyper-masculine world of professional basketball" ("Yo! Yao!"). Leonard makes some reasonable claims in his article, but it was more speculation about the perception of Yao than a researched study. In a more scholarly article, Oates and Polumbaum (2004) examined the global marketing power of Yao, arguing that his ability to be many things to various audiences made him potentially profitable worldwide. Their article is helpful because it highlights the importance of Yao's representation to a global audience, but it does not analyze any particular group that identifies with him.

Method for Analysis

In order to examine how Asians identify with Yao, I conducted a close textual analysis of web posts from his official website, *ClubYao* <http://www.yao mingfanclub.com/>. This website is endorsed by him, and in a message to fans he states, "It is our pledge at *ClubYao* to provide an interesting, informative and friendly fan experience" (Yao, 2006). His message describes the forum as "a home for the best fans anywhere."

As a text to study sports fan culture, Internet discussion is a rich source of study. Either through blogging or participation in discussion boards, this medium is an increasingly popular form of expression for fans. Blogs are websites that contain an individual's thoughts and views on anything. They are usually maintained by the writer and have places for others to leave feedback and comment and add to its content. A blog is what is written on the website, a blogger is the writer, and blogging refers to the act of writing on that website. Linder (2006) cited a Pew Research Institute Study that reported that 12 million American adults blog on a variety of topics. Many blogs are set up like online journals or columns, where the writers talk about their personal experience and how it shapes their views on particular situations. This Pew Research Institute Study explained that 76 percent of bloggers talk about personal experience. For instance, NBA Dallas Mavericks' owner Mark Cuban (2006) maintains a blog where he often comments on issues that affect his team. Most blogs are maintained by a single person. Although Yao's website is not a blog in the sense that one person is writing his/her views, some of the same principles apply to this forum. Blogs are like letters to the editor because people can quickly respond to situations where they have strong personal feelings (Schrank, 2006). Unlike a letter to the editor, the content is posted as is: there is no editorial review process.

The *ClubYao* forum is an appropriate website to evaluate Ming-related, fan-written reaction because it maintains several discussion threads (or topics) that cover a wide variety of Yao Ming–related issues. It also allows registered participants to contribute their viewpoints about a host of Yao-related issues. Also, it is well organized because it has separate discussion threads, which highlight how Yao is represented in the American media. For the purposes of this study, I analyzed messages posted between January 31, 2003, and September 12, 2006. Most of the posts are from 2003 and 2004. The subtopic that all of these writings fall under is "Yao's impact on the Asian community." In these discussion threads, there are three main topics about Yao's identity: how fans identify with Yao, the significance of Yao's Chinese or Asian identity, and the perception that he is "soft."

Identification with Yao

The first relevant theme in these discussions posits that Yao is identifiable because he is Chinese. Several users link Yao's popularity to the fact that he is Asian and Chinese, and other Chinese and/or Asian people want him to do well because they share his ethnic and/or national identity. As explained by participant Bmunchausen66[1] (2003), "Somehow Asians doing well in sports is important. I'm 36 and while growing up the only Asian guy I can recall playing professional sports was Len Sakata with the Baltimore Orioles. Now there's Nomo, Ichiro, Chan Ho Park, Byung Kim, Dat Nguyen, and, of course, Yao." Yao is seen as part of a group of Asian athletes who are changing the perception of Asians globally. Additionally, several users talk about how good it has been that Yao has been successful in the NBA, and how his presence helps break down negative stereotypes associated with Asians. As explained by participant RedDragon (2003), "I was raised in a country where Chinese people were respected for their diligence, entrepreneurial skills and certain physical qualities. Therefore, I was slightly dismayed when I notice that East Asian males are often labeled as diminutive and effeminate by many people in the US. Yao Ming's success in the NBA will help dismantle those demeaning stereotypes."

Because Yao was praised for breaking into the NBA, there were several participants who considered him a pioneer for Asian athletes. For instance, participant Pigstar911 (2003) pointed out that Yao's situation is, "somewhat analogous to that of African-Americans and Jackie Robinson. Sure Yao did not break any major sociological/racial barriers, but the similarity lies in the fact that Yao has the potential to be the first Chinese NBA all-star for years to come." Several other users make this comparison, because Robinson was the first black baseball player to participate in an integrated professional league in the U.S. When Robinson broke the color barrier, he paved the way for other people of color to play baseball.

What is absent from this discussion is how the participants see Yao as a reflection of themselves. These participants clearly distinguish their own personal identity from his, while being supportive of him. They like him because he is Chinese and Asian, but don't see him as an extension of themselves. Given the way that the Yao Ming phenomenon was discussed in more traditional media, such as television shows, magazines, and newspapers, one would think that there would be more discussion of who Yao is as a person, especially among participatory fans. He was admired for sharing a heritage, but for not being an extension of the fans' own identity.

Yao Is Chinese, Not Asian

A second theme found in this discussion thread is that Yao represents what is Chinese, not Asian. As discussed in the literature review, there is a difference between Asian and Chinese, but that distinction is not always made in regards to Yao. For instance, participant Slimpouch (2003) emphasized that Chinese people feel differently about Yao because he is Chinese, and they are more proud, or have more invested in him because they share national identity. "Of course these other Asians do not share exactly the same feelings of pride as a true Chinese blooded person, but I can imagine the feeling is pretty close." Another participant pointed out that Yao is only the beginning of breaking down stereotypes for Asian people, and that as more athletes from different countries come to America, they will dismantle stereotypes depending on their country of origin. As explained by CantonKid (2004, April 4), "I guarantee u once the Japanese, koreans, Filipinos, vietnamese import their products here, azn community will split apart ... Japanese will support Japanese ... korean support Korean ... chinese support Chinese." Not only does Yao represent something uniquely Chinese, he also lets surface some deep cultural conflicts in Asia. For instance, participant Oneofabillion (2004) emphasized a deep conflict between different national identity groups in Asia. "Ichiro? Most Asian hate the Japanese, or at least feel conflicted." This discussion might seem like a side note, but it does seem like an interesting opening to explore the differences between Asian groups. Tensions still exist between Japan and China (Mochizuki, 2007) decades after the two countries were embroiled in bloody wars. Therefore, it would make sense for these conflicts to be articulated through a popular cultural figure.

In these posts, there is no discussion about how the media tends to classify Asians and Chinese as the same. There seems to be in-fighting among the participants about what Yao means, but they do not blame the mainstream media for those classifications. It appears that groupings that do or do not lump Asians and Chinese together are dependant on the location of the speaker. The discussions on Yao's fan website are divergent from how the mainstream American media discusses Yao's Asian and Asian-American fan base. These posts show conflict in how Yao is viewed; not an unquestioning loyalty to him.

Yao Is Soft

The third theme that is present in these discussion threads is that Yao is soft. By soft, I mean that NBA players are expected to be tough, and be able to withstand a long season of being pushed and shoved by other large men. In response to the comment about Yao's inabilities on the court, Chuck_187 (2005) wrote, "Realistically, Yao hasn't changed the view on Chinese athletes. His weaknesses of strength, lack of speed, lack of meanness, lacks quickness, weak under mental pressure, poor handling and other things are well documented stereotypes westerners have of Asians." This comment reinforces some of the ideas about Asian athletes that are used to explain why they are not successful, or why Yao is not successful on the court.

What is absent from these discussions is discourse about how Yao is developing as a player. Most of these discussions took place during his first few years in the league, when players are getting acclimated to the league. Most players need time to adjust to the schedule, the level of competition and the culture of the NBA, regardless of their country of origin. Few players enter the NBA completely ready to be competitive in it. And Yao was an experiment, because he was the first Chinese player drafted number one overall, and there still are very few Asian NBA players, even though Asian people constitute a large percentage of the world's population. There was not a roadmap for him to follow like some other international players from Europe or South America. But that possibility is not discussed here, only that Yao should be competitive and ready to dominate American players.

Implications

This study has two implications. First, it highlights some of the problems created by combining different Asian groups into a single identity. National identity is discussed in some cultural studies scholarship, especially in regards to the difficulty of defining something like Chinese identity (Ang, 1998; Lee, 1996; Tuan, 1998). This study shows that there is a break between Asians who are supposedly Yao fans as a united block, and their own personal identity. It is not like the Tiger Woods commercial, a case of "I am Yao Ming," but instead, an admiration of his achievement, a recognition of the difficulty of his position, but not a situation of vicarious success. Also, these discussion boards show that Yao is a point of contention because people appear to identify more with him, depending on whether they are Chinese or not. If they are not Chinese, they seem not to identify as much with him because they are a different Asian nationality. Just like the term Latino means various things because it represents a broad spectrum of people, this break within Asian identity is also present in this group. And as cited in previous literature, this possibility of diversity within Asians is not often discussed outside of cultural studies literature.

Second, Yao might not be generating the fan base loyalty that is otherwise suggested by popular press sources. There is discussion of a homogeneous Asian block of fans who follow Yao (Abbott, 2003; Abel, 2003; Feigen, 2003; Luo, 2003). Certainly he has generated interest in the NBA because of his connection to Asian countries and people. And he is popular with Asian audiences, as evidenced by ticket sales and his game ratings. Many of the post comments suggest that Yao is not as good as he was expected to be. Instead, they suggest that he is more of a symbolic figure as opposed to the best player ever. This raises interesting questions between ability and identity. How much can identity alone solidify popularity or status within a fan base? Some players gain popularity simply because they are on television frequently or have lucrative endorsement deals. As stated earlier, during the time frame of these writings, and even in 2007, Yao's NBA teams had not won a playoff series. Other international players have, including the international Spurs players who have won multiple championships. Granted, China is a much bigger country than France and Argentina, but even so, Yao's popularity does seem appropriate.

While these posts provide some interesting commentary about Yao's representation and identity, there are limitations to studying blogs and web posts. First, they are a purely participant oriented text. They are written by a small group of people who may be unconcerned with the reaction from their audience. Moreover, the lack of face-to-face communication in these posts may encourage participants to be more inflammatory than in traditional conversations. The users are using pseudo names; they are not taking direct ownership of their words. Also, a user has to have time, access, and computer literacy, and be a registered user, in order to post comments on the website. Consequently, these posts are not a representative sample of Yao Ming's Asian fans. Second, individuals post on the website if they have strong feelings and the inclination to share their opinion. They are similar to a letter to the editor. Most people are not going to spend their time writing letters unless they are extremely upset or happy, or have the time to express these thoughts. Many of the participants who posted on this website had numerous posts, suggesting that they spend a fair amount of time on the discussion boards.

Despite these limitations, web posts are useful to study because they are an emerging medium and a way for individuals to subvert mainstream media by producing their own news. But it is not just private citizens using this technology. Blogs and web posts are used by mainstream sports media outlets as well, including Sportingnews.com, Sportsillustrated.com, and various other news and entertainment outlets. Due to the blending between blogs, web posts, and traditional news sources, the study of *ClubYao* posts helps contribute to the body of literature that examines fans' expression of culture.

In conclusion, examining Yao Ming's fan discussion is important because of its articulation of ethnicity and national identity. Identity is talked about in sports scholarship, but not in terms of these demographic characteristics. Given the high percentage of international players in the league, how does ethnicity and national identity factor into sports fan bases now? Further exploration of this question and ethnic and/or national identity is necessary to understand how fan bases operate in a multicultural and global world.

Note

1. The direct quotes from the participants contain the original grammar and spelling.

FAN MOTIVES

Advances in Theories
of Sports Fans' Motives

*Fan Personal Motives and
the Emotional Impacts of
Games and Their Outcomes*

LLOYD REYNOLDS SLOAN AND DEBBIE VAN CAMP

One billion people worldwide tuned in for the 2006 Super Bowl game. Five billion watched the soccer World Cup the same year. When polled, 92 percent of people indicated that they have a high interest in sports spectatorship, and 71 percent say they have purchased merchandise such as hats or T-shirts (Milne & McDonald, 1999). The major networks and sports channels broadcast over 1.5 million hours of sports in the U.S. annually ("Behind the Numbers," 2002). The cost of actually attending an NFL game is about a third of a family's weekly income, or about $300. Residents of North America, and much of the world, part with their hard earned cash and often travel miles to attend an average of 1.6 sporting events a year. Marketing professionals know well the power and pull of sports for the average American; a thirty-second ad slot during the 2007 Super Bowl game cost at least $2 million. Watching sporting events is among the most, if not the most, predominant forms of leisure behavior in the U.S. In short we watch sports, a lot of sports, and we will give up our time and money to be able to do so.

While the phenomenon of watching sports dates back more than 2000 years and the academic observation that we like to watch sports is far from new, the systematic investigation into precisely *why* we watch sports is relatively recent. Sloan (1989) examined the wide variety of potential motives for sports spectatorship, along with some preliminary data designed to assess which of these motives can adequately explain the experience of viewing sports. At the time, this consideration of sports fans—who they are, why they watch, and how watching sports affects them — represented a new area of interest for psychology. The interim years have seen further theoretical treatments and empirical investigation of these questions by other researchers (Wann, 1995; Wann, 2006). The current chapter will attempt to summarize the major theories used to explain sports spectatorship along with the contemporary empirical research associated with those theories. Next we will present data from a longitudinal study of sports spectators, their motives, and how these motives mediate the affective experience of watching a game, and of winning or losing a game.

Spectators or Fans?

In considering the internal psychological or emotional motivation for watching sports we assume that watching sports satisfies some need in the spectator. We are not therefore considering the casual spectator who can take it or leave it; rather we are interested primarily in the sports fan. The fan is the more enthusiastic and devoted spectator; even more extreme is the fanatic, the person with an intense, sometimes overwhelming, liking of the sport, often with intense uncritical devotion. Fans generally have a "qualitatively different, deeper, and more textured set of expectations and responses" (Gantz & Wenner, 1995), and fanship is considered to have cognitive, affective and behavioral bases and expression. Fans feel themselves to be part of a community of fans, they frequently engage in collective behaviors which provide feelings of belongingness. While spectators are not necessarily fans, precisely how we differentiate between a more casual sports spectator and the devoted fan, and between the die-hard and the fair-weather fan, may be a matter of degree of devotion, with mere observers of the sport on one end of the continuum and highly committed fans on the other (Milne & McDonald, 1999).

Attributes and Consequences of Fandom

True fans are so involved that the team is central to their lives. Fans watch every game, their emotions rising and falling drastically depending upon the outcome. Likewise, fans show physiological changes when watching a game, for example increased heart rate and perspiration (Hillman, Cuthbert, Bradley, & Lang, 2004); there are even differences when it was a win or loss, for example, in testosterone levels (Bernhardt, Dabbs, Fielden, & Lutter, 1998). While they may be affected by losses, the fans' devotion to their team does not waver. At times the fans' devotion to their team can outweigh other personal or work commitments; fans schedule business trips around the team's schedule, and miss weddings, graduations, anything that conflicts with an important enough game, like the playoffs (McKinley, 2000). Furthermore, when the fan is focused on the game nothing else matters; one fan's home burned around him while he listened to a ballgame on a radio headset.

The overwhelming importance of the team to the fans' lives can have serious consequences when things don't go the way that they want. Sports teams failures have led to suicides. While suicides are thankfully not all that common, harming the fans of the rival team is extremely common, and again many examples could be provided. The worst soccer riot in history left over 300 dead and 1,000 injured. While soccer provides perhaps the most extreme examples of this kind of fan behavior, other sports are not immune.

Who Is the Fan?

The profile of the fan varies between individuals and perhaps systematically by sport. However, some commonalities are apparent. Milne and McDonald (1999) surveyed over 1,300 fans concerning frequency of sports spectatorship, as well as reading and talking about sports. Respondents' scores suggested that there are three levels of fans: low-level, medium-level, and high-level fans. Low-level, or social, fans are not highly invested in the sport or a team but are more likely attracted by the entertainment and social aspects of watching sports. For these "fans" the outcome of a given event is less important than the overall entertainment. Medium-level fans are more "focused fans" and have much in common with the higher-level fan. However, their behavior is more directly related to their team's, or a particular player's, performance. Finally, there is the high-level, or vested, fan who is most likely male, under 55, and a previous or current sports participant. These fans have a strong and long-lasting relationship with their team. Their sport or team is part of who they are, they refer to themselves as "we," and they see other fans as part of a community to which they belong. They invest time, money, and emotions into following their team, and while their emotions may drastically rise and fall depending upon how well their team does, their status as fans never wavers. These profiles fall along a continuum, which one can progress along given the right personal predisposition and external factors. Fundamentally, though, understanding why some easily develop from the casual observer to the devoted fan, while others don't, is a matter of understanding why a person consumes sports.

Theoretical Motivations

The Development of Theories of Sport

The philosophical beginnings of sports inquiry were initially addressed within the concept of play, further theorizing differentiated game from play and then sport (Groos, 1898; McDougall, 1918; Spencer, 1873). While sports may have the beneficial aspects of play and recreation, they are most like games in their pursuit of the goal of victory, degree of structure, and rules. The scientific study of sport has occurred primarily within sociology, psychology, and to some extent anthropology, each coming from their unique perspective. Sociology focuses on the function of sports to social organizations and society, psychology on the impact of sports on the individual, and anthropology on the analysis of games content as a means to assess the character of the society. Early psychological work focused on the benefit of play to the development of individuals, and the catharsis perspective shed light on adult involvement with play. The proposed function of sports naturally generated work addressing the question of motivation in sports. Since the time of the previous chapter writing (Sloan, 1989), there have been many scales developed to measure these various motives which do indeed shed some light on why people watch sports. However, empirical data regarding sports motives remain scant, and thus there is particular need to examine fans' personal motivations within the gratifications of sports to inform our understanding of people's desires for sports. It is this challenge that we take up here. While we strive to shed light on established theories for fan-spectators we should recognize newly developing sports contexts. The increasing popularity of fantasy sports leagues, blogs and other web based fan resources, and digital sports games, all represent new and exciting frontiers for sports research, and many pioneering contributions are included in this volume.

It is beyond the scope of this chapter to consider every theory which might account for sports fans' devotion to sports, or to consider any one theory in extensive detail. Sloan (1989) provided a detailed summary of the theoretical views presented. Here we offer a brief summary, noting advances and contributions since the previous chapter, before turning our attention to new data examining sports fans' motives. Most of the hypothesized theories are based on social or psychological need. The theories may be divided into five major categories: salubrious effects theories, stress and stimulation theories, aggression theories, entertainment theories, and achievement seeking/social identity–related theories. Each will be reviewed in turn; including a brief consideration of how winning or losing may impact the fulfillment of the motive or desire.

Salubrious Effects Theories

The salubrious explanation for participation in an activity, in this case sports spectatorship, is that it is favorable to one's health or well being, or that it may provide pleasure to the participant. The most well known salubrious theory is *Recreation Theory*, which states that people restore and rejuvenate themselves by physically using their bodies. This theory seems somewhat more applicable to why we might play sports rather than watch them, although, as suggested by entertainment theories, watching sports can be salubrious also. Related to recreation theory is *Diversion Theory*, which views play as an escape or change of pace. The *Family Contact* motive refers to a sports fan's desire to spend time with other family members in some shared activity, and since this is likely appealing primarily because it is felt to be favorable to one's well-being it may considered under the salubrious category. Many chapters in this volume focus on the formation and uses of web-based communities of fans potentially serving social contact as well as identity representation. In sum, watching sports allows pleasure to be derived by means of restoration, escape, or spending time with one's family or comrades.

Various sports motivation scales include salubrious attraction subscales in their measures. For example, the Sport Fan Motivation Scale (SFMS; Wann, 1995; Wann, Schrader, & Wilson, 1999) includes an escape and a family factor. Similarly, the Motivation Scale for Sport Consumption (MSSC; Trail & James, 2001) includes escape, family, and social interaction factors.

As validation of this motive, researchers have found scores on such subscales to be predictive of game attendance. For example, the salubrious attraction factor of Pease and Zang's (2001) Spectator Motivation Scale (SMS) significantly related to professional basketball game attendance, and Zhang et al. (2001) found their Scale of Attendance (SAM) predicted attendance at minor league hockey games.

Consequences for Spectators. The salubrious motive for sports spectatorship does not require one's team or player to win in order to derive pleasure. Therefore a fan should experience an increase in positive affect, and decrease in negative affect, after watching the sport, as compared to before, regardless of who won. However, an escape motive may predict the opposite or a weaker effect, since once the game is over then so is the opportunity to escape.

Stress and Stimulation Seeking Theories

It is easy to imagine the office worker who spends weeks in a cubicle desiring the thrill and excitement provided by the game on the weekend. Elias and Dunning (1986) and Maguire (1991) suggested that modern society lacks sufficient excitement and variability. Goodger and Goodger (1989) and Zillmann et al. (1989) proposed that watching sports is a ready source of stimulation. The notion that there is an optimal level of stimulation or excitation was first formulated by Wundt (1873/1904), and further developed by Leuba (1955). Zuckerman et al. (1962) developed a scale designed to measure a person's level of sensation seeking. Zuckerman (2007) later defined sensation seeking as the need for "varied, novel, complex, and intense sensations and experiences, and the willingness to take physical, social, legal, and financial risks for the sake of such experience" (p. 49). This trait is considered a stable and basic personality variable which differs meaningfully across individuals, and Zuckerman (1971) postulated that this individual difference would manifest itself in the person's behaviors and activities. The Zuckerman Sensation-Seeking Scale (SSS) was first developed in 1964 (Zuckerman, Kolin, Price, & Zoob, 1964) and has been revised into various forms including the most commonly used, form IV

(Zuckerman, 1994). Since the development of the SSS there have been numerous studies examining the extensive and varied correlates of sensation seeking. For example, people who score higher on the SSS are more extroverted (Eysenck & Zuckerman, 1978), and more likely to be gamblers (Gupta, Derevensky, & Ellenbogen, 2006).

People have a basic need for excitement, and one way or another, they will fulfill it (Zuckerman, 2000). One possible source of this excitement which is readily available in today's society is sports (Zuckerman, 1983). The sensation seeking scale has been applied to the study of high risk sports participation (Malkin & Rabinowtiz, 1998). However, the majority of this research focuses upon that part of the sensation seeking personality that is willing to take risks in the pursuit of sensation. However, Zuckerman has always stressed that it is not the risk itself these individuals want, they are seeking to maintain their own optimal level of sensation and they will engage in risks to get it. In addition, the application of sensation seeking hypotheses to sports frequently focuses on people participating in sports rather than the spectators. However, not everyone is willing or able to take part in sports and it may be that watching sports is one easily available source of sensation (Klausner, 1968). Furthermore, watching sports potentially satiates this need for stimulation irrelevant of the outcome. Perhaps the only necessary component is that one is unaware of the outcome, so one can spend those few hours on the edge of one's seat, riding the emotional, and to some extent physical, rollercoaster that is "watching the game."

The sensation seeking motive for sports spectatorship is reflected in the SFMS (Wann, 1995) which includes a eustress (positive stress) motive. Empirical studies have found that for those motivated by a desire for eustress, watching sports satisfies this need. Results accounted for a significant proportion of post-win positive affect (Wann, Royalty, & Rochelle, 2002), as well as for active participation of sports activities (Cohen & Avrahami, 2005). Likewise the MSSC (Trail & James, 2001) includes a drama subscale whose items reflect the pleasure derived from a close game or one with an uncertain outcome. Finally the SAM (Zhang et al., 2001) has a stress factor validated by findings that it predicts attendance.

Milne and McDonald's (1999) Motivations of the Sport Consumer Scale (MSC) measures 13 motives representing four major factors. Relevant to the current discussion, three motivational subscales may be considered under the general heading of "stress and stimulation": risk-taking, based directly on Zuckerman's optimal stress theories; stresses reducing anxiety and tension; and competition, which asks participants whether their motives are "the thrill of the competition."

Consequences for Spectators. Fans motivated by salubrious effects experience an increase in positive affect and a decrease in negative affect after the game compared to before (regardless of outcome) as a result of experiencing the sought arousal or uncertainty which satiates the need or desire.

Aggression Theories

The violence associated with sporting events is unfortunately all too familiar. However, is it the case that sports viewing results in aggressive tendencies, or that aggressive tendencies are the motivation for watching? Theorists as far back as Aristotle have considered the *concept of catharsis* or reduction in aggressive drive levels which results from participating in controlled and socially acceptable acts of aggression. The notion is that we all have some level of aggressive drive and energy which builds up in us and must be carefully released or it will explode (Lorenz, 1966; Zillmann et al., 1989). Such cathartic release may also be possible from watching others, and thus vicariously experiencing the reduction and release. Of course many predictions from catharsis have not been supported, in fact watching aggressive acts and violence appears to more often result in an increase rather than a decrease in aggression both generally (Bandura, Ross, & Ross, 1961; Berkowitz, 1970, 1975, 1986) and in the specific realm of sports (Arms, Russell, & Sandilands, 1979; Goldstein & Arms, 1971; Sloan, 1979a; Turner, 1970; Wann & Branscombe, 1990b).

The relationship between viewing violence and subsequently behaving aggressively derives directly from *social learning theory* (Bandura, 1971, 1973, 1983). This view holds that observers learn to act a certain way, in this case aggressively, simply by viewing aggression. How these viewed aggressive acts are rewarded or punished will determine the extent to which they are inhibited or disinhibited. The win–loss of the team will serve as information regarding rewards and punishments for aggression. Violence that results in victory should increase aggression, while violence that results in failure should decrease aggression. However, social learning theory is less clear regarding the effects of watching on people's moods. Social learning of emotional moods would appear to allow fans to learn to duplicate moods associated with winning behaviors, but these are difficult for fans to know in a large stadium at great distances and they may be seen to vary across successful (won) games (e.g., from confidence to aggressiveness to desperation, and so forth).

The *frustration aggression hypothesis* (Berkowitz, 1969; Dollard, Doob, Miller, Mowrer, & Sears, 1939) has a different interpretation of the link between viewing aggression and acting aggressively. The hypothesis proposes that aggression is the result of experienced frustration. Its explanation for the link between watching and acting is that seeing acts of violence could serve as a cue for the appropriateness of the observer's own aggression; it could reduce any inhibitions which had hitherto prevented the person from acting on his frustration-induced aggressive drive. This hypothesis also distinguishes between the effects of different game outcomes. A loss produces frustration because the goal of winning was blocked, resulting in increased levels of anger, hostility, dissatisfaction and aggression.

Other aggression-related theories of spectator motivation include the desire to assert dominance to experience feelings of power and self-esteem (Adler, 1927; Cheska, 1978), and the quest for conflict and competition as a source of positive drama (Zillmann et al., 1989).

Social observation and empirical evidence lend much support to the motivational role of aggression in sports spectatorship (Bryant, Zillmann & Raney, 1998). Specifically, the defining characteristic of the televised sports events rated most enjoyable is violence (Raney & Depalma, 2006), and that aggressiveness of play is the most reliable predictor of enjoyment (DeNeui & Sachau, 1996).

It should be noted that the aggressive motive is among the most relevant to understanding people's choice among different sports to watch. An aggressive or violent hockey match may be more desirable and fulfilling than a similarly aggressive tennis match. Using his SFMS, Wann, Schrader, & Wilson (1999) found systematic differences in people's preferences for aggressive or non-aggressive sports, which could be linked to other motives. Those individuals preferring aggressive sports were more motivated by economic concerns (betting) and those preferring non-aggressive sports appeared to be more motivated by the aesthetics of sports.

Consequences for Spectators. The catharsis motive predicts a decrease in negative emotions and an increased sense of calm following a game as compared to before, regardless of whether it was a win or a loss. *Social learning theory* predicts interactions between before and after the game, and win versus loss, on future aggressive behavior but not changes in the person's moods and emotions following wins and losses. *Frustration aggression theory* predicts that losing will produce increased levels of negative affect: anger, hostility, dissatisfaction and aggression.

Entertainment Theories

This group of theories stresses that sports fans watch for the entertainment value. If entertainment is defined as that which gives pleasure or relaxation, then many of the other motives discussed here may be more broadly described as a subset of the entertainment motive. Why is it that we come to find sports spectatorship a source of pleasure and thus entertainment? If we assume that the same processes can explain our attraction to sports as they can to anything else, then the answer revolves around socialization and mere exposure. Boys growing up in the U.S. are encouraged to play and watch football, basketball, or hockey, depending usually on Dad's preference, from a young age. They are given equipment to play sports, taken to games and taught the rules, and given the various paraphernalia which go along with being a fan. They are in fact "fans-in-training." Even if the child initially dislikes football, when he is forced to watch it he will no doubt learn to love it, if for no other reason than that which is familiar is liked (Zajonc, 1968).

Specific to entertainment and not readily subsumed under other theories is the notion that attraction to sports is explained by its aesthetic value. Soccer viewers frequently describe good goals as "beautiful." The skill and artistry inherent in so many sports may well be the thing that makes it so entertaining to many of us. As already alluded to, this motive may be differentially satisfied by different sports. Spectators with a preference for individual (as opposed to team) sports and those with a preference for non-aggressive (as opposed to aggressive) sports score high on the aesthetic motivation scale of the SFMS (Wann, Schrader, & Wilson, 1999). High scores on this factor are also related to active participation in soccer-related activities (Cohen & Avrahami, 2005). So, for those spectators motivated by the aesthetic appeal of watching sports, things like tennis, gymnastics, and auto racing are particularly appealing. As further validation for an entertainment motive, scores on more generally worded entertainment scales such as that of the SMS (Pease & Zhang, 2001) and the SAM (Zhang et al., 2001) are related to game attendance and consumer support of a sport (Funk, Mahony, & Ridinger, 2002).

Another aspect of sport's attractiveness in and of itself is its representation of life's values. Sport is thought to build character, teamwork, perseverance, fairness, hard work, loyalty, and altruism. Duncun (1983) analyzed spectator sport in six categories of symbolism which may account for its appeal: recurring life issues, transcendence of human limitations, rebellion against industrialized society, aesthetic unity and completion, religious overtones, and political dimensions. Szymanski and Zimballst (2005) analyzed ways in which the sport that a nation plays reflects, and is reflected by, its culture. They argue, among other things, that the U.S. and Europeans "have absorbed the structure and rules of their sports into their psyches, turning the arbitrary rules into a way of life" (p. 2). Novak (1976) argued that sport appeals to people because it resembles "primal symbols" rather than the more Calvinistic life values listed. Kruse (1981a) contended that repair strategies and apologies were more successful when the violator adhered to and had not violated the "team ethic of sport."

Wann's (1995) validated SFMS includes both a general entertainment motive and an aesthetic motive. Scores on the entertainment subscale accounted for a significant proportion of post-win positive affect (Wann, Royalty, & Rochelle, 2002), and the aesthetic motive has been linked to preferences for different sports (Wann, Schrader, & Wilson, 1999). The MSSC (Trail & James, 2001) includes an aesthetics subscale as well as physical attraction and physical skills motive subscales. The MSC (Milne & McDonald, 1999) also includes an aesthetics motive scale, whose items talk about sport as beautiful and artistic.

Consequences for Spectators. Simply watching an aesthetically pleasing activity which is entertaining is the source of pleasure. Therefore, negative emotions are predicted to decline and positive emotions increase — regardless of outcome.

Achievement Seeking and
Social Identity Theories

In sports the point is to win. The game or competition ends and there is a winner and a loser, and the winner is the more satisfied of the two. This satisfaction then is based on the idea that something was achieved. Maslow (1943) included the need for achievement in his typology of basic needs— at the esteem level. The question is, as a spectator how does one meet this achievement need? The answer is suggested by the now well known phenomenon Basking in Reflected Glory (BIRG; Cialdini et al., 1976). This refers to the tendency to more closely align oneself as an individual with a group following a win than following a loss, specifically in the wearing of school/team apparel and using the pronoun "we" versus "they." The notion that when our team wins then so do we is reflected in results using the MSSC (Trail & James, 2001), the SAM (Zhang et al., 2001), and the MSC (Milne & McDonald, 1999).

The flip side to the BIRG phenomenon, inherent in the original BIRG findings and developed later (Snyder, Lassegard, & Ford, 1986), is Casting Off Reflective Failures (CORFing), which refers to the tendency to avoid being connected to unsuccessful others— not only did "*we* win," but "*they* lost" (Cialdini et al., 1976). While these are complementary processes, they differ in that BIRGing is typically used to enhance oneself while CORFing is a defensive and self-protective mechanism, as are anticipatory notions such as PADing (Protective Anticipatory Distancing; Sloan, 1989). However, each of these can serve to boost or protect self-esteem (Wann & Branscombe, 1990b; Wann & Branscombe, 1993), which suggests a social identity type process. Indeed both mechanisms can be explained by social identity processes, which is the focus of the next section.

Social Identity Theory   Social identity theory (Tajfel & Turner, 1979, 1986) suggests that an individual's self-concept is in part derived from one's membership in different groups— one's social identity. A positive social identity provides both a sense of belonging in the social world and a source of self-esteem. It follows that we will seek to belong to those social groups which maximize our sense of self-worth, and will view the groups to which we belong as superior, thus protecting our self-esteem. Consequently we are prone to in-group favoritism, attribution biases, social comparisons, and other cognitive processes that allow us to maintain a positive image of the social groups to which we belong. In sum, "I belong to this group, this group is good, therefore I am good."

It is not hard to see how this theory can be applied to the question of why people watch sports, or more precisely why they are fans of certain teams (Jacobson, 2003). The fan group is a source of quasi-intimate relationships and belonging (Melnick, 1993). Being a fan is a way to achieve group membership and a collective social identity that can feed into our individual identity. Becoming a fan is a relatively easy group identity to obtain, with no real skills or qualifications needed, and low costs (Zillman, Bryant, & Sapolsky, 1989). We are motivated to be a part of the winning group; however, once we align ourselves with any team, even if it's the losing one, group processes and biases will come into play to ensure that our allegiance is beneficial to our self-concept.

Other Self-Esteem Seeking and Protecting Biases   While BIRGing and CORFing are the most well documented of self-esteem seeking and self-esteem protecting tactics used by fans, there are others. For example, Sloan (1989) noted that winning and losing have differential effects on intra-group cohesiveness. Fans also seek or maintain self-esteem via differing evaluations and attitudes towards the group following wins and losses. Causal attribution processes regarding team outcomes parallel those for our own successes and failures, thus protecting the team as we would the self, and thereby indeed protecting the self (Sloan, Cherry, Holly, & Schwieger, 1982). In addition to our own attributions for a team, we may also construct narratives with other fans. This is increasingly easy to do with modern technology.

Other evidence for a self-esteem motive comes from empirical research utilizing the various motivation scales. Wann's SFMS (1995) measures two separate motives related to social identity: group affiliation and self-esteem. Both have been found to account for variance in the active participation in sports activities (Cohen & Avrahami, 2005). Likewise, Pease and Zhang's SMS (2001) found the level of fan identification to be significantly related to game attendance. The MSC (Milne & McDonald, 1999) also includes two social identity related factors: affiliation and self-esteem.

Consequences of Identification   The level of identification people have with a team is predictive of whether their self-descriptions will include their status as fans (Wann, Royalty, & Roberts, 2000). Implicit in social identity theory is the notion that the stronger our social identity and group attachment, the more bias we will show. For example, fans who identify with the group (university) rate the team more favorably overall and more favorably after wins than losses (Dietz-Uhler & Murrell, 1999; Sloan, 1979a, 1989), and are biased in their ratings and predictions of players (Wann & Grieve, 2005; Wann et al., 2006). Identification has also been related to involvement with the team, ego-enhancing attributions for wins, positive future expectations, willingness to spend money, and belief that the team is special (Sloan, 1979a, 1989; Wann & Branscombe, 1993). Team identification also predicts enjoyment (Madrigal, 1995). On the negative side, highly identified sports fans derogate self identity threat relevant targets more (Branscombe & Wann, 1994) and are more willing to behave aggressively toward players/coaches on the opposing team (Wann et al., 1999), especially when the outcome of the game was unfavorable (Wann et al., 2005). These caveats aside, being a fan is generally a good thing (Wann & Branscombe, 1990b). Wann (2004) explored this relationship further and predicted that team identification facilitates social psychological well-being by increasing the fan's social connections.

Consequences for Spectators. The achievement motive predicts an interaction between pre–post, and win–loss, on both positive and negative affect; specifically, a marked increase in positive affect following a win and a decrease following a loss.

Other Motives

While we believe that the motives reviewed above are a fairly exhaustive analysis of the most plausible motives, others have been suggested, particularly by those who have developed measurement instruments. For example, Wann (SFMS; 1995) includes an economic motive and suggests that some sports fans watch because they can bet on the outcome. However, the economic motive may be a direct achievement opportunity to gain material and social benefit. Personal investment in gambling predicts the same sorts of emotional outcomes and related consequences as do identity threats and losses. Milne and McDonald (MSC; 1999) include social facilitation, self-actualization motive, and value development motives in their scale. Finally, Trail and James (MSSC; 2001) included an acquisition of knowledge factor which refers to those fans who like to track the statistics of players and teams.

Different Motives for Different Fans for Different Sports

The development of various measures for these motives has allowed for comparative work and the identification of individual differences in sports fan motives across gender, race, and national origin. A few key findings are reviewed here to highlight representative individual differences.

Gender Differences. Men are more likely to be fans, show more emotional investment, and experience more emotional consequences after wins/losses; are more active in their spectatorship; and are more likely to have pre-game rituals (Gantz, 1991). Men watch sports to unwind and/or escape while women watch more for companionship (Gantz, 1991). Men also score higher on the entertainment, economic, eustress, escape, aesthetics, and self-esteem factors; and women score higher on the family scale of Wann's SFMS (1995). Masculinity predicts sports motivations, except the family motive which was explained by femininity scores (Wann & Waddill, 2003).

Ethnic Differences. After finding cross-racial differences in sports fans motives, Bilyeu and Wann (2002) added three factors to the SFMS: representation (background/culture/ethnicity), similarity (having something in common with the player), and support/perceived greater equality (wanting to see one's group succeed). African Americans reported significantly higher scores than Whites on the original factors of self-esteem, escape, entertainment, economics, and family, as well as the three new factors; no differences were found on the eustress or aesthetic scales. Armstrong (2002) found similar results in a motivation scale for Black fans.

National Differences. Kwon and Trail (2001) found that international students score higher on the aesthetic motive than American students. Koreans and Japanese have been found to have different motivations (Won & Kitamura, 2007).

Different Sports. Fans motivated by economics preferred aggressive sports, while those motivated by aesthetics preferred non-aggressive sports and individual sports (Wann, Schrader, & Wilson, 1999). James and Ross (2004) found that motives for watching non-revenue sports centered more around entertainment, skills and drama.

These differences present a problem to the empirical researcher of sports fan motivation. If spectators of different sports have different motivations, then dissecting the puzzle of sports motives may be complicated by the differential uses and gratifications provided by a sport and by the different needs of each fan. While we directly acknowledge that possibility, a reasonable course of action therefore may be to choose sports and fan samples that represent frequently encountered populations and settings and to recognize this limitation when drawing conclusions.

Theoretical Predictions Regarding the Effect of Watching Sports on a Fan's Emotions

As the review of the theoretical motivations suggests, each theory predicts the influence of sport on the spectating fans' emotions. These are summarized in Table 1.

Multiple Motives of Fans

As discussed above, there are some notable differences across fans on the basis of group identities such as gender, race, or nationality. Variations in motives may also result from numerous individual needs, for example loneliness, need for power, or family contact needs. Generally, no single personal motive is suggested as the only motive moderating sports viewing and outcomes effects. Rather, theory and empirical results suggest the existence of multiple sports-related motives. We turn now to a review of the predictions of each theory regarding sports impact.

The *Salubrious Effects motive* for sports spectatorship, or the related concepts of escape, entertainment and family contact, do not require that one's team or player win to derive pleasure. This theory predicts an increase in positive affect and a decrease in negative affect after watching the sport regardless of who won. As a caveat it is plausible that an *escapism motive* may predict the opposite or a weaker positive change, since once the game is over then the

Table 1. Theoretical Predictions Regarding the Effect of Watching Sports on Fans' Emotions

	Upset, sad, irritated, discouraged	Ashamed, depressed	Pleased, happy	Proud, satisfied	Calm	Full of energy
Salubrious effects[a]	□	□	□	—	□	□
Stress and stimulation[b]	□	□	□	—	□	□
Aggression–catharsis	□	□	—	—	□	□
Aggression–frustration aggression theory (loss)	□	□	—	—	—	□
Achievement–win	□	□	□	□	—	—
Achievement–loss	□	□	□	□		

Notes: Only those theories which suggest clear predictions are included. The predictions concerning changes in "full of energy" according to the salubrious effects theoretical position are less certain as they may depend upon how satisfied the person's needs are.

a. The predictions for all theories considered under the heading "salubrious effects" are the same (general, escape, family contact, stress reduction, and entertainment).

b. The predictions for all theories considered under the heading "stress and general stimulation seeking effects" are the same (general, risk taking, excitement seeking, drama and competition).

opportunity to engage in escapism is exhausted. The related *Entertainment theory* does not require one's team or player to win to be satisfied. Therefore negative emotions decline after the game and positive emotions increase — regardless of outcome.

Stress/Stimulation-seeking theory of sports spectatorship also predicts an increase in positive affect and a decrease in negative affect after the game compared to before. Risk-taking predicts the same results as does *Stress Reduction* in theorizing reduced tension and negative affect with increased positive affect. The *Drama theory* suggests pleasure is derived from a close game with an uncertain outcome. While some positive emotion may be high before a game in anticipation of the drama, pleasure should be felt during and after a dramatic game. Finally, *Competition* suggests that fan motives are for "the thrill of the competition" and so will likely show a pattern of results similar to drama. Both drama and competition motives may center on how exciting the game was and depend on the closeness of the game.

The central prediction for both salubrious effects and stress and sensation seeking motives is that both negative and positive affect will show a pre–post change, presumably that positive emotions will rise and negative moods will fall as portrayed in Table 1. However, the anticipation of good feelings may lead to high positive affect before the game that diminishes as needs are ful-filled. Either way, salubrious effects and stress and sensation seeking motives predict simple pre–post change in emotions. Furthermore, these sports motive theories are the only ones to predict any pre–post game change in feelings of "calmness."

Within aggression notions, the *Catharsis motive* predicts a decrease in neg-ative emotions and an increased sense of calm. *Frustration Aggression* theory does not predict any change in pre–post game emotion in winning games. How-ever, lost games should increase negative emotions. *Social Learning theory* pre-dicts interactions between before and after the game, and win versus loss, on behavioral aggression but is less clear whether strong predictions can be made.

The *Self-Esteem/Achievement-seeking motive* predicts a marked pre–post game increase in positive emotions following a win and a decrease following a loss. The *Achievement motive* predicts an interaction between pre–post, and win–loss conditions, for both positive and negative emotional responses. The *Economic motive* affects emotions in the same manner as predicted by Achieve-ment models. This appears to be a specific overt economic risk version of achievement seeking, with the same emotional outcome predictions. Other the-ories of sports motivation such as social facilitation, self-actualization motive, value development, and acquisition of knowledge do not make as clear a set of predictions about fans.

Typical Past Findings and New Approaches

Early research pursued many theories of sports impacts and appeal dis-cussed above. Sloan (1979a) asked fans to report their emotions and moods before or after, won or lost games. Some 16 moods clustered into three factors: (1) angry–upset, (2) pleased–happy and (3) calm–tense. Upset moods were generally low and increased only in a loss. Happy moods were moderately high but dropped in a loss and rose slightly in a difficult win. For both Angry and Happy type moods, the Pre–Post by Game Outcome interaction was the dom-inant effect, although each mood typically showed a moderate Pre–Post main effect and a Game Outcome (Win–Loss) main effect produced by the Pre–Post by Win–Loss interaction. These findings are contrary to implications of Salu-brious Effects, Stress and Stimulation-Seeking, Catharsis and Entertainment theories which anticipated *simple*, uniform pre–post game effects on fans' benevolence, energy, tension, calmness, tiredness or other "positive" feelings, but only interaction-produced effects occurred. Social Learning Theory pre-dictions of greater aggressive feelings following a team success were discon-firmed. Only Achievement and Frustration–Aggression theories predicted increases in Anger variables and decreases in positive emotional variables fol-lowing losses, while Self-Esteem serving Achievement Theory alone hypothe-sized increased Pleasure–Happiness responses after a win. Consequently, Sloan

(1979a; 1989) concluded that only Vicarious Achievement (Self-Esteem) Seeking motives were consistent with the results. This suggests that vicarious achievement seeking for self-esteem enhancement plays a major role in fans' associations.

In contrast, other research discussed above suggested excitement or stimulation seeking motives. Important among these reasons are the possibilities that: (a) more than one of these theoretically proposed phenomena may act simultaneously, conceivably confounding their effects or hindering their detection, and (b) individual differences between fans may lead them to be more influenced by some phenomena than by others. If one or both of these possibilities are true, then it may not be possible to separate effects of diverse phenomena just by the judicious selection of measures. If situational factors at sports contests engage several motives simultaneously, then it may prove difficult to find sports that provide stimulation or entertainment and yet are devoid of achievement opportunities.

Examining Individual Motives to Better Understand Sports Fan Emotional Responses

Another approach to understanding fans' motives is examining the influence of theoretically related individual differences in motivations and needs. Situational determinants of sports contests are not readily controllable in order to determine underlying motives. Alternatively, one can predict and observe the impact of directly measured fans' motives on the degree of fans' emotional responses to sports outcomes. It was this latter approach to deciphering sports fan motives that was employed in the research reported here.

Some Trait-Motive Measures That Appear Likely Related to Theorized Sports Mechanisms

The following individual differences (motives) are among those implicated as motives for sports fandom: (1) sensation-seeking, (2) achievement–power needs, and (3) social contact needs.

Zuckerman's (1971, 1979) *Sensation Seeking Scale* (Form IV) provides a multifaceted measure of individual dimensions of stimulation seeking. It is a refined, reliable scale with extensive construct validation composed of a general (combined) subscale (SSS) and four component subscales. *Thrill and Adventure Seeking* (TAS) measures proclivity for risky, adventurous activities. *Experience Seeking* (ES) deals with seeking arousal through the mind and senses through a spontaneous, unusual, and non-conforming life style. *Boredom Susceptibility* (BS) measures aversion to repetitive experience, work and boring people. *Disinhibition* (DIS) explores traditional modes of stimulation seeking and release through partying, drink, sex and so forth. Examination of Zuckerman's reports of risk, behavioral and experience preferences suggests that the latter three subcomponents are most likely to represent the stimulation-seeking motives described by some sports theorists.

The *Sensation Seeking and Anxiety State Test* (SSAST) is another useful measure of sensation seeking (Neary & Zuckerman, 1976). Respondents reported 36 feelings as a state measure or, as employed here, as a trait assessment reported in terms of how the respondent usually feels. Only the trait Sensation-Seeking subscale is considered here. It is being employed to provide an affective rating alternative measure of sensation-seeking to complement the Zuckerman Sensation-Seeking measure and maximize the potential of detecting sensation seeking dimensions that may moderate fans' emotions.

The *UCLA Loneliness Scale* (UCLA, 1996) may relate to fan motives based upon a desire to be with other fans or family members for social contact. This motive measure shows strong convergent validity with other loneliness measures and a negative relationship to reported social support and interpersonal relationship satisfaction adequacy. The UCLA Loneliness measure was employed to tap strong social contact needs that might draw fans to sports and may interact with pre- versus post-game changes in mood. Notably it correlates positively with introversion, depression and lower self-esteem as potential motives.

The *Sports Need for Achievement and Power Scale* (SNAPS; Sloan, 1987) is a brief measure composed of athletic locker room slogans. The Power/Competitive Achievement Scale most strongly relates to the WOFO (Work and Family Orientation Scale; Spence & Helmreich, 1978) "Competitiveness" achievement subscale. This nPower (SNAPS) subscale appears to measure achievement motives thought to influence fans of competitive sports.

These instruments are individual difference measures of theory-relevant aspects of esteem–achievement motivation, stimulation seeking, and social contact needs. Examining the impact of these individual differences on the effects of watching sports on fans' affective responses also benefits from an alternative research design.

An Alternative Approach to Identifying Fan Motivations

Sport's impacts on fans must, in part, determine fans' situation induced motives. Inferring fan sports' motives by examining changes in emotions and moods before versus after wins or losses has been very useful. Investigating fans' motive-traits and motives' impacts on emotions before and after games offers an alternative view of sports fans' reactions and the potential moderators of those reactions. It is clear, however, that some fans are drawn to different sports and it may be that those fans are impacted differently by virtue of the different needs and motives.

Prior research on sports fans inferred their motives for sports from mood reports of fans either before or after games that had been won or lost — a between-subjects design. Such research designs generally support vicarious achievement theories, and suggest that individual differences in achievement motives might be related to the strength of emotion changes. A within-subjects design allows us to observe directly the actual change in participants' emotional responses in each condition of pre- or post-, won or lost games. We can examine the moderation of those pre–post main effects, win–loss main effects, and their overall interaction.

Hypotheses Regarding Interactions between Fan Motives (Moderators) and Fans' Emotional Responses to Games and Their Outcomes

At a simplistic level, a sports theory's predicted effects of game viewing or outcome on fans' emotional responses should be moderated by a related fan trait-motive.

Self-Esteem and Achievement Seeking theories predict strong impacts of game outcome on emotion changes. Needs for power–achievement should be expected to moderate the pre–post by win–loss interaction and perhaps the simple win–loss main effect, with high power–achievement needs strengthening each of those effects. This may be especially true for the strong increase in negative emotions following losses.

Stimulation Seeking. Stimulation seeking was not inferred from earlier situational effects (pre–post x outcome designs) but has been widely examined. Fans' individual trait motives may reveal their influence in moderating emotion changes at games. Predictions that "Calm" and "Pleased" moods/emotions should rise and that perhaps "Upset" emotions *might fall* should be strengthened by high levels of sensation seeking for fans with active Experience Seeking (ES) and Boredom Susceptibility (BS).

Although more speculative, it is possible that other aspects of sensation-seeking could diminish achievement seeking–caused outcome impacts on emotions. *Disinhibition (DIS) motives* indicate active counter–normative desires which may counter or diminish esteem and achievement seeking concerns and needs. As achievement related outcomes appear very powerful, the opposing sensation seeking impacts may have been simply overwhelmed in earlier research.

Salubrious Effects theories make similar predictions especially based on social contact needs (family and social enjoyment). Paralleling stimulation seeking, salubrious effects notions suggest that after games "Upset" moods would drop and "Happy" and "Calm" moods would rise and fans high in social contact needs/loneliness should intensify these salubrious effects-predicted changes.

Methodology

The current research was conducted on fans attending live basketball and football games for reliability across arenas. It is important to note this, since motives for consuming some sports media may be different and represent a separate field of analysis (Gantz & Wenner, 1995). While potential differences across sports are recognized, common features may be more central for issues here. Basketball and football were chosen as sports that represent qualities of general theoretical concern: skill, individual and team coordination, moderate levels of overt violence, highly competitive and intense, and provide fast-moving action. While we did not include a detailed measure of fandom, participants indicated that they were fans when they were selected to participate.

Participants

Subjects were 76 male and female college student fans of school teams at a medium-sized university in the eastern United States. Participants volunteered for the season-long study as a course-related research experience.

Procedure

Undergraduates at a pre-season meeting completed a survey assessing a number of the proposed motives likely to moderate the game-viewing fans' experience. Specifically, they completed: (1) the Zuckerman (1971) form IV Sensation Seeking Scale, including a general factor (SSS) along with the subscales of experience seeking (ES), boredom susceptibility (BS), thrill and adventure seeking (TAS), and disinhibition (DIS); (2) the SSAST (Neary & Zuckerman, 1976), the sensation-seeking trait–affect subscale (SS); (3) the UCLA loneliness scale (UCLA) (Russell, 1996) and (4) a need for power–competitive achievement measure (nPower) (SNAPS; Sloan, 1987). Participants also received detailed instructions explaining their role in this research.

Respondents were followed throughout the season at each home game. In the twenty minutes before and after each game, participants met one of a group of experimenters who conducted the emotions–mood data collection interview with them. A participant's data were employed only if he or she provided all information before and after at least one victorious game and one lost game in order to examine their reactions to sporting events in a setting with considerable generality and realism. Participants' emotions were obtained on a mood adjective checklist containing a subset of twelve evolved from the Sloan (1989) research. Participants were asked, "how much does this mood or feeling apply to you right now?" Participants responded on a five-point scale from "not at all" to "extremely."

The Design then was a 2 × 2 (Pre–Post Game by Game Outcome [won or lost]) experimental design. Data from all pre-game or post-game periods of a given outcome type (e.g. won or lost) were averaged for the 2 × 2 ANOVA and ANCOVA analyses, which included a participant-fan individual motive measure as the covariate-hypothesized moderator of the 2 × 2 ANOVA effects. This procedure provided a rare opportunity to examine valid within-subjects data collected in the field with high ecological validity for the study of sports fans.

Validating Self-Report with Behavior   An important consideration in obtaining these emotion ratings is that they might reflect experimental demand or that other questionnaire hazards may distort participants' real feelings. Sloan (1989) reports convincing evidence that subjects' mood reports are valid. At the same games a similar adjective checklist was employed along with unobtrusive video recording of fans as they entered and left the game. Facial emotions were rated on five sports theory related dimensions considered accurate and reliable (Ekman, Friessen, & Ellsworth, 1972). Judges' ratings produced results that almost exactly matched those for the self-report checklist. This allowed us to have greater confidence in the accuracy and meaningfulness of the emotion self-report measures.

Results

Analyses of Pre–Post Game by Win–Loss Game Outcomes. Our primary analyses are (1) ANOVA to test the pre–post game by win–loss factors effects on fan emotional responses, and (2) ANCOVA to test the above 2 × 2 design with selected fan motivation scores as covariates. This provides a test of the fan's individual motive's moderation of the effects of the 2 × 2 design. This test indicates whether and how much the fan's motive increases or decreases the specific main effect or interaction.

Game Outcome Effects on Emotions and Implications for Theories. Changes in emotions from before to after won and lost games display findings replicating Sloan's (1979a, 1989) and others' findings. Happy/Pleased emotions rose following wins and fell after losses. Upset/Sad moods displayed the reverse pattern showing great increases in losses but little decrease in wins (see Table 3). This strong pre–post game by game outcome (win–loss) interaction was significant for almost all variables, replicating prior research (Sloan, 1979a, 1989; Sloan, Cherry & Holly, 1988) and appears to best support *Self-Esteem/Vicarious Achievement*–seeking theories of sports' appeal. In addition, only self-esteem/achievement seeking was expected to impact shame and pride as self-esteem related emotions. Notably, "proud" and "ashamed" followed the same positive and negative emotion patterns as would be expected for emotions specifically identified with self-esteem related outcomes. Thus, the notion that many fans seek self-esteem boosts via the benefits of collective achievement (Basking in Reflected Glory; Cialdini et al., 1975) suggests that Self-Esteem/Achievement

Theories offer our only strong understanding and predictions of fan emotion changes at games and hence our best clue to their motivations.

In all cases, the major emotional changes that followed losses resulted in previously low negative moods greatly increasing and positive moods dropping. Likewise, positive moods are quite high before games, possibly fueled by any number of fans' motives for sports viewing. In fact, pre–post and win–loss main effect differences in negative moods both appear to be simple consequences of the increase in negative emotion state following losses. Strong increases in negative emotions following losses are precisely where self-esteem/achievement seeking motives theoretically are expected to produce. Conversely, positive emotions show more impact of winning and so may involve additional or other types of fan motives more extensively.

Table 2. Means in Each Condition (Pre–Post, Win–Loss, Pre–Post × Win–Loss Interaction) and Tests of Significance for Each Effect for Each Emotion (Solid Lines Are Wins)

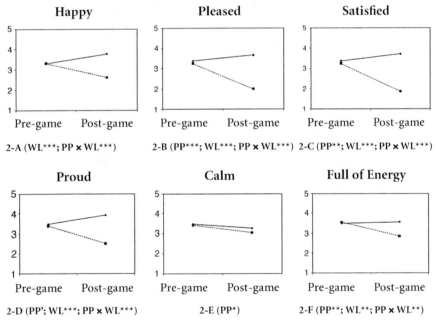

2-A (WL***; PP × WL**)   2-B (PP***; WL***; PP × WL***) 2-C (PP**; WL***; PP × WL***)

2-D (PP'; WL***; PP × WL***)   2-E (PP*)   2-F (PP**; WL**; PP × WL**)

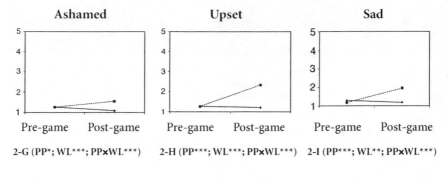

2-G (PP*; WL***; PP×WL***)	2-H (PP***; WL***; PP×WL***) 2-I (PP***; WL**; PP×WL***)

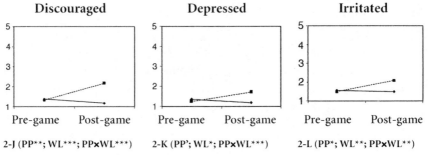

2-J (PP**; WL***; PP×WL***)	2-K (PP'; WL*; PP×WL***) 2-L (PP*; WL**; PP×WL**)

Notes: A solid line with diamonds is a game that was won; a broken line with squares is a game that was lost.

PP denotes pre–post main effect, WL denotes win–loss main effect, PP×WL is the interaction of the two.

Significance tests denoted by † $p < .10$;* $p < .05$;** $p < .01$;*** $p < .001$; all $n = 76$

Factors note: Factor analysis produced 3 factors: (1) Pleased–Happy (also Proud, Satisfied, and Full of Energy) (2) Upset–Sad (also Ashamed, Discouraged, Depressed, and Irritated) and (3) Calm

Emotion change results lent little support to other theories. *Salubrious Effects theories* (entertainment, social contact needs, escapism, drama, and so forth) and *Basic Sensation-Seeking Theories* predict only pre–post game changes as fans' needs are anticipated or satisfied. Simple pre–post game changes were observed only for the "calm" emotion response that was suggested by basic stimulation-seeking and salubrious effects theories of sports' appeal. *Aggression Theories* were not supported except for *Frustration-aggression* positions, if *Achievement seeking failures* could be presumed to be frustrating. *Catharsis* positions were reversed.

Fans' Motives as Moderators of Emotional Responses to Sports and Sports' Outcomes

Despite the strong impact of self-esteem/achievement seeking motives upon fans, it is possible that other theories may continue to draw us to the games but entirely other phenomena may act on us once there. If multiple phenomena impact fans at the games, then we may be able to reflect on those alternative mechanisms by investigating individual difference motives–needs that may moderate the pre–post game and game (win–loss) outcome and their interaction on the emotional changes observed above. That is, while we can try to infer fans' motives from fans' emotional responses to sports, we might also examine fans' motives by directly measuring those hypothesized motives and testing those individual motives' moderating effects on observed fan emotional reactions to games and outcomes.

Do fan motives moderate the pre–post, win–loss interaction effects on fans' emotions that have been so frequently observed as positive and as negative emotions? The research reported below pursued this richer and more complex approach to better understanding sports fans' motives.

Multiple fan motives for sports appear likely. Observed pre-game high positive and low negative emotions suggest that fans may be responding to pre-game hopefulness or other motives causing expectations of enjoyment of the sports event. The fact that fan emotions do not change greatly following a win may reflect a sense that the win merely has satisfied expectations or perhaps simply provided relief from the possibility of failure. In any case, the absence of the emotional impacts of losing may allow the greater expression of other, less powerful, individual trait-motives and their consequences. This may suggest that different motives and needs may moderate positive versus negative emotions and do so rather differently following wins versus losses as compared to simple pre-game, post-game effects.

This and past research has found support for vicarious or shared achievement seeking for the benefit of fans' self-esteem, while other studies have found results suggesting excitement or stimulation seeking or social contact needs, among other motives. To what degree do individual motives for stimulation seeking or social needs or achievement seeking moderate the impacts of game outcomes on fans' moods and emotional responses and are they uniformly separate in their impact?

Fan Trait-Motives' Moderation of Fans' Emotional Responses to Sports

Analysis of covariance (ANCOVA), that is, covarying the various ANOVA effects reported above, will reveal the degree to which that motive strengthens or weakens the effect (e.g., a main effect or the pre–post by win–loss interaction effect) that was observed above. This is an appropriate way to test for the moderation of an inferential effect by an individual difference variable, and is equivalent to regressing a simple index (change score) representing an effect (i.e., main effect or interaction) onto the individual motive-trait to test for moderation of that effect by the tested fan motive.

In Table 3 below, the significance level may serve as an indicator of the degree to which the fan motive moderated the reported effect, while the sign of the regression "b" indicates the direction of the relationship between the motive score and the effect.

The pre–post by won–lost game interaction was moderated by the fans' *need for power-achievement (nPower) for all negative emotions* except "irritated" which wasn't significant (see Table 3). The higher the need for achievement/ esteem seeking (nPower) score, the stronger the impact of outcome. This is in keeping with predictions of the ways that fans' needs for self-esteem/achievement would moderate fans' emotional responses to team wins and losses. Importantly, such blocked achievement (at losses) may have produced frustration which should increase negative emotions but produce little change in positive emotions.

Surprisingly, the pre–post × win–loss interaction for positive emotions was moderated primarily by general Sensation-seeking and Disinhibition-seeking motives. The higher the fan's sensation-seeking score, the weaker the interaction, suggesting that positive emotions are primarily moderated by fans' simple need for specific stimulation–entertainment/sensations and in a manner in opposition to winning-induced happiness effects such as perhaps the joy of elevated self-esteem. The achievement measure may not adequately tap all of the positive emotions of winning (i.e., "joy" versus "dominance over adversaries"). It is noteworthy that the nPower subscale is not significantly correlated to the various Sensation Seeking subscales, indicating that these measures are independent of one another despite having apparently opposite relationships to other common correlates and emotion outcomes.

Pre–post game effects for negative emotions (see Table 3) are strongly moderated by sensation-seeking, but surprisingly so. Increases in negative emotions from pre- to post-game were positively related to increasing stimulation needs. Experience-seeking also predicted decreases in several positive emotions. If high sensation-seeking needs imply greater negative reaction to losses, then this may imply possible interrelationships between sensation-seeking and self-esteem seeking desires—winning may be part of the stimulation sought. This may imply that high sensation-seekers may be satiated well primarily by games that are won, again suggesting an incorporated achievement role.

Notably, Loneliness–social contact motives (UCLA Loneliness Scale) show effects opposite to sensation seeking traits in moderating pre–post game impacts on negative emotions. The lower the fan's loneliness–social contact needs, the more "upset" and "discouraged" they were after games (only losses show increased negative emotions). Lower loneliness is related to higher self-esteem possibly suggesting another self-esteem seeking interrelationship to sports' emotional impact.

Table 3. Fan Traits and Motives That Moderate (Interact with) Pre–Post, Win–Loss, and Pre–Post × Win–Loss Interaction Effects (ANCOVA) on Emotions

Note: Each ANCOVA test indicates the interaction of that ANOVA effect with the covariate.

	Pre–Post Main Effect × Covariate	Win–Loss Main Effect × Covariate	Pre–Post × Win–Loss Interaction × Covariate
Proud	SSS (ES)* b = -1.54 SSS (DIS)* b = -1.50	UCLA* b = -0.61	SSS† b = -0.85
Satisfied	—	UCLA* b = -0.77	—
Happy	—	—	SSS (DIS)* b = -1.63
Pleased	nPower* b = -0.592	(SS† b = -0.24)	SS F* b = -0.26
Full of Energy	SSS (ES)* b = -1.34	nPower† b = -0.71	SSS (DIS)* b = -0.26
Calm	—	UCLA† b = -0.52 (UCLA* b = -0.52)	UCLA† b = -0.53
Upset	SS** b = 0.41 nPower† b = 0.55 UCLA b = -0.55	nPower† b = -0.53 (nPower* b = -0.60)	nPower* b = -0.68
Discouraged	SSS (ES)* b = 1.46 UCLA b = -0.49	(SSS (ES)† b = -1.12) (nPower† b = -0.48)	nPower** b = -0.72
Sad	SSS (BS)† b = 1.33	nPower† b = -0.56 (nPower* b = -0.57)	nPower* b = -0.57
Ashamed	SSS (BS)** b = 2.40	SSS (ES)* b = -1.42 nAchiev† b = -0.48	nPower* b = -0.70
Depressed	SS* b = 0.27	SS* b = -0.37 UCLA* b = 0.54 (nPower† b = 0.54)	nPower* b = -0.60
Irritated	SSS (BS)† b = 2.28	UCLA† b = 0.44	—

Note: SS = sensation mood (SSAST); SSS = sensation seeking scale; SSS (ES) = excitement seeking subscale of the SSS; SSS (DIS) = disinhibition subscale of the SSS; SSS (BS) = boredom susceptibility; nPower = need for power (from SNAPS scale; UCLA = UCLA loneliness scale/need for contact measure.

Significance tests denoted by † $p < .10$;* $p < .05$;** $p < .01$;*** $p < .001$; all $n = 76$.

ANCOVA test for win vs. loss for post game scores only (to emphasize outcome impacts) are displayed in parentheses to distinguish them from full pre–post × win–loss interaction tests.

Win–Loss Game Outcome Effects. Negative emotion increases where they are related to higher needs for Achievement/Self-Esteem (nPower as in interaction findings above), to higher needs for Sensation-seeking (Experience Seeking) and to higher levels of Social Contact needs (Loneliness). Again, these results may suggest that self-esteem/achievement needs may be a related element captured in the sensation-seeking and/or loneliness measure or that these motives have conjoint or opposite impacts.

Game outcome (win–loss) effects on positive emotions reveal that increasing positive emotions (in a win) are related to lower social contact–loneliness needs but only marginally related to lower general Sensation-seeking needs. Perhaps this should not be surprising as the win–loss main effect sums over pre- and post wins versus pre- and post losses, incorporating outcome-produced emotional responses, and may suggest how multiple motives may be at work simultaneously. These findings seem weakly related to the pattern of findings for the pre–post game by win versus loss interaction effect. Of course we would expect that interaction to be more likely to show self-esteem/achievement motive effects on emotion changes because that interaction more strongly tests the impact of winning versus losing.

"Calm" responses show the only simple pre–post game effect uncomplicated by the pre–post by win–loss interaction. Calmness drops from pre-game to post-game, in apparent contrast to some salubrious effects theories, and to some broad sensation-seeking notions if sensation needs are satisfied by sports viewing. This effect however is not moderated by any tested fan motive, although there are marginal interactions with outcome effects suggesting possible relationships with achievement seeking.

Summary and Discussion

Perhaps the most surprising overall finding is that positive versus negative fan emotions are moderated by different fan motive–trait needs even within the same pre–post game and/or game outcome (win–loss) effects. Conventional expectation might have led us to anticipate that positive versus negative emotions would be simple reversals of one another and so would be moderated by similar motives. A possible explanation may lie in the findings of recent personality research that has found contexts in which positive emotions and negative emotions behave independently from one another, not just oppositely. Our findings appear to confirm this seemingly counterintuitive result.

As complex as current theorizing about sports fans' motives is now, our results suggest that there are other key factors that we may not have fully anticipated. While the notion of multiple concurrent motives for sports suggested a complex situation demanding challenging analysis and interpretation, the counterintuitive relative independence of positive and negative emotions has elevated complexity and the tasks of discovery and interpretation even further.

These results strongly indicate that multiple personal motives influence fans' emotional reactions to sports, suggesting the value of further investigation of sports theory implications.

A Summary of Individual Fan Trait-Motives as Moderators of Game and Outcome Effects

Higher Self-Esteem/Achievement needs moderated increasing pre–post game differences between winning versus losing but only for negative emotions. Higher levels of general Sensation-seeking and Disinhibition needs predicted decreased pre–post game differences between winning versus losing, but only for positive emotions. Higher levels of several sensation-seeking needs, Boredom Susceptibility and Experience Seeking, predicted increasing levels of negative emotions from pre- to post-game. Higher levels of Experience Seeking also predict increasingly lower positive emotional responses. Higher levels of Social Contact needs, Loneliness, predicted decreasing levels of negative emotions from pre- to post-game in contrast to the impacts of achievement related trait-motives.

Thus the sensational risk of playing to achieve the self-esteem enhancing win, appears to be but one of several motivations interwoven within the stimulating nature and diverse appeals of the sports contest for the engaged fan. These diverse motivations may vary by the level of fandom-involvement (Milne & McDonald, 1999), including (low) fans motivated by social contacts, (medium) fair-weather fans likely to BIRG to enhance esteem and (high) committed fans who would work even harder (CORFing) to alleviate the pains of negative outcomes. The key moderators identified here (achievement, sensation and social contact needs) were not separable by fan level but they may well have greater impact for some fan types than for others.

Implications for Theories of Sports' Impacts on Fans

The conclusions presented here are based on both sets of findings reported above. They incorporate (1) the pre–post game by win versus loss (2 × 2) ANOVA analyses of fan emotions and (2) the tests of theory related fan personal trait-motives as moderators of those pre–post game by win versus loss effects.

Self-Esteem/Achievement Seeking Theories (Strong Support). Consistent with Self-Esteem/Vicarious Achievement Seeking theories of fan motivation, fans with high power-achievement needs scores showed significantly more extreme pre–post game-by-game outcome interaction effects on negative

Upset/sad emotions, and that interaction was not moderated by other fan motives. This result implies that fans seek self-esteem enhancement via vicarious achievement from their associations with sports. Fans with high individual achievement motives appear to seek even more of that vicarious benefit in showing the strongest emotional responses to wins versus losses. These convergent findings from personal motives and from situational outcomes give increased credibility to the suggested role of self-esteem/achievement seeking motivation in fans' attraction to sports.

Salubrious Effects theories (Modest Suggestive Support) which encompass general enjoyment, escapism, socialization, and entertainment all predicted simple pre–post effects on emotion changes, either increased at the prospect of the experience and diminished afterward or elevated afterward with the past joy of the experience. "Calm" showed the decreasing effect but had no pre–post game moderators. All other emotions' changes were complicated or created by their substantial pre–post game by win versus loss interactions.

Social-Contact/Loneliness Needs (Modest Support) did moderate "upset" and "discouraged" negative pre–post mood changes, such that higher loneliness led to greater negative mood changes. This is consistent with the notion that fans may be present "just for the company" which they lose at games' end. Social-contact/loneliness motives were the only moderators of "calmness" but did so surprisingly in win–loss interaction contexts, suggesting self-esteem achievement needs also may be involved. Notably, higher loneliness is often related to lower self-esteem, which may suggest a connection to achievement seeking.

Sensation-Seeking theories (Substantial but Unexpected Impact) predicted simple pre–post changes in emotions, but only "calm" showed that effect and that effect wasn't moderated by any dimensions of sensation-seeking examined. Sensation-seeking did however play roles in moderating pre–post game changes in all negative emotions and several positive emotions when they were confounded by interaction with the win–loss factor. Surprisingly, high stimulation needs predicted increasingly negative emotions. Higher sensation seeking needs also moderated a diminishing of the pre–post game by win–loss interaction effect on positive emotions, suggesting that these needs somehow operate in contrast to power–achievement needs.

Frustration–Aggression theories (Suggestive Support) predicted negative emotion increases in losses but did not predict observed positive emotion increases in wins. Nonetheless, frustration–aggression notions generally are consistent with pre–post game by win–loss interaction impacts on negative emotions and with those effects' moderation by self-esteem/achievement seeking fan motivations, if achievement failures (losses) are indeed frustrating. Social learning theory wasn't adequately testable as there were no direct aggression measures. Catharsis predictions were contradicted by the results of the pre–post game by win versus loss outcomes because "calm" dropped and negative moods rose after games.

New Opportunities for the Study of Sports Fans' Motives

The Value of Personality by Situation Approaches. As in the past (Sloan, 1979a, 1989), Self-Esteem/Achievement Seeking has been strongly supported as a key fan motive for sports by situational (pre–post game by win–loss outcome) factors. By examining the impact of diverse individual fan motives on situational factors, this research revealed important influences of a number of additional trait-motives. This approach discovered significant predicted influences of fans' personal achievement seeking motives. Importantly, Sensation-Seeking and Social Contact (Salubrious Effects) theories found support only because of the "person by situation interaction" research design employed here. Sensation-Seeking and Social-contact Needs theories found unique new support in fans' trait-motives' moderating effects on otherwise non-definitive or non-predicted situational (e.g., pre–post game by win–loss outcome) effects. These findings taken together provide strong indications of the important roles of self-esteem related vicarious achievement needs, social contact needs, and stimulation-seeking needs within fans' motivations for sports.

The "personality by situational factor interaction" approach employed here has allowed us to begin to sort out the influences of several complex and perhaps somewhat interrelated motives in a setting in which situational factor effects are strong and complex. The continued use of such an approach, considering the fan's personality within the situational interaction, therefore holds some promise of providing both integration of current knowledge and ground breaking new discoveries of the motives of sports fans.

In addition, it seems there is little doubt that fans are influenced by multiple motives in different facets of their emotional responding to sports and that it also is likely that multiple motives may be active and influential simultaneously, thereby creating fan emotional responses which may be rich and complex. For the researcher, such interwoven fan motives and consequent emotional responses to sport create an intriguing, enjoyable and challenging puzzle to attempt to unravel.

Exploring Fandom and Motives for Viewing Televised Sports

ADAM C. EARNHEARDT AND
PAUL M. HARIDAKIS

In this study we sought to identify motives for watching televised sports and to explore the relationship between motivation and perhaps one of the most important antecedents to television sports viewing: fandom.

Various studies have suggested different motives for watching sports, specifically (Kahle, Kambara, & Rose, 1996; Milne & McDonald, 1999; Trail & James, 2001; Wann, 1995), and for watching television, generally (Rubin, 1983). Therefore, our first objective was to identify more clearly a comprehensive typology of motives people have for viewing televised sports. We considered motives from the Television Viewing Motives Scale (TVMS; Rubin, 1983), and specific, sometimes disparate, motives for watching sports gleaned from the literature.

Previous studies have suggested highly avid fans may have different motives for viewing sports than do less avid fans and are more involved with televised sports than are less avid fans (Gantz, 1981; Gantz & Wenner, 1995; Wann, 1995). Consequently, our second objective was to explore the extent to which viewers' level of fandom affects their motives for viewing televised sports. The findings suggest that our predispositions to sports (i.e., level of fandom) may influence our sports television viewing motives. We also discuss the implications of these findings as well as directions for future sports media research.

People build their knowledge of and interest in sports, in part, based on their exposure to and motives for watching televised reports. Twenty-four-hour news and entertainment programming on ESPN and other sports channels and media provide audiences with access to the personal lives of their favorite athletes (Harris, 2004). Other channels focus on specific sports (e.g., golf, motor sports). Televised sports offer something for everyone and often provide the only views into the lives of athletes.

Uses and Gratifications Theory

In this study we apply suppositions of the theory of uses and gratifications to explore viewer motives for consuming sports on television. Uses and gratifications theory is an audience-centered, media-uses-and-effects perspective. A central premise of uses and gratifications is that people are purposive, goal-directed, and motivated in their media use (Katz, Blumler, & Gurevitch, 1974). This theory also suggests that individual factors influence media-use motives, selectivity, other levels of media-use activity, and ultimately, effects of use.

Uses and gratifications theory is built on five tenets: (a) audience members are goal-directed, purposive, and motivated in their selection of media; (b) audience members actively select media based on coherent, self-perceived desires to fulfill goals, with an understanding that some media channels will fulfill certain goals and others will not; (c) audience members' psychological and sociological differences affect media selection and audience members' abilities to fulfill goals; (d) audience members use different media to fulfill needs, suggesting that people will use other forms of media to fulfill the same goals when the desired (or primary) medium is not available; and (e) based on the level of audience initiative and individual characteristics, the audience has the power to be more influential than the media in the audience-media relationship (Katz et al., 1974; Katz, Gurevitch, & Haas, 1973; Rubin, 1986, 2002).

Accordingly, this theory provides media scholars with guiding tenets for understanding individual differences among audience members, media-use activities, and motives for consuming media. Thus, uses and gratifications can offer practical directions for examining the relationship among fandom and motives for viewing sports.

Previous research of audience activity (e.g., selectivity, involvement) and motives may shed light on the use of sports entertainment to fulfill certain goals. Research grounded in this perspective has revealed a variably engaged audience, selective in their media use, variably involved with media content (e.g., Herzog, 1944; Katz et al., 1974; Levy & Windahl, 1984), who display an affinity for specific media channels and content (Rubin & Perse, 1987b). Thus, in the audience–media use–effects relationship, it is the audience member who is most influential. Examining motives people have to watch television is used to help explain this process of media selection, use, and effects (Katz et al., 1974; Rubin, 1981a, 1984). In the following section, we explore literature related to this process by reviewing studies related to fandom followed by a review of research related to television viewing and sports television viewing motives.

Fandom

Gantz and Wenner (1995) noted that a persistent problem in sports media effects research is the different descriptions of "fandom" and what constitutes a "fan." Some researchers have used the term "fan" and "spectator" interchangeably. Yet there are distinct differences between a fan and a spectator. Not all spectators are fans. Sloan (1979b) found that sports viewers range from non-fans, to observers, or spectators, to highly avid fans. In a similar study, James and Ridinger (2002) classified three fandom levels as "strong loyalty," "loyal fan," and "not a fan." Thus, if fandom is placed on a continuum, one end would represent a "fan" and the other would represent a "non-fan."

Gantz and Wenner (1995) also found evidence of varying levels of fandom. They identified three distinct fandom categories: (a) fans, or "true believers," deeply committed to their team; (b) spectators, or mere observers with a minimal level of interest; and (c) non-fans, or those not necessarily interested in sports, but who watch to be with others.

Wann, Dolan, McGeorge, and Allison (1994) found differences between fans' and spectators' perceptions of their influence on outcomes of games. Fans perceived that they had an ability to influence the outcomes of football and basketball games, whereas spectators perceived less influence over those outcomes. Fans who perceived they had greater influence were more likely to watch the contest. Overall, fans with strong loyalty to certain athletes perceived greater connections to athletes and believed they could influence the performance of their favorite athletes.

Similar research has provided evidence of relationships between levels of fandom, exposure to sports, and other factors related to sports television viewing. For example, researchers have examined links between fandom and motives for watching sports (Kahle et al., 1996; Milne & McDonald, 1999; Trail & James, 2001; Wann, 1995), involvement (e.g., perceive sports on television to be valuable, exciting, interesting, etc.) (Shank & Beasley, 1998), watching favorite and disliked athletes (Mahony & Moorman, 2000), community (Wann & Robinson, 2002), mood reactions to wins and losses (Wann et al., 1994), perceptions of influence on contest outcomes (Wann et al., 1994), and gender (James & Ridinger, 2002; Melnick & Wann, 2004).

There appears to be a relationship between media use, sports television viewing, and interest in participating as a fan (Jeffres, Neuendorf, & Atkins, 2002). The more people use media to consume sports, the more they participate as spectators and fans. Researchers have suggested that avid fans display stronger, more salient motives for watching sports on television than do non-fans (Gantz & Wenner, 1991; Trail & James, 2001; Wann, 1995). Therefore, it is necessary to understand the motives and goal-oriented differences of sports television viewers.

Motives

Motivation is a key concept in the study of media effects (Rubin, 2002). Uses and gratifications research has produced several motive typologies to guide research of televised sports effects. Early uses and gratifications studies identified various motives for watching television, including entertainment, social utility, excitement, pass time, companionship, and information (Rubin, 1983), as well as curiosity, diversion, and identity (Blumler, 1979). Later television viewing motives research utilized the same, or similar, typologies (e.g., Haridakis, 2002; Haridakis & Rubin, 2005).

The same cannot be said for studies of sports viewing motives. Researchers have identified particular motives for sports viewing with little consistency among the motive typologies. Therefore, a representative review of television viewing motives research, sports viewing motives research, and a comparison of those motives identified are offered below.

Researchers have linked motives to selecting specific media genres (Katz et al., 1974; Rubin, 1983, 1984) such as soap operas and news (Rubin, 1981a; Rubin & Perse, 1987a, 1987b), and other media channels such as the Internet (Papacharissi & Rubin, 2000). Other researchers have focused on motives for consuming televised sports specifically, albeit with different motive typologies. If, as uses and gratifications suggests, media selection is goal-directed, purposive, and motivated, then it is necessary to examine connections between sports television viewing and viewing motives (Gantz & Wenner, 1991).

Sports-Viewing Motives

Although some research has suggested that some motives for viewing sports, such as entertainment and information-seeking, were similar to motives for general television viewing (Gantz & Wenner, 1991; Wenner & Gantz, 1989), other studies have produced varied sports-viewing motive typologies (Kahle et al., 1996; Milne & McDonald, 1999; Trail & James, 2000; Wann, 1995; Wann & Branscombe, 1993). Rubin (1979) presented a media-use typology as part of a television viewing motives analysis and honed the motive typology in later studies to develop the Television Viewing Motives Scale (TVMS; Rubin, 1981a, 1983). Of the motives that emerged as significant predictors of viewing specific content, Rubin (1981a) found "arousal" to be a salient predictor of sports viewing. However, several other motives (e.g., escape, pass time, relaxation) were weaker but still correlated significantly with television sports viewing.

In a study of motives specific to sports content, Gantz (1981) found slightly different motives for watching sports. The strongest motive was the "thrill of victory." Those who tended to watch for the "thrill of victory" felt better about the game if they cheered for their favorite players, were curious about the outcome, or their favorite athletes won. The next strongest motive was "to let loose," suggesting a form of release. Those who watched for this reason were more likely to let off steam, become excited, and indulge in excessive drinking behaviors. Learning about the game, interest in the players, and passing time were weaker motives for watching sports. These motives may have been weaker because highly avid fans and other informed viewers may already have known about the game and developed interest in favorite athletes (Wenner & Gantz, 1989). For these reasons, it is unlikely that they would watch sports to pass time. Instead, they would watch to be actively engaged in the contest and the outcome.

Gantz and Wenner (1995) suggested that highly avid fans would be more likely to view sports from a deeper and qualitatively different set of experiences than non-fans. Consistent with previous uses and gratifications studies (Rubin, 1981a, 1983; Rubin & Perse, 1987a), 15 motive statements were factor analyzed to reveal nine significant motives factors. Outcome (i.e., which team and/or athlete won), drama (i.e., enjoy the tension involved), and information-seeking (i.e., learn more about the athletes) were the strongest motives for sports fans. Interestingly, for non-fans, watching with family and friends was a significant motive for watching sports, simply because everyone else was watching sports.

One motive from the original TVMS (Rubin, 1983) that appears frequently in the sports viewing motives literature is escape. Wann, Allen, and Rochelle (2004) found that people used sports as a way to escape boredom and stress. Respondents were motivated to view sports as an escape from over-stimulation and under-stimulation (i.e., to lessen or increase arousal).

Wann (1995) developed a Sports Fan Motivation Scale (SFMS). Wann identified motives for watching sports. These included eustress (euphoric stress or drama), self-esteem, escape, entertainment, economics, aesthetics, group affiliation, and family. Motives such as aesthetics (i.e., watch sports for the beauty and grace of the game) and self-esteem (i.e., watch for feelings of self-respect and confidence) were strongly correlated with viewing sports.

Trail and James (2001) constructed their own measure, entitled the Motivation Scale for Sports Consumption (MSSC). Motives for watching sports on television included (a) achievement (e.g., to feel accomplishment when an athlete wins), (b) knowledge (e.g., to learn about sports), (c) aesthetics (e.g., to experience the beauty of sports), (d) drama (e.g., to experience excitement), (e) escape (e.g., to forget about the pressures of everyday life), (f) to be with family, (g) physical attraction (e.g., to watch attractive athletes), (h) physical skills (e.g., to learn physical skills required to compete), and (i) social utility (e.g., to watch with others).

Robinson and Trail (2005) examined sports viewing motives in relation to perceived levels of attachment to athletes. Using a shortened version of the MSSC, they found that achievement, a significant predictor of sports viewing in previous studies, was the strongest predictor of attachment to favorite athletes. This finding is significant because it suggests a connection between motives for watching televised sports and an outcome of watching sports.

Hypothesis and Research Questions

We know that various motives for watching television (e.g., arousal, entertainment) influence media use and effects (Rubin, 1983). Similar motives have been linked to watching televised sports (Gantz, 1981; Gantz & Wenner, 1991). Some scholars have suggested there are other motives specific to watching televised sports. Three specific motives identified for watching sports are achievement, aesthetics, and self-esteem (Milne & McDonald, 1996; Trail & James, 2000; Wann, 1995). Therefore, the following hypothesis was proposed:

H: *Higher levels of fandom will be related positively to achievement, aesthetics, and self-esteem motives for watching televised sports.*

Rubin (2002) noted that an early criticism of motive research was the lack of clearly defined purposive and habitual motives people have for using particular media content. Although researchers have speculated about a variety of other motives people may have for viewing televised sports, to date, a comprehensive and consistent typology for televised sports viewing motives has not been identified. Therefore, the following research question was posed:

RQ1: *What are the motives people have for watching televised sports?*

In addition, uses and gratifications posits that predispositions influence viewer motivation. In the case of sports, it is important to consider the influence of fandom, because it still is unclear what motives people have for watching televised sports when varying levels of fandom are considered. Thus, the following research question was proposed:

RQ2: *What is the relationship between fandom and viewer motivation?*

Methodology

A principal purpose of this study was to examine the relationship among fandom and motives for viewing televised sports. A questionnaire was used to gather information from television viewers about their levels of fandom and motives for viewing televised sports. Demographic information (e.g., age, gender, and ethnicity) was collected to describe the sample.

Sampling Procedure

The sample in this study consisted of undergraduate students from two Midwestern universities ($n = 347$). Because fandom and interest in sports is evident in every age, gender, and ethnic group (Bilyeu & Wann, 2002; Gantz & Wenner, 1991; Robinson & Trail, 2005), there was no evidence to suggest a sample of college students would differ greatly from other segments of the population in the United States (James & Ridinger, 2002). Researchers have found that college students watch a significant amount of television (Busselle & Shrum, 2003; Diddi & LaRose, 2006). It is possible, then, that college students watch television, in part, to fill sports viewing goals.

The mean age was 21.40 years. There were more women ($n = 197$) than men ($n = 149$). The ethnic composition of the sample was primarily Caucasian ($n = 286$), followed by African-American ($n = 36$), Asian ($n = 7$), Hispanic ($n = 5$), American Indian ($n = 2$), and other ($n = 9$). One participant did not report age, gender, and education level; two did not report ethnicity.

Fandom

Wann's (2002) Sports Fandom Questionnaire (SFQ) was used to gauge respondent fandom level. This index assessed self-perception of fandom. Response options ranged from 5 (*strongly agree*) to 1 (*strongly disagree*). Sample items included "I consider myself to be a sports fan" and "Being a sports fan is very important to me."

This instrument has proven to be a valid and reliable measure of fandom in prior research (see, e.g., Melnick & Wann, 2004; Wann, 2002; Wann et al., 2004). Items were summed and averaged to get a fandom score ($M = 3.23$, $SD = 1.15$, alpha = .94).

Motives

Rubin's (1983) TVMS was adapted to measure motives for viewing televised sports. Respondents were asked to rate their reasons for watching sports on television using response options that ranged from 5 (*exactly*) to 1 (*not at all*). The revised scale assessed motives from the TVMS that also have been identified in some sports viewing studies. These included: (a) relaxation, (b) companionship, (c) habit, (d) pass time, (e) entertainment, (f) social interaction, (g) information, (h) arousal, and (i) escape. In addition to motives on the TVMS, we included three additional motives gleaned from previous studies of sports television viewing (James & Ridinger, 2002; Melnick & Wann, 2004; Robinson & Trail, 2005; Wann, 1995). These were (a) aesthetics, (b) self-esteem, and (c) achievement.

As with previous uses and gratifications research in which items were factor analyzed to reveal motive structure (e.g., Rubin, 1983; Rubin, Haridakis, & Eyal, 2003), a principal components factor analysis with varimax rotation was conducted on the motive measure to extract the sports television viewing motive factors. There were 36 items on the scale. Items that loaded on each factor were summed and averaged to form indexes for each viewing motive. The results of the factor analysis and means and standard deviations of each motive factor identified are provided in Table 1 and are discussed in the results section below.

Results

RQ1: Motives for Watching Televised Sports

RQ1 inquired about the reasons fans have for watching televised sports. The motives people have for watching sports were identified by subjecting the responses to items in the motive measure to factor analysis (see Table 1). Six motive factors explaining 67.62 percent of the variance after rotation were identified.

Table 1. Factor Loadings of the Revised Television Viewing Motives Scale

Motive Items	Sports Television Viewing Factors					
	ENTR	SELF	COMP	LEAR	PASS	APAT
Entertaining Relaxation						
Because it's enjoyable	**.85**	.17	-.03	.22	.16	-.03
Because it's exciting	**.83**	.19	-.01	.26	.07	-.01
Because it entertains me	**.83**	.17	-.01	.16	.13	.10
Because I just like to watch	**.80**	.05	-.05	.16	.25	.04
Because it's thrilling	**.77**	.30	.00	.24	.08	.03
Because it amuses me	**.72**	.16	.03	.23	.23	.05
Because it allows me to unwind	**.71**	.21	.22	.05	.32	-.01
Because there's a natural beauty to sports	**.68**	.35	.31	.17	.01	-.11
Because it's a pleasant rest	**.62**	.22	.35	-.05	.24	-.02
Self-Esteem/Achievement						
So I can feel a personal sense of achievement when my team does well	.22	**.84**	.15	.11	.05	.07
So I can feel proud when my team plays well	.24	**.79**	-.01	.20	.11	-.11
So I can feel like I've won when an athlete wins	.18	**.79**	.05	.09	.13	.07
Because it gives me confidence	.25	**.78**	.18	.14	.21	-.10
Because it increases my feelings of self-esteem	.19	**.76**	.25	.09	.14	-.03
Companionship						
So I won't have to be alone	.03	.16	**.75**	.14	.11	.11
Because it makes me feel less lonely	-.00	.41	**.56**	.13	.29	.04
When there's no one else to talk to or be with	.12	.16	**.54**	.11	.41	.25

Motive Items	Sports Television Viewing Factors					
	ENTR	SELF	COMP	LEAR	PASS	APAT
Learning/Social Interaction						
So I can learn about sports	.23	.18	.11	**.81**	.12	-.07
So I can learn things about sports which I didn't know before	.30	.11	.25	**.76**	.00	.04
So I can be with other members of the family or friends who are watching	.14	.19	-.00	**.65**	.23	.13
Pass Time/Escape						
Because it gives me something to occupy my time	.39	.18	.13	.14	**.66**	.20
So I can get away from what I'm doing	.36	.29	.21	.20	**.60**	.04
Apathetic						
When I have nothing better to do	-.02	-.10	.14	-.01	.12	**.85**
Just because it's there	-.05	.00	.04	.05	.06	**.84**
Eigenvalue	15.09	2.81	2.57	1.61	1.25	1.01
Variance Explained	41.93	7.81	7.13	4.46	3.48	2.81
Cronbach Alpha	.94	.91	.74	.77	—	—
Pearson *r*	—	—	—	—	.60*	.59*
M	3.52	2.17	1.85	3.28	2.80	2.82
SD	0.96	1.03	0.78	0.95	1.04	0.95

Note. ENTR = entertaining relaxation, SELF = self-esteem/achievement, COMP = companionship, LEAR = learning/social interaction, PASS = pass time/escape, APAT = apathetic. $* p < .001$

Factor 1, *entertaining relaxation motivation*, included all entertainment items ("Because it entertains me," "Because it's enjoyable," and "Because it amuses me"), two relaxation items ("Because it allows me to unwind" and "Because it's a pleasant rest"), two arousal items ("Because it's exciting," "Because it's thrilling"), one habit item ("Because I just like to watch"), and one aesthetic item ("Because there's a natural beauty to sports").

Factor 2, *self-esteem/achievement motivation*, included all achievement items ("So I can feel a personal sense of achievement when my team does well," "So I can feel like I've won when my team wins," and "So I can feel proud when my team plays well") and two self-esteem items ("Because it increases my feelings of self-esteem" and "Because it gives me confidence").

Factor 3, *companionship motivation*, included all companionship items ("So I won't have to be alone," "When there's no one else to talk to or be with," and "Because it makes me feel less lonely").

Factor 4, *learning/social interaction motivation*, included two information items ("So I can learn things about sports which I didn't know before," "So I can learn about sports") and one social interaction item ("So I can be with other members of the family or friends who are watching").

Factor 5, *pass time/escape motivation,* included one pass time item ("Because it gives me something to occupy my time") and one escape item ("So I can get away from what I'm doing").

Finally, factor 6, *apathetic motivation,* included one pass time item ("When I have nothing better to do") and one habit item ("Just because it's there").

Hypothesis 1 and RQ2: Relationships among Fandom and Sports Television Viewing Motives

Our hypothesis posited that fandom would be specifically related to motives of achievement, aesthetics, and self-esteem. As noted earlier, the factor analysis revealed a self-esteem/achievement motivation. There was a significant positive correlation between fandom and self-esteem/achievement motivation ($r = .58, p < .01$). Aesthetics, however, did not emerge as a motivation after the factor analysis. One aesthetics item ("Because there's a natural beauty to the game") loaded as part of the entertaining relaxation motivation. There was a significant positive correlation between fandom and entertaining relaxation motivation ($r = .79, p < .01$). These findings partially supported the hypothesis.

The second research question (RQ2) inquired about a wider array of motives fans may have for watching televised sports. To answer this question, we correlated fandom with each of the six motives identified via factor analysis.

As noted above, there were significant positive correlations between fandom and entertaining relaxation motivation ($r = .79, p < .01$), and fandom and self-esteem/achievement motivation ($r = .58, p < .01$). Additionally, there were significant positive correlations between fandom and companionship motivation ($r = .35, p < .01$), learning/social interaction motivation ($r = .42, p < .01$), and pass time/escape motivation ($r = .52, p < .01$). There was a significant negative correlation between fandom and apathetic motivation ($r = -.11, p = .05$). These results suggest that people who exhibited higher levels of fandom were more likely than their counterparts to view sports for entertainment, relaxation, self-esteem, achievement, companionship, learning about sports, interacting socially with family and friends, passing time, and escape. On the other hand, people who exhibited higher levels of fandom were less likely than their counterparts to view televised sports out of apathy (i.e., nothing better to do).

Discussion

Uses and gratifications provided a guiding framework for exploring fandom and motives. Because this theory has been used to explain the process of media selection to fulfill goals and the outcomes related to that process (Katz et al., 1974; Rubin, 1981a, 1984) it was logical to apply it to the study of viewing televised sports. Uses and gratifications also has been used in previous studies of motives for using sports media (Gantz, 1981; Wenner & Gantz, 1989).

The objectives of this study were (a) to identify more clearly motives for viewing televised sports and (b) to explore the relationships between fandom and sports television viewing motives. Because several previous studies suggested different motives for watching sports (Kahle et al., 1996; Milne & McDonald, 1999; Robinson & Trail, 2005; Trail & James, 2001; Wann, 1995), it was important to identify a comprehensive motive typology before exploring relationships to fandom.

Motives

Rubin (2002) argued that audience members are goal-directed, purposive, and motivated in their selection of media. Studies have identified reasons why people watch certain types of television programming. However, few studies have explored motives people have for watching sports on television with any relative consistency in motive typologies. Combining Rubin's TVMS with additional specific motives identified in previous sports viewing research, the findings in this study suggested that people watched sports on television for a variety of reasons. Of the 36 items on the revised TVMS, several loaded on meaningful motive factors (entertaining relaxation, self-esteem/achievement, companionship, learning/social interaction, pass time/escape, and apathetic motivations).

Entertaining relaxation motivation surfaced as a primary reason people have for watching televised sports. This is consistent with previous studies of sports viewing motivations (Gantz, 1981; Wann, 1995). This finding is consistent with studies that found similar motives for sports and general television viewing (Gantz & Wenner, 1991; Rubin, 1981a, 2002; Wenner & Gantz, 1989). This finding also lends support to Gantz' (1981) finding that people watched sports "to let loose," or to relax and be entertained while watching sports. Respondents in our sample tended to be motivated to watch sports on television because: (a) the content was enjoyable and thrilling, but at the same time (b) the content was relaxing and restful.

Self-esteem, achievement, and aesthetics motives were added to the TVMS from previous studies because they consistently emerged as reasons why people watched sports on television (Milne & McDonald, 1999; Trail & James, 2001; Wann, 1995). In this study, self-esteem and achievement emerged on a single factor for watching sports on television. This finding corroborates previous studies of sports television viewing that found people watched sports on television to build self-esteem (Milne & McDonald, 1999; Wann, 1995) and for a sense of achievement (Milne & McDonald, 1999; Trail & James, 2001). That one aesthetics item loaded as part of the entertaining relaxation motivation suggests a need for further investigation of this motive. This finding does, however, lend some support to previous studies that found people watched for the "natural beauty of sports" (Trail & James, 2001; Wann, 1995).

It has long been known that companionship is a motivation people have for watching television (Rubin, 1983). In previous television viewing motive studies, people reported using television as a companion, thus motivated by a sense of companionship (Rubin, 1983; Rubin & Perse, 1987b). However, prior to this study, companionship motivation was absent from sports television viewing studies. When included in this study, the three items related to companionship loaded on their own factor (i.e., I watch sports on television "so I won't have to be alone," "when there's no one else to talk to or be with," and "because it makes me feel less lonely").

Learning/social interaction motivation might suggest something about the co-viewing nature of sports television. In this study, when people were watching to learn about sports, they were watching with other people. This finding, that people watch television, in part, to be with family, lends some support to Lull's (1980) finding that people used television to be with their family. This substantiates the findings of Wenner and Gantz (1989) who identified "learning about the game" as a reason some fans watch sports on television. This also corroborates prior research findings that watching with family and friends served as a motive for watching sports (Gantz & Wenner, 1995).

Pass time/escape motivation emerged as a reason people watched sports on television. It appears that respondents in this study were motivated to watch sports on television to "get away from the rest of the family" (i.e., escape) and to occupy their time (i.e., pass time). This lends support to prior findings that suggest people watch television to pass time (Rubin, 1981a, 1983; Rubin & Perse, 1987b) and escape (Rubin, 1981a, 1983; Wenner & Gantz, 1991).

There is some precedent in the study of sports television viewing for suggesting that some viewing takes place out of pure apathy. In this study, apathetic motivation consisted of watching sports out of habit (e.g., just because it's there) and to pass time (e.g., boredom). This type of motivation was identified in previous television (Rubin, 1981a, 1983; Rubin & Perse, 1987b) and sports television viewing studies (Wenner & Gantz, 1995). However, watching televised sports out of habit did not appear in previous sports television viewing motive typologies. Nonetheless, it appears as though watching out of habit may be a relevant reason to consider when exploring the reasons why people view televised sports.

Fandom

Fandom is a background characteristic that people bring with them to the sports television viewing setting. More importantly, fandom helped to explain why people approach and use sports media differently. According to uses and gratifications, it is important to consider background characteristics of media users that influence motives for sports media use. Fandom is but one of many background characteristics (e.g., gender, age, socio-economic status) that should be examined in relation to sports television viewing motives in future research.

Because achievement, aesthetics, and self-esteem motives appeared consistently in previous sports media studies with varied motive typologies (e.g., Milne & McDonald, 1996; Trail & James, 2000; Wann, 1995), it was relevant to include these motives in the current examination. Our hypothesis predicted that fandom would be related positively to achievement, aesthetics, and self-esteem motivations for watching televised sports. As expected, respondents in the current study who reported being fans of sports were motivated to watch to fulfill achievement (e.g., "So I can feel proud when my team plays well") and self-esteem goals (e.g., "Because it gives me confidence").

These findings support previous findings that viewers watch sports for reasons of achievement (Milne & McDonald, 1996; Trail & James, 2000), self-esteem (Milne & McDonald, 1996; Wann, 1995), and aesthetics (Milne & McDonald, 1996; Trail & James, 2000).

Fandom also linked directly with entertaining relaxation, self-esteem/achievement, companionship, learning/social interaction, and pass time/escape motivations. These findings lend support to previous studies that found links between fandom and entertainment motivation (Wann, 1995), relaxation motivation (Milne & McDonald, 1999; Trail & James, 2000; Wann, 1995), learning motivation (Trail & James, 2000), social interaction motivation (Milne & McDonald, 1999; Trail & James, 2000; Wann, 1995), and escape motivation (Trail & James, 2000; Wann, 1995).

Limitations and Future Directions

There were a few notable limitations to this study. Two significant limitations pertain to the sample selected and the number of variables included. First, a convenient sample of college-aged students was used. Therefore, the sample was not representative or inclusive of all sports television viewers. These results may be generalized to college-aged sports television viewers in the United States, but generally, the profile of a sports television viewing audience would include viewers of all ages, in various parts of the world, and with varied socio-economic backgrounds. Future research should assess the motives of a wider array of diverse samples of sports viewers to see if the motive structure uncovered in this study is corroborated across samples of varying diversity.

Second, there were more women than men in the sample. This may have skewed the results related to sports television viewing motives and fandom. We know that more men than women watch sports on television (Gantz & Wenner, 1991) and that men and women watch different types of sports on television. Sargent (2003) found that women tended to watch sports like figure skating (e.g., stylistic sports) and men tended to watch sports like boxing (e.g., combative sports). Future research should assess the motives for watching different types of sports, and gender differences in the motives for watching sports, to ascertain whether men and women differ in their motives and the influence of their motives on selection of sports genres.

Here we examined the relationship between one audience background factor (i.e., fandom) and sports viewing motivation. There are likely many other variables related to motives for viewing televised sports. Future studies might consider the contributions of variables such as co-viewing, experience with sports, socio-economic differences and other social/psychological factors. For example, one motivation that continues to emerge in studies of sports television viewing is social interaction. Therefore, co-viewing, or the process of watching television with others, might provide some interesting insight related to sports media use.

Uses and gratifications researchers have found evidence that suggests audience members' psychological and sociological differences affect media selection and abilities to fulfill goals. Those differences lead to certain effects. Thus, such differences likely affect not just motives for viewing sports, but also selection of fare and a variety of effects that result from viewing sports.

This study was proposed, in part, to explore the relationship between sports-viewing motives and fandom. The focus, therefore, was on the analyses of simple bivariate relationships. Future studies should continue to examine fandom and motives by exploring the types of relationships people have with athletes (i.e., parasocial interaction, identification) and how those relationships impact motives for viewing sports.

We have only begun to understand the number, combination, and complexity of variables that explain those motives and the influence of those motives on effects. As future studies are conducted and new combinations of variables are considered, we may develop better methods for explaining sports television use.

NASCAR Fans in
Their Own Words

Motivation Expressed in Narratives

LAWRENCE W. HUGENBERG AND
BARBARA HUGENBERG

Reasons or motives for following NASCAR play important roles in fan communication. Since NASCAR began six decades ago, there have been few communication studies of NASCAR fans and their narratives. Moreover, scholars and reporters have spent the majority of the past sixty years stereotyping NASCAR fans as "conservative, Southern rednecks" (Hagstrom, 1998; Howell, 1997; Huler, 1999; Lord, 2001; MacGregor, 2001; Ronfeldt, 2000). As NASCAR grew in popularity in the late 1990s, its fan demographic became very diverse, and the fan base, formerly concentrated in the southeastern United States, spread to different areas of the country. NASCAR expanded its racing schedule to disparate places, and the geographic center of "NASCAR Nation" moved further west and north. Raceways were built in Arizona, California, Delaware, Illinois, Michigan, Missouri, and Nevada—far removed from traditional NASCAR tracks in Florida, Georgia, North Carolina, South Carolina, Tennessee and Virginia. Additionally, NASCAR Busch Series races have been run in Mexico City since 2006 and Montreal since 2007. NASCAR continues to be interested in building tracks in or near New York City and Seattle. This migration has influenced the NASCAR fan base in the following ways: more affluent, more urban, more educated, more technologically savvy, and more youthful ("Weekends with the NASCAR Family," 2005).

Part of the development of this recent NASCAR fan base diversity can be attributed to the expanded weekly television and cable coverage of each NASCAR race, making racing more accessible to more people in more population centers. What accounts for this surge in interest in and appreciation for NASCAR across the United States and our neighboring countries? What has changed with the NASCAR organization? Have perceptions regarding the sport shifted and have these shifting perspectives spread fandom of NASCAR across wider demographics?

NASCAR Nation

NASCAR is the fastest growing spectator sport in the United States (Hagstrom, 1998; Howell, 1997; Hugenberg & Hugenberg, 2008; Huler, 1999; MacGregor, 2005; "Growth of NASCAR," 2007). The historic popularity of NASCAR in the southeastern United States as a predominantly white, "good ol' boys'" sport has gradually shifted to become a national pastime enjoyed by well-educated, middle-class professionals (Ronfeldt, 2000; Varvus, 2007). At the same time, NASCAR sought to become a technology-integrated sport capitalizing on the younger fans' interest in and comfort with developing applications of technology to communicate fan data and race information. This progressive evolution of NASCAR is also evident in the current circuit's title sponsorship. Nextel replaced Winston cigarettes, a subsidiary of R. J. Reynolds Tobacco, that sponsored the NASCAR title, *Winston Cup Championship*, from 1970 to 2003, and changed the name of the championship to the *Nextel Cup*. This evolving NASCAR demographic profile, and subsequent corporate sponsorship, contributes to increased participation from non-traditional NASCAR fans—young women and men.

Although the fan base is spreading to all corners of the country, what are the commonalities shared among members of this fan culture, and how are they different from other sports fans? Hugenberg and Hugenberg (2008) argued that NASCAR fans differ in several areas including loyalty to sponsors, loyalty unfettered by geographic location, and loyalty to the individual drivers. These loyalties are demonstrated in fans' purchasing behaviors. Approximately 80 percent of NASCAR fans purchase products of their favorite driver's sponsors, and 88 percent of NASCAR fans for five years or more reported they make an effort to purchase products endorsed by their favorite driver (*Sports Illustrated*, 2004). NASCAR fandom is unique in its live viewing format. Professional sports teams hold sporting events near large urban centers equipped to handle sizeable crowds via mass transit and urban road infrastructure. This is not the case with many NASCAR races, which occur in more rural settings with infrastructures built to support daily activities, not hundreds of thousands of fans. The mass entrance and egress of these throngs create untenable traffic scenarios, and many fans travel more than a few hours to attend races. Many NASCAR fans camp near racetracks in mobile homes for days prior to events. Based on our experiences at multiple tracks in various locations, this scene creates an atmosphere of revelry, much like tailgating near baseball and football stadiums, but on a much larger scale in numbers of people *and* time spent. The fan base is changing, the fan experiences are evolving, but what about the stories fans tell about why and how they became and remain NASCAR fans? To understand the attraction to NASCAR among more youthful fans, one of the fastest growing demographics, we sought to discover common threads woven in the narrative tapestries. We relied on their stories and their voices to build greater understanding of how and why the sport factors into their lives.

The Narrative Paradigm

When asked to participate in this research, young NASCAR fans were more than willing to tell (or write) their stories. Riessman (1993) stressed the importance of these stories in defining narratives as "first-person accounts by respondents of their experience, putting aside other kinds of accounts (e.g., our descriptions of what happened in the field and other research narritivizations, including the 'master narratives' of theory)" (pp. 1–2). Fisher (1984) examined the narrative paradigm in a different manner:

> The presuppositions that structure the narrative paradigm are: (1) humankind are essentially storytellers; (2) the paradigmatic mode of human decision-making and communication is "good reasons" which vary in form among communication situations, genres, and media; (3) the production and practice of good reasons is ruled by matters of history, culture, and character along with the kinds of forces identified in the ... language action paradigm; (4) rationality is determined by the nature of persons as narrative beings— their inherent awareness of *narrative probability*, which constitutes a coherent story, and their constant habit of testing *narrative fidelity*, whether the stories they experience ring true with the stories they know to be true in their lives...; and (5) the world is a set of stories which must be chosen among to live the good life in a process of continual recreation [pp. 7–8].

In giving narrative analysis focus and purpose, Riessman (1993) concluded, "Narrative analysis allows for systematic study of personal experience and meaning: how events have been constructed by active subjects" (p. 70). Later, Stevenson and Greenberg (1998) used event structure analysis (ESA) which provided specific rule-governed techniques to clarify linkages between events and the narrators' stories. Expanding narrative analysis, Fraser (2004) explored a particular line-by-line application of narrative analysis to individuals' stories. Other scholars have applied the narrative paradigm in cross-disciplinary and inter-disciplinary settings with varying degrees of success in illuminating the narratives themselves (Appel & Richter, 2007; Bradley, Lupei & Ray, 2007; Mazzocco, Green & Brock, 2007; Schiffrin, 2003; Triss & Breen, 2007).

The collected written records, thus, provide information to help us better understand and appreciate their fandom motives. Swiss and Chevrel (2002) suggested narratives are frequently the result of the ones storytellers anticipate sharing with others. Although these narratives could be contrived in anticipation of a specific communication context, the narratives result from the cumulative experience of the narrator in telling her or his story. Georgakopoulou

(2006) noted that narratives, and the narrator's willingness to tell them, are the result of past events and personal experience. This idea informed our research because we believe young NASCAR fans' interest in NASCAR is the result of positive experiences with other NASCAR fans in their families *and* their willingness to communicate with each other about their fan-ness. De Angelis (2007) suggested that people create and share stories to identify with others—who share similar goals, behaviors, and interests.

Burke (1968) developed the dramatistic pentad that has been used as a critical methodology to assess written and oral forms of communication. Even though we appreciate the pentad and its applications, perhaps Burke's most important contribution to the study of communication was *identification*. To assist our understanding of the processes of *identification*, Burke (1968) added another element to the dramatistic pentad (now a hexad)—attitude. However, Burke left a question unanswered: How does the inclusion of "identification" help us understand communicators' motives?

It is impossible to separate the communicator's motives from the communication act (Bitzer, 1968). Burke (1974) contended, "linguistic motive involves kinds of persuasion guided not by appeal to any one local audience, but by the logic of appeal in general" (p. 129). The individual fans' motives, as articulated in their narratives, are essential data. Even though narrative analysis is decades old, other qualitative methods continue to fall short in offering insights into a person's motives—much less a sports fan's motives.

People make sense of experiences by putting them into narrative form (Riessman, 1993, p. 4). Personal narratives allow communicators to select from many competing alternatives—both strategic and practical. These two issues assisted Fisher (1984, 1985, 1987a, 1987b) in developing the narrative paradigm. In his initial essay, Fisher (1984) wrote, "The narrative paradigm does not deny reason or rationality; it reconstitutes them, making them amenable to all forms of human communication" (p. 2). Rybacki and Rybacki (1991) described narratives as "Discourse in narrative form [which] occurs in live public speaking, messages transmitted or recorded electronically ... and the print media" (p. 107). Fisher (1984, 1985, 1987a, 1987b) explained that narratives offer many insights into communicative realities. Rybacki and Rybacki (1991) concluded, "One of the advantages of the narrative approach is that it allows examination of media as a purveyor of social values. It also provides a way to account for what an audience does with a narrative" (p. 124).

Clegg (1993) suggested that "language is more or less transparent; it reveals a reality outside itself to which it refers and defers. Its stories are the stories of everyday life trimmed and shaped into narrative by the skilled storyteller" (pp. 31–32). Sigman, Sullivan, and Wendell (1988) illustrated the goals of conversation analysis: determining the "interaction role(s) and their social role(s) ... rather than the predictive values of previously abstracted social role(s) for produced behavior" (p. 167). Burke (1974), interpreting Mead, suggested that narration begins with the interactive dialogue between the "I" and the "me" (p. 38). Although recognizing the importance of this internal dialogue, narratives must be analyzed as an external dialogue. Narrative can be examined for narrator motives by uncovering recurring symbols used in storytelling that indicate themes and framing the message in a context (Hugenberg & Schaefermeyer, 1983).

Narrative Analysis

Over two decades have passed since Fisher published his initial essay on narrative criticism, yet few studies have explored or expanded the utility or applications of the narrative paradigm. Foss (1989) concluded soon after Fisher introduced narrative analysis, "[T]he notion of narrative has not been used extensively in rhetorical criticism as have some of the other concepts that guide other approaches" (p. 239). The narrative approach is the *best* way to examine human motives surrounding specific behaviors. The elements of narrative analysis offer insight into the narrator's motives. Fisher (1985) argued, "The primary function of the [narrative] paradigm is to offer a way of interpreting and assessing human communication that leads to critique, a determination of whether or not a given instance of discourse provides a reliable, trustworthy, and desirable guide to thought and action in the world" (p. 351).

Narrative Standards Fisher (1985) suggested the following standards for the critic to use in applying the narrative paradigm: (a) the truth standard, (b) the aesthetic standard, (c) the results standard, and (d) the ethical standard. The *truth standard* examines the narrative against what is commonly held to be true. When listening to a narrative, we conclude certain things to be true or false. We examine whether the narratives are consistent with commonly held truths. Rybacki and Rybacki (1991) concluded, "The truth of a narrative is a combination of what the rhetor intends and the audience interprets in any rhetorical act" (p. 108). The *aesthetic standard* focuses on the elements the storyteller uses to deliver the narrative and includes language selection, the communicator's point of view, and other decisions made by the communicator in preparing the narrative. Traditionally, this standard sheds minimal light on the communicator's motives. Although all the decisions made by the communicator reflect her or his motives, there is not necessarily a direct cause and effect relationship. The *results standard* examines the consequences of the narrative or its impact. We examine how the narrative was accepted over competing or similar narratives. In addition, we explore actual consequences of the narrative. One of those consequences is that people become known by the stories they tell. Fisher (1985) concluded, "The only way to determine whether or not a story is a mask for ulterior motives is to test it against the principles of narrative probability and fidelity" (p. 364). Finally, the *ethical standard* judges the morality of the narrative and, by association, the morality of the narrator.

Ettema and Glasser (1988) wrote, "Narrative is an instrument for the assertion of moral authority" (p. 8). The ethical standard is the most important of Fisher's four standards of narrative criticism. This research adds a *practical standard* to the discussion of narrative analysis. It is important to interpret the motives revealed in any narrative as the narrator's attempt to identify with others. As social creatures, humans seek identification with others through communication and action. Through storytelling, human identification with others is communicated. Including the standard, then, focuses examination of narrative on the level of identification communicated as the narrator reveals specific behaviors and cognitions.

Finally, Burke (1968, 1989b) suggested a primary motive for communicating with others is to identify with them — to show that people belong to the same group or club with others. He suggested that identification is the primary (and perhaps sole) reason why people engage in rhetorical activities. Identification and one's narratives are intertwined. Sports-fans-as-narrators cannot identify with others unless the following occurs: (a) the sports-fan-as-narrator knows the narratives of others, (b) the sports-fan-as-narrator likes or agrees with these narratives, (c) others recognize the sports-fan-as-narrator's narrative as similar to their own; and (d) others want to identify with the sports-fan-as-narrator because of these narratives. These four elements of identification offer the practical reasons why humans use narratives—*to succeed through identifying with others.*

This analysis intertwines narrative criticism and identification as critical devices to understand the motives of young NASCAR fans as expressed in narrative form.

The Narratives of Young NASCAR Fans

Subjects

This study focused on the demographic NASCAR suggests is its fastest growing demographic — young adults. Students in an introductory communication course at a large Midwestern university ($N = 186$) who indicated that they were NASCAR fans responded to the statement: *Please tell us about your reasons for following NASCAR.*[1] Student participation in research or completion of an alternative assignment is a course requirement. Of the student-respondents, 115 were male (62 percent), 58 were female (31 percent), and 13 (7 percent) declined to specify their gender. The sample consisted of 164 Caucasians (88 percent), 14 African-Americans (8 percent), 4 Asian-Americans (2 percent), and 2 Hispanic Americans (1 percent), and 2 students (1 percent) did not report their ethnic background. The sample consisted of participants who described their families to be upper middle class ($n = 87$, 47 percent) or middle class ($n = 84$, 45 percent). Only 4 respondents (2 percent) considered their families to be lower middle class and 4 more respondents (2 percent) considered their families to be lower class. All quotations in the text are presented exactly as written by the subject. No editorial corrections were made by the authors.

Results

The Family-Time Motive   A common unifying theme in the stories of young NASCAR fans is their family-oriented motives for becoming NASCAR fans—a form of identification. The narratives examined suggest that watching a NASCAR race facilitated their relationships with members of their family — typically immediate members of their family such as parents, siblings and grandparents. One fan noted simply, "I'm not really a NASCAR fan, but I watch NASCAR when my family is watching it." Another fan noted, "My father is a fan of NASCAR and some of my aunts and uncles are also NASCAR fans. Sometimes I will sit down and watch it with them." Another reported, "It's something my family does and it brings me closer to them." Reiterating the importance of family and following NASCAR, one male fan wrote, "I have followed NASCAR because I see how into it my brother is and it got me interested in watching it." Another fan noted, "It is a way to get together with my brother and relax on the weekends." One fan noted that he started to like NASCAR because "my family watches it all together so I watch it with them." Another female fan stated, "My family are huge fans so in which case I watch along with them at family events. It's just a fun thing for all of us to do together at times."

One male fan wrote about trying to stay close to his family's interests in NASCAR, writing, "I follow NASCAR because my uncle's are big fans of NASCAR so when I'm at their houses on a holiday or around them they'll usually watch a race or talk about racing. I like to be part of the conversation or action, so I watch the races and give them my opinion on subject matters." Another fan reiterated the same motive, stating, "Because I grew up with it. Every family event we would all watch NASCAR. So as I got older, I started to become a fan. Also my uncle is a huge NASCAR fan and he works on the trailers of Tony Stewart and other big name drivers." Another fan reported, "My extended family watches NASCAR and every time we get together the race is on and we have a good time yelling at the TV."

One fan reported his mother's influence, stating, "Mainly since my parents got into it. With my Mom being a die-hard Rusty Wallace fan when he raced, the house would usually be filled with cheers for him and curses at Jeff Gordon. So I started to get into it since they did. Usually ends up a pretty fun Sunday." Another fan reported a NASCAR bond with his father, stating, "I follow NASCAR because I have come to enjoy the competitiveness and speed involved. Initially, I started watching it to have something in common with my dad, but now I have really come to like it." One male fan noted, "It is a time that my dad and I can share together — going to a race talking about things we never have a chance to talk about. After my mom and dad divorced, she tried to keep us seperated; however our interest in NASCAR has kept us close." Similarly, another fan concluded he became a NASCAR fan "Because my Dad always watches it; so I started to as well."

One female fan noted, "I follow NASCAR because my father is a huge NASCAR fan. I began to watch it when I was young and it became a natural thing to watch. Every time I watch it, I ask my dad more and more questions about it and especially about the skills and the mechanics required." Another female fan wrote, "I really enjoy watching NASCAR because my father got me hooked on it when I was a little girl." A male fan wrote, "I follow NASCAR because my father watches it all of the time. I watch it to spend time with him and to have something to talk about. I think if he did not watch it that I would never have gotten interested in it." Similarly, another fan suggested, "I watch NASCAR because my Dad and Grandpa have loved it for years and I think they just want to share it with me. I don't follow it closely. I do get excited to watch it with my family because of my Dad." Another fan noted the influence of his grandfather, "Me and my grandfather have a close relationship. I try and follow it as much as I can so I can relate to things we talk about, or bring up in conversation."

Another female fan reported, "I just recently became interested because of a family member's love for the sport, so I am slowly learning little bits and pieces about it. Eventually I would like to know more. For now, when it's on, I watch and pick up something new every time." A female fan reiterated the importance of her family in developing her interest in NASCAR, stating, "My whole family, grandparents and all have been big NASCAR fans since I was born and they've attended many races and they are the ones who got me to like NASCAR." Another fan wrote, "For the most part, I only watch NASCAR when I am with my Dad's side of the family. They go to about 4 races a year and are big fans, and its always fun to bond with them and watch a race." Another fan noted his family's interest in cars influencing his interest in NASCAR, writing, "I follow NASCAR mainly because my dad and brother are total 'motorheads' and watch anything with a motor."

In a society that reports fewer and fewer family dinners, the generation gap, and classic sibling rivalries, sharing a common interest in anything is noteworthy. An interesting feature of many students' stories is that they "grew to like it" perhaps because NASCAR viewing afforded opportunities to develop common interests and shared language within the familial context. However, the young NASCAR fans we studied were also eager to share stories about how the sport aided with other types of interpersonal relationships and communication.

Social Motive A second motive for young fans enjoying NASCAR incorporates the importance of their interpersonal relationships with significant others, friends and acquaintances—a form of identification. One fan wrote, "I got into it with an old boyfriend." Another noted, "I went to a NASCAR race because my friend at the time had an extra ticket." A young male fan wrote, "The reasons I will catch an occasional race is because it's a social situation...." Another male reported, "I have a friend who is a fan and I really enjoy watching it with him, mostly for social reasons." Another fan concluded, "It is something I like to watch with friends when they are interested." One young fan concluded, "My friends turned me into a NASCAR fan." A male fan noted, "I watch NASCAR to relax and socialize and have a good time." A female fan reported, "I follow NASCAR because my former boss watched it all the time so he basically got me hooked and I watch it as often as I am able to. I enjoy watching it with my friends and family. I also follow it because it something my boss and I would do all of the time. I would really enjoy it when customers also watched along with us." Finally, another fan wrote, "It is a fun atmosphere to get together with a bunch of NASCAR fans."

One fan noted, "It is also a great way to meet other people and the tensions between fans of different drivers is great." One female fan reported, "My-ex-boyfriend was a huge fan and got me started watching it. I also work with a group of guys who watch the races every Sunday while we're at work, so I tend to watch it with them." Another female fan noted, "I follow NASCAR because my boyfriend likes ... it and watches it a lot." One fan noted his interest in NASCAR was supported by the time spent playing video games with his neighbor, writing, "When I was young my neighbor was obsessed. We would play NASCAR videogames and discuss our favorite drivers." Another male fan wrote, "My girlfriend's dad likes to watch it whenever its on and so I started watching it so I could relate with him, then slowly I became a fan and still am growing as a fan."

One male fan reported he became interested with his friends in high school, noting, "I follow NASCAR because a lot of my friends did throughout high school. Once I picked up on it, I found I really enjoyed and there was more to it than a bunch of turning." Another fan wrote, "I follow NASCAR because my roomate does and my dad does. It gives us things to talk about." A female fan noted, "Some of my family and friends watch it so I just watch it because when I am with them the race can get addicting. It is like cheering for your home team to win the race and it is fun to have your favorite racer win over one of your friend's."

The fans reported bonding within the family and with friends and co-workers, social drives probably not uncommon among fans of any sport, but we were also interested to note that NASCAR races provided a type of vicarious thrill unlike many other sports. These ritualized behaviors (Rubin, 1984) focusing on weekly family-member viewing of NASCAR races reveal motives consistent with other ritualized family get-togethers that become important to the individuals and impact their decisions and behaviors.

Thrill-of-the-Sport Motive   A third motive identified by young NASCAR fans is the excitement or thrill these young fans experience watching NASCAR races—especially the likelihood of high-speed wrecks. One fan wrote, "I like cars. It's exciting, high speeds. The thrill of watching cars speed in circles for hours is intense." A second fan noted, "The race is exciting and I enjoy watching the strategies that go into the sport. The speed, the crashes, the intensity of the races. The drivers must think fast and react even faster. It's a joy to watch. I must say I enjoy the crashes as well—as long as no one gets hurt." A related motive is the danger inherent in NASCAR. One fan noted, "I like to see a crash, but I don't want them to get hurt. I think it is cool that they can go that fast and have control of a car." Another fan reiterated this sense of danger in writing, "I follow NASCAR because it is fun and exciting. Watching cars go in circles is amazing. It's fun to see who is going to win. It could be any car because anything can happen to a race car at any given time." Another fan stated, "I like to watch NASCAR to see the wrecks that may happen and watching the danger in the pit stops." Another fan concluded, "I'm impressed by the speed and power of the cars." Another fan, trying to rationalize his motives, wrote, "I like the competition and strategy involved, but mostly I like to watch the crashes." A male fan wrote, "I believe that it is the fastest growing sport in America. It's thrilling and exciting especially since the point standings were introduced."

One fan combined his interest in cars and women, writing, "I like fast cars and women. NASCAR happens to contain both." Another fan noted his interest in NASCAR by writing, "I like car racing. It is an excitement to see fast motion, meaning high speech. The ability to surpass long distances in controlled high speeds. It also shows me the excellence of human achievement both the skill and the car." A male fan wrote, "I watch NASCAR because it gives me a rush to see crashes/accidents. I bealieve that a clean race with no crashes is not even half as interesting as one with crashes." Another fan concluded, "I enjoy racing and the thrill of speed. I love the cars and how loud they are. I love the atmosphere and the fans at the races."

A male fan concluded, "I watch NASCAR because the competition is fast and fierce. The speed of the races are really fast. This is something these guys live for. NASCAR is extreme and definately exciting." Another fan reported, "I like the strategy involved in passing and drafting. I also like bump drafting and close finishes. So basically the competition involved." Another fan noted, "I like the competitive feeling, I think the excitement that comes from the race is unbelievable." Another fan wrote, "I follow NASCAR because the races are exciting. They are unlike any other sport and it is something I could probably never do."

So many of the young narrators were more than willing to admit that they enjoyed the sport based on the possibility of life-threatening crashes—and some admitted it was *because* of the crashes. Watching groups of talented racers travel in circles at speeds often reaching 220 miles per hour, bumper-to-bumper, and inches apart from each other, according to many of the young fans, provides a thrill unlike anything else. Yet, for some fans, there seemed to be more than the titillation of high speeds and the promise of crashes that provided motive for their love of NASCAR.

Escape or Enjoyment Motive Some fans expressed the reason they watch NASCAR was to escape from their daily routines and obligations. One fan reported that NASCAR is his escape from school, stating "I think it is fun to sit on the couch and eat lunch after church with my dad and get to forget about school and everything else." Another fan noted, "The reasons I watch NASCAR are basically because it takes me away from all the worries and tension of everyday life; when I watch a race I put all my worries aside and focus only on the race." Vorderer, Klimmt, and Ritterfield (2004) seemed to merge the escape motive with the entertainment motive in concluding, "One possible motive for seeking entertainment may be the media users' temporary interest and desire to escape from the social world in which they actually live" (p. 399).

Zillmann and Bryant (1994), Slater (2002), Nabi and Krcmar (2004) and Vorderer et al. (2004) explicated the enjoyment motive for media use. The collected narratives reveal an entertainment motive for watching NASCAR consistent with their findings. A young male fan wrote, "Because it provides a good and exciting source of entertainment." One fan noted that she watches only "the big races, such as the Brickyard and the Daytona." Another fan concluded that she follows NASCAR "because it is a different sport option from football and basketball. Definitely has an adrenalin rush watching, always something happening at the split second it changes." A male fan noted, "Watching a good performance is something nice to see. Also, it's a nice way to be able to sit and relax while watching something I enjoy." Another fan wrote, "I follow NASCAR for the same reason as any other sport — it's entertaining and passes time." Another fan concluded, "I follow NASCAR because it is enjoyable to watch." Another noted, "I follow NASCAR for the simple reason that it is fun to watch. I enjoy the excitement of watching a good race and the energy all the drivers have." In addition to the escape and entertainment motives for being a NASCAR fan, respondents reported their identification with a specific driver was the reason they followed NASCAR.

Relationship with Driver Motive Another motive expressed by young NASCAR fans is the relationship they have with individual drivers, one form of narrator identification. A unique fan experience was reported when one fan stated, "I follow NASCAR because my dad went to high school with one of the drivers — Dave Baliney. He isn't very well known in NASCAR but its fun to follow him." One female fan wrote, "The only reason I watch it is to look at the drivers." One fan who used to live in Florida suggested that his reason for being a NASCAR fan is associated with that fact that his "family knows a few of the drivers and it got me hooked on cars." A fan noted that her interest in NASCAR increased after identifying a driver to cheer for: "I really got into it, and then when I found a driver to follow, I began to get into NASCAR more and follow his career."

Another fan noted his support of Dale Earnhardt as motive for watching NASCAR, "I started following NASCAR because of Dale Earnheardt. After his death, I continued following his son." One fan reported, "I follow NASCAR because I like Jeff Gordon. I like to see him win." Another fan concluded, "When I was young, I loved cars and automobiles and one day I was watching a race and saw Bill Elliot's McDonald's car and thought it was really cool. I then followed the sport a lot until he retired and after he left I began to like Tony Stewart." A female fan noted her identification with Jeff Gordon, "I really enjoy Jeff Gordon because he is good looking and also is active. He has a lot of sponsors I like. He has commercials, posters and memerablia everywhere because he is so well respected."

Fans' motives are often mixed. They enjoy watching with the family, but really love it because of a handsome driver or a cool car, and it provides some well-needed escape from life's pressures. The following illustrates fans' mixed motives.

Mixed Fan Motives   Each combination of motives reveals an idiosyncratic combination for each student narrator. One male fan mixed enjoyment and social motives for his interest in NASCAR, "I enjoy watching it. I would like to try it. It relaxes me. I feel a sense of comfort. I watched it growing up. And a lot of my friends watch it." One fan incorporated family, social and excitement motives into her reasons for being a NASCAR fan, stating, "It's an exciting sport to watch. I grew up watching it with friends and family and I like to watch the cars go fast. It's a sport I can talk about with my friends and family and enjoy doing so."

One fan noted rooting for Dale Earnhardt with his Dad (family) was a fond memory, and their current support of Dale Earnhardt, Jr. (identification with a driver), are their motives for watching NASCAR: "When I was little, it was a big bonding thing between my dad and I. Our favorite driver was Dale Sr. and when he died, I guess we both somewhat lost interest. Dad still watches every Sunday pretty much religiously, but I'll watch it with him if I'm around. We both like Dale Jr. (obvious reasons), but I guess it brings back good memories we shared and it's a way to bond and enjoy each other's company."

Another fan watches NASCAR to spend time with her Dad (family) but also uses the races as an escape when she stated, "For as long as I can remember, my dad has always been a fan so I tended to watch it with him as a child. As I grew older, I found NASCAR to be an event that I looked forward to each week. I also found the race to be a time that I can actually enjoy to the fullest and not have to constantly worry about work or school." Yet another fan noted her interest in NASCAR grew as a result of her Dad's interest (family) and the excitement of the races, writing, "My dad is a huge NASCAR fan and would always watch the races at home and I guess I just got hooked on it. I enjoy the rush/thrill of the race and admire their stamina."

Another fan revealed excitement, enjoyment, and social motives for following NASCAR: "I have always liked cars, and find it exciting and entertaining when they are pushed really hard and to the limit. I also find it a good way to sit back, relax and enjoy the time. It's also a good way to meet and interact with others, especially when I do go to the races." Another fan reported his interest in NASCAR related to his cousins (family) and the excitement of the races, "I follow NASCAR because I think it is exciting to watch and because my cousins are very into it. So I try to stay up on it because it will give me something to talk about with them." Similarly, a female fan combined the social, driver identification, and excitement motives: "I think NASCAR is very interesting and exciting to watch. I think the drivers are cute and it always keeps me on the edge of my seat. I watch it with a lot of my guy friends and it is a really great time."

Another fan combined the entertainment and social motives for his interest in NASCAR, reporting, "I just like to watch it on TV. It's a good form of entertainment. It also gives me time to be with friends and family which I value very much."

Practical Standard and Identification

Identification with their family, friends, or driver emerged as three of the dominant motives of NASCAR fans; therefore the practical standard was affirmed. NASCAR fans revealed their attitudes toward the sport and their actions to gain identification with others. The narrator told her or his fan story to identify with family members, friends and acquaintances, and/or their favorite driver. A limitation to the affirmation of the practical standard in examining narratives of sports fans is the narrow focus of this study — NASCAR. To affirm the practical standard in this genre of narrative, additional narratives of young fans of other sports should be evaluated for clear motives that are similar to or disparate from those motives identified in this research.

These NASCAR fan narratives were examined and five different motives identified. The narratives indicated three identification motives as young NASCAR fans explained their fandom. These three identification motives are shared by NASCAR fans and are effective in creating a clearly identified fan community. Depending upon the explicated levels of fandom, information dispensed in each fan's narrative determines the degree to which identification is realized and the target of the narrator's identification specified. In other words, how practical is the motive of NASCAR fans as an identification-creating communicative strategy?

Conclusion

The analysis and comparison of young NASCAR fan narratives provide cumulative insights into their collective motives for their sport fandom — in this case, specifically NASCAR fans. Mumby (1993), in describing the importance of narrative analysis, observed, "The articulation of social actors as *homo narrans* provides one alternative to the model of rationality that has characterized Western thought" (p. 1). Adding the practical standard enabled us to identify and reveal three different identification motives of NASCAR fans: identification with members of their family, identification with friends and acquaintances, and identification with their favorite NASCAR drivers. Sometimes the motives for a person telling a story are more revealing than the story itself. The practical motives for young NASCAR fans communicating their stories offer insight into their selected identification strategies. This analysis affords greater understanding of young NASCAR fans' motives, and, in our view, young NASCAR fans have a dominant motive for telling their fan stories— to identify with and spend time with members of their family. The social motive of friendship and being able to talk with friends about NASCAR was also revealed as an important motive for young NASCAR fans. Additional young NASCAR fans' motives discovered in this analysis of their narratives include: being a fan of the sport and watching it for its thrills (crashes, speed, etc.), escaping from daily routines, entertainment, identification with a driver, or a combination of two of more of these specific motives.

Sports communication and sports fandom scholars should seek additional opportunities to use the practical standard. This standard will assist in the recreation of a storyteller's identification motives for the way they tell their narratives and to whom they tell their stories. Communication scholars may gain enhanced understanding of how the complex identification motives are revealed by narrators. To confirm the conclusions of this research, it will be necessary to compare the results of narrative analysis of stories from young fans of different sports. For example, it would be interesting to compare the narratives of football, baseball, hockey, or soccer fans and the reasons offered for supporting their chosen teams. Future research could pose the following questions: "Why do some fans root for individuals on a team and other fans support teams and not individuals?" or "Why are some people fans of individual sports and others are fans of team sports?" It might prove interesting to separate women's and men's narratives to discover possible differences in fan motives based on gender. Similarities in narrative strategies might be discovered, thus solidifying the consistent set of identification motives for fan behavior. Another necessary research step to confirm the identification motives of young NASCAR fans, the focus of this study, would be to examine the narratives of older NASCAR fans, or those traditional fans who have been fans for a long period of time, and others who more recently became fans of the sport.

   With additional research, studying fans' narratives will illuminate the study of sport fandom and fan behaviors, not with certainty but with probability. Acknowledging the importance of sports fans' identification motives is an important extension of motive analysis *and* sports fan and sports communication research. Discovering the communicator's identification motives has been difficult because scholars relied on survey instruments. Examining specific narratives for identification motives more readily revealed individual narrators' motives, but also permitted the classification of identification motives. This study attempted to extend the examination of narratives to sports fans, specifically young NASCAR fans, to broaden the range of narrative study *and* add additional information to the discussion of sports fandom. Finally, this research added the practical standard to enhance our understanding of communicated identification motives.

Exploring the Motives
of Fantasy Sports
A Uses-and-Gratifications Approach

JOHN S. W. SPINDA AND PAUL M. HARIDAKIS

Fantasy sports, once a niche hobby conducted by calculating box scores from newspapers, has become a popular vicarious experience for sports fans worldwide. According to Rainie (2005), "Fantasy sports teams are created by fans who 'draft' individual professional athletes to be part of their team. The 'team' is an artificial assembly of players from a variety of real teams. The basic statistics of those players are then aggregated after each real world game to determine how well the team is doing. Fantasy leagues are organized either 'rotisserie' style, meaning team standings are based on cumulative player statistics over the entire season, or 'head-to-head,' meaning win loss records [sic] based on point totals in individual game-day match-ups" (p. 1). Although there are a plethora of fantasy sports options available for Internet users (e.g., fantasy NASCAR, fantasy baseball, fantasy basketball, fantasy hockey), fantasy football has emerged as the top fantasy sport, with usage estimates ranging from 10 million players (Rainie, 2005) to 15 million players (Sager, 2006) in the United States.

Esser (1994) suggested that the first organized fantasy sports league was formed in the early 1960s. This league used a scoring system to assign point values to individual players for an assortment of football-related statistics (e.g., touchdowns scored, yards gained, field goals kicked, etc.). Using a calculator, points were tallied after each week's games; the team with more accrued points won the weekly head-to-head matchup. At the end of the season, the team with the top record won the title. Eventually, this pastime was dubbed *fantasy football*, and a number of variations of the league emerged for other sports (e.g., baseball, basketball, hockey, auto racing, collegiate sports). In addition, a number of international sports have fantasy leagues, such as professional soccer leagues.

It is clear that the media, and the diffusion of home computers and the Internet, in particular, have given fantasy sports the fuel to become the phenomenon it is today. Not only does the Internet provide automated, instant calculation of statistics, it also provides a mediated forum for interaction over league bulletin boards. The Internet also supplies a wealth of information about individual player statistics and individual player news. Because of this, nearly all fantasy leagues have migrated to the Internet.

In this study, we explored online fantasy sports playing from a uses-and-gratifications (U&G) perspective. Specifically, we created an index of fantasy sports motives based on three studies. In the first study we used an open-ended essay question format to glean from respondents why they play fantasy sports. In the second study, we transformed motives identified from these essays into motive statements that could be measured with a Likert-type scale. We then combined these motive statements with communication motive items identified in previous U&G research (e.g., Rubin, 1981a; Rubin, Perse, & Barbato, 1988) and with motive statements adapted from sports motives scales (Trail & James, 2001; Wann, 1995). We pre-tested our resulting motive index among a group of college-aged fantasy sports players. In the final study, our pre-tested Fantasy Sports Motives Scale was administered to a large, diverse sample of online fantasy sports players.

In this chapter we outline our three-study method and explore how these fantasy sports motives relate to psychographic audience variables, such as audience activity (e.g., involvement, using Internet to track fantasy players) and aspects of creativity. Additionally, we discuss the implications of the Fantasy Sports Motives Scale as well as provide suggestions for future research pertaining to motivation for playing fantasy sports.

A Uses-and-Gratifications Approach

U&G has been described as being "concerned with the (1) social and psychological origins of (2) needs, which generate (3) expectations of (4) the mass media or other sources, which lead to (5) differential patterns of media exposure (or engagement in other activities), resulting in (6) need gratifications and (7) other consequences, perhaps mostly unintended ones" (Katz, Blumler, & Gurevitch, 1974, p. 20).

U&G research has focused extensively on motives people have for using media and other channels. For example, U&G studies have revealed motives associated with general television viewing (Greenberg, 1974; Rubin, 1981a) as well as for interpersonal communication (Rubin et al., 1988). However, the perspective begins with the premise that motives are influenced by one's social (e.g., demographics, context of media use) and psychological (e.g., personality) circumstances.

Individual Circumstances

As noted earlier, current estimates suggest that 10 to 15 million people play fantasy sports online (Rainie, 2005; Sager, 2006). Rainie (2005) found that fantasy sports participants generally were young (63 percent under 40 years of age), males (86 percent of participants), had significant Internet experience (76 percent had more than six years' experience online), and had relatively high incomes (12 percent made more than $75,000 per year, 5 percent made less than $30,000 a year). However, at this point, there is a lack of empirical research on fantasy sports to link such player background characteristics and motives for playing fantasy sports. Therefore, we asked:

RQ1a: *What is the relationship between demographic factors and motives for playing fantasy sports?*

RQ1b: *How are Internet usage and experience with fantasy sports related to fantasy sports motives?*

Fandom or Creativity?

In addition to player characteristics such as those referenced above, at this point it is not certain whether fantasy sports participants engage in fantasy sports primarily due to their liking of a particular sport(s) or because they desire to "make believe" they are real sports managers. Examining the trait-based creativity of players may be helpful in exploring this issue. Eysenck (1995) argued that creativity is a multi-dimensional concept that has at least five under-lying components: (1) creative engagement (e.g., enjoying and spending time on creative activities), (2) creative cognitive style (e.g., related to intelligence, divergent thinking, problem solving), (3) spontaneity (e.g., impulsive and excitement seeking), (4) tolerance (e.g., flexibility with openness to others' ideas), and (5) fantasy (e.g., daydreaming and imagination) (Kelly, 2006, p. 300). Kelly (2004) developed a measure of creative behaviors (SCAB; Scale of Creative Attributes) applying these five components of creativity. Because we are unsure whether creativity impacts motives for playing fantasy sports, we asked:

RQ2: *Is creativity related to fantasy sports motives?*

Examining the Motivated and Active Nature of Fantasy Sports

The inherent nature of fantasy sports would strongly suggest it reflects active, instrumental media use as opposed to passive, ritualistic media use (see Rubin, 1984, for a description of instrumental and ritualistic viewing orientations). Participants must actively select their "lineups" on a weekly or daily basis, depending on the fantasy sport and type of league involved. Many fantasy sports players also actively check the status of their chosen players because of injuries and potential matchups that may favor them.

When examining an active, goal-directed audience, communication scholars have often turned to U&G as a framework for exploring the motives for using various media such as television (e.g., Greenberg, 1974; Rubin, 1981b, 1984) and the Internet (Papacharissi & Rubin, 2000); particular media content such as violent programs (Haridakis, 2002) and sports (Trail & James, 2001; Wann, 1995); as well as motives for interpersonal communication (Rubin et al., 1988). However, because of a scarcity of empirical findings on motives specific to playing fantasy sports, we asked:

RQ3: *What motives are associated with playing fantasy sports?*

U&G research also has linked motives with audience activity. For example, more purposive instrumental motives have been linked to higher levels of viewer attention to (Rubin, 1984) and involvement with (Haridakis & Rubin, 2003) media. In the case of sports specifically, Wann (1995) found that motives for watching sports moderately to strongly correlated with a measure of sports involvement.

Fan Involvement and Motives for General Sports Viewing

Wann (1995) developed the Sport Fan Motivation Scale (SFMS) to measure general sports fan motivations. In all, he identified eight motives for sports fandom, including: (1) eustress (i.e., positive stress and arousal associated with sports), (2) self-esteem, (3) escape, (4) entertainment, (5) economic, (6) aesthetics, (7) group affiliation, and (8) family. As noted above, this study linked these motives to involvement. In addition, involvement is an aspect of audience activity that U&G researchers have consistently linked to media use gratifications (see Metzger & Flanagin, 2002; Rubin, 2002, for reviews), and because fantasy sports should generally involve high levels of sports fandom and media use, we propose that:

H1: Motivations for playing fantasy sports will predict involvement in fantasy sports.

Building on Wann's (1995) SFMS, Trail and James (2001) created the Motivation Scale for Sport Consumption (MSSC). These authors identified nine motives for being a sports fan. Five of these nine motives are similar in composition to those in the SFMS (aesthetics, escape, family, achievement/self-esteem, social/group affiliation), while four new motives emerge on the MSSC. These motives included: (1) knowledge (e.g., knowing records, statistics, box scores), (2) drama (e.g., enjoyment of a dramatic or close contest), (3) physical attraction (e.g., watching physically attractive athletes), and (4) physical skills (e.g., appreciation of the skills of athletes). Trail and James (2001) also found certain motives (e.g., achievement, escape, physical skill, social interaction) to be positively related to increases in consumption of media content concerning a favorite team. As noted earlier, media consumption concerning athletes and their playing status should be of importance to fantasy sports players. Therefore, we proposed that:

H2: Fantasy sports motives will predict increased fantasy sports information seeking behavior.

Measures

To help clarify how antecedent variables and Internet use variables may impact motives for playing fantasy sports, we collected data on age, daily Internet use (in hours), Internet experience (in years), number of years playing fantasy sports, and types of fantasy sports. We also examined audience activities related to fantasy sports.

Activity

We examined two activities related to fantasy football: reading status reports (e.g., injuries, increased/decreased playing time) related to fantasy sports players, and reading general items related to fantasy sports (e.g., expert advice, strategy). These two activities were measured with a six-item response scale that gauged frequency of use, ranging from "*at least a few times a day*" to "*rarely, if ever.*"

An adapted eight-item version of Zaichkowsky's (1985) Personal Involvement Inventory (PII) was used to measure involvement with fantasy sports (Shank & Beasley, 1998). This measure contains seven-point semantic differential scale items on which respondents rated feelings (expressed in adjectives) about fantasy sports. The PII demonstrated excellent reliability ($\alpha = .89$) in our study.

Creativity

We measured creativity with the 20-item Scale of Creative Attributes and Behavior (SCAB, Kelly, 2004). The SCAB examines the five components of creativity noted earlier in this paper (Kelly, 2006, p. 300). The entire SCAB measure was used in the second study, returning good reliability overall ($\alpha = .80$). However, only the creative cognitive style subscale returned significant, positive correlations to preliminary motive items. Thus, we employed only the creative cognitive style subscale (e.g., related to intelligence, divergent thinking, problem solving) for the final analysis, where it demonstrated sound reliability ($\alpha = .82$).

Study One: Preliminary Index Development of the Fantasy Sports Motives Scale

Following Greenberg's (1974) celebrated method of deriving motives for media use, in study one we asked students at a large, Midwestern university ($N = 50$) to write an open-ended essay stating why they play fantasy sports. These essays were then reviewed for stated motivations (e.g., "I play fantasy football because it gives me the opportunity to act as a coach") as well as latent motivations for playing fantasy sports (e.g., "Fantasy football is a wonderful way to stay connected to the game of football"). These motivations were then taken verbatim or slightly modified and added to the pool of items that measured the motivations for playing fantasy sports. In all, 36 items were garnered from the essays.

In addition, items from scales of sports fan motivation (MSSC, Trail & James, 2001, SFMS, Wann, 1995) were added to the item pool. A few relevant escapist items from past studies of media use (Television Viewing Motives Scale, Rubin, 1981a) were added to verify the instrumental nature of fantasy sports (e.g., "I play fantasy sports when I have nothing better to do"). Additionally, some interpersonal motive items (Interpersonal Motives Scale, Rubin et al., 1988) were added to examine the interpersonal/social dimensions that may exist in fantasy sports. In all, 29 items were added to our instrument from this existing literature.

Study Two: Fantasy Sports Motivation Index Pre-Testing

To pre-test our 65-item fantasy sports motives scale we again recruited college student participants. Students earned points toward a research practicum for their participation by either filling out the questionnaire, provided they played fantasy sports ($N = 42$), or by proctoring one or two questionnaires to people they knew who played fantasy sports ($N = 50$). In the latter procedure, questionnaires and instructions were given to student proctors, who had two weeks to return the questionnaire to receive practicum credit. As a validity check, participants had to fill out the name of the fantasy sports website they used most often to play fantasy sports. Respondents who failed to provide this information were discarded from the analysis. Our first two analyses focused on quantitatively identifying a wide range of potential motives for fantasy sports and pre-testing an extensive motives scale.

Study Three: Fantasy Sports Motives Scale

Our third study focused on further developing the fantasy sports motives scale by sampling a larger, more representative population of fantasy sports players with the more refined motives scale. We recruited participants ($N = 829$) from a variety of websites and message boards dedicated to fantasy sports by asking participants to complete our questionnaire online. Because a vast majority of fantasy sports leagues are conducted online, using the Internet to gather participants seemed not only tenable but appropriate for our analysis. Additionally, this method provided the opportunity to sample a diverse group of fantasy sports players with a plethora of fantasy sports interests. Participants were provided a link to an online questionnaire where they were provided with an informed consent form from the researchers. Similar to study two, respondents were asked to provide a fantasy sports website as a validity check to verify their involvement in fantasy sports.

Our survey respondents were generally similar to the profile of fantasy sports players presented by Rainie (2005). They were predominately young ($M = 28.23$, $SD = 5.83$), male (95 percent), with high Internet experience (50 percent reported more than 11 years of Internet experience, 93 percent reported more than eight years of experience), and high income (83 percent reported household income of more than \$40,000 annually, 41 percent reported household income between \$60,000 and \$120,000). In addition, 81 percent of respondents noted playing one to three fantasy sports ($M = 2.45$, $SD = 1.36$), with professional football (NFL) easily being the most popular fantasy sport (96 percent reported playing). Professional baseball (MLB) was a distant second in participation (61 percent reported playing), followed by professional basketball (NBA), which was a distant third (27 percent reported playing). On the average, respondents stated that they had played fantasy sports for approximately seven years ($M = 7.04$, $SD = 3.98$).

Results

Demographics, Internet Use, and Fantasy Sports Experience

The first research question (RQ1a) asked what relationships exist between demographic variables and motives for playing fantasy sports. RQ1b asked about the relationship between motives for playing fantasy sports and Internet use and between motives and fantasy sports experience. Our findings in study three indicated no noteworthy relationships between fantasy sports motives and our battery of demographic variables (e.g., age, gender, income, and ethnicity). Moreover, there were no significant relationships between Internet use factors (e.g., years using Internet, daily time online) and experience playing fantasy sports (e.g., years playing fantasy sports, current number of fantasy sports played) and fantasy sports motives.

Fantasy Sports Motives: Pre-testing

To answer the question of which motives are associated with playing fantasy sports (RQ3), we employed a two-step process that involved pre-testing our scale in study two, which informed our final motives scale that emerged in study three. To pre-test our fantasy sports motives scale ($N = 92$), we used principal components analysis with varimax rotation to determine how many factors arose from the fantasy sports motives scale items. A preliminary factor analysis indicated that 16 items had weak factor loadings and these were eliminated from the motives scale, leaving 49 items overall. After running a secondary factor analysis, a four-factor solution was achieved, explaining 52.74 percent of the post-rotation variance. Factor 1, *Ownership* (eigenvalue = 5.30), explained 18.27 percent of the overall post-rotation variance. It contained seven items that indicate fantasy sports participants enjoyed the control aspects afforded by fantasy sports, such as picking favorite players, or feeling like a coach/manager ($M = 3.70$, $SD = .96$, $\alpha = .91$). Factor 2, *Socialization* (eigenvalue = 3.66), explained 12.62 percent of the variance. This factor consisted of five items that reflected fantasy sports participants' enjoyment of negotiating trades or talking with others about sports ($M = 3.27$, $SD = 1.08$, $\alpha = .83$). Factor 3, *Exciting Achievement* (eigenvalue = 3.44), explained 11.87 percent of the variance and suggested that fantasy sports participants take a great deal of pride in their ability to pick winning teams and enjoy the excitement and bragging rights that go along with winning at fantasy sports ($M = 2.76$, $SD = .77$, $\alpha = .74$). Factor 4, *Escape* (eigenvalue = 2.893), explained 9.98 percent of the variance and indicated that fantasy sports are used by people to get away from their everyday lives ($M = 2.48$, $SD = 1.09$, $\alpha = .78$).

Fantasy Sports Motives: Study 3 Analyses

Employing the identical method from study two, principal components analysis with varimax rotation was used to determine how many factors arose from the motives scale items ($N = 829$). Results indicated a six-factor solution emerged from the 49-item pool (see Appendix A), explaining 47.69 percent of the total post-rotation variance.

Similar to study two, Factor 1 was *Ownership* (eigenvalue = 5.03), which explained 10.26 percent of the overall post-rotation variance. This motive contained six items that indicated fantasy sports participants enjoy the control aspects afforded by fantasy sports, such as feeling like a coach/manager, picking one's favorite players, and controlling the lineup, unlike actual sports teams ($M = 2.72$, $SD = .85$, $\alpha = .85$). Factor 2, *Achievement/Self-Esteem* (eigenvalue = 4.86), explained 9.91 percent of the variance. This factor consisted of four items that reflected fantasy sports participants' feelings of achievement, basking in victory, stimulation, and increased self-esteem from doing well in fantasy sports (M = 3.29, SD = .79, α = .77). Factor 3, *Escape/Pass time* (eigen-value = 4.55), explained 9.28 percent of the variance and indicated that fantasy sports are used by people to get away from their everyday hassles and troubles as well as to find a way to occupy their time (M = 2.33, SD = .86, α = .89). Factor 4, *Socialization* (eigenvalue = 3.93), explained 9.03 percent of the variance and consisted of items that imply fantasy sports are viewed as a way to socialize, spend time with friends, and enjoy the camaraderie of others (M = 3.39, SD = .80, α = .84). Factor 5, *Bragging Rights* (eigenvalue = 2.54), explained 5.18 percent of the variance and contained three items that relate to being able to boast about one's victory in fantasy sports and possessing either a monetary or symbolic token of that victory (M = 3.08, SD = .99, α = .65). Lastly, Factor 6, *Amusement* (eigenvalue = 2.44), explained 4.99 percent of the variance and indicated that respondents use fantasy sports to keep themselves amused because it's "good clean fun" and it's "something different to do" (M = 3.01, SD = 1.01, r = .59).

Hypothesis one predicted that fantasy sports motives would predict involvement with fantasy sports. This hypothesis was supported, R = .518, F (6, 817) = 49.92, p < .001. Four motives predicted involvement: achievement/self-esteem (β = .25, p < .001), ownership (β =.15, p < .001), bragging rights (β =.14, p < .001), as well as socialization (β = .12, p < .001).

Hypothesis two proposed that fantasy sports motives would predict fantasy sports information seeking behaviors (e.g., reading articles and checking status reports on fantasy sports and athletes). This hypothesis was supported. First, fantasy sports motives predicted reading articles related to fantasy sports, R = .364, F (6, 818) = 20.76, p < .001. Specifically, reading articles was predicted by three motives: achievement/self-esteem (β = .27, p < .001), bragging rights (β = .14, p < .001), and amusement (β = -.08, p = .023). In addition, fantasy sports motives also significantly predicted the frequency with which fantasy sports owners checked the status/statistics of their fantasy athletes, R = .312, F (6, 821) = 14.76, p < .001. This behavior was predicted by three motives: achievement/self-esteem (β = .23, p < .001), socialization (β = .08, p = .031), and amusement (β = -.08, p = .048).

Lastly, we posed a research question (RQ2) pertaining to the relationship among creativity and fantasy sports motives. The creative cognitive style subscale discussed earlier included four items that tap divergent thinking and problem solving skills. This subscale was the only subscale related to all four motives found in the second study. Therefore, in the third study, we employed this measure of creative cognitive style again to explore the relationship between creativity and fantasy sports motives. Surprisingly, none of the motives derived in our final analysis were positively related to the creative cognitive style subscale. Thus, based on these results, the relationship between creativity and fantasy sports motives remains unclear.

Discussion

The research presented in this chapter was designed to explore motives people have for playing fantasy sports and to develop a valid and reliable index to measure fantasy sports playing motives. We drew on motive items gleaned from prior research on media-use, interpersonal, and sports-viewing motivation. Prior U&G research has suggested that people have ritualistic (e.g., diversionary, habitual) and instrumental (e.g., utilitarian) orientations toward media and media content (Hawkins & Pingree, 1981; Rubin, 1981b, 1984). Our results suggest that fantasy sports participants also exhibit instrumental and ritualistic orientations.

Our early findings indicate that people play fantasy sports for various reasons such as the fun of vicariously owning a team, the excitement involved with achieving success in fantasy sports, socially interacting and competing with others, and as a diversion from everyday life. Our findings also indicate that involvement was predicted by more instrumental (utilitarian) motives.

Specifically, factor analysis of the motives index identified six specific motives for playing fantasy sports: ownership, achievement/self-esteem, escape/pass time, socialization, bragging rights, and amusement. The strongest motives for playing fantasy sports were socialization, achievement/self esteem, bragging rights and amusement. The relationship between these motives and player activity (e.g., involvement, seeking information related to fantasy sports) suggests that for this group of participants, participating in fantasy sports was a purposive, instrumental, and active media-use endeavor — as opposed to a passive or habitual pastime to consume time.

For example, ownership, bragging rights, and socialization motives positively predicted involvement with fantasy sports. Those who played fantasy sports looking for reasons such as the enjoyment of victory, feeling like a coach controlling lineups, and socializing and spending time with others, tended to be more involved with fantasy sports than were their counterparts. This is consistent with prior research that suggested that using media for such utilitarian reasons is more involving than more diversionary use such as using media to escape and pass time (e.g., Perse, 1990; Rubin & Perse, 1987b).

The instrumental and active media-use orientation of this sample of fantasy sports players also is reflected in links between motives and players' information-seeking behavior. Those who played fantasy sports for purposes of achievement/self-esteem and bragging rights motivation, but not for the more diversionary motive of amusement, tended to spend more time than their counterparts reading articles related to fantasy sports. Those who played fantasy sports for purposes of achievement/self-esteem and socialization, but not for amusement, tended to spend more time than their counterparts checking the status/statistics of their fantasy athletes.

More purposive use (e.g., ownership, socialization, bragging rights, achievement/self-esteem) predicted greater audience activity, whereas more diversionary use (e.g., playing for reasons of escape, passing the time, and amusement) either did not predict audience activity (in the case of escape and passing the time) or was a negative predictor of activity (in the case of amusement, negatively predicted activity). This supports prior research regarding the relationship between motives and audience activity (e.g., Perse, 1990; Rubin & Perse, 1987b), and therefore also provides some initial evidence for the construct validity of the motive index used in this study.

Prior U&G research suggests that one's background characteristics (e.g., psychological and social circumstances) influence motives for using media. Here, we assessed the influence of one particular characteristic, creative cognitive style, that we felt would be an important attribute in an activity that requires the construction of a fantasy team of players. We did not find the expected links between player motivation and this background characteristic. However, this finding does not suggest that player background is not important. Future research should be directed at identifying those psychological and social factors that may be most relevant to influencing motives for playing fantasy sports and predicting media-use attitudes and behaviors associated with fantasy sports. For example, fandom and the extent to which players identify with teams and/or particular athletes are two factors that should be explored. Scholars have noted that the experience of being a sports fan is not constant across people. In addition, individuals, including those who play fantasy sports, may vary in their levels of fandom, based on their level of emotional involvement and team identification (Wann & Branscombe, 1993; Wann & Pierce, 2003; Wann, Royalty, & Rochelle, 2002).

Conclusion

An intuitive, yet very preliminary, conclusion one can make looking at the motives and relationships would be that fantasy sports are quite similar to popular fantasy board games, where players can fulfill fantasies such as being real estate moguls and achieving phenomenal wealth. The highest loading motive items seemed to indicate that fantasy sports participants enjoyed pretending to be professional sports coaches, general managers, or owners. Another area of fantasy sports that deserves research attention is the quickly expanding world of spin-off fantasy games. One particular example of this is fantasy gossip leagues, where participants are given points based on the number of times their chosen celebrities appear in tabloid magazines. These leagues already have earned endorsement deals with large multi-national corporations (Sager, 2006). Our hope is that this preliminary investigation has revealed some latent variables that may help us explore the fascinating world of fantasy games participants.

Appendix A

Factor Analysis for Fantasy Sports Motives Scale:
Study Three (N = 829)

Fantasy sports motive factors
"I play fantasy sports..."

	Fantasy Sports Motive					
	1	*2*	*3*	*4*	*5*	*6*
Factor 1: Ownership						
So I can feel like the GM or owner of an actual sports team	.86					
So I can feel like the coach of a team	.80					
Because its like having a pro team at my hands	.77					
Because I love the feeling of ownership	.75					
Because I control the lineup, unlike actual sports teams	.65					
So I can manage players like a business-person manages assets	.63					
Factor 2: Achievement/Self-Esteem						
Because I feel a personal sense of achievement when my fantasy team does well		.78				
Because I feel like I have won when my fantasy team wins		.67				
Because I like the stimulation I get from playing fantasy sports		.62				
Because winning at fantasy games improves my self-esteem		.61				
Factor 3: Escape/Pass time						
Because it takes me away from life's hassles			.82			
Because it helps me get away from life's troubles			.82			
So I can forget about school or other things			.79			
Because it passes the time away, particularly when I am bored			.76			
Because it gives me something to do to occupy my time			.71			
Because it's something to do			.67			
Factor 4: Socialization						
So I can spend time with friends who are playing				.81		
Because I enjoy the camaraderie of playing with other people				.79		
Because it helps me keep in touch with people I care about or like				.78		
Because I like to socialize				.71		

Fantasy sports motive factors
"I play fantasy sports..."

	Fantasy Sports Motive					
	1	2	3	4	5	6
Because I enjoy social events, like drafting fantasy teams live				.61		
Because most of my friends are sports fans				.59		
Factor 5: Bragging Rights						
Because I love to "trash talk" and tell other owners how much better my team is					.65	
Because playing for money or a reward only adds to the excitement of fantasy sports					.63	
Because winning my fantasy league will give me bragging rights all year long					.59	
Factor 6: Amusement						
Because it's good clean fun						.73
Because it's something different to do						.72

FAN-PRODUCED CONTENT

"Let the Domination Begin"

Sports Fans' Construction of Identity in Online Message Boards

KELLY A. BERG AND ALLISON HARTHCOCK

As new media technologies become more commonplace, the ability of fans to interact with other fans has increased dramatically in recent years (Baym, 2007; Ford, 2006). The proliferation of opportunities to engage in sports fandom online ranges from fantasy sports and gambling to merchandising and message boards. Yet, online fandom has been relatively neglected as a subject of study (End, 2001; End, Eaton, Campbell, Kretschmar, Mueller, & Dietz-Uhler, 2003). Understanding sports fandom has primarily focused on fandom in offline settings (Gantz, Wang, Paul, & Potter, 2006; Gantz & Wenner, 1995; Hirt, Zillman, Erickson, & Kennedy, 1992; Wann, 1994; Wann & Branscombe, 1990a, 1991; Wann, Melnick, Russell, & Pease, 2001).

Multiple studies have demonstrated sports fandom's impact on several areas of fans' lives. The effects of fandom can range from behavioral to psychological. Behaviorally, fans can react by becoming verbally aggressive toward another team or even other fans. It is not unusual to see a fan "blast" the opposition in an attempt to make others perceive a favorite team in a positive light (Cialdini & Richardson, 1980; End, 2001). In the mind of the fan, derogating the competition will bring a positive perception of the favorite team, and, perhaps, oneself.

The emotional and psychological impacts of fandom are strongly related to the level of identification a fan feels with a particular team (Wann, Friedman, McHale, & Jaffe 2003; Wann, Inman, Ensor, Gates, & Caldwell, 1999). One study found the "positive affective reactions to successful team performance were, in most cases, as intense as the negative emotional reactions to poor performances" (Wann et al., 2003, p. 934). The ups and downs can affect some fans' self esteem.

For these fans, team identification is used to construct a particular social identity directly tied to the performance of their team. A fan's identity is positively impacted as a favored team wins and negatively impacted as that team loses, creating a threat to the fan's social identity (End, 2001, 2002; Raney, 2006). Hirt et al. (1992) found that fans' own beliefs about their future performance and competencies are impacted by a favorite team's win or loss. They also found that mood and self-esteem are positively related to a team's success.

The link between psychological and emotional health and the strength of identification to a particular team leads some fans to utilize strategies that will help them maintain a balance despite losses. Fans will bask in the reflected glory (BIRG) of their team's wins and cut off reflected failure (CORF) to distance themselves from a loss (Wann & Branscombe, 1990a). Basking in reflected glory includes behaviors such as wearing team paraphernalia or using terms such as "we" when discussing the team. Cutting off reflected failure includes behavior such as using terms such as "they" when discussing the team. Highly identified fans have a more difficult time engaging in CORF behavior than fans with a lower level of identification (Branscombe & Wann, 1991; End, 2001, 2002).

Fandom Online

Most professional and college sports teams have Web sites with message boards dedicated to all things team-oriented. In the case of many sporting events, particularly the NCAA Men's Basketball Tournament, fans often are unable to attend all or any of the games due to timing, location, and money. Yet fans are able to find an outlet for their energies by turning to online sources of information and interaction, such as message boards.

Non–school-affiliated discussion boards, such as Rivals.com, ESPN.com, or CSTV.com, are frequented by fans. These non–school-affiliated discussion boards open a unique arena for fans to express themselves and support their school in a manner that is different from message boards associated with a specific school or team. For example, fans on a team- or school-affiliated message board can assume that most others on the board also are fans, which creates a particular climate on the board. However, when the message board is unaffiliated with a specific team, fans cannot make that assumption and, presumably, must take extra steps to support their team or assert an identity. How fan identity is created and maintained in an online environment is unclear.

Though research in online fandom is still growing, some researchers have established support for previous findings and identified new areas for inquiry. End (2001) found that sports fans who use message boards are likely to engage in several self-presentational behaviors, such as blasting and basking in reflected glory. However, End did not examine the ways in which self-presentation is constructed or contributes to the culture of the community. Additionally, the features of the technology — among them anonymity and the lack of face-to-face cues—are likely to alter fan identification. Message boards are relatively anonymous, so fans may worry less about self-presentation after a team loss than fans engaged in face-to-face discussions (End, 2003). The lack of visual and nonverbal cues also may affect the approach taken to maintain or build fan identity and the level of aggression displayed.

This chapter expands on the research that currently exists on sports fandom, utilizing an approach not commonly used in sports fan research. The study is a qualitative analysis of strategies for constructing individual and collective identity among fans communicating via an online message board. Research using direct observation of fans' interactions in message boards adds a key component to understanding the role of message boards in helping individuals not only display their identification with a team but construct and negotiate identity around major sporting events. Examining online sports fandom in this way can provide a more well-rounded understanding of sports fandom and its expression by illuminating new areas for understanding and for studying both online and offline fandom. Additionally, examining sports fans' online interactions offers what much research of sports fan behavior has not offered: fans' behavior in context.

March Madness Fandom

With its status as the second most bet-upon sporting event in the United States behind only the Super Bowl (McCarthy, 2007), the NCAA Men's Basketball Tournament, March Madness, generates much fan interest. Traffic to sports-related Web sites traditionally sky-rockets during the tournament period (Nielsen, 2001, 2004, 2006). On the first day of March Madness in 2006,[1] traffic to NCAA–related Web sites increased "21 percent to 9.7 million unique visitors" (Nielsen, 2006). CBS Sportsonline.com was at the top in visitors and growth, in large part because it began streaming games live on its site (Nielsen, 2006).

CSTV.com (the college sports Web site of CBS—the network that airs the men's tournament) hosts a message board that serves as the community for this study of the 2007 NCAA Men's Basketball Tournament. In addition to ties with CBS, more than 200 collegiate athletic programs have given management of their Web sites to CSTV.com (CSTV.com, 2007). CSTV.com provides a link to "Community" that includes blogs, message boards, and the ability for fans to post video. The message boards serve as a reasonable and easily accessible touchstone for March Madness fans. On the message boards, participants can choose from a variety of college sports to discuss. Each sport has its own forum. Once in a given forum, fans can read and observe or participate in the discussion if they are registered members.

To examine fandom while still in its formative years online, this study examines the "Men's Basketball" forum on the CSTV.com message board, looking at all the posts (messages) in each thread (new topic) from Selection Sunday evening, March 10, 2007, through the day after the championship game, Tuesday, April 3, 2007. This forum allows examination of fandom during a sporting event that garners intense attention by fans. This study focuses on the methods participants used in the message boards to express individual fan identification and a social identity as part of the community of fans.

Fan Identification

When fandom moves online, traditional methods for constructing and expressing identity may be unworkable. Fans must find new ways to express their identity by selecting what aspects of the "self" to use in constructing an online fan identity. In the Men's Basketball forum on CSTV.com, the characteristics presented often related to a particular team. Thus, fans were able to "claim" aspects of their team to create a first impression, similar to taking steps in face-to-face interaction to portray a preferred identity to others. The technology of the message board created alternative opportunities for fans to express identity through screen names, avatars, and signature lines.

Screen Names

The screen names participants used when they joined the CSTV.com community represented the persona, or identity, by which each person wished to be recognized. Screen names in this community typically corresponded with a particular school's team name, team nickname, or team slogan. The screen names on the message board occasionally expressed an individual's personality outside of sports, but that was the exception.

The screen names were unique in that no one else was allowed to sign onto the site with the same name. As a result, participants had to be creative in selecting a name that expressed their identity as a fan. Examples of screen names associated with the team's name included: AlaCyclone and IllinoisGator. These participants expressed both a geographical association and an association with a particular team. The first, AlaCyclone, presented a "self" linked to the Iowa State Cyclones, yet noted a current location of Alabama. The second, IllinoisGator, indicated loyalty to the Florida Gators even while geographically distant. These names demonstrate Crawford's (2004) point that sports fandom communities are not relegated to geographically limited regions. The use of screen names that express regionality along with team loyalty allows geographically distant fans to express identity as an individual and invite community around their team or geographical location.

In addition to reflecting individual identity, screen names help reinforce a collective identity that characterizes the culture of the boards. Participants could interact in various areas of the message boards and forums besides the

Men's Basketball section, such as the general discussion and football forums.[2] A key aspect of the culture is the expression of fandom of sport, in general, and of a team, in particular. Choosing a team- or school-related nickname could signal allegiance with other members of the message boards through recognition of similarities in team loyalties or region.

Other screen names allowed fans to reinforce team identification and social identity through boasting and blasting. WolfPackisBack and GoDuke03 boasted, while screen names such as FuofM or I'msogladIwenttotheUofM served the purpose of blasting or expressing rivalries. By virtue of their screen names, fans could continue to express their fan identity consistently without the extra effort of doing so within a message. The name stood as a continual reference point for other participants.

Avatars

Avatars immediately proclaim, as wearing team apparel might, which team a fan supports. An avatar is an image — graphic, photo, or illustration — that the participant can upload as an attachment to his/her user profile. That avatar is attached to each message the participant posts, appearing on the left side of the message under the participant's screen name. It substitutes for the physical presence of the fan.

CSTV.com members had the freedom of choosing an avatar from their own digital files. They could make any number of creative choices for an avatar, such as photos of themselves or other fans, other photo or graphic images, sports memorabilia images, and an almost infinite number of non–sports-related images. However, the range of avatars displayed was quite narrow and, in all but two instances, fans adhered to a consistent image rather than switching avatars. Three categories of avatars were dominant on the forum: school-related logos, images for other aspects of the school, and non–sports-related avatars.[3]

One common option for an avatar was the standard image/logo for the team. A team's mascot was one of the most commonly used team-associated images. Another common image was a school's "flag." Because more than one participant supported the same team, using the same mascot or flag image limited one's ability to express individuality as a sports fan but still showed the fan's bond to that team.[4] With so many fans using this type of avatar, a collective fan identity was evident instead.

Some members displayed an avatar for a particular player or players, both for basketball and for other college sports. For example, one fan exhibited a UCLA football player in action. A Notre Dame football fan displayed an image of Notre Dame football legends riding horses, with the caption: "Nowhere but where Legends Live Forever Notre Dame." A Tennessee fan used an image of Tennessee basketball player Chris Lofton shouting on the court. Research on fans' offline associations has found that identification with player characteristics is one cause of team-related identification (Wann, 2006b). The choice of these avatars on the message boards expressed fan identification in a more specific and distinguishing manner than flags or mascots.

Others tried to be creative and produce an avatar/image that showed a rivalry between teams. One avatar displayed the logos of both Ohio State and the University of Michigan with a "greater than" math sign between them and the words "simple math" underneath the logos. An Ohio fan's avatar displayed the image of a Michigan football helmet with a circle surrounding it and a line crossing it out. Like verbal chants or holding up a sign at a game blasting another team or team's fans, fans engaged in a heated rivalry such as the one between Ohio State and Michigan could use avatars to blast their rivals each time they posted, even without using words to do so.

Signature Lines

Another feature of the message boards that allowed fans to construct an identity was the common practice of attaching a "signature line" to a posting. Although it would be difficult and awkward for fans to insert a "quote" or saying each time they spoke to someone, fans could insert one or more of these at the end of each of their messages on the message board. A signature line was not required, but members often used the signature line function of the boards to express a connection to a team. The signature lines on the message board during March Madness fell into four categories: team identification, team success/status, rivalry, and non–sports-related quotes or sayings.

Team identification–related signature lines expressed strength of fandom and loyalty. Examples included:

Eat, Sleep, Ohio State
Eating and Sleeping optional[5]

and

I bleed ORANGE and BLUE!!!
National Champions '96, '06 The Gator Nation

Such signature lines allowed the fan to express loyalty and to demonstrate the *extent* of their fandom through zeal or knowledge.

Team status/success signature lines can be one way for a participant to bask in the reflected glory (BIRG) of the favored team. For example, the following signature line: "2006 NCAA BASEBALL NATIONAL CHAMPS!!" allowed the participant to savor a school victory, thereby providing the participant with the glory of a school's wins in another sport to enhance his or her identity, even if the school's basketball team failed to bring home a title.

It also is possible to express rivalry through a signature line, such as "P.S. Carolina Sucks" or "If only the Huskies could play the Cougars every weekend." The signature lines gave some fans an opportunity to express their loyalty by playfully disparaging others and repeatedly blasting a hated or primary rival for the favored team. Like rivalry-related avatars and screen names, these signature lines gave some fans the opportunity to reiterate their team support or dislike for rivals each time they posted, no matter what the content of a particular message was.

Other fans used signature lines to express an aspect of their personality beyond their fandom. For example, participants could express their political identity by using a quotation from the president of the United States. One participant celebrated the birth of his nephew by announcing his birth and welcoming him to the world. Much like using avatars that are unrelated to sports, using signature lines that are about content other than sports provided other participants with a broader framework in which to understand a participant in the community. In this way, participants also contributed to the community of fans by bypassing team identification in favor of other methods of bonding over more than sports topics.

Fandom Community

The culture of fandom in this particular community was established through the strategies participants used in designing the messages they posted to the boards. Fans not only expressed their identity but also worked to construct a common social or community identity as fans of college basketball and college sports. Rather than focusing only on a particular team when discussing a particular event such as the March Madness tournament, participants created an opportunity for fans to form identity that extended beyond team or player identification. Strategies evident on the message boards included adhering to a particular "fan type," using bandwagon appeals, asserting one's own authority, aggression, and using softeners.

Fan Type

On this particular message board, participants encouraged one another to be fans of the sport itself, not simply fans of a particular team. Failing to contribute to interactions in a way that adhered to a broader sports fan identity could have resulted in dismissal of that fan's contributions by other participants. Those fans who were team- rather than college sports–oriented were labeled "homers." Homers are fans whose analysis appeared to glorify a favorite team while failing to address events in an unbiased manner.

Blah-blah-blah.

Most folks would root for Al Queda State vs Duke so your comment really means squat.

Homer you are, plain and simple [sic].

In this example, the fan dismissed the interpretation of another participant due to the perceived demonstration of team loyalty over "objective" analysis of the game. Although each participant may have worked to construct an
individual fan identity, the board culture ultimately preferred an atmosphere
about fandom of college sports, rather than a team- or school-based identity.

Bandwagon Appeals

To assert their views as the prevailing understanding of events, fans called
on others on the board to support their interpretations:

Thread — Am I the only one?

Message — who thinks Oden and Noah are COMPLETELY overrated?

This thread was a negotiation about how to determine whether a player deserved
the mantle of "good" or whether he was overrated. In asking this question rather
than simply offering an interpretation, the poster used a bandwagon appeal to
get others to agree. The bandwagon appeal is a persuasive strategy in which
users attempted to convince others that everyone else on the board believed or
was acting in a particular way and that they should have felt or done the same.
In trying to get others to agree, the fan worked to establish the dominant interpretation to bolster his/her identity. Additionally, by posting a leading question, the fan assumed that others *would* agree. The bandwagon approach could
then be used to bring together other forum members as a community.

Another bandwagon appeal included linking one's analysis to another participant or outside "expert." Fans could demonstrate their own expertise by
providing reinforcement for their interpretation. By connecting their analyses
to another member of the message board, participants acknowledged the respect
due to particular members of the boards and assured that they were afforded
credibility and respect as well. In this way, the community acknowledged that
particular members were valued highly. By relying on the collective identity and
knowledge of its members of status, fans built their own identity and status
within this community of fans.

Fans also provided links to outside sites or articles that supported their
own status as "experts." When fans provided links to those who agreed with
them, they not only gave an interpretation, but they also provided their own
bandwagon by demonstrating that there were those who already agreed with
them and that, therefore, others should, too. Additionally, they could reiterate
the opinion of another media analyst in the process of providing their own
interpretation to strengthen the bandwagon appeal. This was seen as acceptable, as long as it was acknowledged that this was not the poster's original idea.
In one thread, a participant posted a comment, to which another fan responded,
"I knew someone would regurgitate Seth Davis in this thread...." By indicating that another member's analysis reflected the opinions of *Sports Illustrated*

author Seth Davis, the fan derided the original fan for not providing an original, but informed, analysis. Additionally, by posting this statement, this fan enhanced his/her own credibility by demonstrating knowledge of outside analyses.

Asserting One's Own Authority

Fans tried to bolster their own identity by demonstrating their authority. They asserted authority through pools or brackets, claiming experience as a fan or citing their geographic location as providing weight to a contribution. Participants also tried to elevate their authority simply by "claiming" knowledge, such as "knowing all along" what an outcome would be.

> I said it all along, Ohio State is the #1 team and I believe they will win the national championship.

The features of the technology could help a participant avoid questions about such claims as "I said it all along," providing the fan with a feeling of automatic authority.

Fans frequently discussed their bracket picks and bracket standings, referencing both the shared bracket set up on Yahoo by one participant and their other brackets both offline and online. While brackets could be serious business for participants, bantering about pools and brackets was also a playful bonding strategy on the CSTV.com message boards that contributed to creation of a feeling of collective identity. They poked fun at themselves for their poor picks, consoled one another, and used bracket discussion as an opportunity to show off and to play. In a thread titled "Has anybody signed us up for a, Pool" [*sic*] this banter could easily be seen.

> Not yet. I always wait until the brackets come out. We should get a game together with board people so I can prove my superiority.

> ——
> All those in favour of ** being the official pool setter-upper for March Madness, signify by saying "EH?"

> ——
> (These are followed by a half dozen "eh"s and "yea"s.)

> ——
> I like to wait until the last minute to make my final decisions as I am a stat wh0re who does research. Oh, and "eh"

> ——
> Oh snap I'm in. It's ON!!!! x(

> ——
> You're gonna lose. :D

> ——
> Reported for lying.

The online pools and brackets could have been a way for fans to "prove" who was superior in analyzing basketball teams. In one thread, titled "I would like to thank all you little people., Can't be caught" [*sic*], a participant flaunted his/her knowledge in a "performance" for other participants.

> As of tonight I can not be caught in the yahoo tourney pick'em. so I want to thank you all for allowing me to whoop up on ya!
>
> Who's yer basketball daddy?!! :D

When they were unsuccessful, participants could fall back on superiority of reasoning, statistical support, or historical knowledge of teams to aid them in asserting their authority.

Claiming to be a long-time fan through thick or thin or having historical knowledge of games and players was a common strategy for asserting one's authority.

> I remember watching the couches burn in Dayton when Negele Knight and co. knocked off the 35 Illini in round 1 back in 1990.

Though fans did not necessarily need to have been physically present with teams of years gone by, having knowledge of a team's past wins and losses could be used in the same way.

> No, you didn't choke in 2005. You just had the refs turn a blind eye to your thuggery on defense vs Arizona during the final 5:00 regulation and in OT of the regional final. That was the sorriest officiating job in the history of the NCAA Tournament. The second worst was the 2nd half of the national championship game vs. Carolina, when they turned a blind eye to all of those illegal moving screens you were setting....

Dedication to a team over many years could also elevate one's status.

> It's like you Hokie fans come from 11 years of hibernation and suddenly we see like 5 of you in a matter of 2 days lmao. Probably just started liking the team 3 weeks ago.
>
> ———
>
> Yes, Hokie fans are excited to see our team back in the NCAA's after many years of basketball mediocrity. Live with it! Check profiles before you start spouting off. There are several of us Hokie fans who have been posting on the football boards for many years — some since it was Fansonly. Personally, I'm a 1985 graduate.

One fan criticized fans of another team, laughing at the seemingly sudden appearance on the message boards of fans of that team and disparaging them for being brand new followers rather than true fans. The respondent tried to regain authority by using experience as a long-time fan, pointing to active participation in other message boards and suggesting the complainant was not savvy enough to check profile pages before making judgments of community members. Though they argued, both agreed that experience as a fan was significant and each tried to assert their own experience as superior to the other's experience.

Simply living near the location of a team under discussion could provide someone with an automatic authority as being more likely to be "in the know."

It's kind of known around these parts that Knight won't build a new basketball arena as long as Ernie is the coach or Moos was the AD. Moos is gone now and Knight installed a close friend. They've refused to give rnie a new AD is pretty good friends with Few. Few also grew up here. Ernie Kents personality isn't (sic) the best either, lol. Ernie is making it touch on them to pull the trigger on the firing by going so deep into the tournament. The next few days should tell the story, I would imagine.

Through geographic proximity to a team, fans suggested they had "insider knowledge" about a team that only those in the area could know. The assumption was that their interpretations carried more authority, bolstering their identity by raising their status within the community.

Aggression

Aggression can be a strategy for protecting one's sense of self, much like blasting or basking in reflected glory. Although aggressive behavior is, in part, an outcome of the technological features of the communication medium, studies of offline fan behavior (Wann et al., 2001) suggested that aggression and insults also are a method of asserting dominance over other sports fans. Online, this could come in the form of complaining about someone's lack of knowledge of the English language and name calling, a common complaint in other fan message boards, as well (Berg, 2002). For example, in response to a fan's post in which poor grammar and all capital letters prevailed, another fan offered a particularly vehement insult.

1) turn off the caps lock, you look like a jagbag. 2) study grammar, 3) build a time machine and go back in time. Tell your mom to swallow the load.

The original poster tried to use an aggressive approach, with one sentence of his/her message in all capital letters, to assert his/her dominance. His/her response to the insult was to use aggression in return:

JEALOUSLY SAYS A LOT HUH CYCLONE FAN?
OH AND I'LL KEEP MY CAPS TO ANNOY YOU.

Using all capital letters serves as the equivalent of yelling offline. In this example, the aggressive exchanges continued and triggered aggression among other participants. Others jumped into the fray to say their piece, which often involved repeated name calling, scarcely hidden expletives, and insulting others' grammatical skills. Though aggressive interactions with other fans do happen offline, the technology may make this a more prevalent area for insult because of the lack of other information about an individual, one's own anonymity, and the importance placed on the written word in message boards (Alonzo & Aiken, 2004).

The use of name-calling on the message boards was intended to put others "in their place." Making fun of the favorite team's players by correlating them to women ("Congrats, ladies. :D") and reinventing the team's nickname into a slur (for example, "tarholes" instead of Tarheels and "pukies" for Duke fans or players) was common. Such behavior diminished other fans' contributions without even addressing the interpretation or information they offered. By teasing and harassing other fans, a feeling of individual fan identity was strengthened.

Softeners

To maintain a sense of community, participants frequently would "soften" their messages. Participants on the CSTV.com message boards had to adjust their form of expression to accommodate the lack of vocal and visual cues on the forum and avoid the potential for misconstruing one's message as aggressive or to ameliorate aggressive verbiage. The use of softening strategies allowed bonding as a collective to occur despite the lack of nonverbal and visual cues traditionally relied on in offline interaction.

Softening commonly manifested itself through use of humor or playful banter. In the following instance, a participant jokingly insulted the team coach of another fan, then added:

> ... just busting your chops. I don't like Duke, but I respect your posts. I agree that they simply are not as good as they usually are. However, they are still as good as most teams.

In this case, in addition to humor, acknowledging respect for another participant's involvement on the message boards provided a blanket softener for future posts that might be aggressive or insulting regarding that participant's team or posts, inviting development of a sense of community, or communal identity, on the board.

Fans would qualify their analyses to encourage others to be open to the ideas presented in a message. Qualification often occurred through the use of acronyms such as "IMHO" (in my humble opinion) or "JMHO" (just my humble opinion). Admitting one's "homer" status up front also mitigated likely criticism of a point. In qualifying their posts, participants could avoid potential hostile reactions at seeming too confident. Qualifying allowed a comfortable "out" for participants if their interpretations were less authoritative than another fan's. For newer participants or fans with less respect on the boards, such a move could open the pathway to becoming a "member" of the community.

The use of emoticons, or "smileys," was one method of showing members' tone or attitude and softening the content of a message in the absence of vocal and facial cues. The use of these emoticons softened the interpretation while allowing the participant to express context-based mood. This provided other members of the community with a framework for interpreting the intent of the statement. In doing so, emoticons contributed to the construction of the community.

Discussion

Exploring the interactions on the CSTV.com site provides more detailed support of fan identification behaviors recognized in previous studies. Expressions of fan identity manifest themselves online just as they do offline (Wann et al., 2003), albeit in a different manner. As offline fans do, online fans engaged in behaviors such as blasting and basking in reflected glory (Cialdini & Richardson, 1980; End, 2001; Wann & Branscombe, 1990a). Online, blasting and basking in reflected glory were evident in the screen names chosen. Choosing one's own team-related nickname likely would be viewed negatively offline, but it is a requirement of participation in an online community. Fans exploit that function of the technology to creatively express identification.

New findings also are evident. Creative use of the technology's features helped participants negotiate both individual and collective fan identities. A common bond drew fans to the site: a love of college men's basketball. However, their bond was limited, at times, by their identification as fans of one or more particular teams. It may have been limited further by differing interpretations of important aspects of the sport or of fandom itself. While many fans displayed loyalty to a team, this particular forum developed a community that was not only about individual fandom, but also about sports fandom and enthusiasm for college men's basketball in particular. This displayed itself in the alternation between team and sports fandom identification depending, in part, on whether favorite team(s) were doing well. This led to some difficult interactions and mixed expressions, such as "homer" being both a point of pride and criticism.

The negotiation of individual and collective identity was displayed in a variety of ways. Through screen names and avatars, fans expressed individual identity by identification with a team or school. Yet choosing a screen name that mirrored the team/school identification choices that others on the forum made could signal to other participants a broader fan identity related to college sports.

The connection that participants felt to the images associated with their online identity was evident in the consistent use of avatars on the boards. Though avatars generally remained the same for most participants throughout the data collection period, a few changes did occur. Because of a lost bet to another participant, one fan switched his/her avatar so that it displayed the flag of Kansas State. When a participant did change an avatar, others commented on or questioned the change, which reflected the normative behavior on the board of staying with one avatar.

Other strategies not previously noted in research for creation of both an individual and a collective fan identity include using bandwagon appeals, asserting one's own authority, aggression, and softeners. Bandwagon appeals implied that others in the community felt similarly and challenged additional participants to join in on the agreement. When the bandwagon approach was used to elevate one's own status as a fan, though, it could be said to reinforce an individual identity, as well.

Similar to the bandwagon appeal, asserting one's own authority also reinforced individual identity and elevated one's status in the community. When fans engaged in self-promotion based on pools or brackets, experience, and locale, they contributed to the construction of their fan identity through a form of bragging, which demonstrated authority as part of their social identity. This also had the potential to elevate a fan's status within the community. By boasting about their authority, fans attempted to enhance their credibility with other members of the community.

Although it was noted in prior research that aggressive behaviors are part of sports fandom, the findings in this study also revealed an element of aggression among fans that focused on the technological aspects of the interaction. Critiques on grammar, spelling, and punctuation in online communities are common. In the Men's Basketball forum, these critiques were used to protect one's own identity and bolster it in front of other members of the forum. In this instance, aggression was intended for individual identity-building.

Aggression also could be part of the playful or not-so-playful banter on the boards. Name-calling, both friendly and unfriendly, was a common occurrence. When used in a playful manner, this type of aggression was also seen as part of the collective identity that was constructed by these fans. Although some of the aggressive behavior detracted from the collective identity, the playfulness on the boards could contribute to bonding among participants.

While sports fans condoned and expected the "use of aggression in sporting contexts" (Wellard, 2002, p. 239), on the CSTV.com site, the sense of anonymity afforded by the technology affected the atmosphere of the interaction. On the CSTV.com message boards, fans interacted in an environment that allowed them to remain anonymous, which differed from face-to-face interactions. Thompsen (1993) found that people who communicate online often are more hostile and less civil in their computer-mediated interactions. Thompsen asserted that this hostility is directly linked to the anonymity and lack of nonverbal cues. Anonymity can create a sense of distance from other participants. This distance also reduced one's sense of responsibility to others, leading to fewer inhibitions on emotions or actions and freeing participants to experiment with their responses. Yet the lack of cues also can lead to misinterpretation, which can lead to hostile behavior that is not necessarily motivated by lack of ties to others.

As one way of reducing aggression and enhancing the sense of collective identity and community, participants frequently used softeners. These words and visual representations of emotions helped keep the atmosphere on the forum more civil. The atmosphere is a significant contributor to the ability of any group to cohere and establish communal goals and identity.

This study was an examination of the ways in which fans created and displayed individual and collective fan identity. Because the tournament spanned several weeks and viewers often watched teams of which they were not fans, the interactions that occurred on this site and at this time may differ from expressions of identity that occur at other times for sports fans online. Further, this study focused on the messages as they were presented. Areas of future research might include interviews to explore how fans make sense of their online fandom and the identities they have developed.

Notes

1. The last date for which Nielsen figures were publicly available.

2. Despite the fact that it occurred on other message boards and that the technology allows it, there was no evidence that participants were operating under more than one screen name during the time of this study. There is evidence, however, that this sort of activity did occur on the CSTV.com boards at other times, as participants in "The Sideline" section of the boards have conversed in at least one thread about a participant who has attempted to interact with other members under more than one name to hide his/her identity.

3. Non–sports-related avatars did not occur often on the board and encompassed a wide range of images. Because the appearance of these avatars was less frequent, they did not appear to contribute significantly to the collective identity.

4. It would be a mistake to assume that all team-related avatars represented a participant's team preference. In one discussion, for example, a participant was asked by another fan why his/her avatar appeared to be unrelated to the team he textually proclaimed to favor. He responded that the avatar was a nod to a relative who loved the team and to his/her own childhood association with the team.

5. Screen names are intended to personify some aspect of a participant and assist in creating the culture and atmosphere of a community while protecting the offline identity of communicators. Though the participants on CSTV.com participated in a public venue, some were minors and others may have been unaware that their words could be traced to a particular person through all of their online interactions, particularly since some included their offline names in their screen names or profiles. Therefore, representation of messages in this chapter avoids attribution to particular posters in order to provide a layer of protection for the identity of the fans.

Additionally, messages included are presented as closely as possible to their on-screen presentation. Grammar, spelling, and punctuation "errors" made by participants in their messages remain in the examples used in this chapter to help preserve and more accurately represent the culture created on the message board. However, messages are single-spaced for space reasons. When multiple messages in a thread are included, some messages are missing both for space reasons and to focus on the key point being made. Lines (_____) are included to demonstrate the transition to another participant's message.

"It's (Not) in the Game"

The Quest for Quantitative Realism and the Madden Football *Fan*

ANDREW BAERG

Introduction

"It's in the game!" So proclaim the athletes at the end of advertisements promoting various digital sports games published by industry juggernaut Electronic Arts (EA). EA's corporate slogan betrays a game design philosophy centered on an accurate simulation of sport. In doing so, the company aims to place sports fans within the sports they so passionately follow by allowing them to take control of their favorite teams and players.

One of EA's most popular franchises is the *Madden Football* series. The game's annual release date has come to be marked with anticipation by its considerably large fan base. In this chapter, I identify and explicate one of the ways in which a specific group of these fans understood their engagement with the digital sports game. A qualitative textual analysis of message board discourses surrounding the release week of *Madden Football 2006* (2005) revealed two recurring and interrelated themes. First, users expressed a concern for the quantitative realism of their experience. Second, users deployed discourses and practices associated with scientific experimentation and community labor to solve the realism problem they perceived as endemic to the game. This scientifically informed pursuit of quantitatively realistic digital football implicitly gendered the community's activity within traditionally masculine discursive frames.

Literature Review

In performing this study, I begin to take up Leonard's (2006) call for scholars to address the digital sports game more seriously. He argued that "the field of sports game studies represents a barren wasteland of knowledge. As of yet, there has been little work examining the centrality of race or gender, representation of sport, notions of realism or the related competitions" (p. 393). The study reported here sought to discern the most salient aspects of this fan group's experience with *Madden*. In this data set, concerns about the game's realism appeared prominent, suggesting that one dimension of Leonard's call for scholarly interest also interests *Madden*'s fans. By focusing on how this group of *Madden Football* fans engaged the game's realism and how these fans attempted to achieve it, this chapter explores relatively uncharted territory.

The question of perceived realism in media and its potential effects on audiences has occupied scholars for the better part of three decades. Television effects researchers have been particularly interested in perceived realism. The many studies concerning the subject include work focusing on realism and children's perception of television programs (e.g., Hawkins, 1977; Reeves, 1978; Weintraub, Austin, Roberts, & Nass, 1990). Others have attempted to locate perceived realism as a dynamic process related to the viewer's construction of the text (Barker, 1988) and studied perceived realism's relationship to the age of viewers and to televisual content (Dorr & Kovaric, 1990). The impact of perceived realism on viewers also has been examined in the context of cultivation theory (Busselle, 2001; Busselle, Ryabalova, & Wilson, 2004; Potter, 1986). More recent work has aimed to explain how prior knowledge positively correlates to the perceived realism of a narrative (Green, 2004).

Defining realism has also been a concern of this work. Potter (1988) codified existing studies of perceived realism to argue for a multidimensional definition oriented around the style and meaning of the message, the viewer's perception of the message's utility, and the degree to which a television character may influence a viewer's life. To this understanding, Busselle and Greenberg (2000) added the dimension of the likelihood of an event's occurring in the real world. Realism also has been defined in terms of how a media text typifies a range of people, its factual relation to the real, its narrative consistency and general level of production values (Hall, 2003).

However, television serves as a representational medium rather than the simulation medium that is the digital game. Although there have been those who have argued for continuities between representational and simulation media (e.g., Crawford, 2003; Mateas, 2004; Murray, 2004), others have argued for a break, stating that simulation media like the digital game operate through different mechanics than their representational counterparts. In contrast to older media, simulation media allow for both input and output, subsequently offering those who use them a dynamic experience with each encounter. The new simulation medium of the digital game enables audiences to configure the text and subsequently create their own experience rather than experiencing the same text in each encounter with it (Eskelinen, 2003; Frasca, 2003; Galloway, 2004).

Given this different form of experience, it seems notions of perceived realism ought to be revisited in the context of the new medium of the digital game. Yet, this literature remains relatively sparse. In addressing perceived realism conceptually, McMahan (2003) theorized that realism in the digital game ought to be discussed in terms of (a) social realism, how social interactions in the game replicate those of the real world; and (b) perceptual realism, how the objects in the game match those in the real world. In a similarly conceptually-oriented essay, Galloway (2004) focused on social realism and the digital game in grounding his work in film theory's understanding of the socially realistic text as critical of existing power structures (Aitken, 2006; Hipkins & Cooke, 2006; McKerrow, 1993). Although multiple studies of video game players and their engagement with violent games have been conducted (e.g., Alloway & Gilbert, 1998; Anderson, 2004; Farrar, Krcmar, & Nowak, 2006; Goldstein, 2005; Unsworth, Devilly, & Ward, 2007), it seems only Maillet's (2006) study of adolescents and perceived realism has begun to address how gamers playing non-violent digital games related their activity to the material world.

This study of *Madden* fans' online discussion postings supplements previous work on digital games and the question of realism by examining how this segment of users engaged the game as a realistic representation of football. The ensuing discussion of *Madden* fans lends concrete illustration to the ways in which they understood realism and attempted to achieve it in a new medium enabling them to configure their experience of the text. This configuration was oriented around quantitative and self-proclaimed "scientific" discourses that position them within traditionally masculine discursive frames.

To explain why these fans focused on quantitative realism is to situate these discourses in a broader context acknowledging that enumeration most often has been practiced by men. Anderson (1992) draws our attention to the gendered nature of statistics as a form of knowledge when tracing the field back to the late 17th and early 18th centuries. Anderson noted that data collection and production was an elite Western male enterprise mirroring the values of the dominant legal, political, and economic arrangement of the society in which statistics arose. Oates and Durham (2004) posited the power to measure as one of the ways in which white males validated their position in social and cultural relations. In referencing the masculine counting of slaves and colonial subjects and the measurement of female beauty contestants and models, they argued for the historical prevalence of enumeration as a particularly male project. Recent scholarship on girls' perceptions of and participation in mathematics education betrays the anxiety that an engagement with numbers has been a masculine preserve for far too long (Anderson, 2005; Herzig, 2004; Kennedy, 2005; Mendick, 2005).

This fan discourse also positions the fan within football's longer historical articulation to a rationality grounded in a scientific masculinist orientation. Football has been cited as playing a key role in furthering American cultural myths linked to both technology (Lindquist, 2006; Real, 1975) and masculinity (Hartmann, 2003; Lalvani, 1994; Nauright, 1996; Oriard, 1981). These links also have been made in the context of the uniformed football body and increasingly augmented by protective technologies (Jirousck, 1996). It seems that these ideas have been ingrained in the sport since its inception. In a series of essays on the game, penned for *Harper's Weekly* in the late 1880s and 1890s, football pioneer Walter Camp argued for the virtue of football from a technocratic point of view: "If ever a sport offered inducements to the man of executive ability, to the man who can plan, foresee, and manage, it is certainly the modern American foot-ball" (Camp, quoted in Oriard, 1991, p. 13). The game of football offered a cultural space in which the values of masculine scientifically-informed authoritative organization and order could be upheld, encouraged and disseminated in order to engender maximum efficiency. Camp's considerable influence on the rule structures of football transformed the game from the loosely configured running and kicking of rugby to the more reasoned and ordered sport he envisioned — the sport he would label a "scientific contest" necessitating "scientific planning" (Oriard, 1993, pp. 42, 45). Camp's organization of the game neatly paralleled Frederick Winslow Taylor's four principles of scientific management for businesses: "Science, Harmony, Cooperation and Maximum Output" (Oriard, 1993, p. 45). For Camp, it was not the "woman of executive ability" who could play football. It also does not seem as though he would expect a woman to possess the ability to practice Taylor's principles of scientific management. To Camp's mind, both football and the scientific approach informing the sport appeared to function as domains of strictly masculine activity.

Even as this study contributes to the literature on perceived realism and digital game fans, it also supplements these studies by hypothesizing about why this set of fans focused on the quantitative aspect of realism in their engagement with *Madden*.

Methodology

This study involved a qualitative textual analysis of discussion board threads during the week of August 8–15, 2005, in the "Madden Football" sections of two of the more popular sports game Internet message boards, *Operation Sports* (www. operationsports.com, hereafter OS) and *Madden Mania* (www.maddenmania.com, hereafter MM). This week proved unique for the community in that it heralded the release of *Madden Football 2006* (2005) for the Xbox and Playstation 2 game consoles. Therefore, analyzing fan discourse from this particular week provided the greatest potential for considering what had occupied the community over the previous year in its consumption of *Madden Football 2005* (2004) and anticipation of *Madden Football 2006* (2005). At the time of data collection, OS had just under 40,000 members. A moderator at MM reported just under 20,000 members, but stated that the community had often had more than 20,000 members before inactive memberships had been deleted (personal communication, January 23, 2006). For this project, the 10 threads garnering the greatest number of views from both of these respective boards were saved. Each message in these threads was collected, and then the messages were qualitatively analyzed for recurrent themes.

This methodology provided the benefit of allowing the discourse to flourish organically without prompting from the researcher. Previous audience studies on perceived realism in media typically have involved focus groups where interviewees have been asked to respond to questions posed by the researcher (e.g., Hall, 2003; Maillet, 2006). Busselle et al, (2004) noted prompting by researchers as one of the methodological challenges of studies on perceived realism. In examining the online sports gaming message boards, this study was grounded in fan-initiated rather than researcher-initiated discourse. As a consequence, the fans in this study explained and related how they understood realism uninfluenced by a specific research question.

It is important to acknowledge that the fans posting on these boards may not represent the broad panoply of the game's players. Therefore, the findings may not be generalizable. However, this data set may provide researchers with insight into the kinds of meanings of the game from the most passionate fans. Additionally, considering this kind of fan discourse also furthers an understanding of how these fans respond to the way the game positions them. As such, it has broader implications for the study of digital game players as well.

Before proceeding, a brief explanation of *Madden*'s setup is necessary. As part of a way to deal with the potential problem of different user skill levels, playing styles and perceptions of what constitutes realistic football, EA ships the game with a set of customizable options called "sliders." The notion of a slider comes from the representation of these game options on the screen as something akin to a bead sliding back and forth on an abacus wire. In many digital sports games, this virtual bead can be moved back and forth across a visually represented wire as a way to alter game variables like, in the case of *Madden*, penalty frequency or the overall ability of all players to catch passes or to tackle. Pushing the pass catching slider all the way to the right will make it easier for receivers and running backs to catch passes thrown their way and minimize dropped balls during the game. Pushing this slider all the way to the left will yield the opposite effect. Sliders may operate on a variety of scales from 1–5, 1–10, and 1–100, depending on how customizable the game's designers situate a given gameplay variable. These sliders enable users to modify their experience of the game by tweaking aspects of gameplay to their liking. Thus, novice users can make the game easier, whereas expert users can make the game more challenging. However, users often employ the sliders for far more than altering the game's respective level of difficulty. Many of them experiment with these sliders to generate what they perceive to be a realistic game rather than using them as difficulty modifiers. Slider settings can then be posted online for community feedback and/or refinement.

Realism and Madden Football

A commitment to realism served as one of the most prevalent user responses to the *Madden* experience. A survey of threads in this data set yielded a number of invocations of the terms "realism," "realistic" and their derivatives. For example, the terms "realistic," "unrealistic" and "realistically" appeared 92 times in the MM thread entitled "1st Against the Run" and 124 times in the "Brit Pitbull and Sm27's [two users] Madden 2005 'Manifesto' How to Fix the Game" threads alone. Given the number of times users employed the notion of realism and/or realistic in their forum postings, they provided a clear sense of how they understood what counted as realistic in their experience. However, it was quantitative realism that appeared most salient in the context of this set of fan discussion.

This desire for quantitative realism positioned this set of fans within the parameters of a factually grounded perceived realism akin to that of fans engaging traditional representational media (Hall, 2003). This particular focus on quantitative rather than other dimensions of realism also links these fans to a historically masculine interest and power as expressed in numbers.

Quantitative Realism and Madden Fans

The posts on discussion boards at OS and MM clearly manifested the importance of quantitative realism. It seems that the numbers provided a frame these fans mobilized in their responses to their experience. In this case, fans communicated their expectation that the *Madden* experience should be quantitatively realistic through an expressed desire for statistical outcomes mirroring those of National Football League averages from the previous or current season's campaign. Without this reflection of real world statistical data, users scoffed at any claims that the game could ever be deemed realistic.

An important aspect of their discussion and the game itself concerned the difference between simulated games (truncated as "simmed" for "simulated" in its verb form or "sims" for "simulated games" in its noun form) and played games. The option to simulate games enabled users to have the computer calculate the result of a given contest and then display and compile statistics from the game apart from any direct user activity. Users did not see the game being played graphically, but saw only the final score and each team's and player's generated statistics. A played game, by contrast, directly involved a user's input in that users physically moved the controller to manipulate their players and teams on the virtual field against cpu (computer) or human opponents. Simmed games typically required only a second or two of calculation, whereas played games required anywhere from 15 minutes to two hours to complete.

This community of *Madden* users devoted themselves to ensuring that both the simmed and played games yielded what they perceived to be realistic statistics. One user carefully measured *Madden*'s generated statistics against NFL totals while playing the game in posting, "I constantly have NLF.com up and Cnns sports site so i can see all the team stats at all times."[1] Another shared screenshots of numbers that did not agree with expectations in stating, "attached are pics to show just how messed up the stats engine is.... All i will say is EVERY category was messed up in some way, especially qb stats which appeared as if the NFL season decreased to 12 games from 16." The importance of accurate statistical totals also appeared in a protracted debate over a reported bug involving what happened to passing yardage totals when a quarterback was tackled in the backfield. One fan chided another who was not familiar with the way in which the rules worked in stating, "I really hope you're kidding because if you have been 'watching pro football since 1985' and dont know what when a QB gets sacked the amount of yardage that is lost on the sack is deducted from the QB's pass yardage." Another user argued for the importance of quantitative realism in positing that, "Having accurate stats helps us gauge the effectiveness of the various units on our franchise, it's neat to see if you can get the #1 offense, defense, whatever." Another fan suggested that distorted statistical totals ruined the game in saying, "So simulated RB stats are busted and unrealistic? No fix for this eh? Sigh ... that's a gamebreaker for me." One of the more astute fans criticized the unrealistic statistical outcomes evident in excessive passing yards over rushing yards in making an argument about a perceived key problem with the game: "the cpu doesn't pass enough against each other in simmed games which causes schewed stats for every possible aspect of the game. Consider how the lack of a passing game effects the number of INT, how too much running increases pancake stats and how tackles are distributed. In played games the opposite is true, the cpu wil pass all over you and will have absolutely no interest in a running game. The effect that this has on the realism of your franchise is obvious, (we're all top against the Run, worst against the pass, etc)." In this example, this fan contrasted the quantitative realism of played games versus simmed games by arguing for a statistical domino effect in which one quantitative problem — in this case, the computer's refusal to pass the ball during simmed games — generated a series of others. For this user, the result was an obviously unrealistic experience.

Users posted litanies of statistics as the primary source of evidence to support their positions about how realistic or unrealistic *Madden* might be in simulating real world football. In attempting to generate a set of sliders that would yield quantitatively realistic outcomes, many users reported statistics for individual games they played as a way for the community to measure *Madden*'s realism and the effects the sliders may have been having on statistical totals. The granularity of these reported statistics extended from team performances to unit performance (e.g., offense, defense, offensive line, linebackers, special teams, etc.) and, finally, to specific, individual player performance as well. A representative post would include detailed information like the following: "QB Drew Henson: 68.2% rtg, 15/22/191yds, 1 TD, 2 Int, 1 sack." Some users even went so far as to chart the particular plays called, the time of the game when these plays were called, and the subsequent outcome of each of these plays, as in: "11:56 left in Qtr 1, 1&10 own 30 run — HB Toss Weak, 2&5 pass — Anderson option, 1&10 own 41 run — HB Counter." This kind of data sharing was followed by commentary from each user about the relative realism of the generated statistics or simply reported for community observation. The numbers were then analyzed and evaluated by other forum members to generate aggregate data about the degree to which *Madden*'s statistical model fared against NFL averages using a given slider set. Where this aggregate data approximated these real world figures, the users deemed the experience realistic. Where the data did not approximate actual NFL statistics, users rejected the game as unrealistic.

"Looks like we may have nailed it" — Fixing *Madden '05*

Perhaps more interesting than the evidence offered as proof of *Madden*'s lack of realism was the action fans took to deal with what they perceived to be these quantitative problems. In working to tweak sliders, these *Madden* fans expressed themselves through discourses of experimentation as part of a self-proclaimed scientific project designed to make *Madden* more quantitatively realistic. These fans were not necessarily practicing a stringent scientific methodology, but they explicitly labeled their activity in scientific terms. As part of their scientific endeavor, these users aimed to master the internal workings of the software in order to bend the game to do their will so that they could achieve the realistic experience they desired. These fans manipulated in-game variables and assessed the effects of changes to various options. In doing so, they responded tangibly to their perception of the game's realism and took advantage of how this new medium was enabling them to configure their experience.

As they related their thoughts and ideas, users discussed their activity by evoking the metaphors of the lab and experimentation. In wanting to encourage further tweaking of the game's variables, one poster exhorted fellow users, "Keep it commin' guys ... you'll be deserving of some sort of 'Nobel Prize' as the true research scientists of 'Sliderology.'" Another fan referenced a user who was experimenting with a way to solve a gameplay problem in reporting that, "the flaw isn't a big deal because it can be stopped. I labbed tonight with Kobra from VG so we found a way to stop this. It'll take some more lab time to see if it consistently stops it." After some initial attempts at generating realistic quantitative totals, one fan evoked a discursively scientific methodology in declaring, "Our next step should be to come up with a controlled cohesive method to experiment and test and get this done." One fan related gratitude to "everyone out there testing" while another became devoted to addressing a potential problem with the game in finally declaring, "I just specifically went and tested the so-called INT [interception] yards glitch and there is NO SUCH THING." In the Madden Mania thread entitled "1st Against the Run/31st Against Pass" alone, the word "test" and its derivatives appeared 287 times over a three-and-a-half-week-period.

As part of this testing process, this group of fans discussed how to modify sliders in order to generate the desired numerical outcomes. One discussant commented on the problems with the amount of rushing yards being gained with a comparison to NFL averages before invoking a slider tweak, "Way way way too many carries for the running backs. Looks like I'm going to have to control every team and edit their pass/run slider and RB1/RB2 [RB=running back] sliders until the stats are on point." Another alluded to the same issue in saying, "those rushing stats are a little high. But, not too high. I'd say they're getting about 10–15 yards too many per game. Might be something where you could adjust the RB1/RB2 slider just slightly and give a few more carries to the backup and completely fix it." A third poster commented on how difficult it was to match offensive and defensive rankings, in spite of the sliders, given the way in which *Madden* had been designed. This user claimed, "When you make a set of sliders to replicate actual NFL stats in the games you play against the cpu it does not matter since the cpu simmed games will not replicate the actual NFL stats." This person's frustration identified statistical problems derived from slider problems, the very device EA inserted into the game to deal with differing playing styles. Changing sliders from one position to another in order to yield realistic played games failed to deal with the problem of unrealistic simmed games which generated statistics that, for this fan, did "not replicate the actual NFL stats."

Not only did these fans identify the nature of their work as scientific, they also consistently pointed out the importance of working in the context of a pseudo-scientific community to accomplish what they perceived to be the immense nature of the task at hand. One poster insisted on the collective effort of the community in volunteering to help other forum members: "i'm offering to run some tests with you, but remember, this must be a team work, not individual." Later in the same thread, another thanked the community for their input in stating, "I know it is a lot of typing and recording of stats to finally once and for all figure this stuff out, but they're is NO WAY I was going to do this myself, I am glad we are working together on this." A third also expressed this need for community involvement by claiming, "the point of this thread is to get as much input and contribution from from the madden players out there, so that we can actually really nail the gameplay and finally allow people to have their best games. One or two people cannot do this, it takes feedback and ideas from a range of people to imagine, create, and test everything. So all input is greatly appreciated." At times some forum members chastised others who failed to function within the scientific paradigm they had delineated for the community. One user angrily addressed a poster who was not taking the project seriously enough by saying: "All you are telling me is that once again, you expect me or somebody else to do all of the work for you. You expect the game to work perfectly for you. You have contributed nothing to this project and just expect us to do everything for you. You are not exhibiting the behavior that this thread and our project is all about. In case you didn't bother to read it, this is a TEAM EFFORT. All with a common goal of helping each other along VERY SPECIFIC LINES of testing." With these kinds of posts, one could surmise that this kind of collective project served as a form of fraternal bonding in which this pseudo-scientific community accepted a challenge, moved forward in attempting to overcome the challenge, and then worked to complete it.

It would appear that these discussants configured their experience with virtual football in a similar way to Walter Camp's interpretation of the material game. Camp described football as a sport privileging "science, perfectibility through hard work, hierarchical control and corporate cooperation, an aristocracy of merit based on absolute equality of opportunity" (quoted in Oriard, 1991, p. 13). It seems that these users adopted these kinds of perspectives in their approach to fixing *Madden* and generating what they perceived to be a realistic experience as well.

Discussion

This chapter has provided insight into how one group of fans explained their experience of the digital sports game through an analysis of *Madden* fan discourse reported on the popular digital sports game websites *Madden Mania* and *Operation Sports*. In looking at this set of fans' desire for quantitative realism and the self-proclaimed scientific approach they took to achieving this goal, their discourse reveals how they used the configurative character of a new medium to generate their own realistic experience. Their focus on quantitative realism and the means they used to achieve it appears to position them within traditionally masculine discursive frames cited earlier.

In this group of fans' scientifically informed approach to generating quantitative realism, at least one user explicitly outlined the otherwise implied masculine nature of the project in responding to another poster, "I myself and GMBreaker, BritPitbul, Adembroski2, Fj47, and a whole lot of *the men* I have listed in the "Credits" post, (post #10) Have spent SO much time on this." Certainly, these kinds of explicit pronouncements about the sex of those involved are rare in this data set. Whether this fan truly knows the sex of those working on this project is open to speculation. Additionally, given the nature of online discussion forums, it is extremely difficult for the researcher to identify the sex of posters.

However, it appears that the discussants assumed a historically masculine subjectivity in the process as they perceived realism through the lens of quantitative discourses. For these fans, to perform their project rationally is to act scientifically. To act scientifically is to perform their masculinity in dominating the technological environment in which they live. If we combine Camp's discussion of football as "a scientific contest" and the historically gendered nature of quantification, then this group of *Madden* fans' emphasis on quantitative realism and their quest to achieve it perfectly accords with what we might expect a stereotypically masculine fan interested in football to deem important. It is precisely the scientized expression of this kind of power over the number that serves as the epistemological frame through which *Madden* users interpreted the game's lack of realism. The technological manifestation of the sport of football in the medium of the digital game serves as a prime exemplar of the nexus of gender, science and mediated sport.

It would seem that much more could be garnered from this data set in asking questions about how these fans seemed to be instrumentalizing virtual athletes through quantification and in theorizing about the potential effects of this activity on their engagement with so-called "real" sport. The current study also suggests further research ought to investigate how digital sports game fans interpret their experience of virtual sport and are shaped by their involvement in this increasingly popular activity. This future research might explore the degree to which other digital sports game fans perceive and configure realism in their interaction with sport in this new medium.

Additional study might also further engage how the configurative nature of new media shape and influence what it means to be a sports fan, and how this fandom is experienced. This study implied that members of this group of *Madden Football* fans were not fully convinced by EA's marketing slogan, and that the slogan may actually contradict their ability to mold their experience with the game. Based on this data set, one might surmise that they would respond to the company's advertising punch line "It's in the game!" with a loud chorus of "Only if we put it there."

Note

All quotations in the text are presented as posted by the contributor. No editorial corrections were made by the author. In order to avoid interrupting the flow of the postings, the author avoided inserting (sic) to note spelling and grammatical errors.

Virtual Sports Consumption, Authentic Brotherhood

The Reality of Fantasy Football

MICHAEL SERAZIO

For the fantasy football fanatic, the seventh day is hardly an occasion for rest. From the moment he[1] wakes, the clock begins ticking toward kickoff. There are statistical match-ups to analyze; weather and injury reports to consult; imaginary rosters to juggle. He is still a fan, but a very different kind of fan, and while he may be alone in managing and cheering on his particular fantasy squad, he is not at all alone in his quest for fantasy success.

With the help of the Internet, fantasy sports leagues have blossomed over the past decade from fringe subculture phenomenon to robust social obsession. Estimates vary, but even the ballpark figures are staggering. In 2004, 10 million fantasy football participants spent an average of $154 each on sports statistics magazines, league entry fees, and assorted draft services (Tedeschi, 2004). Moreover, with participants spending an average of six hours a week maintaining their teams both at home and in the office, companies brace for millions of dollars in lost employee productivity (Flood, 2004; Petrecca, 2005). This fantasy world thus has very real consequences.

A few definitions are in order. Fantasy football is usually defined as leagues in which participants draft real players from assorted professional teams to their imaginary rosters in order to compete against other participants' imaginary rosters. Points for a fantasy team roster accumulate through the individual performances of real athletes, helping fantasy coaches or general managers succeed in league competition. Decisions from draft day through kickoff each week are made under the guise that the participant is actually in charge and that, though still a spectator, he somehow shares in the action and the glory of the players he "owns." Players are typically selected for critical "skill" positions like quarterback, running back, tight end and kicker, and statistical measures generally tabulate performance in terms of touchdowns and yardage gained.

Although a social analysis of fantasy sports leagues cannot avoid accounting for their Internet context, it is important to register the fact that fantasy sports leagues far predate their popular emergence in the online world. Moreover, I argue that their meaning and utility has not fundamentally changed with the dawn of the Internet era, even if cyberspace has accelerated the convenience.

Many have pointed to 1979 as the definitive birth of fantasy baseball, and some trace fantasy football to more than a decade earlier (Wendel, 2004). The explosive growth of fantasy leagues, however, had to wait for the ease of statistical tracking via the Internet, which allows for instantaneous translation of on-field performance into fantasy points. Marketers have watched with keen interest as this consumer demographic has evolved. A recent report claimed more than 50 percent of players are between 25 and 44 years old, 37 percent have at least a bachelor's degree, and 33 percent take home $75,000 or more in annual income — an enviable market indeed (Kang, 2005).

A quantitative sketch of these fantasy enthusiasts does not, however, answer certain qualitative questions about what is at work with this new form of sports consumption. What are the emotions and values — and uses and gratifications — that come with assuming the position of fantasy sports fan? How does being a fantasy competitor alter the dynamics of the experience from "real" fandom?[2] This chapter examines and evaluates those deeper meanings of fantasy football consumption and participation.

Concurrent Cravings: Community and Competition

The sociology of fantasy sports leagues has a rather thin literature to date. Here, I propose slicing the theoretical framework into two core foundations. The first main theme situates fantasy sports participation within the context of fandom as a means to community. In this formulation, consuming fantasy sports is an occasion for social interaction; it is an opportunity to form, maintain, and strengthen social bonds. This locates the consumption of sports as an inherently social process that affords the personal gratification that comes with unity and kinship. King's (1997) use of Durkheim's totem worship is an apt starting point: "This love which the lads feel for their team is simultaneously also a love for the feeling of solidarity which they experience every time they attend the game and participate in the communal practice of drinking and singing. Just as Durkheim suggested aboriginal tribes worship their society through the totem, so do the lads reaffirm their relations with other lads through love of the team.... The team, and the love invested in it, is a symbol of the values and friendships which exist between the lads" (p. 333).

I will clarify how fantasy sports maintain participants' feeling of solidarity by creating an environment that allows participants to reaffirm their relations with others. Furthermore, I explore how this solidarity is possible despite dissecting "real" professional teams and effectively fragmenting that shared totem of allegiance. In a purely fantasy world, the fractured totem no longer offers a clear and unifying mode of fandom whereby relations with others are maintained by cheering for a single professional club — that traditional sort of uncomplicated obedience and veneration that produces kinship and identity among groups of fans. In fantasy football, allegiances to the real team and to other fans of the real team are frayed from the start. Still, participation in fantasy leagues "promotes the formation of social groupings," as Huizinga (1970) stated about sport (p. 13). Segrave (2000) further framed sport as "a flight from loneliness, the end, as Nietzsche might say, of the principle of individuation" (p. 67). The fantasy world, I believe, does not depart from that.

This is because fantasy sports do not merely offer that point of transcendence through interaction; they are predicated on it and, in a way, necessitate it. Much like traditional fandom, with its potential for "invoking a deeper sense of commonality, one that transcends the normative order" of race, politics, and language barriers, a shared passion for fantasy sports generates its own gratifying communal experience (Segrave, 2000, p. 68). Wenner and Gantz (2000), in summarizing five core motivations for viewing sports on television based on extant research, labeled this the "companionship dimension" that lures the fan (p. 237). Because message board interaction (and the attendant "smack talk" between competitors) seems not merely incidental but rather integral to fantasy football gaming, the companionship dimension is a crucial motivation for participation.

A second main theoretical framework for the study emphasizes the vicarious experience of sports competition. Here fantasy participation and experience is reduced from the macro-level of sociology to the micro-workings of psychology, as Wann, Melnick, Russell and Pease (2001) framed it. Research has not only found that "desires to thrill" in victory are among the strongest motivations for watching sports, but that a preferred team or player's success finds viewers reveling in the reflected glory (Wenner & Gantz, 1989, 2000). In their research, Branscombe and Wann (1992a) noted that, through rooting for favored teams, fans engage in vicarious competition. The players are, in a way, avatars of the ego, and perhaps the illusion of sport, at some level, engages that fan subconscious. In choosing and cheering for specific players, fans may indeed be projecting themselves into the bodies of the athletes performing on the field. How else to explain that adrenaline-pulsing, gut-churning quality of the sports viewing experience — that simulated rush of experiencing the professional athlete's success and failure? This projection would be made explicit in the consumption of fantasy football. Wann, Melnick, Russell and Pease (2001) termed this the "eustress motive" (p. 38). They quoted Brill's (1929) early comment on the pleasure — the "why" — of sports fandom: "The life of man in America or in any of the industrialized countries today, laboring on the farm, in the factory, in the office, is not the natural life of the man. He is still an animal formed for the battle and conquest, for blows and strokes and swiftness, for triumph and applause. But let him join the crowd around the diamond, the gridiron, the tennis court or the ring.... Let him identify himself with his favorite fighter, player or team.... He will achieve exaltation, vicarious but real" (p. 434).

In fantasy football, that vicarious exaltation is achieved with even greater precision than in traditional sports fandom. By evoking the illusion that a participant owns and manages a set of professional players, the illusion of their success mirroring the participant's is made literal; the vicarious experience is lived because that is what the fantasy construction is meant to facilitate. Shipman (2001) invoked Eco's concept of watching sports as voyeurism in posing the question: "Do fantasy players somehow equate their actions and results to those of the athletes on the field?" (p. 5). The answer here, I believe, is a resounding affirmative.

As a part of these two frameworks, gender — and, more precisely, masculinity — is very clearly a huge factor. Both popularly and in academic study, it has long since been perceived that "sports and sports fandom are ... sites of male bonding" (Sabo & Jansen, 2000, p. 205). Moreover, sport legitimizes the socializing process for men. It gives them a respectable cover, an excuse for bonding. As Fasteau (1975) argued: "Sports is one of the few things men feel they are allowed to become emotional about. Sitting in a bar, grunting, groaning, elbowing each other in the ribs and exclaiming over the ebb and flow of a football game on the owner's TV is the closest a lot of men come to sharing strong feelings with another man" (p. 110).

More recently, sports talk radio has been studied for this quality. Nylund (2004) found that "sports talk provides a safe haven for men to bond and reaffirm their essential masculinity" (p. 149). He called upon Messner's notion of "covert intimacy" to explain the emotional appeal of sports talk radio. He claimed by "doing things together rather than mutual talk about inner lives," the male is allowed to forge relationships in ways that do not imperil his projected masculinity (p. 165). Furthermore, this is made possible by the lack of a female presence. According to Wenner (1998), "much of the cultural power of sports is linked to its functioning as a male rite of passage and the role sports spaces and places play as a refuge from women" (p. 308).

This chapter seeks to understand the experience of the fantasy sports participant in a context of fan empowerment: "making couch potatoes into coach potatoes" as Williams (2003) cleverly put it. Fiske (1992) and Grossberg (1992) posited as much in their work, arguing that fanship is a participatory, empowering, active process. Indeed, this chapter demonstrates that fantasy football fanship is also very much a "contact" sport.

Methods

Whannel (2000) foregrounded the problem of studying sports fandom through televised viewing: "The problems of method stem from our lack of a reliable means of getting at the complexities of response that we may have to media images.... What goes on in their heads as they watch [television] is a process that is peculiarly resistant to analysis" (p. 229). Put simply, "pleasures cannot simply be articulated" (p. 230).

I initially attempted to make contact with participants by posting a general inquiry on nearly a dozen of the most popular fantasy sports boards on the Internet. This posting stated: "I'm doing research on sports and culture and, as part of a project on fantasy football, I'm posting on message boards like this to see if anyone would be game to fill out a short, pretty simple questionnaire on opinions and experiences with fantasy football. I could send it by e-mail, it would take maybe five minutes, and would help out tremendously." After posting the notice twice within the course of a month and soliciting graduate students on an e-mail listserv, I collected 18 paper interviews.

The open-ended questions were formulated in an attempt to appraise some of the aforementioned themes; the answers were categorized and interpreted informally on a post hoc basis. Questions included some of the following: "Why do you play fantasy football?" "What makes it enjoyable?" "How do you prepare?" "How do you interact with the other members of the league?" "What do you use the message boards for?" "What do you think it means when your fantasy team does well?" "What do you think of the job of professional GMs?" "How do you compare being a fantasy football participant with being a 'traditional' fan?" "Do you feel or think differently?" "What happens when your fantasy players go against your favorite NFL team?"

Responses ranged from the literal and terse to much more detailed, richly descriptive elucidations of the psychological and social experience that accompanies fantasy football. I then conducted six semi-structured, in-depth interviews (by phone or in person) with those who agreed to discuss the topic further. The interviews lasted approximately 30 minutes each and were based upon the questionnaire responses. All names in the study have been changed to protect respondents' confidentiality and anonymity. Given that this research was limited to a small group of respondents, and because those I interviewed may not be perfectly representative of all fantasy sports players, the results may be rich and useful but not necessarily generalizable.

Fantasy football was chosen as the exemplar among sports because 93 percent of fantasy sports participants play it (Petrecca, 2005). Respondents in my research were between the ages of 16 and 49. The mean age was 30. In all, 16 of the 18 respondents were White (2 did not identify their race), and all but 1 were male. On average, they spent between $50 and $100 per season on fantasy football and about 10 to 15 hours a week watching or reading about football or fantasy football.

Findings

The main theoretical themes of community and competition appeared in and were articulated through the pleasures of fantasy football in intriguing ways. Findings from this qualitative inquiry will be presented in accordance with the thematic order suggested above, though in some cases wholly extrapolating the community experience from the competition experience is not feasible.

Fantasy Fandom and Community: Familiar Networks

Not every fantasy football player likely experiences the romantic, almost premodern social fabric on display in Steve's league, but his words provide an idealistic point of entry: "Our league is in its 15th year, and we're all from the same small town. We may watch some of the games together, but we also patronize each other's business [sic]. One member runs a garage, another is an investemetn [sic] advisor, another a stone engraver, etc. After all these years we resemble a family — we've gone through a lot together on a personal level — marriages, divorces, births, deaths or parents, hospitalization, etc. As with all families, we occasionally have some spats."

As male sports kinship goes, this 49 year old appears to have a found a small slice of fantasy utopia. Their virtual competition didn't solely precipitate that strong connection and the sentimentality that now accompanies it. It did, however, help engineer and solidify the group's bond. Moreover, in a world of multi-league fantasy addicts, Steve's participation in just one league resists the tendency of fantasy football competitors to head up multiple teams. Still, no matter how many leagues an individual participates in, evidence confirmed the first theoretical foundation of this study: Fantasy football is a means to community.

Trent's experience, though he participates in wholly different leagues than Steve, is paradigmatic. Responding to a question probing his motive for playing fantasy football, he wrote, "As someone who likes to organize and set up social activities, this is one I can do with my sports-crazed friends." His two leagues are composed of family, friends, and friends of friends. They get together for a draft night in August, during the season to watch night games, and for a large Super Bowl party at the end of the year. "We are very interactive," he said.

In a follow-up interview, Trent, 30, who started playing fantasy football 16 years ago when his father introduced him to it, explained how fantasy sports helps preserve friendships:

We started this league about seven years ago when we were finishing up college ... and throughout the years we started with 10 people and we still have 8 of the original owners. ... This really gives people, at least in my group, an excuse to get together for pizza and a beer once a month and talk about fantasy football and let that conversation cruise into work or how the new girlfriend is.... So it has definitely kept us as close as when we were in the dorm rooms.... And I can pretty much say that fantasy football has been a part of that because some of the people I was friends with that are not participants, we've drifted a little bit farther. We still exchange Christmas cards and calls, but that's a few times a year.

This model of friends, particularly college friends, using fantasy football as a de facto impetus for staying in touch was seen in numerous respondents. Even Jake, 41, further removed from his university years, noted in an interview that, in one of his four leagues: "My roommate from college and I had not conversed much at all in the eight or nine years after we graduated.... But the past three years in league together, we've got e-mails flying back and forth every few days. It's a much closer world of communication for us than before fantasy football so that's been sort of fun to sort of reestablish connection." Here, consuming and participating in fantasy football is a way of resurrecting social networks — tracking down and keeping hold of old friends.

For Jake, that functionality is multi-generational. His wife has not bought into the fantasy attachment. (Jake spends between 90 minutes and 3 hours a day on fantasy football and jokes that fantasy football has taken up his time since retiring from the school board.) But his two teenage daughters share the passion: "It's a pretty active topic, and the girls have been sucked into this.... When I go traveling on business, I'll call home for info [on football] and they'll pass it along." Furthermore, he is consciously planning to use fantasy football as a way of keeping in touch when his oldest daughter goes off to college: "It won't have to be a thing of where Dad is keeping track of her life, but you can bet that they'll [sic] be a few crazy trade offers going back and forth every week."

Others repeated this benefit of being united by fantasy sports in cyberspace, particularly among social networks diffused geographically and ever more often frayed by the relentlessly transient rhythms of contemporary life. Aaron, 32, reported, "Most of the guys I play with are spread across the country, so it keeps us in touch." Joey, 28, said, "It's a chance to share an activity with people who live far away." His wife, Lisa, 29, who plays in the same league, added, "Some of them are in NYC, some in D.C., and some in Texas. It lets us play together even though we're so far apart." Brian, 25, repeated this theme: "I use [sic] to go to college with a lot of the guys in the league, but don't keep in touch very well except through the message board and through smack talk." With easy Internet accessibility, fantasy gaming knows no borders. While most players locate their fantasy companions within the United States, Jake played last season with a Peace Corps volunteer based in South Africa. He noted, "The time zones were difficult to say the least."

Fantasy Fandom and Community:
New Affiliations

Kerry, 28, plays in seven leagues and, like others, initially got involved because of old friends. In an interview, he commented: "Other guys—we decided to get them into this. It kind of keeps the community open because it kind of keeps them into the bullshit and such.... It is a way to keep in touch. It's also a way to meet new people." He plays in one league in the Philadelphia area that was, at first, full of unknown competitors who became friends. This highlights a second social dimension of fantasy participation, a subtheme of community: forging new relationships. "It's a bunch of guys who never met before and got together for a draft and that's how a bunch of these leagues start up," he said.

The "meet new people" aspect of fantasy gaming seems to be of less importance than its utility in preserving already established relationships, but it is not wholly absent from respondents' experiences. Jake, who estimated that he has posted 3,000 messages on a particular public message board ("The Huddle"), pointed out how close that group has gotten: "Once I got so I knew some of these different folks and I knew their football allegiances and political allegiances and stories and such, it's been fun to keep up.... This year when Katrina hit, one of the Huddlers set up a PayPal fund to benefit Huddlers affected by Katrina." He noted: "We raised and distributed over 5,000 dollars," because "these folks had risen to a point of communication that it was like, 'Ok, well, let's help these folks out.'"

Mark, 29, noted that fantasy football is even a conversation lifeline at times: "If I'm in a social situation ... it's an immediate topic of conversation. And to me that's the best part, if your conversation has died, anybody can go to fantasy football and go on and on with that." For him, the fantasy game thus serves as the antidote to awkward silences.

How, specifically, are both old and new communities fostered? According to the questionnaires and interviews, respondents stay connected through e-mail, instant messenger, private and public Internet message boards, as well as getting together to watch games, and talking by phone or in person at parties, work meetings, or bars. Topics include league and rule announcements, sharing NFL news, dangling trade offers, celebrating and bemoaning the day's performances, and seeking gaming advice or commentary. "We exchange trash-talking e-mails, borderline-baseless predictions, trade offers, and general banter related to players on each other's rosters," Jake said.

These modes of communication seem to be primarily for entertainment value as opposed to being informative about sports or the league. According to Kerry, "We bust each other's stones." Thus, "smack talk" emerges as the *raison d'être* for much fantasy discussion. Returning to Steve's fantasy utopia, he stated: "I would say a quarter of the posts are about football. One quarter are about personal interests. One half are jokes & insults!" At this end of the spectrum, football is almost secondary, merely incidental, to the give-and-take evidenced in the fantasy forum. For Joey, too, his interaction with other fantasy members is "generally unrelated" to fantasy football. Even so, the message boards are cherished. Brian, 25, wrote: "I primarily use the message boards to talk trash. This is one of the best aspects of the fantasy football season (second only to draft night).... We can say things on here that we wouldn't say anywhere else. We also use it to make arrangements to get together, to complain to the commish, post polls and anything else football or not football related really."

Fantasy Fandom and Competition: Simulated Experiences

Some of the stray comments from respondents thus far likely demonstrate ample evidence of the second core theoretical theme: vicarious competition. Nearly every respondent mentioned some variation on "the thrill of competition" as part of their participation motivation. "I am athletic, competitive, obsessive, and analytical by nature — so Fantasy Football feeds my soul," wrote Jake. Asked what makes fantasy football enjoyable, Chad responded simply, "I am a competitive person, I want to win." Drew delivered a similarly pithy response to the same question: "Competition, camaraderie, it helps make the games more interesting."

Clearly, however, the enjoyment of competition is enhanced by the socialization underpinning the experience. Several respondents claimed that competition was all the more enjoyable if you knew who you were squaring off against and if you had some substantial social connection to that opponent. We desire to play and we desire to win. Interestingly, though, victory quenches our passion doubly if it is a good friend or family member whom we have beaten.

What is at work here? Steve likes competition, but he was quite specific about the context: "I enjoy the competition with my friends." Donovan continued along these lines: "I like to compete with my friends to demonstrate that I am the best." Kerry also thrills in the competitive edge of fantasy sports but said that, in an anonymous public setting like some of his leagues, the rush just isn't the same. "If you're in a free league with no guys you know, there's nothing to motivate you," he says. "I pay attention to that league, but not nearly as much as I pay attention to my other leagues." This competitiveness thus cannot be extricated from the community benefits that many fantasy participants enjoy; one complements the other in a kind of playful tension.

Because of that, "bragging rights" — an oft-cited subset of "smack talk" — represent the ultimate goal. "It is fun to win against friends — just to have some bragging rights for a week, that sort of thing," Joey wrote. Trent added: "I enjoy when my team does well, especially against close friends or family members. It gives me 'bragging rights' until we play again. Winning doesn't say anything of substance, but it does say, 'I was smarter than you' on that particular day."

Here we arrive at a significant departure from traditional fandom: the meanings inferred from the successes on the field. When assuming the position of traditional fan, rooting for one "real" NFL team, an individual divines a certain ineffable sense of pride from her team's success. It breeds an affective product: excitement, conquest, and the trappings of tribal victory. But it is clearly a brawny upshot of fandom. It is the vicarious thrill of one's team being tougher, stronger, more graceful than another, and its ineffability can nonetheless be traced in vaguely physical terms. That is the sensation of the traditional fan, the "real" fan.

Within the fantasy world, pride goes from brawny to brainy. Trent, who revealed something significant in his choice of phrasing fantasy success as being "smarter than you," continued on this point in an interview: "I still get a sense of excitement, but it's, 'I knew more than you did.' 'I picked a better player.' 'I made a better trade.'" Pride, in this context, is contained in one's smarts or shrewdness. It is the thrill of the coldly calculating front-office GM, a far cry from the imagined and vicariously simulated exploits of player grunt in the heat of the battle. Winning affirms knowledge to the group; it serves as kind of football IQ test and, hence, testimonial for the crowd. It also ratifies work ethic, particularly if, like Kerry, you've spent long hours in the late summer months preparing your fantasy game plan. "To see that translate into a good fantasy season, it definitely is fulfilling. It shows that my research worked, and it paid off," he said. Brian wrote, "It makes me feel like I know what I'm doing, and I know a lot about football." Jake added: "I can get cocky when my team(s) is (are) doing well—just as I can when I'm winning at anything.... That impish grin starts to creep in and the fun begins.... If my team is performing well, it means I've done a good job with the week's analysis, making predictions, trading/waivering, and setting my roster.... If they're stinking it up, it's typically a sign that I'm not as smart as I think I am."

Here Jake demonstrated that, by not doing well in fantasy, it's a reflection of *not* being smart enough. Self-esteem and satisfaction are tied together, at least in some small measure, with skillfully sizing up football talent. It is a curious departure from how fans traditionally reflected on and celebrated football games prior to fantasy sports. Before, the young fan might have watched a game and perhaps simulated that experience by pretending to be a pro player in recreational schoolyard games. Now one might conclude fantasy sports is breeding a nation of fans who fancy themselves the next stat-crunching suit seated up in the luxury boxes. We no longer dream of growing up to be the next Joe Montana; we dream of being the next "Vice President—Player Personnel." Or do we?

Fantasy Fandom and Competition:
Professional Perceptions

The surveys included a question that attempted to parse just how respondents thought about the role of professional general managers. I expected that respondents would display a large measure of confidence that they could do a better job than the "real life" executives in charge. (Tuning in to just five minutes of sports talk radio surely makes one believe this. Indeed, within the football subculture, terms like "armchair quarterback" or "Monday morning quarterback" show just how integral the second-guessing fan is to a game's popularity.) Yet the survey responses to this subtopic — perceptions of the professional analogy of fantasy competition — were quite unexpected, most notably in their deferential attitudes.

"It's hard, really hard," Aaron said about real life GMs. "I have neither a salary cap nor an owner to work under." Trent said, "Playing fantasy football and being a professional GM have nothing to do with one another.... They have responsibilities the public doesn't even know about.... Spending a few hours a day, or more, on fantasy football doesn't even scratch the surface." Peyton added, "The job of a real GM is so much more involved that it is hard to compare the two." Brian concluded, "I think it makes too many fantasy football owners think they really understand the complexities of being a GM. Really most of us are just morons pretending we know what we're doing." Matt agreed with the moron part, but, amusingly, placed himself above that assessment: "A large chunk of fantasy players probably believe that they could be successful GMs. Most would not be however. That said, I would be one, because of my knowledge of the game and players."

Some, like Donovan, did reflect some of the envy that I expected the question to elicit: "It's the best job in the world." But others took the question more hesitantly, evaluating what the job demands. As Jake said: "I can't imagine having players' careers (and their lives and family existences) in my hands as I waive and trade.... Loyalty and compassion would be an even bigger impediment to progress in the real world. I'd much rather stay out here in Fantasy Land."

Conclusion

Chad stated simply, "Fantasy has changed football." Matt added, "Fantasy football has totally reconfigured my thinking about the NFL." Brian passed judgment on that fact: "I think fantasy football corrupts the way we watch the games." One respondent after another agreed with the overarching sentiment that by taking on a fantasy football role, the game changes shape for the individual, even if, in reality, nothing has changed at all on the field of play. We seem to watch the game differently. We relate to it in new ways. Clearly, an uncontested consequence of this is that now the fantasy player has an abiding interest in all games on any given Sunday. "With being a fan, you just care about your team winning," Daunte said. "With fantasy football, you care about every turnover, every catch a lot more." In that, fantasy gaming has been perhaps the greatest boon to the NFL since the invention of the football itself.

The greatest challenge for fantasy participants occurs when their favorite team goes up against their fantasy players. Discomfort reigns. Donovan calls it "a very uncomfortable situation." Jake wrote: "It's awkward — like taking two girls to the same dance without telling either one. Before FF, I only cared about games that directly impacted Pittsburgh's chances of making the playoffs. I find myself much more interested in all the teams and much more interested in all the divisions than prior to FF." The fan is torn between the "real" dimension of fandom and the priorities of its virtual realm.

Respondents seemed somewhat split on which dimension commands greater loyalty — the fan's fantasy team or the fan's favorite professional team — with perhaps a small majority claiming they would rather see their "real" team do well. "It has changed many peoples [sic] perspectives.... Its tough [sic], but I still will take a Giant win any day," Brett said. Byron said, "I'd rather the Bengals win than my fantasy team." Brian declared, "I always want my NFL team to win."

Others, however, are fully converted with respect to fandom. For example, Aaron stated: "I used to cheer for the Giants and Cowboys, now I don't much care anymore. Now I want my players to do well, and I want to see a good football game, in that order. I rarely care who actually wins until playoff time." Identity as "real" fan is abandoned in this case; Aaron wholly engages with the game at a purely imaginary level. Moreover, fantasy corrupts the social experience at a different level. As has been established, the fantasy realm clearly has benefits for solidifying social networks through competition. Yet something gained is something lost. To get to it, one must take a step back and reappraise the general, traditional, "real" experience of fandom and camaraderie. A few respondents offered decent inroads.

Jake, for instance, described himself as a Pittsburgh Steelers fan marooned, "trapped," in New England Patriots country: "I guess I kind of stick out." Yet because of that social dislocation, he finds a more intense connection with his black-and-gold comrades: "There's not many of us, so when you see somebody wearing Steelers gear, you can pick 'em out, there's an instant camaraderie of brotherhood there." That instantaneous connection is lost, dissolved, disintegrated into the postmodern rosters of the fantasy experience. Jake realized that. "You miss that true, absolute brotherhood of being a Packer fan or a Steeler fan in fantasy football. You don't have the experience of being at the stadium with fantasy football, and that's a miss for the experience," he said in an interview. There is something very deep at work there. It harkens back to King's (1997) use of Durkheim's totem worship. The common NFL team becomes a projection of the common bond, of love for one another as long as you salute the right flag.

Football fans have long since appropriated teams as part of their own identity, taking ownership of "my" Colts, as Steve says, or "my" Chargers, as I often say. That choice of words is telling. It indicates not only a sense of commitment, but also an extension of identity. Who we cheer for is who we are. We brand ourselves with their apparel and, if it is genuine, believe that the relationship is more than jersey-deep. Some even believe that you do not choose your allegiance; it is chosen for you and you are predestined to one tribe based upon birthright. "When you talk about the Eagles doing well, that's a pride since I was born — that's built into me," Kerry said. Trent said, "I've been a 49er fan since I was able to walk or read or what not, so I would much rather see the 49ers win every game than my fantasy team win." He said that with that identity he can strike up a conversation anywhere if he spots a 49ers hat, even if a total stranger is wearing it. For Trent, there's an implicit togetherness: "It connects you to all kinds of people. There's a connection there that you have a sense of accomplishment and pride that you've been with them for many years, and here's the fruits of my labor." The team's sacrifice and the individual's commitment, especially in dire straits, are intertwined. And the team's success, unlike the fantasy world, imprints itself on a cultural zeitgeist in a way that is palpable, in a way that sweeps the individual off his or her feet and carries them away with the collective that shares the allegiance. As Lisa stated: "I think in the end I would rather be part of a winning city than a winning fantasy team.... It's fun when you're all rooting for the same team together like when you watch an Eagles game in Philly. It's a nice community kind of thing that the fantasy league just doesn't come close to."

Indeed, the fantasy realm shatters that particular notion of community or, at the very least, complicates it. Doing so sets up an intriguing parallel. Fantasy football reduces teams to individual performances. It also takes fans who previously formed communities based upon allegiances to those teams and reduces them to individuals rooting for patchwork lineups. Fantasy football effectively divorces them from the city as "team" and scraps the fabric that a sports community creates as bound by geography. The very notion of a fantasy football "team" is obviously a fabrication. Players do not actually work together as on the field in real life. But it is a fabrication that is invented for the benefit of the individual and represents a fitting sports extension of the themes apparent in an individual-centered, personally-tailored media era.

Some themes could not be located precisely in this research. The most salient of these is the challenge in trying to parse that psychological level of participation by fantasy participants. Do they subconsciously project themselves into the bodies of the players they choose? A few answers hint at this possibility. Brian, 25, assumed the posture of a nostalgic jock hero when he wrote, "I play [fantasy football] because it gives me an outlet for my football fanaticism since I am no longer playing the real thing." Peyton stated: "It feels great when your team does well. I think it is just because you pick players whom you think should perform, and when they do, it it's like you had something to do with it." Is the fantasy being extended in a more serious way here?

Kerry confided: "I started playing fantasy football about eight years ago. I can't imagine what I would do if I couldn't participate in any leagues." The fantasy realm is full of real world consequence. It offers an occasion for upholding social networks and for reuniting old friends, and its greatest virtue might be its ability to facilitate community forged in the fire of competition. It is an empowering and active realm, but it is not without drawbacks. Many of these issues remain open to further exploration. What seems firmly established here is the fascinating undercurrent that finds teams, leagues, friendships, and emotions all predicated on something fundamentally illusory and intrinsically imagined. As Jake said, "There is nothing but this imagined pride and imaginary championship involved, and yet we are hanging on the ends just waiting to see who gets it."

Note

1. According to a recent survey, 93 percent of the time it is indeed a "he" (Aamidor, 2005). Given the overwhelming male participation in fantasy football — and the attention that will be given to gender as a relevant factor — the author and editors have chosen, after careful deliberation, to use gender-specific pronouns.

2. The term "real" fandom will be used throughout this paper to mean the more traditional formulation of fandom: rooting for one unified professional team. While using a term like "real" presents its own set of complications (namely, that traditional fandom can be considered arbitrary and fabricated in its own right), it seemed an appropriate label given the dichotomization that a term like "fantasy" sets up.

The Florida Gator Nation Online

REBECCA B. WATTS

"The message boards are ... the grassroots of fandom."
— Marty Cohen, publisher, Gatorbait.com

Swamp Gas. Gator Bait. GatorSports Forum. The Gator Board. These are the online homes of such University of Florida sports fans as FearNoSpear, gatorlady, and G8rGrowl. They are Internet discussion boards for anyone interested in all things related to Gator athletics, especially football. Depending on the year and the season, there is also discussion of basketball, baseball, other sports, and especially recruiting. One of the most popular gathering places for the Gator Nation online is gatorcountry.com, now affiliated with espn.com, which had over 90,000 unique users per month and 28,000 visits per day in 2005. The Gatorcountry site, which includes the Swamp Gas message boards, boasts 9 million average hits per month during football season, and 1 million hits on National Signing Day (the day each February when high school seniors can officially commit to NCAA college football teams) alone. Another popular fan site is gatorbait.com, now affiliated with rivals.com and Yahoo! Sports. Gatorbait reported an average of 2 million hits per month and 3.5 million hits in January 2005, up due to the heightened interest in recruiting leading up to National Signing Day (Watson, Internet culture special, *Sports Talk Live*, 1 August 2005).

In short, these boards and the users who post and lurk there are part of the online presence of what is increasingly referred to as the Gator Nation. Fans' discussions on these and other Gator-focused Web sites allow them the opportunity to build community with one another, become active participants in reporting team-related news, express their opinions, and even become activists for causes in this online town hall. A case study of the Florida Gator Nation online will illustrate how sports fans, through their participation online, have the opportunity to build community with one another as well as report and even create news about their team, which empowers fans to gain agency and a sense of involvement in regard to their chosen team.

Virtual Communities and Social Capital

Howard Rheingold (2000), who created the term "virtual communities," defined them as "social aggregations that emerge from the Net when enough people carry on those public discussions long enough, with sufficient human feeling, to form webs of personal relationships in cyberspace." Rheingold (2000) hypothesized that "one of the explanations for this phenomenon" of the exponentially increasing popularity of participation in online communities "is the hunger for community that grows in the breasts of people around the world as more and more informal public spaces disappear from our real lives." In contemporary America, people spend more of their time isolated in their cars for long work commutes and less time walking shoulder to shoulder on the sidewalk. Ours is a society in which fast-food restaurants and convenience stores dominate, and in which the old general store where locals could loaf on the front porch is but a memory of times past. These are the sorts of "informal spaces" for conversation that are disappearing, but such spaces are being recreated in online communities.

While Rheingold (2000) did not argue that virtual communities could replace "real" communities, he cited many examples of how virtual communities could serve as a healthy supplement, widening one's circle of friends and colleagues, in some cases paving the way for future face-to-face interactions with online contacts, and enriching the very texture of the life of the mind by enabling us to toggle back and forth between our real and virtual communities. Rheingold's description of toggling back and forth between virtual and real communities to the point that they blur into one reality rings true with the experiences to be had in online sports fan communities such as the Gator Nation online. One moment a sports fan's consciousness may be focused on matters at work or home, and the next moment his or her consciousness may be transfixed by the latest thread in the online discussion that is virtual life on the Gator boards. Another moment a Gator fan may be cheering the team on in person at Ben Hill Griffin Stadium or gathered with fellow fans at the local sports bar, but soon will hurry back to his or her laptop after the game to see what other fans have to say about how the game went that day. Or, perhaps closer to the experience Rheingold described, a fan can simultaneously watch the Gators play on television while participating in the online discussion in real time as the game unfolds—all the while keeping up with whatever else may be going on in the home or the office, not to mention multitasking on the computer by keeping one window on the Gator boards, another on e-mail, and perhaps yet another on a project for work.

For social capital scholar Robert Putnam, sharing geographic space (not just cyberspace) is a crucial catalyst to creating community bonds. His ideal virtual community is one that complements rather than replaces geographic place. Thus, he prefers online communities rooted in local communities rather than solely in specialized interests (Putnam, Feldstein, & Cohen, 2003). Putnam et al. valued "the startling immediacy and localness" of the postings found on craigslist.org, as well as "member participation in defining norms of the group" (such as through flagging of offensive posts and the creation of list-specific vocabulary) and the fact that its sense of community is born of "aims and purposes beyond that of simply being together" (p. 240).

The fans whose discussions create the Gator Nation online are also an instance of a virtual community rooted in the local space of Florida, where many Gators reside, and more specifically in the geographic space of Gainesville, where many resided in their college days and gather still for game days and other occasions. So, too, do those in online Gator communities work together to define norms—whether formally by serving as moderators and disciplining flamers, or informally by creating a shared vocabulary of terms and allusions that serve to further cement the social bonds of the Gator Nation. Finally, online Gators are not simply self-disclosing ad nauseum (as is often the case with bloggers), nor are they there simply to see and be seen as on social networking sites. Online Gators participate in their virtual community to voice their opinions on all things related to University of Florida athletics with likeminded others, but they are also there to report information on practices attended, the latest recruiting news gathered, and staffing rumors heard; to sell or exchange tickets; to ask for advice on what to do when visiting other SEC towns; and even to seek prayer and support for Gator friends and family in need. What happens on these Gator-focused Web sites and message boards complements events that happen in real time (sports seasons) and space (Florida and the Southeastern Conference), thereby making it more likely that "virtual social capital" does indeed result from the aggregate of Internet interactions that are the Gator Nation online.

Creating Community

Through the content of their posts and their online interactions with one another, sports message board posters give one another support, rapport, and a sense of connectedness. As the *St. Petersburg Times'* Ernest Hooper (2000) observed: "The Internet has long been known as the super information highway, but for people ... who immerse themselves in team-specific Web sites, chat rooms and message boards, it's also a portal to passion. No voices are heard, no faces are seen, but the emotion that fuels such sites is as evident as a broad smile or a grimace" (p. 1C). One instance of such community-building activity specific to the Gator message boards revolved around Greg See, a tight end turned defensive tackle who came to the Gators on scholarship in 1995. Redshirted his first year, he left in spring 1996 because of homesickness for his native Pennsylvania. However, he came back to the Gators in 1997 as a walk-on and had worked his way into being "in position to contend for playing time" by spring 1998. But at that time See's dreams of finally seeing playing time for the Gators were dashed when he was diagnosed with brain cancer. Gators fans, including and especially those online, rallied to See's cause.

Many Gators showed their support for See through the Greg See Scholarship Foundation, which was founded after a discussion that took place on the Gator Country Web site. Ray Hines, a Web designer who created Gator Country in 1996, had a longtime friend and fellow Gators fan who died after a long battle with cancer. Hines felt that serving as one of 12 board members for the See Foundation was a way to remember his own friend's memory through helping others. In addition to helping direct the Foundation, Hines used his Web designing expertise to create a Web page about See on the Gator Country site where he posted updates on See and on the charity golf tournament held in his honor. Of online Gators' enthusiasm for helping See and the scholarship established in his name, Hines observed, "You know how Gators are.... We feel like brothers and sisters. We go to football games and it's like there are no strangers on game day. It's the same thing on Gator Country. We're all just like that" (quoted in Neiswanger, 1999).

Before See left his Gainesville hospice to return home to Philadelphia, a going-away party was organized for See. While organizers tried to keep the crowd of well-wishers small, word spread on the message boards, and over 200 people stopped by the hospice to wish See well. When See succumbed to the cancer in July 2000, "Scott Costello of Gainesville, a moderator on two message boards ... said he received more than 200 e-mails about See" the next day (Auman, 2000, p. 2C). Greg Auman reported that weekend in the *St. Petersburg Times*, "Message boards on University of Florida football Web sites were overloaded with postings from fans Friday [the day after See's death].... Hundreds were mourning the loss of a player who never made it on the field but found a way to touch their lives in a greater way" (p. 2C). The story of how Gator fans connected online to show See their support, raise funds, and mourn his loss is a touching example of how fans can initially be brought together by the mutual love of their team but eventually come to create a community that moves beyond merely rehashing statistics, speculating about recruits, and complaining about coaches.

Just as the story of Gator fans coming together online and in person to support Greg See points to the altruism and goodwill that can be encouraged through participation in sports message boards, another example of community-building amongst online Gators has more to do with the bonding to be had through using creativity to poke fun at rival teams, especially their fans and coaches. While the message boards of old were simply long lists of messages to be scrolled through in what today seems an archaic text-only format (such as the original Swampy message board of the early 1990s), today's message boards allow users to post graphics and photographs as well as hypertext links along with the traditional text postings. Combine the ability to post photos with the ease and availability of Photoshop and the desire to bring down sports rivals using the weapon of humor, and you have a recipe for one of the longest running jokes of the Gator Nation online.

Lulu and Junior are the names online Gators bestowed on a couple of Tennessee Volunteers fans spotted in the stands at the 2001 SEC Championship game in which the Vols played the Louisiana State University Tigers. CBS Sports, which broadcast the game, panned to the stands to show a shot of some Vols fans and focused on a man and woman decked out in full orange-and-white Vols regalia. Many Gators fans watching the SEC Championship (as the Gators are also an SEC team) saw the close-up of the couple and went online to talk about them.

As the proprietor of the Lulu and Junior's World Travel Web site recalled, "This all started with a frame capture from the CBS telecast of the 2001 SEC championship game between LSU and UT. We were all set to see our Vols romp LSU but to our horror — well, the picture tells the story." The original Lulu and Junior screen still was first posted unaltered by an LSU Tigers fan with the username of BradyJ, but then was given its first alteration when it was made into a MasterCard–like ad: "SEC Championship Tickets ... $90, Hot Dog & Coke ... $35 (2 Each), Hair Perm & Goatee Trim ... $25. The Look after LSU goes up on Tennessee with 3 minutes left to lose all hope of Rose Bowl: PRICELESS." From the perspective of online Gators, Lulu and Junior are typical Vols fans. The names Lulu and Junior seem to have been drawn from similarly named characters from the old *Hee Haw* television show, whom Lulu and Junior very much resemble in their physical appearance.

In the user-generated *Wikipedia* entry devoted to Lulu and Junior, they are described as "two disgruntled, middle-aged, and portly Volunteers fans," whose Tennessee roots mean that many of their altered images "involve redneck stereotypes." After this initial appearance of Lulu and Junior on the Gator boards, a popular pastime became using Photoshop to place Lulu and Junior in a variety of other contexts— thus, Lulu and Junior's World Travels. In all, over 40 works of Photoshop-driven humor are posted in this particular Lulu and Junior gallery, many of which made their Web debut posted on the Gator message boards. Not only do these images of Lulu and Junior bring Gators together, but as attested by the guestbook on the Lulu and Junior's World Travels site, fans of all sorts of Tennessee rivals come together in the laughter inspired by Lulu and Junior. As of September 2007, over 62,600 visits have been made to this site to pay homage to what may be the world's— or at least the Internet's— most famous Tennessee Volunteers fans (Lulu and Junior's World Travels).

In Lulu and Junior's presence on the Gator message boards, both in images and in the text responses generated by those images, we see how Gator fans have used humor as many before them have: to gain power over rivals, especially over those in whom there is some perceived threat. Online Gators skewer rivals, as personified by Lulu and Junior, as a way of gaining power over them online even in years when they may not win against them on the football field. Whether rallying in support around cancer victim Greg See or rallying in humor around the altered images of Lulu and Junior, online Gators have used their message boards as a way to cope in power struggles, whether the life-or-death struggle against cancer or the win-or-lose struggle against threatening football rivals.

Reporting News

Sports reporters for traditional media such as television, radio, newspapers, and magazines realize perhaps more than anyone else the power wielded by sports message board posters. On August 1, 2005, the Florida television network Sun Sports devoted an hour-long episode of its show *Sports Talk Live* to the impact of the "Internet Culture" on sports reporting. Representing the new media in this discussion were Marty Cohen (gatorbait.net), Jim Lamar (warchant.com), and Sean Delaney (miami-hurricanes.com). The perspectives of the "old media" were represented by Mike Bianchi of the *Orlando Sentinel*, Brady Ackerman of Sun Sports' *Tailgate Saturday*, Pat Dooley of the *Gainesville Sun*, Steve Ellis of the *Tallahassee Democrat*, and Sun Sports' Watson. Among the topics discussed was the increasing role that message boards and other forms of "new media" are playing in reporting rumors and breaking news, which has changed the traditional media's approach to reporting standards and timeframes. Fans can now be reporters alongside those with the official press passes, and, increasingly, sports sites' reporters are being granted the same press credentials as members of traditional print and broadcast media (Watson, Internet culture special, *Sports Talk Live*, 1 August 2005).

A theme emphasized on *Sports Talk Live* was how rumors reported online eventually get picked up by and reported on in the traditional media. The perception that information can be posted online by anyone without going through the more rigorous system of editors and fact-checkers that is (or should be) the norm in traditional media is as disturbing to some as it is liberating to others. Franz Beard, managing editor of *Gator Country*, and Ray Hines, publisher of *Gator Country*, who appeared together in a taped segment on the *Sports Talk Live* Internet special, discussed the accuracy of their journalistic stories versus rumors that appeared on the message board component of their site. Beard explained that, "What we demand is the fairness and the accuracy when we're reporting. Now, what goes on the message boards, that's a different story, because there's every different version of the story we can imagine." Hines described his site's process of "rumor control": "We all get together when something comes out. We have like a team of 10 moderators on the board. When a rumor comes up, most of the time they pull it and put it somewhere else. Then they call us and let us know. Then we can find out what's going on, if it's true or not. But there's always one that will slip by ... That's what gives the Internet a bad reputation sometimes."

Likewise, when asked how he decides what's offensive and what's simply smack talk, *Gator Bait* publisher Marty Cohen observed that: "There's a real gray area there. It's almost each individual post you have to look at it, and sometimes it depends on your mood. I mean you might know you've seen this guy post a thousand times, he's just stepped over the line today and he's out of here." But despite the element of chaos caused by rumors or out-of-control posters, Cohen felt optimistic about the democratizing, equalizing potential of the Gator message boards, arguing that: "The message boards are ... the grass-roots of fandom. You've got every sort of fan.... And there's a lot of truth that comes out of the message boards and there's also a lot of insanity. So drawing the line is really difficult to do, it takes a lot of time. That's almost harder to do than gathering news sometimes."

Despite these safeguards, new media such as blogs and message boards are making it possible for anyone to report sports news. As Whit Watson observed: "If a fan walks down the street in Gainesville and goes into a restaurant or a club and sees an athlete or a coach engaged in something they shouldn't be engaged in, in essence you've got thousands upon thousands of reporters there who can post on a message board whenever they want. They're not account-able, they're not trained, they're hiding behind a screen name" (Watson, Internet culture special, *Sports Talk Live*, 1 August 2005).

Similarly, Mike Bianchi of the *Orlando Sentinel* expressed his view that "the message boards are the ultimate democracy. Everybody has their say." He elab-orated on this later, characterizing the many voices represented on the fan forums as "a thousand sources out there, that's the way I look at it ... not a high percentage [pan out as stories] ... but like I said earlier, there have been some huge stories that have been broken on the Internet." This comment points to the new symbiosis that exists between fans and sports reporters. As Bianchi argued to Pat Dooley of the *Gainesville Sun*, part of a sports columnist's or reporter's job is to patrol the fan forums: "If you're a traditional beat writer at a newspaper now ... if you don't check the message boards everyday, you're not a very good beat writer. I think you have to check them." Dooley agreed that much of what his and other sports writers' jobs now entail is looking online for "fires to put out." But, at the same time, Dooley admitted that, "If you don't check it out, there may be 10 things on there in a month. Nine may not be true, but the one you don't [take the time to] check out turns out to be true."

Marty Cohen of *Gator Bait* likened the posting of information online to throwing spaghetti against a wall: "Some of it's going to stick, most of it's going to fall, but some of it's going to stick, so you just keep throwing it." He added that the "thirst to be first" to break a story encourages taking the risk to post a story as it continues to unfold, as in the case of speculations about whether Urban Meyer would be taking the job at Notre Dame or at Florida. Fan sites of both Notre Dame and Florida posted stories saying he was coming to their school, and media sites in their respective markets cited those stories—but only one side's story could have been true (Watson, Internet culture special, *Sports Talk Live*, 1 August 2005).

But as discussed on *Sports Talk Live*, there is a blurring between fan-oriented sites and journalism-driven sites, with many sites such as Gator Country and Gator Bait existing as hybrids that feature both fan- and journalist-created content, though in separate areas of their respective sites. Other hybrids are formed when traditional media such as newspapers, television networks, and radio stations create Web sites incorporating both online versions of their print sports coverage as well as message boards. The idea that new sports media and old sports media could possibly come together and complement one another's coverage is, to Watson, exciting because it means more information for the always information-hungry sports fan: "Who wins in this deal? You do. More is more, especially during football season."

The fans win in the sense that they are empowered by new media such as message boards to be more active participants in the discourse surrounding their sports. Fans can start a Web site calling for the firing of a just-signed coach (as they did upon the hiring of Ron Zook as the Gators football coach), thus disturbing the new coach and the athletic director who hired him. Fans can post reports about sighting a suspended player such as UF's Marcus Thomas walking to practice, thus disturbing the coach (Urban Meyer) who is then forced to comment on it to the traditional media. (Meyer was paraphrased as stating that "Thomas merely was working out on his own") ("Thomas' status" 2006, p. 4).

As University of Florida Athletic Director Jeremy Foley observed in the midst of the fireronzook.com era: "The Internet has changed the landscape.... You dismiss a lot of it as malicious and ignore it because it could be coming from anyone, like an opponent, but, yes, if something credible comes up, you do have to check it out.... The line between what's fact and fiction on the Internet is blurred.... People tend to see it and believe some of it" (Roberts, 2003, p. 9).

Or a fan can post a photo of a supposedly new Florida uniform that looks reminiscent of the style of another team, perhaps realizing the photo is not authentic, but posting it as a way of floating the design in a public forum so as to bring the design to the attention of those who do have control over such things. As Marty Cohen conjectured: "Verification of information is tough, but I tell you what, there is an impact on the process because folks look at it. Jeremy Foley is on our Web site, Urban Meyer says he looks at the site.... I hope that he looks at it. People who make decisions look at it, and obviously they're not swayed by what fans or message boards think, but I think it all does have an effect" (Watson, Internet culture special, *Sports Talk Live*, 1 August 2005).

Related to this, the Gators' former "ol' ball coach" Steve Spurrier, now coach of the rival South Carolina Gamecocks, closed practices to the general public midway through preseason practices in August 2006 "because he said too much about what happens is being reported on Internet sites" ("Spurrier Closes Practice," 2006, p. C7). For athletics directors and coaches such as Foley, Meyer, and Spurrier, the power to control decision-making and strategy is compromised when sports fans make their opinions and observations open to public view online, 24 hours a day, 7 days a week.

Expressing Opinions and Becoming Activists

When sports fans want to express how they feel about the current issues in their respective sports worlds, they turn to the Internet. When Florida Gators fans were unhappy with the fact that coach Urban Meyer was giving too much playing time to lackluster senior Chris Leak rather than to freshman fireball Tim Tebow, they vented their frustrations and debated the relative strengths (and weaknesses) of their quarterbacks on the Gator boards: "The major Gators fan-site was loaded with people defending their boos or explaining why they booed, and another group pledged its support of Leak" (DiRocco, 2006, p. E-1).

When fans feel frustrated by the current Bowl Championship Series system of determining the NCAA Division I football title, as opposed to the playoff system used in all of the other NCAA college football divisions, they argue their points online: "The Sports Fans of America Association has made five proposals for a Division I playoff system on its Web site, which the group says entertains 175,000 unique visitors each month" (Strasen, 2001, p. 2). Sports message boards give fans the opportunity to vent their frustrations, to articulate their opinions and arguments, and even become activists in ways that have implications beyond the Internet. Some see this freedom of expression in a positive light. George Johnson, a fan who posts regularly on the sptimes.com message boards, reflected, "It's sort of like being on a debate team.... You want to compare notes. I guess people just want to share their feelings, their theories. Part of the appeal is being able to speculate on what the team is going to do, how are they going to handle the pressure" (quoted in Hooper, 2000, p. 1C).

But others, especially some reporters for traditional media outlets, are cynical, skeptical, and sensationalistic in their presentation of sports message board participants. Representative of this more negative perspective is Selena Roberts of the *New York Times*, who described online sports fans as people who "manipulate the careers of coaches from their basements, cubicles and breakfast nooks while wearing suits, curlers and khakis. They boot up to take down rivals using D.S.L., dial-ups and wireless magic as they tap out rage, rumors and revelations.... Masked by the mousepad, they wield fantasy-camp–like powers via the online message board — a venting place that provides cyberfanatics a chance to toy with the lives of sports figures they loathe and love" (Roberts, 2003, p. 9).

To portray sports message board posters in this manner is an attempt to bring them down a rung, to disempower their voices by equating their freedom of expression with mere game-playing and attacking their character by calling them crazed "cyberfanatics." One could read Roberts' description as merely a colorful, attention-getting lead. But when one considers her position as a reporter for one of the most influential traditional media outlets in the world, her words can be read as the reaction of someone who, as part of the entrenched power structure, feels threatened by the increasing influence of the more grass-roots new media. Howard Rheingold (2000) cited social psychologist Sara Kiesler's contention in the *Harvard Business Review* that "computer-mediated communications can break down hierarchical and departmental barriers, standard operating procedures, and organizational norms." Even Robert Putnam, though not the proponent of virtual communities that Rheingold is, admitted that one advantage of such online discussions is the ability to break down traditional hierarchies and allow voices usually muted or silenced to be heard (2000).

On a practical level, the ones who are most directly impacted by the "rage, rumors and revelations" posted online are those coaches whose careers message board posters are out to "manipulate" from the comfort of their "breakfast nooks." The coach Roberts likely had in mind when she wrote those words was then–UF football coach Ron Zook, embroiled in controversy from the moment he was revealed as the replacement for departing coach Steve Spurrier. The prospects for Zook were bleak from the start, considering Spurrier's success at Florida and long association with the university from his days as Heisman-winning quarterback in the 1960s to his days as the coach who turned around Florida football with multiple SEC championships and ultimately the National Championship in the 1996 season. When Spurrier announced his resignation on January 4, 2002, within 10 minutes of the initial posting on gatorsports.com (associated with the *Gainesville Sun* newspaper), "those boards—like many sites related to Florida football — were overwhelmed by a flood of Gator fans trying to find out if their worst nightmare had come true. It was five hours before traffic subsided enough to allow the boards back up for widespread consoling."

Gatorcountry.com was similarly overloaded, so much so "that it had to scale back its page to a single confirming headline and link to *The Sun*'s site. The message boards at Gator Country were down most of the afternoon." According to Gator Country's Ray Hines, "This is unspeakable — it just went crazy and the servers crashed several times.... We had people telling us that even *ESPN* went down for a little while" (Auman, 2002, p. 7C). Considering this extreme online activity at the news of Spurrier's departure, it is not surprising that fans displeased with his replacement would soon be overloading sites devoted to ousting his replacement.

Possibly the best known, and perhaps the most effective, instance of Gators' online activism is the example of the online reaction against the Gators' next football coach, Ron Zook. On the same day Athletic Director Jeremy Foley announced his decision to hire Zook, disbelief and dissension hit the message boards, and a Web site specifically devoted to voicing such sentiments could be found at fireronzook.com. The site was up for Zook's entire tenure at UF, which spanned from his hiring in early 2002 to his departure after the bowl game in January 2005, and the site can still be accessed today in its final, victorious form. The URL was actually purchased when Zook was only mentioned as a possible replacement, "when seven fraternity brothers chatting on an Internet message board shared their dismay over the pursuit by their alma mater ... of Ron Zook" (Thamel, 2004, p. D1).

Just as there were some Zook defenders present alongside the Zook haters on the various Gator message boards, so, too, was there a rival www.support-zook.com site (Woods, 2002, p. E-1). Competition to cover breaks in the developing Zook saga was fierce, as Bianchi noted: "The Internet has changed the way we do business.... Look at the stories the Internet has broken.... Ron Zook, when he went to the frat house and got into the altercation, that was on the Internet three days before [it was covered in] the traditional media (Watson, Internet culture special, *Sports Talk Live*, 1 August 2005). So the collective pressure to fire Zook remained quite constant and was channeled through both old and new media. That, coupled with a less-than-stellar record, resulted in Zook's being fired before his third season was complete, after an unforgivable loss to Mississippi State on October 23, 2004. Zook's firing came the following Monday, October 25. In the brief interval between the most embarrassing of losses and Foley's announcement of Zook's firing, the Gator message boards went wild, and the Fire Ron Zook site was so popular that "users got a 'service unavailable' message ... as frustrated Gator fans logged on to pile on their beleaguered coach" (Staples, 2004, p. 6).

Fireronzook.com was online and updated regularly from January 2002 through December 2004, beginning when Ron Zook was named head coach of the Florida football team and ending in December 2004, after his second and final season as Gators coach was complete. The author/creator of Fireronzook.com was never revealed on the site. The only attribution apart from a credit to FATT Webdesigns appeared on the Editor's Note page, which always featured a photo of a person with a brown paper bag over his head, with a comical smiley face drawn on it in black marker. This author mug shot was accompanied by the caption "The Webmaster, Loyal Gator: The Webmaster is an Alumnus of the University of Florida and knows that most Gator fans own shot guns ... just in case you were wondering about the bag."

However, the author of the site did reveal himself in the days following Zook's demise. Mike Walsh, a 1996 UF alum living in New York, told the Associated Press that the day Zook was fired was: "a great day for any Florida fan.... But my reaction wasn't what I thought it would be. I thought I would leave work and go have champagne. ... But I was bitter. I was bitter that we were right. I was bitter that we wasted 2½ years with Zook. I was bitter that a bunch of Florida grads could see that he had no qualifications while athletic director Jeremy Foley, who gets paid a lot money, couldn't" (quoted in Long, 2004).

The main content of the site was contained in the "Editor's Notes," the first of which was posted on January 17, 2002, just days after Zook was hired, and the last of which was posted on December 8, 2004, after the campaign to fire Zook finally proved successful and a new coach, Urban Meyer, had been named. These substantial notes, written in the first-person style of sports opinion columns, were posted roughly every week during football seasons. In a similar vein, there was also a more limited set of "Sermons" by a different author who depicted himself with a photo of a plastic action figure with a pirate patch over one eye and a minister's collar attached to his black shirt.

These "Notes" and "Sermons" not only functioned to embody Florida fans' frustrations with Zook and AD Jeremy Foley (who hired him), but also served to accumulate a critical mass of arguments and evidence as to why the Zook era of Florida football should never have begun, and once started, should have been ended as quickly as possible. Each week, the authors would accumulate evidence from that week's games and relevant outside events related to Zook to construct an ever more convincing argument that Zook was not qualified to lead the team. Additional evidence against Zook was compiled in a compact chart called "The Tale of the Tape," which listed statistics related to Zook's two years as associate head coach in the 1990s in one column and the FRZ.com interpretation of those statistics in a second column.

Just as Gators used humor as a weapon against rivals in the form of Photoshop-enhanced images of their fans and coaches, Florida fans also used humor to deal with the stress of having Ron Zook as their head coach. To help cope with their frustration toward Athletic Director Jeremy Foley, the site featured a section linked under the title "Help Foley" and headlined, "My Career is in Your Hands: A list of suitable career options for soon to be former Florida Athletic Director Jeremy Foley: Because we're dedicated to helping Foley find his next job." Job leads offered to Foley included paramedic in Lee County, Florida; mobile home salesperson, manager at Denny's restaurant, and ticket office intern at Iowa State University. Readers of fireronzook.com were also afforded the opportunity to contribute content to the site in the form of "Letters to Foley." Users were also asked to submit any replies they received from Foley, but only one such reply was posted to the site. Fans could also post "Love Letters" to the authors of the site as a way of voicing their feedback. Also, during the period when the site was actively updated, a message board was available to fans as an additional venue for shared ranting and venting about the continued downfall of Florida Gators football while coached by Zook.

In October 2004, when the end was imminent, two entries linked under "Our Picks" and headlined "If FRZ.com=UF Athletic Director" offered lists of coaches considered by the authors to be much more qualified than Zook and, thus, candidates to replace him should the Fire Ron Zook campaign be successful. The first entry was actually a list of coaches who should have been considered and offered the job in late 2001/early 2002 instead of Zook, while the second entry listed four criteria a Zook replacement must exhibit (with elaboration on each): 1) "Must have proven himself to be a winner as a head coach;" 2) "Must be committed to the University of Florida and not see the job as a stepping stone;" 3) "Must have an offensive mind and like to 'pitch' the ball around;" and 4) "Must not be babbling clown in front of TV cameras." Of course, this list was as much an indictment of Zook as it was a depiction of fans' ideal next coach. Eight candidates were then named with arguments given as to why each would bring improvement to Florida's football program. Included in this list was Urban Meyer, who eventually took the Florida job after turning down an offer to coach Notre Dame.

Not surprisingly, when Zook was fired and Spurrier was again available (having left the Washington Redskins after his lackluster two seasons there), bringsteveback.com sprung up (English, 2004, p. 4C). When the Spurrier return was ruled out, the two top candidates for the coaching job appeared to be Utah's Urban Meyer and Boise State's Dan Hawkins. One cautious UF alum, Andy Judah, actually bought the domain names fireurbanmeyer.com and firedanhawkins.com as a pre-emptive strike against any future efforts by online Gators to undermine their next coach's success before it even had a chance to begin: "I just didn't think it was an appropriate way for fans and alumni to act in the hiring of a new coach.... Ron Zook never had a chance here at Florida, so I'm doing this to block someone else doing the same thing" (Thamel, 2004, p. D1). Jeremy Foley, maligned almost as severely by fireronzook.com as Zook himself, reflected, "I always thought it [the site] was unfair to Ron.... As the noise built it became divisive. It became apparent it wasn't going to work." Though Foley still argued that "Fans don't make [coaching] decisions," he conceded that "fans can create a climate that's not healthy to success. There's no question, with the different forms of communication today, the noise can get turned up very loudly" (Mandel, 2007, pp. 93–94, 109). As Stewart Mandel concluded, though possibly with tongue in cheek, "perhaps the college football world owes a debt of gratitude to Mike Walsh, the visionary Florida fan who, in following his whim and launching fireronzook.com, unknowingly empowered a new generation of fans" (Mandel, 2007, p. 109).

Conclusion: Agency through Online Activism

A case study of the Florida Gator Nation online illustrates how sports fans, through their participation in such online fora as message boards and Web sites, have the opportunity to build community with one another as well as report and even create news about their team, which empowers fans to gain agency and a sense of involvement in regard to their chosen team. Howard Rheingold has called virtual communities contemporary agora (2000). Likewise, as reporter Tom Robinson so astutely described, "the town square of the 21st century" is "the Internet message board" (Robinson, 2003, p. C1).

In the town squares of the Gator Nation, online Florida fans can commune with one another in ways that offer social support as well as empower themselves through creativity and humor. In the town squares of the Gator Nation, online Florida fans can participate in gathering and reporting the news of their team, whether through reporting on potential recruits, attending and reporting on team practices, or spreading rumors of changes in staff or strategy. In the town squares of the Gator Nation, online Florida fans can agitate for the removal of an unlikely coach and campaign for a more effective one. As Mandel argued, the existence of fan activist sites such as fireronzook.com has given "newfound weight to the voice of the people. In a sport where the fans often find themselves ignored ... there's no denying their increased influence in many schools' coaching decisions. Today's fans may be unrealistic, overly demanding, and, in some cases, delusional, but one thing they are not is ignored" (Mandel, 2007, p. 109).

Similarly, while Selena Roberts did not seem to take online sports fans seriously in terms of their motivations, she did appear to have some grasp on the sea-change in the fan experience that has accompanied the advent of online sports-fan communities: "Not that long ago, as in the '90s, fans' voices didn't carry much farther than their seats at the stadium. There was talk radio, but venom tends to evaporate through the airwaves. The chat rooms provide some permanence because the messages are in writing. Given the power of the word, the Internet is a tool of technology the overzealous fans have longed for: finally, they have a way to manipulate their teams, their heroes and their enemies. Why sit in the stands when you can take part in the game through cyberspace?" (Roberts, 2003, p. 9). Online sports discussion sites, such as those frequented by Florida Gators fans, empower fans through opportunities to become community-builders, active participants in the creation of sports information, and activists for the direction in which they, along with every fan base, hope to see their team progress— toward victory. In football, only 11 players can be on the field at any given time. But with the development of online sports fan sites, every team — and especially the Florida Gators—can have a Twelfth Man in spirit, online.

References

Aamidor, A. (2005, June 25). Millions of sports fans participate in fantasy sport leagues. *Associated Press Newswires*. Retrieved October 8, 2005, from Factiva database.

Abbott, H. (2003, May). Yao's rocket ride. *Inside Stuff*, 46–51.

Abel, A. (2003, January 27). The man who would be Ming. *Sports Illustrated*, 63–67.

Abercrombie, N., & Longhurst, B. (1998). *Audiences*. London: Sage.

Adler, A. (1927). *Understanding human nature*. Garden City, NY: Garden City Publishing.

Ahrens, F., & Farhi, P. (2002, June 19). Gol-gol-gol gooaaalll! Univision's soccer win; Spanish-language network's announcers lure fans from ESPN. *Washington Post*, p. C1.

Aitken, I. (2006). The European realist tradition. *Studies in European Cinema, 3*, 175–188.

Alabarces, P., Tomlinson, A., & Young, C. (2001). Argentina versus England at the France '98 World Cup: Narratives of nation and the mythologizing of the popular. *Media, Culture, and Society, 23*, 547–566.

Alloway, N., & Gilbert, P. (1998). Video game culture: Playing with masculinity, violence and pleasure. In S. Howard (Ed.), *Wired-up: young people and the electronic media* (pp. 95–114). London: UCL Press Limited.

Alonzo, M., & Aiken, M. (2004, January). Flaming in electronic communication. *Decision Support Systems, 36*, 205–213.

Ancheta, A. N. (1998). *Race, rights, and the Asian American experience*. New Brunswick, NJ: Rutgers University Press.

Anderson, B. (1983). *Imagined communities*. London: Verso.

Anderson, C. A. (2004). An update on the effects of playing violent video games. *Journal of Adolescence, 27*, 113–122.

Anderson, D. I. (2005). A portrait of a feminist mathematics classroom: What adolescent girls say about mathematics, themselves and their experiences in a "unique" learning environment. *Feminist Teacher, 15*, 175–194.

Anderson, M. (1992). The history of women and the history of statistics. *Journal of Women's History, 4*, 14–37.

Ang, I. (1998). Can one say no to Chineseness? Pushing the limits of the diasporic paradigm. *Boundary 2, 25*, 223–242.

Appel, M., & Richter, T. (2007). Persuasive effects of fictional narratives increase over time. *Media Psychology, 10*, 113–134.

Araton, H. (2005). *Crashing the borders: How basketball won the world and lost its soul at home*. New York: Free Press.

Arms, R. L., Russell, G. W., & Sandilands, M. L. (1979). Effects on the hostility of spectators of viewing aggressive sports. *Social Psychology Quarterly, 42*, 275–279.

Armstrong, K. L. (2002). Race and sport consumption motivations: A preliminary investigation of a Black consumers' sport motivation scale. *Journal of Sport Behavior, 25*, 309–331.

Auman, G. (2000, July 22). Fans flood Internet site to mourn ex–Gator. *The St. Petersburg Times*, p. 2C. Retrieved November 1, 2006, from Lexis Nexis News database.

Auman, G. (2002, January 5). Stunned Gator fans swamp sites. *The St. Petersburg Times*, p. 7C. Retrieved November 1, 2006, from Lexis Nexis News database.

Ballard, C. (2006, March 27). Writing up a storm: The Internet is changing sports coverage. *Sports Illustrated, 104*(3), pp. 58–65.

Bandura, A. (1971). *Social learning theory.* Morristown, N.J.: General Learning Press.

Bandura, A. (1973). *Aggression: A social learning analysis.* Englewood Cliffs, N.J.: Prentice-Hall.

Bandura, A. (1983). Psychological mechanisms of aggression. In R. G. Geen & E. I. Donnerstein (Eds.), *Aggression: Theoretical and empirical reviews* (Vol. 1). New York: Academic Press.

Bandura, A., Ross, D., & Ross, S. A. (1961). Transmission of aggressions through imitation of aggressive models. *Journal of Abnormal and Social Psychology, 63*, 575–582.

Barker, D. (1988). "It's been real": Forms of television representation. *Critical Studies in Mass Communication, 5*, 42–56.

Barthes, R. (1973). *Mythologies.* London: Paladin.

Baudrillard, J. (2000). Beyond use value. In M. J. Lee (Ed.), *The consumer society* (pp. 19–30). Oxford: Blackwell.

Bauman, Z. (1998). *Work, consumerism, and the new poor.* Buckingham: Open University Press.

Baym, N. (2007). *Social sports explosion.* Online fandom: News and perspectives on fan communication. Retrieved September 17, 2007, from <http://www.onlinefandom.com/archives/social-sports-explosion/>.

Behind the numbers: How U.S. sports dollars are spent. (2002, March 11–17). *Street and Smith's Sports Business Journal, 4*(47), 30–39.

Benoit, W. L. (1995). *Accounts, excuses and apologies: A theory of image restoration strategies.* Albany, NY: State University of New York Press.

Benoit, W. L., Gullifor, P., & Panici, D. A. (1991). President Reagan's defensive discourse on the Iran-Contra affair. *Communication Studies, 42*, 272–294.

Benoit, W. L., & Hanczor, R. S. (1994). The Tonya Harding controversy: An analysis of image restoration strategies. *Communication Quarterly, 42*, 416–433.

Berg, K. (2002). *Interpretive community and The X-Files fan forum: An ethnographic study.* Unpublished doctoral dissertation. University of Missouri, Columbia.

Berkowitz, L. (1969). The frustration-aggression hypothesis. In L. Berkowitz (Ed.), *Roots of aggression.* New York: Atherton Press.

Berkowitz, L. (1970). The contagion of violence: An S-R mediational analysis of some effects of observed aggression. In W. J. Arnold & M. M. Page (Eds.), *Nebraska Symposium on Motivation.* Lincoln: University of Nebraska Press.

Berkowitz, L. (1975). *A survey of social psychology.* Hinsdale, Ill.: Dryden Press.

Berkowitz, L. (1986). *A survey of social psychology* (3rd ed.). New York: Holt, Rinehart and Winston.

Berkrot, B. (2002, February 1). No destiny in charge to Super Bowl; we made it happen, say "rag-tag" Patriots. *The Advertiser*, p. 65.

Bernhardt, P. C., Dabbs, J. M., Jr., Fielden, J. A., & Lutter, C. D. (1998). Testosterone changes during vicarious experiences of winning and losing among fans at sporting events. *Physiology & Behavior, 65*, 59–62.

Berry, B., & Smith, E. (2000). Race, sport, and crime: The misrepresentation of African-Americans in team sports and crime. *Sociology of Sport Journal, 17*, 171–197.

Billings, A. C., Halone, K. K., & Denham, B. E. (2002). "Man, that was a pretty shot": An analysis of gendered broadcast commentary surrounding the 2000 Men's and Women's NCAA Final Four Basketball Championships. *Mass Communication & Society, 5*, 295–315.

Bilyeu, J. K., & Wann, D. L. (2002). An investigation of racial differences in sport fan motivation. *International Sports Journal, 6*, 93–106.

Bitzer, L. F. (1968). The rhetorical situation. *Philosophy and Rhetoric, 1*, 1–14.

Black, E. (1980). A note on theory and practice in rhetorical criticism. *Western Journal of Communication, 44*, 331–336.

Blank, H., & Nestler, S. (2006). Perceiving events as both inevitable and unforeseeable in hindsight: The Leipzig candidacy for the Olympics. *British Journal of Social Psychology, 45,* 149–160.

Blinebury, F. (2002, September 1). Wave of Yaomania ready to crest for Chinese. *The Houston Chronicle,* p. 14.

Blumler, J. G. (1979). The role of theory in uses and gratifications studies. *Communication Research, 6,* 9–36.

Bmunchausen66 (2003, October 19). Why is Yao so popular? *YaoMania!Forum Index: Yao's Impact on the Asian Community.* Retrieved September 12, 2006, from <http://www.yaomingmania.com/forum/viewtopic.php?p=21416&highlight=while+growing+asian+guy+recall+playing+professional+sports#21416>.

Booth, W. C. (1998). Why ethical criticism can never be simple. *Style, 32,* 351–364.

Bradley, S., Lupei, B., & Ray, M. (2007). The power of storytelling. *Information Outlook, 11,* 12–17.

Branscombe, N. R., & Wann, D. L. (1991). The positive social and self–concept consequences of sports team identification. *Journal of Sport & Social Issues, 15,* 115–127.

Branscombe, N. R., & Wann, D. L. (1992). Physiological arousal and reactions to outgroup members that implicate an important social identity. *Aggressive Behavior, 18,* 85–93.

Branscombe, N. R., & Wann, D. L. (1994). Collective self–esteem consequences of outgroup derogation when a valued social identity is on trial. *European Journal of Social Psychology, 24,* 641–657.

Brennan, C. (2005, September 1). Sports world cries for the big easy. *USA Today,* p. C12.

Brewer, M. B. (1991). The social self: On being the same and different at the same time. *Personality and Social Psychology Bulletin, 17,* 475–482.

Brill, A. A. (1929). The why of the fan. *North American Review, 228,* 429–434.

Brown, J. A. (1997). Comic book fandom and cultural capital. *Journal of Popular Culture, 30*(4), 13–31.

Bryant, J. (1989). Viewers' enjoyment of televised sports violence. In L. A. Wenner (Ed.), *Media, Sports and Society* (pp. 270–289). London: Sage.

Bryant, J., Brown, D., Comisky, P. W., & Zillman, D. (1982). Sports and spectators:

Commentary and appreciation. *Journal of Communication, 32,* 109–119.

Bryant, J., Zillmann, D., & Raney, A. A. (1998). Violence and the enjoyment of media sports. In L. A. Wenner (Ed.), *MediaSport* (pp. 252–265). London: Routledge.

Burke, K. (1931). *Counterstatement.* Berkeley, CA: University of California Press.

Burke, K. (1937). *Attitudes towards history.* Berkeley, CA: University of California Press.

Burke, K. (1950). *A rhetoric of motives.* Berkeley, CA: University of California Press.

Burke, K. (1950). *A rhetoric of motives.* New York: Prentice-Hall.

Burke, K. (1968). Dramatism. In *International encyclopedia of the social sciences* (V. 7, pp. 445–452).

Burke, K. (1969). *A grammar of motives.* Berkeley, CA: University of California Press.

Burke, K. (1974). *A rhetoric of motives.* Berkeley, CA: University of California Press.

Burke, K. (1989a). The nature of human action. In J. R. Gusfield (Ed.), *On symbols and society* (pp. 53–55). Chicago: Chicago University Press.

Burke, K. (1989b). *On symbols in society.* Chicago: The University of Chicago Press.

Burke, K. (1989c). Identification. In J. R. Gusfield (Ed.), *Kenneth Burke: On symbols and society* (pp. 179–191). Chicago: The University of Chicago Press. (Original work published in 1969.)

Busselle, R. W. (2001). Television exposure, perceived realism, and exemplar accessibility in the social judgment process. *Media Psychology, 3,* 43–67.

Busselle, R. W., & Greenberg, B. S. (2000). The nature of television realism judgments: A reevaluation of their conceptualization and measurement. *Mass Communication & Society, 3,* 249–268.

Busselle, R. W., Ryabovolova, A., & Wilson, B. (2004). Ruining a good story: Cultivation, perceived realism and narrative. *Communications, 29,* 365–378.

Busselle, R. W., & Shrum, L. J. (2003). Media exposure and exemplar accessibility. *Media Psychology, 5,* 255–282.

CantonKid (2004, April 4). Why is Yao so

popular? *YaoMania!Forum Index: Yao's impact on the Asian community.* Retrieved September 12, 2006, from <www.yao mingmania.com/forum/viewtopic.php? t=9&postdays=0&postorder=asc&start= 70>.

Carroll, N. (2000). Art and ethical criticism: An overview of recent directions of research. *Ethics, 110,* 350–387.

Cevallos, D. (2002, June 17). U.S. wins a harsh blow to national pride. *Inter Press Service* [Electronic Version]. Retrieved December 18, 2002, from <http://lw7fd. law7.hotmail.msn.com>.

Chan, J. M. (2002). Disneyfying and globalizing the Chinese legend Mulan: A study of transculturation. In J. M. Chan & B. T. McIntyre (Eds.), *In search of boundaries: Communication, nation-states, and cultural identities* (pp. 225–248). Westport, CT: Ablex Publishing.

Chea, T. (2004, April 3). NBA wants to turn Yao Ming admirers into full fledged fans. *The Associated Press.* Retrieved October 14, 2004, from Lexis Nexis Academic Universe.

Cheska, A. T. (1978). Sports spectacular: The social ritual of power. *Quest, 30,* 58–71.

Chow, R. (1998). Introduction: On Chineseness as a theoretical problem. *Boundary 2, 25,* 1–24.

Chuck_187 (2005, March 21). The Yao Ming Phenomenon. *YaoMania!Forum Index: Yao's Impact on the Asian Community.* Retrieved September 12, 2006 from <http://www.yaomingmania.com/forum/view topic.php?p=170809&highlight=docu mented+stereotypes#170809>.

Cialdini, R. B., Borden, R. J., Thorne, A., Walker, M. R., Freeman, S., & Sloan, L. (1976). Basking on reflected glory: Three (football) field studies. *Journal of Personality and Social Psychology, 34,* 366–375.

Cialdini, R. B., & Richardson, K. D. (1980). Two indirect tactics of image management: Basking and blasting. *Journal of Personality and Social Psychology, 39,* 406–415.

Clegg, S. R. (1993). Narrative, power, and social theory. In D. K. Mumbry (Ed.). *Narrative and social control: Critical perspectives* (pp. 15–45). Newbury Park, CA: Sage.

Coakley, J. J. (1986). *Sport in society: Issues and controversies* (3rd ed.). St. Louis, MO: Times Mirror/Mosby College Publishing.

Cohen, A., & Avrahami, A. (2005). Soccer fans' motivation as a predictor of participation in soccer-related activities: An empirical examination in Israel. *Social Behavior and Personality, 33,* 419–434.

Collins, T., & Vamplew, W. (2002). *Mud, sweat, and beers: A cultural history of sport and alcohol.* New York: Berg.

Comisky, P., Bryant, J., & Zillman, D. (1977). Commentary as a substitute for action. *Journal of Communication, 27,* 150–153.

Consalvo, M. (2003). Cyber-slaying media fans: Code, digital poaching, and corporate control of the Internet. *Journal of Communication Inquiry, 27,* 67–86.

Crawford, C. (2003). Interactive storytelling. In M. J. P. Wolf & B. Perron (Eds.), *The video game theory reader* (pp. 259–273). New York: Routledge.

Crawford, G. (2004). *Consuming sport: Fans, sport, and culture.* London: Routledge.

Crisp, R. J., Heuston, S., Farr, M. J., & Turner, R. N. (2007). Seeing red or feeling blue: Differentiated intergroup emotions and ingroup identification in soccer fans. *Group Processes and Intergroup Relations, 10,* 9–26.

CSTV.com (2007). Services. Retrieved September 17, 2007, from <http://www.cstv. com/online/services/collegesports-services.html>.

Cuban, M. (2006, September 26). Suspending officials? A business lesson. *Blogmaverick: The Mark Cuban weblog.* Retrieved September 27, 2006, from <http://www. blogmaverick.com/>.

Curry, T. J., & Jiobu, R. M. (1984). *Sports: A social perspective.* Englewood Cliffs, NJ: Prentice Hall.

Danto, A. C. (1982). Narration and knowledge. *Philosophy and Literature, 6,* 17–32.

Dasgupta, N., Banaji, M. R., & Abelson, R. P. (1999). Group entiativity and group perception: Association between physical features and psychological judgment. *Journal of Personality and Social Psychology, 75,* 991–1005.

De Angelis, R. (2007). Narrative triangulations: Truth, identity and desire in Ford Maddox Ford's *The Good Soldier. English Studies, 88,* 425–446.

Deaux, K., Reid, A., Mizrahi, K., & Ethier, K. A. (1995). Parameters of social identity. *Journal of Personality and Social Psychology, 68,* 280–291.

Delgado, F. (2003). The fusing of sport and politics: Media constructions of U.S. versus Iran at France '98. *Journal of Sport and Social Issues, 27,* 293–307.

DeNeui, D. L., & Sachau, D. A. (1996) Spectator enjoyment of aggression in intercollegiate games. *Journal of Sport & Social Issues, 20,* 69–77.

Diddi, A., & LaRose, R. (2006). Getting hooked on news: Uses and gratifications and the formation of news habits among college students in an internet environment. *Journal of Broadcasting & Electronic Media, 50,* 193–210.

Dietz-Uhler, B., End, C., Demakakos, N., Dickirson, A., & Grantz, A. (2002). Fans' reactions to law-breaking athletes. *International Sports Journal, 6,* 160–170.

Dietz-Uhler, B., End, C., Jacquemotte, L., Bentley, M., & Hurlbut, V. (2000). Perceptions of male and female sport fans. *International Sports Journal, 4,* 88–97.

Dietz-Uhler, B., Harrick, E. A., End, C., & Jacquemotte, L. (2000). Sex differences in sport fan behavior and reason for being a sport fan. *Journal of Sport Behavior, 23,* 219–231.

Dietz-Uhler, B., & Murrell, A. (1999). Examining fan reactions to game outcomes: A longitudinal study of social identity. *Journal of Sport Behavior, 22,* 15–27.

Dimmock, J. A., Grove, J. R., & Eklund, R. C. (2005). Reconceptualizing team identification: New dimensions and their relationship to intergroup bias. *Group Dynamics: Theory, Research, & Practice, 9,* 75–86.

DiRocco, M. (2006, September 27). Fans' boos are news to Gators starter Leak; quarterback says he was too busy to hear jeers during Kentucky game. *The Florida Times-Union,* p. E-1. Retrieved November 1, 2006, from Lexis Nexis News database.

Dixon, T., & Linz, D. (2000). Overrepresentation and underrepresentation of African Americans and Latinos as lawbreakers on television news. *Journal of Communication, 50,* 131–148.

Dollard, J., Doob, L., Miller, N., Mowrer, O., & Sears. R. (1939). *Frustration and aggression.* New Haven: Yale University Press.

Doosje, B., Ellemers, N., & Spears, R. (1999). Commitment and intergroup behaviour. In N. Ellemers, R. Spears, & B. Doosje (Eds.), *Social identity* (pp. 84–106). Oxford, UK: Blackwell.

Dorr, A., & Kovaric, P. (1990). Age and content influences on children's perceptions of realism of television families. *Journal of Broadcasting & Electronic Media, 34,* 377–398.

Douglas, M. (1966). *Purity and danger: An analysis of the concepts of pollution and taboo.* London: Routledge & Kegan Paul.

Drill: Players, fans show their true colors. (2001, September 24). *The Washington Post,* p. D9.

Duncun, M. C. (1983). Symbolic dimension of spectator sport. *Quest, 35,* 29–36.

Eaglestone, R. (2004). Postmodernism and ethics against the metaphysics of comprehension. In S. Connor (Ed.), *The Cambridge companion to postmodernism* (pp. 182–195). Cambridge: Cambridge University Press.

Eagleton, T. (2003). *After theory.* New York: Basic Books.

Eitzen, D. S. (1999). *Fair and foul: Beyond the myths and paradoxes of sport.* Lanham, MD: Rowman & Littlefield Publishers.

Ekman, P., Friesen, W. V., & Ellsworth, P. (1972). *Emotion in the human face.* New York: Pergamon Press.

Electronic Arts, Inc. (2004). *Madden football 2005™.* Tiburon.

Electronic Arts, Inc. (2005). *Madden football 2006™.* Tiburon.

Elfin, D. (2001, September 23). Games return after terrorist attacks. *The Washington Times,* p. C5.

Elias, N., & Dunning, E. (1986). *Quest for excitement: Sport and leisure in the civilizing process.* Oxford: Blackwell.

Elliot, S. (2007, February 26). The know list 6: Work that net. *Sporting News, 231*(9), p. 5.

End, C., Birchmeier, Z., & Mueller, D. (2004, September). *How time and group reactions influence sport fans' online defensive reactions to various sources of identity threat.* Paper presented at the annual meeting of the Association for the

Advancement of Applied Sport Psychology, Minneapolis, MN.

End, C. M. (2001). An examination of NFL fans' computer mediated BIRGing. *Journal of Sport Behavior, 24,* 162–181.

End, C. M. (2002). *The influence of ingroup/outgroup norms on sports fans' aggressive responses to social identity threat.* Unpublished doctoral dissertation, Miami University.

End, C. M., Dietz-Uhler, B., Harrick, E. A., & Jacquemotte, L. (2002). Identifying with winners: A reexamination of sport fans' tendency to BIRG. *Journal of Applied Social Psychology, 32,* 1017–1030.

End, C. M., Eaton, J., Campbell, J., Kretschmar, J. M., Mueller, D., & Dietz-Uhler, B. (2003). Outcome's influence on sport fans' computer-mediated attributions. *International Sports Journal, 7,* 128–140.

English, A. (2004, January 2). Despite it all, Gators see gains. *The St. Petersburg Times,* p. 4C. Retrieved November 1, 2006, from Lexis Nexis News database.

Enzenberger, H. M. (1972). Constituents of a theory of the media. In D. McQuail (Ed.), *Sociology of Mass Communication* (pp. 99–112). Harmondsworth: Penguin.

Eskelinen, M. (2003). Video games and configurative performances. In M. J. P. Wolf & B. Perron (Eds.), *The video game theory reader* (pp. 195–220). New York: Routledge.

Esser, L. (1994). *The birth of fantasy football.* Retrieved November 2, 2006 from <http://www.fantasyindex.com/Birth.html>

Ettema, J. S., & Glasser, T. L. (1988). Narrative form and moral force: The realization of innocence and guilt through investigative journalism. *Journal of Communication, 38,* 8–26.

Eysenck, H. J. (1995). Creativity as a product of intelligence and personality. In D. H. Saklofske & M. Zeidner, (Eds.), *International handbook of personality and intelligence.* New York: Plenum Press.

Eysenck, S., & Zuckerman, M. (1978). The relationship between sensation-seeking and Eysenck's dimensions of personality. *British Journal of Psychology, 69,* 483–487.

Farrar, K. M., Krcmar, M., & Nowak, K. L. (2006). Contextual features of violent video games, mental models and aggression. *Journal of Communication, 56,* 387–405.

Fastau, M. F. (1975). *The male machine.* New York: Dell.

Fatsis, S., Wonacott, P., & Tkacik, M. (2002, October 22). Great leap: A basketball star from Shanghai is big business. *Wall Street Journal,* p. A1. Retrieved February 23, 2003, from Lexis-Nexis News database.

FATT Webdesigns. (2002, January 17, through 2004, December 8). *FireRonZook.com.* Retrieved June 1, 2007, from <http://www.fireronzook.com>.

Feigen, J. (2003, January 3). Yao laps Shaq in All-Star race. *The Houston Chronicle,* p.1.

Feigen, J. (2004, March 24). Yao's presence felt and heard in win. *The Houston Chronicle,* p. 01.

Fish, S. (1980). *Is there a text in this class? The authority of interpretive communities.* Cambridge, MA: Harvard University Press.

Fisher, W. R. (1984). Narration as a human communication paradigm: The case of public moral argument. *Communication Monographs, 51,* 1–22.

Fisher, W. R. (1985). The narrative paradigm: An elaboration. *Communication Monographs, 52,* 347–367.

Fisher, W. R. (1987a). *Human communication narration: Toward a philosophy of reason, value, and action.* Columbia, SC: University of South Carolina Press.

Fisher, W. R. (1987b). Judging the quality of audiences and narrative rationality. In J. L. Golden & J. J. Pilotta. (Eds.), *Studies in honor of Chaim Perelman.* Boston: D. Reidel.

Fiske, J. (1989). *Reading the popular.* London and New York: Routledge.

Fiske, J. (1992). The cultural economy of fandom. In L. A. Lewis (Ed.), *The adoring audience: Fan culture and popular media* (pp. 30–49). London: Routledge.

Flood, J. P. (2004). Winners or losers. *Parks & Recreation, 39,* 74–79.

Ford, S. (2006, December 30). Fox Sports to make championship bowl games available online. *MIT Convergence Culture Consortium.* Retrieved September 17, 2007, from <http://www.convergenceculture.org/weblog/2006/12/fox_sports_to_make_championshi.php>.

Foss, S. (1989). *Rhetorical criticism: Exploration and practice.* Prospect Heights, IL: Waveland.

Foster, M. (2002, January 28). Super Bowl this year a red, white and blue zone [Electronic version]. *The Associated Press Online.* Retrieved March 3, 2006, from <http://web.lexis-nexis.com>.

Fox Sports Blog (2006, July 12). Retrieved July 2, 2007, from <http://community.foxsports.com/blogs/BobbyMcMahon/2006/07)12/Zidane_apologizes>.

Fraser, H. (2004). Doing narrative research: Analyzing personal stories line by line. *Qualitative Social Work, 3,* 179–201.

Frasca, G. (2003). Simulation versus narrative: Introduction to ludology. In M. J. P. Wolf & B. Perron (Eds.), *The video game theory reader* (pp. 221–235). New York: Routledge.

Funk, D. C., & James, J. (2001). The psychological continuum model: A conceptual framework for understanding an individual's psychological connection to sport. *Sport Management Review, 4,* 119–150.

Funk, D. C., Mahony, D. F., & Ridinger, L. L. (2002). Characterizing consumer motivation as individual difference factors: Augmenting the Sport Interest Inventory (SII) to explain the level of spectator support. *Sport Marketing Quarterly, 11,* 33–43.

Galloway, A. R. (2004). Social realism in gaming. *Game Studies: The International Journal of Computer Game Research,* 4(1). Retrieved August 15, 2006 from <http://www.gamestudies.org/0401/galloway/>.

Gantz, W. (1981). An exploration of viewing motives and behaviors associated with television sports. *Journal of Broadcasting, 25,* 263–275.

Gantz, W. (1991). Men, women, and sports: Audience experiences and effects. *Journal of Broadcasting & Electronic Media, 35,* 233–243.

Gantz, W., Wang, Z., Paul, B., & Potter, R. F. (2006). Sports versus all comers: Comparing TV sports fans with fans of other programming genres. *Journal of Broadcasting & Electronic Media, 50,* 95–118.

Gantz, W., & Wenner, L. A. (1991). Men, women, and sports: Audience experiences and effects. *Journal of Broadcasting & Electronic Media, 35,* 233–243.

Gantz, W., & Wenner, L.A. (1995). Fanship

and the television sports viewing experience. *Sociology of Sport Journal, 12,* 56–74.

Gardner, W. L., & Gabriel, S. (2004). Gender differences in relational and collective interdependence: Implications for self-views, social behavior, and subjective well-being. In A. H. Eagly, A. E. Beall, and R. J. Sternberg (Eds.), *The psychology of gender* (pp. 169–191). New York: Guilford Press.

Garofoli, J. (2002, June 18). Melting pot boils over for World Cup — Immigrants' loyalties tested. *San Francisco Chronicle,* p. A13.

Gatorbait.net Message Boards. *Gator Sports Forum.* Retrieved November 1, 2006, from <http://www.florida.rivals.com>.

The Gator Board. *Gator Sports Discussion.* Retrieved November 1, 2006, from <http://www.thegatorboard.com/bb>.

Gatorsports Forum. *The Gainesville Sun Gatorsports.com.* Retrieved November 1, 2006, from <http://www.gatorsportsforum.com/forums>.

Geertz, C. (1973). Thick description: Toward an interpretive theory of culture. In *The interpretation of cultures* (pp. 3–30). New York: Basic Books.

Georgakopoulou, A. (2006). The other side of the story: Towards a narrative analysis of narratives-in-action. *Discourse Studies, 8,* 235–257.

Gerdy, J. R. (2002). *Sports: The all–American addiction.* Jackson, MS: Mississippi University Press.

Ghanem, S., & Wanta, W. (2001). Agenda-setting and Spanish cable news. *Journal of Broadcasting & Electronic Media, 45,* 277–289.

Giulianotti, R. (2002). Supporters, followers, fans, and flaneurs: A taxonomy of spectator identities in football. *Journal of Sport and Social Issues, 26,* 25–46.

Goldberg, D. (2001, September 24). NFL's return smiles on the big apple. *Charleston Daily Mail,* p. B1.

Goldstein, J. (2005). Violent video games. In J. Raessens & J. Goldstein (Eds.), *Handbook of computer game studies* (pp. 341–357). Cambridge, MA: The MIT Press.

Goldstein, J. H., & Arms, R. L. (1971). Effects of observing athletics contests on hostility. *Sociometry, 34,* 83–90.

Goodger, J. M., & Goodger, B. C. (1989).

Excitement and representation: Toward a sociological explanation of the significance of sport in modern society. *Quest, 41*, 257–272.

Governor responds to Saints' announcement. *State of Louisiana, Office of the Governor website* (2005, December 30). Retrieved Feb. 23, 2006, from <http://www.gov.state.la.us/index.cfm?md=newsroom&tmp=detail&catID=3&articleID=1568&navID=27>.

Green, M. C. (2004). Transportation into narrative worlds: The role of prior knowledge and perceived realism. *Discourse Processes, 38*, 247–266.

Greenberg, B. S. (1974). Gratifications of television viewing and the correlates for British children. In J. Blumler & E. Katz (Eds.), *The uses of mass communication: Current perspectives of gratifications research* (pp. 71–92). Beverly Hills, CA: Sage.

Gregory, M. (1998). Ethical criticism: What it is and why it matters. *Style, 32*, 194–220.

Groos, K. (1898). *The play of animals.* New York: Appleton.

Grossberg, L. (1992). Is there a fan in the house? The affective sensibility of fandom. In L. A. Lewis (Ed.), *The adoring audience: fan culture and popular media* (pp. 50–65). London: Routledge.

Growth of NASCAR over the past decade: 1997–2006. (2007). Retrieved April 7, 2007, from <http://www.nascar.com>.

Guardian Blog (2006, July 12). Retrieved June 29, 2007 from <http://blogs.guardian.co.uk/news/archives/2006/07/12/zidane_je_ne_regrette_rien.html>.

Gupta, R., Derevensky, J. L., & Ellenbogen, S. (2006). Personality characteristics and risk-taking tendencies among adolescent gamblers. *Canadian Journal of Behavioral Science, 38*, 203–213.

Hagstrom, R. G. (1998). *The NASCAR way: The business that drives the sport.* New York: John Wiley & Sons.

Halling, N. (2005, September 10). American football: Saints march on to give battered city sense of hope. *The Independent,* p. 62.

Haridakis, P. M. (2002). Viewer characteristics, exposure to television violence and aggression. *Media Psychology, 4*, 323–352.

Haridakis, P. M., & Rubin, A. M. (2003). Motivation for watching television violence and viewer aggression. *Mass Communication & Society, 6*, 29–56.

Haridakis, P. M., & Rubin, A. M. (2005). Third-person effects in the aftermath of terrorism. *Mass Communication & Society, 8*, 39–59.

Harris, R. J. (2004). Sports and music: Emotion in high gear. In R. J. Harris (Ed.), *A cognitive psychology of mass communication* (4th ed., pp. 151–186). Mahwah, NJ: Lawrence Erlbaum.

Hartley, J. (1984). Encouraging signs: TV and the power of dirt, speech, and scandalous categories. In W. Rowland & B. Watkins (Eds.), *Interpreting television: Current research perspectives* (pp. 119–141). Beverly Hills, CA: Sage.

Hartmann, D. (2003). The sanctity of Sunday football: Why men love sports. *Contexts, 2*(4), 13–19.

Hastorf, A. H., & Cantril, H. (1954). They saw a game: A case study. *Journal of Abnormal and Social Psychology, 49*, 129–134.

Hatch, J. B. (2006). Beyond *apologia*: Racial reconciliation and apologies for slavery. *Western Journal of Communication, 70*, 5–24.

Hawkins, R. P. (1977). The dimensional structure of children's perceptions of television reality. *Communication Research, 4*, 299–321.

Hawkins, R. P., & Pingree, S. (1981). Uniform messages and habitual viewing: Unnecessary assumptions in social reality effects. *Human Communication Research, 7*, 291–301.

Hearit, K. M. (1999). Newsgroups, activist publics, and corporate *apologia*: The case of Intel and its Pentium chip. *Public Relations Review, 23*, 217–232.

Hearit, K. M., & Brown, J. (2004). Merrill Lynch: Corporate *apologia* and business fraud. *Public Relations Review, 30*, 459–466.

Herzig, A. H. (2004). "Slaughtering this beautiful math": Graduate women choosing and leaving mathematics. *Gender & Education, 16*, 379–395.

Herzog, H. (1944). What do we really know about daytime serial listeners? In P. F. Lazarsfeld & F. N. Stanton (Eds.), *Radio Research 1942–1943* (pp. 3–33). New York: Duell, Sloan & Pearce.

Hilliard, D. C., & Hendley, A. O. (2004, November). *Celebrity athletes and sports imagery in advertising during the NFL telecasts.* Paper presented at the annual meeting of the North American Society for the Sociology of Sport, Tucson, AZ.

Hillman, C. H., Cuthbert, B. N., Bradley, M. M., Lang, P. J. (2004). Motivated engagement to appetitive and aversive fanship cues: Psychophysiological responses of rival sport fans. *Journal of Sport & Exercise Psychology, 26,* 338–351.

Hills, M. (2002). *Fan cultures.* London: Routledge.

Hinkle, S., & Brown, R. J. (1990). Intergroup comparisons and social identity: Some links and lacunae. In D. Abrams & M. A. Hogg (Eds.), *Social Identity Theory: Constructive and Critical Advances* (pp. 48–70). New York, NY: Springer-Verlag.

Hipkins, D., & Cooke, P. (2006). Introduction: Realism in European cinema and beyond. *Studies in European Cinema, 3,* 171–173.

Hirt, E. R., Zillmann, D., Erickon, G. A., & Kennedy, C. (1992). Costs and benefits of allegiance: Changes in fans' self–ascribed competencies after team victory versus defeat. *Journal of Personality and Social Psychology, 63,* 724–738.

Hoberman, J. (1997). *Darwin's athletes: How sport has damaged black America and preserved the myth of race.* Boston: Houghton Mifflin.

Hooper, E. (2000, July 19). Sports unlimited. *The St. Petersburg Times,* p. 1C. Retrieved November 1, 2006, from Lexis Nexis News database.

Horne, J. (2005). *Sport in consumer culture.* New York: Palgrave Macmillan.

Howell, M. (1997). *From moonshine to Madison Avenue: A cultured history of the NASCAR Winston Cup Series.* Bowling Green, OH: Popular Press.

Hugenberg, L. W., & Hugenberg, B. S. (2008). If it ain't rubbin,' it ain't racin': NASCAR, American values and fandom. *Journal of Popular Culture* (in press).

Hugenberg, L. W., & Schaefermeyer, M. H. (1983). Soliloquy as self–disclosure. *Quarterly Journal of Speech, 69,* 180–190.

Hugenberg, L. W., & Spinda, J. (2007 November). *An empirical study of NASCAR fandom: Motivation, identification and involvement.* Paper presented at the annual meeting of the National Communication Association, Chicago, IL.

Huizinga, J. H. (1970). *Homo ludens: A study of the play element in culture.* London: Paladin.

Huler, S. (1999). *A little bit sideways: One week inside a NASCAR Winston Cup race team.* Osceola, WI: MBI Publishing.

Hyman, M. (2006, February 6). Welcome footsteps: Sports play a vital role in New Orleans' recovery from Katrina. *The Baltimore Sun,* p. D10.

Iliff, L., & Case, B. M. (2002, June 15). Border war: Beware team USA, Mexico takes its soccer seriously. *Dallas Morning News,* Sports.

Iser, W. (1974). *The implied reader: Patterns of reading in prose fiction from Bunyan to Beckett.* Baltimore, MD: Johns Hopkins University Press.

Iser, W. (1978). *The act of reading: A theory of aesthetic response.* Baltimore: Johns Hopkins University Press.

Iser, W. (2006). Reception theory: Iser. In W. Iser (Ed.), *How to do theory* (pp. 57–69). Oxford: Blackwell.

It's unanimous: Jets award ball to city of New York (2001, September 24). *Providence Journal-Bulletin,* p. C3.

Jacobson, B. (2003). The social psychology of the creation of a sports fan identity: A theoretical review of the literature. *Athletic Insight: Online Journal of Sport Psychology, 5,* 1–10.

James, J. D., & Ridinger, L. L. (2002). Female and male sports fan: A comparison of sport consumption motives. *Journal of Sport Behavior, 25,* 260–279.

James, J. D., & Ross, S. D. (2004). Comparing sport consumer motivations across multiple sports. *Sport Marketing Quarterly, 13,* 17–26.

Jeffres, L. W., Neuendorf, K., & Atkins, D. (2002). Media use and participation as a spectator in public leisure activities: Competition or symbiosis? *Leisure Studies, 22,* 169–174.

Jenkins, H. (2000). *Star Trek* rerun, reread, rewritten: Fan writing as textual poaching. In H. Newcomb (Ed.), *Television: The critical view* (6th ed., pp. 470–494). New York: Oxford University Press.

Jenson, J. (1992). Fandom as pathology: The consequences of characterization. In L. A. Lewis (Ed.), *The adoring audience:*

Fan culture and popular media (pp. 9–29). London: Routledge.

Jirousek, C. A. (1996). Superstars, super-heroes and the male body image: The visual implications of football uniforms. *Journal of American Culture, 19*(2), 1–11.

Johnson, A. L., Crawford, M. T., Sherman, S. J., Rutchick, A. M., Hamilton, D. L., Ferreira, M. B., & Petrocelli, J. V. (2006). A functional perspective on group memberships: Differential need fulfillment in a group typology. *Journal of Experimental Social Psychology, 42*, 707–719.

Jones, I. (1997). A further examination of the factors influencing current identification with a sports team, a response to Wann et al. (1996). *Perceptual and Motor Skills, 85*, 257–258.

Kahle, L. R., Kambara, K. M., & Rose, G. M. (1996). A functional model for fan attendance motivations for college football. *Sport Marketing Quarterly, 5*(4), 51- 60.

Kang, S. (2005, August 29). Football (A special report). *The Wall Street Journal.* Retrieved October 8, 2005, from Factiva database.

Katz, E., Blumler, J. G., & Gurevitch, M. (1974). Utilization of mass communication by the individual. In J. G. Blumler & E. Katz (Eds.), *The uses of mass communications: Current perspectives on gratifications research* (pp. 18–33). Beverly Hills, CA: Sage.

Katz, E., Gurevitch, M., & Haas, H. (1973). On the use of the mass media for important things. *American Sociological Review, 38*, 164–181.

Kellner, D. (2000). Cultural studies and philosophy: An intervention. In T. Miller (Ed.), *A companion to cultural studies* (pp. 139–153). Oxford: Blackwell.

Kellner, D. (2001). The sports spectacle, Michael Jordan, and Nike: Unholy alliance? In D. L. Andrews (Ed.), *Michael Jordan, Inc.: Corporate sport, media culture and late modern America.* New York: SUNY.

Kelly, K. E. (2004). A brief measure of creativity among college students. *College Student Journal, 38*, 594–596.

Kelly, K. E. (2006). Relationship between the five-factor model of personality and the scale of creative attributes and behavior: A validational study. *Individual Differences Research, 4*, 299–305.

Kendall, L. (2000). "Oh no! I'm a Nerd!" Hegemonic masculinity on an online forum. *Gender and Society, 14*, 256–274.

Kennedy, K. (2005). A collaborative project to increase the participation of women and minorities in higher level mathematics courses. *Journal of Education for Business, 80*, 189–193.

Kimball, G. (2001, September 23). Football: Patriots day; The Jets: New Jets coach Herman Edwards has been thrust into a crisis situation. *The Boston Herald*, p. B23.

King, A. (1997). The lads: Masculinity and the new consumption of football. *Sociology, 31*, 329–346.

Kirkwood, W. G. (1983). Storytelling and self–confrontation: Parables as communication strategies. *Quarterly Journal of Speech, 69*, 58–74.

Kirkwood, W. G. (1992). Narrative and the rhetoric of possibility. *Communication Monographs, 59*, 34–39.

Klausner, S. Z. (1968). Empirical analysis of stress-seekers. In S. Z. Klausner (Ed.) *Why man takes chances.* Garden City, NY: Anchor Books, Doubleday.

Kruse, N. W. (1977). Motivational factors in non-denial *apologia. Central States Speech Journal, 28*, 13–23.

Kruse, N. W. (1981a). Apologia in team sport. *Quarterly Journal of Speech, 67*, 270–283.

Kruse, N. W. (1981b). The scope of apologetic discourse: Establishing generic parameters. *Southern Speech Communication Journal, 46*, 278–291.

Kwon, H., & Trail, G. (2001). Sport fan motivation: A comparison of American students and international students. *Sport Marketing Quarterly, 10*, 147–155.

Lalvani, S. (1994). Carrying the ideological ball: Text, discourse and pleasure. *Sociology of Sport Journal, 11*, 155–174.

Lange, R. (2001, September 24). Jets win comes from the heart; Giving game ball to city. *The Record*, p. S1.

Lanter, J. R. (November, 2000). *Sport spectator identification and involvement in a spontaneous sport victory celebration.* Paper presented at the meeting of the North American Society for the Sociology of Sport, Colorado Springs, CO.

Lanter, J. R., & Blackburn, J. Z. (October, 2004). *The championship effect on college*

students' identification and university affiliation. Paper presented at the meeting of
the Association for the Advancement of
Applied Sport Psychology, Minneapolis,
MN.

Layden, T. (2003, May 19). Caught in the
net: Everyone's a reporter in the world of
fan-driven, rumor-mongering college
websites, forcing coaches and players to
watch their every step. *Sports Illustrated*,
98(2), 46–47.

Leach, E. (1976). *Culture and communication*. Cambridge, England: Cambridge
University Press.

Leuba, C. (1955). Toward some integration
of learning theories: the concept of optimal stimulation. *Psychological Reports, 1*,
27–33.

Lee, R. E., & Barton, M. H. (2003). Clinton's rhetoric of contrition. In R. E. Den-
ton & R. Holloway (Eds.), *Images,
scandal and communication strategies of
the Clinton presidency* (pp. 219–246).
Westport, CT: Greenwood.

Lee, S. J. (1996). *Unraveling the "model
minority" stereotype: Listening to Asian
American youth*. New York: Teacher's
College Press.

Leonard, D. (2003). Yo, Yao!; What does the
"Ming Dynasty" tell us about race and
transnational diplomacy in the NBA?.
Color Lines, 6(2), 34–36.

Leonard, D. (2006). An untapped field:
Exploring the world of virtual sports
gaming. In A. A. Raney & J. Bryant (Eds.),
Handbook of sports media (pp. 393–407).
Mahwah, NJ: Lawrence Erlbaum.

Levy, M. R., & Windahl, S. (1984). Audience
activity and gratifications: A conceptual
clarification and exploration. *Communication Research, 11*, 51–78.

Lewis, T. (2005, December 31). Ticket or
leave it. *Times-Picayune*, p. 9.

Lickel, B., Hamilton, D. L., Wieczorkowski,
G., Lewis, A., Sherman, S. J., & Uhles, A.
N. (2000). Varieties of groups and the
perception of group entiativity. *Journal
of Personality and Social Psychology, 78*,
223–246.

Linder, J. (2006, September 9). World Wide
Gab. *The Baltimore Sun*, p. 2D.

Lindquist, D. C. (2006). "Locating" the
nation: Football game day and American
dreams in central Ohio. *Journal of American Folklore, 119*, 444–488.

Ling, D. A. (1970). A pentadic analysis of
Senator Edward Kennedy's address to the
people of Massachusetts, July 25, 1969.
Communication Studies, 31, 81–86.

Long, M. (2004, October 24). Web site part
of Zook's lasting legacy. *Associated Press
Online*. Retrieved September 1, 2007,
from Lexis Nexis News database.

Lord, L. (2001). The fastest-growing sport
loses its hero. *U.S. News & World Report,
130*(9), 52.

Luo, M. (2003, February 5). Rockets' Yao
Ming carries Asians in America to new
heights. *The Associated Press State and
Local Wire*. Retrieved February 23, 2003,
from Lexis Nexis database.

Lorenz, K. (1966). *On aggression*. New York:
Harcourt Brace.

Lull, J. (1980). The social uses of television.
Human Communication Research, 6, 197–
209.

Lulu and Junior. *Wikipedia: the free encyclopedia*. Retrieved November 1, 2006, from
<http://en.wikipedia.org/wiki/Lulu_and
_Junior>.

Lulu and Junior's world travels. Retrieved
November 1, 2006, from <http://home.
att.net/~luluandjunior/wsb/html/view.
cgi-home.html-.htm>.

MacCambridge, M. (2004). *America's game:
The epic story of how pro football captured
a nation*. New York: Random House.

MacGregor, J. (2005). *Sunday money: Speed!
Lust! Madness! Death! A hot lap around
America with NASCAR*. New York:
HarperCollins.

Machor, J. L., & Goldstein, P. (Eds.) (2001).
*Reception study: From literary theory to
cultural studies*. London: Routledge.

Mackie, D. M., & Smith, E. R. (1998). Intergroup relations: Insights from a theoretically integrative approach. *Psychological
Review, 105*, 499–529.

Madrigal, R. (1995). Cognitive and affective
determinants of fan satisfaction with
sporting event attendance. *Journal of
Leisure Research, 27*, 205–227.

Maguire, J (1991). Towards a sociological
theory of sport and the emotions: A fig-
urational perspective. *International Review for the Sociology of Sport, 26*, 25–
36.

Mahony, D. F., Madrigal, R., & Howard, D.
(2000). Using the psychological commitment to team (PCT) scale to segment

sport consumers based on loyalty. *Journal of Sport Marketing, 9*, 15–25.

Mahony, D. F., & Moorman, A. M. (2000). The relationship between the attitudes of professional sports fans and their intention to watch televised games. *Sport Marketing Quarterly, 9*(3), 131–139.

Maillet, S. (2006). An exploration of adolescents' perceptions of videogame realism. *Learning, Media and Technology, 4*, 377–394.

Malkin, M. J., & Rabinowitz, E. (1998). Sensation seeking and high-risk sensation. *Parks and Recreation, 33*, 34–40.

Mandel, S. (2007). *Bowls, polls, and tattered souls: Tackling the chaos and controversy that reign over college football.* Hoboken, NJ: John Wiley & Sons.

Mannix, K. (2001, September 23). Football: Patriots day: The Jets: The NFL; back to work. *The Boston Herald*, p. B19.

Manufacturing consent: Noam Chomsky and the media (1994) [Video]. Wintonick, P. (Director). [Available from Zeitgeist Video].

Margolis, J. (1999). *Violence in sports: Victory at what price?* Berkeley Heights, NJ: Enslow Publishers.

Markman, K. D., & Hirt, E. R. (2002). Social prediction and the "allegiance bias." *Social Cognition, 20*, 58–86.

Martin, W. (1986). *Recent theories of narrative.* Ithaca, NY: Cornell University Press.

Marx, K. (1990). *Capital: A critique of political economy.* New York: Penguin.

Maslow, A. (1943). A theory of human motivation. *Psychological Review, 50*, 370–396.

Mateas, M. (2004). A preliminary poetics for interactive drama and games. In N. Wardrip-Fruin & P. Harrigan (Eds.), *First person: New media as story, performance and game* (pp. 19–33). Cambridge, MA: The MIT Press.

Mayeda, D. T. (1999). From model minority to economic threat. *Journal of Sport and Social Issues, 23*, 203–217.

Mazzocco, P. J., Green, M. C., & Brock, T. C. (2007). The effects of a prior storybank on the processing of a related narrative. *Media Psychology, 10*, 64–90.

McCallum, J. (2003, February 17). Really big show. *Sports Illustrated*, pp. 58–62.

McCallum, J. (2003, February 10). Sky rocket. *Sports Illustrated*, pp. 34–39. Re-

trieved from October 1, 2003, from Lexis Nexis Academic Universe.

McCarthy, M. (2007, March 28). College kids caught in gambling madness: Basketball tournament increases interest in wagering. *USA Today*, p. 1C.

McDougall, W. (1918). *Social psychology.* New York: J. W. Luce & Co.

McGuire, J. (2002). Selective perception and its impact on the evaluation of radio play-by-play announcers. *Journal of Radio Studies, 9*, 51–64.

McKerrow, R. E. (1993). Visions of society in discourse and art: The failed rhetoric of social realism. *Communication Quarterly, 41*, 355–366.

McKinley, J. (2000, August 11). Sports psychology; It isn't just a game: Clues to Avid Rooting. *New York Times.*

McMahan, A. (2003). Immersion, engagement and presence: A method for analyzing 3-D video games. In M. J. P. Wolf & B. Perron (Eds.), *The video game theory reader* (pp. 67–86). New York: Routledge.

Melnick, M. J. (1993). Searching for sociability in the stands. A theory of sports spectating. *Journal of Sport Management, 7*, 44–60.

Melnick, M. J., & Wann, D. L. (2004). Sport fandom influences, interests, and behaviors among Norwegian university students. *International Sports Journal, 8*(1), 1–13.

Mendick, H. (2005). Mathematical stories: Why do more boys than girls choose to study mathematics at A-level in England? *British Journal of Sociology of Education, 26*, 235–251.

Messner, M. A., & Montez de Oca, J. (2005). The male consumer as loser: Beer and liquor ads in mega sports media events. *Signs, 30*, 1879–1909.

Metzger. M. J., & Flanagin, A. J. (2002). Audience orientations toward new media. *Communication Research Reports, 19*, 338–351.

Milne, G. R., & McDonald, M. A. (1999). *Sport marketing: Managing the exchange process.* Toronto: Jones and Bartlett Publishers, Inc.

Mochizuki, M. M. (2007). Japan's shifting strategy toward the rise of China. *Journal of Strategic Studies, 30*, 739–776.

Montgomery, G. (1996). Film realism: A

comment. *Historical Journal of Film, Radio & Television, 16*, 269–271.

Moreland, R. L. (1987). The formation of small groups. In C. Hendrick (Ed.), *Review of Personality and Social Psychology* (Vol. 8, pp. 80–110). Newbury Park, CA: Sage.

Morris, B. S., & Nydahl, J. (1983). Toward analyses of live television broadcasts. *Central States Speech Journal, 34*, 195–202.

Mumby, D. K. (1993). Introduction: Narrative and social control. In D. K. Mumbry (Ed.), *Narrative and social control: Critical perspectives* (pp. 1–12). Newbury Park, CA: Sage.

Murray, J. (2004). From game-story to cyberdrama. In N. Wardrip-Fruin & P. Harrigan (Eds.), *First person: New media as story, performance and game* (pp. 2–11). Cambridge, MA: The MIT Press.

Murrell, A. J. & Dietz, B. (1992). Fan support of sports teams: The effects of a common group identity. *Journal of Sport and Exercise Psychology, 14*, 28–39.

Nabi, R. L., & Krcmar, M. (2004). Conceptualizing media enjoyment as attitude: Implications for mass media effects research. *Communication Theory, 14*, 288–310.

Nauright, J. (1996). Writing and reading American football: Culture, identities and sports studies. *Sporting Traditions, 13*, 109–127.

Neary, R. S., & Zuckerman, M. (1976). Sensation seeking, train and state anxiety, and the electrodermal orienting response. *Psychophysiology, 13*, 205–211.

Neiswanger, R. (1999, June 29). In memory of his late friend, a Greg See Foundation founder is hoping he can help See find ... one last miracle. *The Independent Online Alligator*. Retrieved November 1, 2006, from <http://www.alligator.org>.

Nelson, J. (1984). The defense of Billie Jean King. *The Western Journal of Communication, 48*, 92–102.

Nichols, B. (1996). Image and reality: The real story. *Historical Journal of Film, Radio & Television, 16*, 267–268.

Nielsen Company (2007, August 30). Nielsen reports growth of 4.4% in Hispanic and 3.9% in Asian U.S. households for 2007–2008 television season [Electronic Version]. Retrieved September 1, 2007, from <http://www.nielsenmedia. com>.

Nielsen/Netratings (2001, March). March Madness slam dunks 167 percent more traffic to finalfour.net, according to Nielsen/Netratings. Retrieved September 17, 2007, from <http://www.nielsen-net ratings.com/pr/pr_010323.pdf>.

Nielsen/Netratings (2004, March). March Madness draws college hoop fans online, according to Nielsen/Netratings. Retrieved September 17, 2007, from <http://www. nielsen-netratings.com/pr/pr_040319_2. pdf>.

Nielsen/Netratings (2006, March). March Madness spurs nearly 10 million sports fans to jump online the first day of the NCAA tournament for news and live video, according to Nielsen/Netratings. Retrieved September 17, 2007, from <http://www.nielsen-netratings.com/pr/ pr_060321.pdf>.

Novak, M. (1976). *The joy of sports*. New York: Basic Books.

Nylund, D. (2004). When in Rome: Heterosexism, homophobia, and sports talk radio. *Journal of Sport & Social Issues, 28*, 136–168.

Oates, T., & Polumbaum, J. (2004). Agile big man: The flexible marketing of Yao Ming. *International Review of Asia and the Pacific, 77*, 187–210.

Oneofabillion (2004, April 4). Why is Yao so popular? *YaoMania!Forum Index: Yao's Impact on the Asian Community*. Retrieved September 12, 2006, from <www.yaoming mania.com/forum/viewtopic.php?t= 9&postdays=0&postorder=asc&start= 70>.

Oriard, M. (1981). Professional football as cultural myth. *Journal of American Culture, 4*(3), 27–41.

Oriard, M. (1991). *Sporting with the gods: The rhetoric of play and game in American culture*. Cambridge: Cambridge University Press.

Oriard, M. (1993). *Reading football: How the popular press created an American spectacle*. Chapel Hill, NC: University of North Carolina Press.

Ouwerkerk, J. W., Ellemers, N., & de Gilder, D. (1999). Group commitment and individual effort in experimental and organizational contexts. In N. Ellemers, R. Spears, & B. Doosje (Eds.), *Social iden-*

tity (pp. 184–204). Oxford, UK: Blackwell.

Papacharissi, Z., & Rubin, A. M. (2000). Predictors of Internet use. *Journal of Broadcasting & Electronic Media, 44*, 175–196.

Pease, D. G., & Zang, J. J. (2001). Sociomotivational factors affecting spectator attendance at professional basketball games. *International Journal of Sport Management, 2*, 31–59.

Pells, E. (2002, February 3). Super Bowl more than a game in post–Sept. 11 world. *The Associated Press Online.* Retrieved March 3, 2006, from <http://web.lexisnexis.com>.

Perse, E. M. (1990). Audience selectivity and involvement in the newer media environment. *Communication Research, 17*, 675–697.

Petrecca, L. (2005, August 25). Marketers tackle participants in fantasy football. *USA Today.* Retrieved October 7, 2005, from Factiva database.

Pigstar911 (2003, February 6). Why is Yao so popular? *YaoMania!Forum Index: Yao's Impact on the Asian Community.* Retrieved September 12, 2006 from <www.yaomingmania.com/forum/viewtopic.php?t=9>.

Platow, M. J., Durante, M., Williams, N., Garrett, M., Walshe, J., Cincotta, S., Lianos, G., & Barutchu, A. (1999). The contributions of sport fan social identity to the production of prosocial behavior. *Group Dynamics: Theory, Research, and Practice, 3*, 161–169.

Potter, W. J. (1986). Perceived reality and the cultivation hypothesis. *Journal of Broadcasting & Electronic Media, 30*, 159–174.

Potter, W. J. (1988). Perceived reality in television effects research. *Journal of Broadcasting & Electronic Media, 32*, 23–41.

Prentice, D. A., Miller, D. T., & Lightdale, J. R. (1994). Asymmetries in attachments to groups and to their members: Distinguishing between common-identity and common-bond groups. *Personality and Social Psychology Bulletin, 20*, 484–493.

Putnam, R. D. (2000). *Bowling alone: The collapse and revival of American community.* New York: Simon & Schuster.

Putnam, R. D., Feldstein, L. M., & Cohen, D. (2003). *Better together: Restoring the American community.* New York: Simon & Schuster.

Rainie, L. (2005, June). *One in twelve Internet users participates in sports fantasy leagues online.* Retrieved June 24, 2005, from <http://www.pewinternet.org/PPF/r/158/report_display.asp>.

Raney, A. A. (2006). Why we watch and enjoy mediated sports. In A. A. Raney & J. Bryant (Eds.), *Handbook of sports media* (pp. 313–329). Mahwah, NJ: Lawrence Erlbaum.

Raney, A. A., & Depalma, A. J. (2006). The effect of viewing varying levels and contexts of violent sports programming on enjoyment, mood, and perceived violence. *Mass Communication & Society, 9*, 321–338.

Real, M. R. (1975). Super bowl: Mythic spectacle. *Journal of Communication, 25*, 31–43.

RedDragon (2003, February 14). Why is Yao so popular? *YaoMania!Forum Index: Yao's Impact on the Asian Community.* Retrieved September 12, 2006, from <www.yaomingmania.com/forum/viewtopic.php?t=9>.

Reeves, B. (1978). Perceived television reality as a predictor of children's social behaviour. *Journalism Quarterly, 55*, 682–695.

Reuters Blog (2006, July 14). Retrieved August 8, 2007 from <http://in.rediff.com/cms/print.jsp?docpath=//sports/2006/jul/14zid.htm>.

Rheingold, H. (2000). *The virtual community: Homesteading on the electronic frontier* (revised ed.) Cambridge: The MIT Press. Retrieved September 1, 2007, from <http://www.rheingold.com/vc>.

Rhode Island businessman's bracelets inspire Patriot Andruzzi (2002, February 2). *The Associated Press Online.* Retrieved March 3, 2006, from <http://web.lexisnexis.com>.

Riessman, C. K. (1993). *Narrative analysis.* Newbury Park, CA: Sage.

Riffe, D., Lacy, S., & Fico, F. G. (1998). *Analyzing media messages: Using quantitative content analysis in research.* Mahwah, NJ: Lawrence Erlbaum.

Roberts, S. (2003, July 27). Sports of the times: A feeding frenzy on the Web shoves sanity right out the door. *New*

York Times, p. 9. Retrieved November 1, 2006, from Lexis Nexis News database.

Robinson, M. J., & Trail, G. T. (2005). Relationships among spectator gender, motives, points of attachment, and sport preference. *Journal of Sport Management, 19*(1), 58–80.

Robinson, T. (2003, July 1.) Suddenly, UVa.'s prez stands tall in Hokie Nation. *The (Norfolk) Virginian-Pilot,* p. C1. Retrieved November 1, 2006, from Lexis Nexis News database.

Rodriguez, A. (1996) Objectivity and ethnicity in the production of the *Noticiero Univision. Critical Studies in Mass Communication, 13,* 59–76.

Rondfeldt, D. (2000). Social science at 190 MPH on NASCAR's biggest speedways. *First Monday, 5*(2), 1–29.

Rubin, A. M. (1979). Television use by children and adolescents. *Human Communication Research, 5*(2), 109–120.

Rubin, A. M. (1981a). An examination of television viewing motivations. *Communication Research, 8,* 141–165.

Rubin, A. M. (1981b). A multivariate analysis of *60 Minutes* viewing motivations. *Journalism Quarterly, 58,* 529–534.

Rubin, A. M. (1983). Television uses and gratifications: The interactions of viewing patterns and motivations. *Journal of Broadcasting, 27,* 37–51.

Rubin, A. M. (1984). Ritualized and instrumental television viewing. *Journal of Communication, 34*(3), 67–78.

Rubin, A. M. (1986). Uses, gratifications, and media effects. In J. Bryant & D. Zillmann (Eds.), *Perspectives on media effects* (pp. 281–302). Hillsdale, NJ: Lawrence Erlbaum.

Rubin, A. M. (2002). The uses-and-gratifications perspective of media effects. In J. Bryant & D. Zillmann (Eds.), *Media effects: Advances in theory and research* (pp. 525–548). Mahwah, NJ: Lawrence Erlbaum.

Rubin, A. M. (2004). Personal involvement inventory. In R. B. Rubin, P. Palmgreen, & H. E. Sypher (Eds.), *Communication research measures: A sourcebook* (pp. 286–290). Mahwah, NJ: Lawrence Erlbaum.

Rubin, A. M., Haridakis, P. M., & Eyal, K. (2003). Viewer aggression and attraction to television talk shows. *Media Psychology, 5,* 331–362.

Rubin, A. M., & Perse, E. M. (1987a). Audience activity and soap opera involvement: A uses and effects investigation. *Human Communication Research, 14,* 246–268.

Rubin, A. M., & Perse, E. M. (1987b). Audience activity and television news gratifications. *Communication Research, 14,* 58–84.

Rubin, R. B., Perse, E. M., & Barbato, C. A. (1988). Conceptualization and measurement of interpersonal communication motives. *Human Communication Research, 14,* 602–628.

Russell, D. (1996). The UCLA Loneliness Scale (Version 3): Reliability, validity, and factor structure. *Journal of Personality Assessment, 66,* 20–40.

Ryan, H. R. (1982) Kategoria and apologia: On their rhetorical criticism as a speech set. *Quarterly Journal of Speech, 68,* 256–261.

Rybacki, K., & Rybacki, D. (1991). *Communication and criticism: Approaches and genres.* Belmont, CA: Wadsworth.

Sabo D., & Jansen, S. C. (2000). Prometheus unbound: Constructions of masculinity in the sports media. In L. A. Wenner (Ed.), *Mediasport* (pp. 221–232). London: Routledge.

Sager, I. (2006, October 27). The other online fantasy leagues. *Business Week Online.* Retrieved November 4, 2006, from Academic Search Premiere database.

Saints will return to Superdome on Sept. 24 (2006, February 6). *The Associated Press Online.* Retrieved March 3, 2006, from <http://web.lexis-nexis.com>.

Sandomir, R. (2006, July 11). *Cup ratings are up, but fans deserve better.* Retrieved December 6, 2006 from <http://www.nytimes.com/2006/07/11/sports/soccer/11sandomir.html?ex=1310270400&en=1ad955d799db99dd&ei=5088&partner=rss-nyt&emc=rss>.

Sandvoss, C. (2005). *Fans: The mirror of consumption.* Cambridge: Polity.

Saraceno, J. (2006, September 17). For stumbling Saints, this ain't '06 [Electronic version]. *USA Today,* p. C7.

Sargent, S. L. (2003). Enjoyment of televised sporting events: Evidence of a gender gap. *Communication Research Reports, 20*, 182–188.

Schiffrin, D. (2003). We know that's it: Retelling the turning point of a narrative. *Discourse Studies, 5*, 535–561.

Schrank, D. (2006, August 28). Blogging under the radar. *The Washington Post*, p.C01.

Schwarz, N., Strack, F., Kommer, D., & Wagner, D. (1987). Soccer, rooms, and the quality of your life: Mood effects on judgments of satisfaction with life in general and with specific domains. *European Journal of Social Psychology, 17*, 69–79.

Segrave, J. O. (2000). Sport as escape. *Journal of Sport & Social Issues, 24*, 61–77.

SFGate Blog (2006, July 12). Retrieved July 2, 2007 from <http://sfgate.com/cgi-bin/blogs/sfgate/detail?blogid=27&entry_id=7035>.

Shank, M. D., & Beasley, F. M. (1998). Fan or fanatic: Refining a measure of sports involvement. *Journal of Sport Behavior, 21*, 435–443.

Shapiro, L. (2002, Feb. 4). Red, white, and true; Final kick gives Patriots victory in all–American event. *The Washington Post*, p. A1.

Shepperd, J. A., Ouellette, J. A., & Fernandez, J. K. (1996). Abandoning unrealistic optimism: Performance estimates and the temporal proximity of self–relevant feedback. *Journal of Personality and Social Psychology, 70*, 844–855.

Shipman, F. M. (2001, April). *Blending the real and virtual: Activity and spectatorship in fantasy sports.* Paper presented at the Fourth Annual Digital Arts and Culture Conference, Providence, RI.

Sigman, S. J., Sullivan, S., & Wendell, M. (1988). Conversation: Data acquisition and analysis. In C. H. Tardy, (Ed.), *A handbook for the study of human communication: Methods and instruments for observing, measuring, and assessing communication processes* (pp. 163–192). Norwood, NJ: Ablex.

Simons, H. W. (2000). A dilemma-centered analysis of Clinton's August 17th *apologia*: Implications for rhetorical theory and method. *Quarterly Journal of Speech, 86*, 438–453.

Slater, J. (2002, Jan. 30). Super Bowl finds new focus after September 11 tragedy. *Agence France Presse.* Retrieved March 3, 2006, from <http://web.lexis-nexis.com>.

Slater, M. D. (2002). Entertainment-education and the persuasive impact of entertainment narratives. In T. Brock, J. J. Strange, & M. C. Green (Eds.), *Narrative impact: Social and cognitive foundations* (pp. 157–182). Hillsdale, NJ: Lawrence Erlbaum.

Slimpouch (2003, May 26). Why is Yao so popular? Page 3 of 9. *YaoMania!Forum Index: Yao's Impact on the Asian Community.* Retrieved September 12, 2006, from <http://www.yaomingmania.com/forum/viewtopic.php?p=8355&highlight=course#8355>.

Sloan, L. R. (1979a). Winning and losing: The effects of outcome on spectators. In Goldstein, J. H. (Ed.), *Sports, games and play* (pp. 219–262). Mahwah, NJ: Lawrence Erlbaum.

Sloan, L. R. (1979b). The function and impact of sports for fans: A review of theory and contemporary research. In J. H. Goldstein (Ed.), *Sports, games, and play: Social and psychological viewpoints* (pp. 219–262). Hillsdale, NJ: Lawrence Erlbaum.

Sloan, L. R. (1987). Achievement motivation: Its influences on fans' reactions to sport's outcomes and development of a sports need for achievement and power scale. *Sociedad Interamericana de Psicologia, 21*, Graficas Roche, Caracas.

Sloan, L. R. (1989). The motives of sports fans. In J. H. Goldstein (Ed.), *Sports, games, and play: Social and psychological viewpoints* (2d ed., pp. 175–240). Hillsdale, NJ: Lawrence Erlbaum.

Sloan, L. R., Cherry, A., & Holly, L. (1988). What do fans need from sports? Individual differences in responses to contest outcomes suggest multiple motives in sport's appeal. *International Congress of Psychology Proceedings*, 24. Sydney, AUS: Int'l Union of Psychological Sciences.

Sloan, L. R., Cherry, A., Holly, L. and Schwieger, P. K. (1982). *Sports' appeal and consequences for fans: Achievement needs and attributions for game outcomes.* Paper presented at the annual meeting of the Eastern Psychological Association.

Snyder, C. R., Lassegard, M., & Ford, C. E. (1986). Distancing after group success and failure: Basking in reflected glory and cutting off reflected failure. *Journal of Personality and Social Psychology, 51,* 382–388.

Sorlin, P. (1996). That most irritating question: Images and reality. *Historical Journal of Film, Radio & Television, 16,* 263–266.

Spence, J. T., & Helmreich, R. L. (1978). The Work and Family Orientation Questionnaire: An objective instrument to assess components of achievement motivation and attitudes toward family and career. *JSAS Catalog of Selected Documents in Psychology, 8,* 35 (Ms #1677).

Spencer, H. (1873). The principles of psychology. New York: Appleton. Cited in H. C. Lehman & P. A. Witty (1927), *The psychology of play activities.* New York: A. S. Barnes.

Sports Illustrated (2004). NASCAR Special Collector's Issue.

Spurrier closes practice. (2006, August 16). *The Orlando Sentinel,* p. C7.

Staples, A. (2004, October 24). Anti–Zook talk grows as struggles continue. *The Tampa Tribune,* p. 6. Retrieved November 1, 2006, from Lexis Nexis News database.

Steele, D. (2005, September 15). Big-game revenue doesn't add up to equality [Electronic version]. *The Baltimore Sun,* p. D1.

Stein, K. A. (2006, February). *Antapologia in the 2001 spy plane incident.* Paper presented at the annual meeting of the Western States Communication Association, Palm Springs, CA.

Stein, K. A. (2007, February). *Mel's Hell: Public discourse in response to Gibson's multiple attempts at absolution.* Paper presented at the Western States Communication Association Conference, Seattle, Washington.

Stein, K. A. (in press). *Apologia, antapologia* and the 1960 Soviet U-2 Incident. *Communication Studies.*

Stein, K. A., Larson, S., & Grady, L. A. (2007). *Antapologia arguments during the Hurricane Katrina disaster.* In F. H. Eemeren, J. A. Blair, C. A. Willard, and B. Garssen (Eds.), *The Proceedings of the Sixth Conference of the International Society for the Study of Argumentation* (pp. 1337–1344).

Stevenson, W. B., & Greenberg, D. N. (1998). The formal analysis of narratives

of organizational change. *Journal of Management, 24,* 741–762.

Strasen, M. (2001, December 12). Sports' fans group pitches playoff over BCS. *The Tampa Tribune,* p. Sports 2. Retrieved November 1, 2006, from Lexis Nexis News database.

Sullivan, D. B. (1991). Commentary and viewer perception of player hostility: Adding punch to televised sports. *Journal of Broadcasting & Electronic Media, 35,* 487–504.

Sullivan, D. B. (2006). Broadcast television and the game of packaging sports. In A. A. Raney & J. Bryant (Eds.), *Handbook of sports and media* (pp. 131–169). Mahwah, NJ: Lawrence Erlbaum.

Summary box: Super Bowl–Katrina (2006, February 5). *The Associated Press Online.* Retrieved March 3, 2006, from <http://web.lexis-nexis.com>.

Swamp Gas Forums. Gator Country Web site. Messages posted to <http//www.gatorcountry.com/swampgas>.

Swiss, T., & Chevrel, S. (2002). The narrative you anticipate you may produce. *Postmodern Culture, 12,* 136–153.

Szymanski, S., & Zimbalist, A. (2005). *National pastime: How Americans play baseball and the rest of the world plays soccer.* Washington, DC: Brookings Institution Press.

Tajfel, H. (1978). Social categorization, social identity, and social comparison. In H. Tajfel (Ed.), *Differentiation Between Social Groups: Studies in the Social Psychology of Intergroup Relations* (pp. 61–76). New York: Academic Press.

Tajfel, H., & Turner, J. (1979). An integrative theory of intergroup conflict. In W. G. Austin and S. Worchel (Eds.), *The social psychology of intergroup relations* (pp. 33–47). Monterey, CA: Brooks Cole.

Tajfel, H., & Turner, J. C. (1986). The social identity theory of intergroup behavior. In S. Worchel & W. Austin (Eds.), *Psychology of intergroup relations* (2nd ed., pp. 7–24). Chicago: Nelson-Hall.

Tedeschi, B. (2004, August 23). Advertisers discover the value of young men with time and money to spend on fantasy sports on the Web. *New York Times.* Retrieved September 29, 2005, from Lexis Nexis News database.

Thamel, P. (2004, November 25). Web sites stirring up criticism of coaches, even unbeaten ones. *New York Times*, p. D1. Retrieved November 1, 2006, from Lexis Nexis News database.

Thomas' status for LSU game still uncertain (2006, October 4). *The Tampa Tribune*, p. Sports 4. Retrieved November 1, 2006, from Lexis Nexis News database.

Thompsen, P. A. (1993, February). *A social influence model of flaming in computer-mediated communication.* Paper presented at the annual meeting of the Western States Communication Association, Albuquerque, NM. (ERIC Document Reproduction Service No. ED 355572).

Tomlinson, A., & Young, C. (2006). *German football, history, culture, society.* London: Routledge.

Tompkins, J. P. (Ed.) (1980). *Reader-response criticism: From formalism to post-structuralism.* Baltimore: John Hopkins University Press.

Trail, G., & James, J. (2001). The motivation scale for sport consumption: A comparison of psychometric properties with other sport motivation scales. *Journal of Sport Behavior, 24,* 108–127.

Trish, L., & Breen, L. (2007). Young people's perceptions and experiences of leaving high school early: An exploration. *Journal of Community and Applied Social Psychology, 17,* 329–346.

Tuan, M. (1998). *Forever foreigners or honorary whites? The Asian ethnic experience today.* New Brunswick, NJ: Rutgers University Press.

Tudor, A. (1992). Them and us: Story and stereotype in TV World Cup coverage. *European Journal of Communication, 7,* 391–413.

Tudor, A. (2006). World Cup worlds: Media coverage of the soccer World Cup 1974–2002. In A. A. Raney & J. Bryant (Eds.), *Handbook of sports and media* (pp. 217–230). Mahwah, NJ: Lawrence Erlbaum.

Turner, E. T. (1970). The effects of viewing college football, basketball and wrestling on the elicited aggressive responses of male spectators. *Medicine and Science in Sports, 2,* 100-105.

Tykocinski, O. E., Pick, D., & Kedmi, D. (2002). Retroactive pessimism: A different kind of hindsight bias. *European*

Journal of Social Psychology, 32, 577–588.

Univision broadcast of Mexico–USA game the most-watched sporting event in history of U.S. Spanish-language TV: 2002 FIFA World Cup (2002, June 18). *Business Wire, Incorporated* [Electronic Version]. Retrieved December 19, 2002, from <http://lw7fd.law7.hotmail.msn.com>.

Unsworth, G., Devilly, G. J., & Ward, T. (2007). The effect of playing violent video games on adolescents: Should parents be quaking in their boots? *Psychology, Crime & Law, 13,* 383–394.

Varvus, M. D. (2007). The politics of NASCAR dads: Branded media paternity. *Critical Studies in Media Communication, 24,* 245–261.

Vorderer, P., Klimmt, C., & Ritterfield, U. (2004). Enjoyment: At the heart of media entertainment. *Communication Theory, 14,* 388–408.

Waitzkin, H. (1993). Interpretive analysis of spoken discourse: Dealing with the limitations of quantitative and qualitative methods. *The Southern Communication Journal, 51,* 128–147.

Wander, P. (2005). The ideological turn in modern criticism. In C. R. Burgchardt (Ed.), *Readings in Rhetorical Criticism* (3rd ed.) (pp. 96–114). State College, PA: Strata Publishing.

Wann, D. L. (1993). Aggression among highly identified spectators as a function of their need to maintain a positive social identity. *Journal of Sport and Social Issues, 17,* 134–143.

Wann, D. L. (1994). The "noble" sports fan: The relationships between team identification, self-esteem, and aggression. *Perceptual & Motor Skills, 78,* 864–867.

Wann, D. L. (1995). Preliminary validation of the Sport Fan Motivational Scale. *Journal of Sport and Social Issues, 19,* 377–396.

Wann, D. L. (1997). *Sport psychology.* Upper Saddle River, NJ: Prentice Hall.

Wann, D. L. (2002). Preliminary validation of a measure for assessing identification as a sport fan: The Sport Fandom Questionnaire. *International Journal of Sport Management, 3,* 103–115.

Wann, D. L. (2004). Understanding the positive social psychological benefits of sport team identification: The team identification social psychological health model.

Group Dynamics, Theory, Research and Practice, 10, 272–296.

Wann, D. L. (2006a). Understanding the positive social psychological benefits of sport team identification: The team identification-social psychological health model. Group Dynamics: Theory, Research, and Practice, 10, 272–296.

Wann, D. L. (2006b). The causes and consequences of sport team identification. In A. A. Raney & J. Bryant, (Eds.), Handbook of sports and media. Mahwah, NJ: Lawrence Erlbaum.

Wann, D. L. (2006c). Examining the potential causal relationship between sport team identification and psychological well-being. Journal of Sport Behavior, 29, 79–95.

Wann, D. L., Allen, B., & Rochelle, A. R. (2004). Using sport fandom as an escape: Searching for relief from under-stimulation and over-stimulation. International Sports Journal, 8(1), 104–113.

Wann, D. L., & Branscombe, N. R. (1990a). Die-hard and fair-weather fans: Effects of identification on BIRGing and CORFing tendencies. Journal of Sport and Social Issues, 14, 103–117.

Wann, D. L., & Branscombe, N. R. (1990b). Person perception when aggressive or non-aggressive sports are primed. Aggressive Behavior, 16, 27–32.

Wann, D. L., & Branscombe, N. R. (1991). The positive social and self concept consequences of sports team identification. Journal of Sport & Social Issues, 15, 115–127.

Wann, D. L., & Branscombe, N. R. (1993). Sport fans: Measuring degree of identification with the team. International Journal of Sport Psychology, 24, 1–17.

Wann, D. L., & Branscombe, N. R. (1995). Influence of identification with a sports team on objective knowledge and subjective beliefs. International Journal of Sports Psychology, 26, 551–567.

Wann, D. L., Brewer, K. B., & Royalty, J. L. (1999). Sport fan motivation: Relationships with team identification and emotional reactions to sporting events. International Sports Journal, 3, 8–18.

Wann, D. L., Culver, Z., Akanda, R., Daglar, M., De Divitiis, C., & Smith, A. (2005). The effects of team identification and game outcome on willingness to consider anonymous acts of hostile aggression. Journal of Sport Behavior, 28, 282–294.

Wann, D. L., Dimmock, J. A., & Grove, J. R. (2003). Generalizing the team identification-psychological health model to a different sport and culture: The case of Australian Rules Football. Group Dynamics: Theory, Research, and Practice, 7, 289–296.

Wann, D. L., & Dolan, T. J. (1994). Attributions of highly identified sports spectators. The Journal of Social Psychology, 134, 783–792.

Wann, D. L., Dolan, T. J., McGeorge, K. K., & Allison, J. A. (1994). Relationships between spectator identification and spectators' perceptions of influence, spectators' emotions, and competition outcome. Journal of Sport and Exercise Psychology, 16, 347–364.

Wann, D. L., Fahl, C. L., Erdmann, J. B., & Littleton, J. D. (1999). Relationship between identification with the role of sport fan and trait aggression. Perceptual and Motor Skills, 88, 1296–1298.

Wann, D. L., Friedman, K., McHale, M., & Jaffe, A. (2003). The Norelco Sport Fanatics Survey: Examining behaviors of sport fans. Psychological Reports, 92, 930–936.

Wann, D. L., & Grieve, F. G. (2005). Biased evaluations of ingroup and outgroup spectator behavior at sporting events: The importance of team identification and threats to social identity. Journal of Social Psychology, 145, 531–545.

Wann, D. L., & Grieve, F. G. (in press). Use of proactive pessimism as a coping strategy for sport fans: The importance of team identification. Journal of Contemporary Athletics.

Wann, D. L., Grieve, F. G., & Martin, J. (2006). Use of retroactive pessimism as a method of coping with identity threat: The impact of group identification. Manuscript submitted for publication.

Wann, D. L., Hamlet, M. A., Wilson, T., & Hodges, J. A. (1995). Basking in reflected glory, cutting off reflected failure, and cutting off future failure: The importance of identification with a group. Social Behavior and Personality: An International Journal, 23, 377–388.

Wann, D. L., Haynes, G., McLean, B., & Pullen, P. (2003). Sport team identification and willingness to consider anonymous acts of hostile aggression. *Aggressive Behavior, 29*, 406–413.

Wann, D. L., Hunter, J. L., Ryan, J. A., & Wright, L. A. (2001). The relationship between team identification and willingness of sport fans to consider illegally assisting their team. *Social Behavior and Personality, 29*, 531–536.

Wann, D. L., Inman, S., Ensor, C. L., Gates, R. D., & Caldwell, D. S. (1999). Assessing the psychological well-being of sport fans using the Profile of Mood States: The importance of team identification. *International Sports Journal, 3*, 81–90.

Wann, D. L., Koch, K., Knoth, T., Fox, D., Aljubaily, H., & Lantz, C. D. (2006). The impact of team identification on biased predictions of player performance. *The Psychological Record, 56*, 55–66.

Wann, D. L., Melnick, M. M., Russell, G. W., & Pease, D. G. (2001). *Sport fans: The psychology and social impact of spectators*. New York: Routledge.

Wann, D. L., Metcalf, L. A., Adcock, M. L., Choi, C. C., Dallas, M. B., & Slaton, E. (1997). Language of sport fans: Sportugese revisited. *Perceptual and Motor Skills, 85*, 1107–1110.

Wann, D. L., Morris-Shirkey, P. A., Peters, E. J., & Suggs, W. L. (2002). Highly identified sport fans and their conflict between expression of sport knowledge and biased assessments of team performance. *International Sports Journal, 6*, 153–159.

Wann, D. L., Peterson, R. R., Cothran, C., & Dykes, M. (1999). Sport fan aggression and anonymity: The importance of team identification. *Social Behavior and Personality, 27*, 597–602.

Wann, D. L., & Pierce, S. (2003). Measuring sport team identification and commitment: An empirical comparison of the sport spectator identification scale and the psychological commitment to a team scale. *North American Journal of Psychology, 5*, 365–372.

Wann, D. L., & Pierce, S. (2005). The relationship between sport team identification and social well-being: Additional evidence supporting the team identification social psychological health model. *North American Journal of Psychology, 7*, 117–124.

Wann, D. L., & Robinson, T. N. (2002). The relationship between sport team identification and integration into and perceptions of a university. *International Sports Journal, 6*(1), 36–44.

Wann, D. L., Royalty, J., & Roberts, A. (2000). The self–presentation of sport fans: Investigating the importance of team identification and self–esteem. *Journal of Sport Behavior, 23*, 198–206.

Wann, D. L., Royalty, J. L., & Rochelle, A. R. (2002). Using motivation and team identification to predict sport fans' emotional responses to team performance. *Journal of Sport Behavior, 25*, 207–216.

Wann, D. L., & Schrader, M. P. (1997). Team identification and the enjoyment of winning a sporting event. *Perceptual and Motor Skills, 84*, 954.

Wann, D. L., & Schrader, M. P. (2000). Controllability and stability in the self–serving attributions of sport spectators. *Journal of Social Psychology, 140*, 160–168.

Wann, D. L., Schrader, M. P., & Adamson, D. R. (1998). The cognitive and somatic anxiety of sport spectators. *Journal of Social Psychology, 140*, 160–168.

Wann, D. L., Schrader, M. P., & Wilson, A. M. (1999). Sport fan motivation: Questionnaire validation, comparisons by sport, and relationship to athletic motivation. *Journal of Sport Behavior, 22*, 114–139.

Wann, D. L., Shelton, S., Smith, T., & Walker, R. (2002). Relationship between team identification and trait aggression: A replication. *Perceptual and Motor Skills, 94*, 595–598.

Wann, D. L., Tucker, K. B., & Schrader, M. P. (1996). An exploratory examination of the factors influencing the origination, continuation, and cessation of identification with sport teams. *Perceptual and Motor Skills, 82*, 995–1001.

Wann, D. L., & Waddill, P. J. (2003). Predicting sport fan motivation using anatomical sex and gender role orientation. *North American Journal of Psychology, 5*, 485–498.

Wann, D. L., & Waddill, P. J. (2007). Examining reactions to the Dale Earnhardt crash: The importance of identification with NASCAR drivers. *Journal of Sport Behavior, 30*, 94–109.

Wann, D. L., Walker, R. G., Cygan, J., Kawase, I., & Ryan, J. (2005). Further replication of the relationship between team identification and psychological well-being: Examining non-classroom settings. *North American Journal of Psychology, 7*, 361–366.

Wann, D. L., Zaichkowsky, L., & Mattigod, V. (2005, October). *Team identification and belief in team curses: The case of the Boston Red Sox and the curse of the Bambino.* Paper presented at the meeting of the Association for the Advancement of Applied Sport Psychology, Vancouver, BC, Canada.

Ward, A. (2006, Aug 23). Katrina rhetoric does little to calm growing storm among poor blacks. *Financial Times*, London edition, p. 7.

Ware, B. L., & Linkugel, W. A. (1973). They spoke in defense of themselves: On the generic criticism of *apologia. Quarterly Journal of Speech, 59*, 273–283.

Washington Post Blog (2006, July 12). Retrieved August 8, 2007, from <http://blog.washingtonpost.com/worldup/2006/07/zidane_news_conference.html>.

Watson, W. (Moderator). (August 1, 2005). Internet culture special [television series episode]. In P. Kennedy (Sports Director), *SportsTalk Live*. Orlando: Sun Sports Network.

Watson, W. (2005, August 4). Irony can be pretty ironic sometimes. *Sports Talk Live: Whit Watson Blog*. Retrieved November 1, 2006, from <http://whitwatson.sunsportstv.com/2005_08_01_archive.html>.

Weekends with the NASCAR family: Treating fans like kinfolk. (2005, April 15). *Life*, p. 15.

Weintraub, A. E., Roberts, D. F., & Nass, C. I. (1990). Influences of family communication on children's television interpretation processes. *Communication Research, 17*, 545–564.

Weiss, J. (2002, February 4). Patriots 20, Rams 17; Super Bowl XXXVI: The locals were vocal. *Boston Globe*, p. C18.

Wellard, I. (2002). Men, sport, body performance and the maintenance of "exclusive masculinity." *Leisure Studies, 21*, 235–247.

Wendel, T. (2004, September 20). How fantasy games have changed fans. *USA Today*. Retrieved October 8, 2005, from Factiva database.

Wenner, L. A. (1991). One part alcohol, one part sport, one part dirt, stir gently: Beer commercials and television sports. In L.R. Vande Berg & L. A. Wenner (Eds.), *Television Criticism: Approaches and Applications* (pp. 388–407). New York: Longman.

Wenner, L. A. (1994). The dream team, communicative dirt, and the marketing of synergy: USA basketball and cross-merchandising in television commercials. *Journal of Sport and Social Issues, 18*, 27–47.

Wenner, L. A. (1998). In search of the sports bar: Masculinity, alcohol, sports and the mediation of public space. In G. Rail (Ed.), *Sport and postmodern times* (pp. 301–332). Albany, NY: State University of New York Press.

Wenner, L. A. (2004). Recovering (from) Janet Jackson's breast: Ethics and the nexus of media, sports, and management. *Journal of Sport Management, 18*, 315–334.

Wenner, L. A. (2007). Towards a dirty theory of narrative ethics: Prolegomenon on media, sport and commodity value. *International Journal of Media and Cultural Politics, 3*, 111–129.

Wenner, L. A. (2008). Gendered sports dirt: Interrogating sex and the single beer commercial. In H. Hundley & A. Billings (Eds.), *Examining identity in sports media*. Thousand Oaks, CA: Sage.

Wenner, L. A., & Gantz, W. (1989). The audience experience with sports on television. In L. A. Wenner (Ed.), *Media, sports, & society* (pp. 241–269). Newbury Park, CA: Sage.

Wenner, L. A., & Gantz, W. (1998). Watching sports on television: Audience experience, gender, fanship, and marriage. In L. A. Wenner (Ed.), *Mediasport* (pp. 233–251). London: Routledge.

Wenner, L. A., & Gantz, W. (2000-Reprint). Watching sports on television: Audience experience, gender, fanship and marriage. In L. A. Wenner (Ed.), *Mediasport* (pp. 233–251). London: Routledge.

Whannel, G. (2000). Reading the sports media audience. In L. A. Wenner (Ed.), *Mediasport* (pp. 221–232). London: Routledge.

White, H. (1980). The value of narrativity in the representation of reality. *Critical Inquiry, 7*, 5–27.

Williams, D. (2003, October 5). Fantasy football scores big with fans. *The Commercial Appeal.* Retrieved September 29, 2005, from Factiva database.

Won, J., & Kitamura, K. (2007). Comparative analysis of sport consumer motivations between South Korea and Japan. *Sport Marketing Quarterly, 16,* 93–106.

Wong, P., Lai, C. F., Nagasawa, R., & Lin, T. (1998). Asian Americans as a model minority: Self perceptions and perceptions by other racial groups. *Sociological Perspectives, 41,* 95–118.

Woods, M. (2002, October 16). Giving Zook quick hook is cyber chic. *The Florida Times-Union,* p. E-1. Retrieved November 1, 2006, from Lexis Nexis News database.

Wu, F. H. (2002). *Yellow: Race in America beyond black and white.* New York: Basic Books.

Wundt, W. (1904). *Principles of physiological psychology.* Translated from the Fifth German Edition (1902) by Edward Bradford Titchener. London: Swan Sonnenschein.

Yao, M. (2006). To my fans. *Club Yao: The Official Fan Website.* Retrieved September 30, 2006, from <http://www.yaomingfanclub.com/>.

Zaichkowsky, J. L. (1985). Measuring the involvement construct. *Journal of Consumer Research, 12,* 341–352.

Zajonc, R. B. (1968). Attitudinal effects of mere exposure. *Journal of Personality and Social Psychology Monograph Supplement, 9,* 1-27.

Zhang, J. J., Pease, D. C., Lam, E. T. C., Bellerive, L. M., Pham, U. L., Williamson, D. P., Lee, J. T., & Wall, K. A. (2001). Sociomotivational factors affecting spectator attendance at minor league hockey games. *Sport Marketing Quarterly, 10,* 43–56.

Zillmann, D., & Bryant, J. (1994). Entertainment as media effect. In J. Bryant & D. Zillmann (Eds.), *Media effects: Advances in theory and research* (pp. 437–461). Hillsdale, NJ: Lawrence Erlbaum.

Zillman, D., Bryant, J., & Sapolsky, B. S. (1989). The enjoyment of watching sports contests. In J. G. Goldstein (Ed.), *Sports, games, and play: Social and psychological viewpoints* (2nd ed., pp. 241–278). Hillsdale, NJ: Lawrence Erlbaum.

Zuckerman, M. (1971). Dimensions of sensation seeking. *Journal of Consulting and Clinical Psychology, 36,* 45–52.

Zuckerman, M. (1979). *Sensation seeking: Beyond the optimal level of arousal.* Hillsdale: Lawrence Erlbaum.

Zuckerman, M. (1983). Sensation seeking and sports. *Personality and Individual Differences, 4,* 285–293.

Zuckerman, M. (1994). *Behavioral expressions and biosocial bases of sensation seeking.* New York: Press Syndicate of the University of Cambridge.

Zuckerman, M. (2000). Are you a risk taker? *Psychology Today, 33,* 52–58.

Zuckerman, M. (2007). The sensation seeking scale V (SSS-V): Still reliable and valid. *Personality and Individual Differences, 43,* 1303–1305.

Zuckerman, M., Albright, R. J., Marks, C. S., & Miller, G. L (1962). Stress and hallucinatory effects of perceptual isolation and confinement. *Psychological Monographs, 76,* 1–15.

Zuckerman, M., Kolin, E. A., Price, L., & Zoob, I. (1964). Development of a sensation-seeking scale. *Journal of Consulting Psychology, 28,* 477–482.

Zylinska, J. (2005). *The ethics of cultural studies.* London: Continuum.

About the Contributors

Greg G. Armfield (Ph.D., University of Missouri–Columbia) is an assistant professor in the Department of Communication Studies at New Mexico State University. Dr. Armfield specializes in the study of organizational culture and the intersection of cultural influences on mass media use. His past research has appeared in the *Journal of Communication*, the *Journal of Communication and Religion*, and the *Journal of Media and Religion*.

Andrew Baerg (Ph.D., University of Iowa) is an assistant professor of communications at the University of Houston–Victoria and teaches courses on mass communication and digital gaming. His primary research interests involve the study of digital games with specific focus on the ideologies resident in digital sports games. His most recent work focused on EA Sports' *Fight Night Round 2, Tiger Woods PGA Tour 2004, MVP Baseball 2005*, and *Madden Football 2005*.

Matthew H. Barton (Ph.D., University of Nebraska–Lincoln) is an assistant professor of communication at Southern Utah University. His research interests focus on the relationship between politics and religion, *apologia* rhetoric and popular culture. In addition to numerous conference presentations, he has published work exploring the Clinton–Lewinsky scandal/apology and the discourse surrounding 9/11 and the challenges to religious pluralism.

Kelly A. Berg (Ph.D., University of Missouri–Columbia) is an assistant professor of communication at St. John's University/College of St. Benedict. She has studied online fandom, exploring interpretive strategies of *The X-Files* fans in online message boards in her dissertation. She also had two chapters published in *Communication Theories for Everyday Life* (2004).

Amanda Breitenfeldt (B.A., Ripon College) currently works as the Client Services Coordinator in the marketing department of the Green Bay Packers, in Green Bay, WI.

Beth Dietz-Uhler (Ph.D., University of Pittsburgh) is a professor of psychology at Miami University. Her research interests include sport fan identification, gender differences in sport fans, and group identity. She has published in such journals as *European Social Psychology, Journal of Sport and Exercise Psychology*, and *Journal of Basic and Applied Social Psychology*.

Adam C. Earnheardt (Ph.D., Kent State University) is an assistant professor of communication studies at Youngstown State University. His research interests include sports media uses and effects, fandom, media ethics, new media technologies, and computer-mediated communication. In 2003, he earned the Duquesne University Graduate Student Fellow award for his work in photojournalistic ethics.

David Fingerhut (M.S., M.A., University of Illinois–Chicago) is a doctoral student in clinical psychology at the University of Illinois at Chicago. His masters degrees are in sport psychology and clinical psychology. His research interests include motivational strategies of health behaviors such as exercise maintenance.

Walter Gantz (Ph.D., Michigan State University) is professor and chair of the Department of Telecommunications at Indiana University. In addition to a long-standing interest in studying media and sports, he has conducted a number of massive content analyses related to public health.

Frederick G. Grieve (Ph.D., University of Memphis) is an associate professor of psychology, Coordinator of the Clinical Psychology Master's Program at Western Kentucky University, and a licensed psychologist in the Commonwealth of Kentucky. He completed pre–doctoral internships at the University of Mississippi Medical Center and Harriett Cohn Mental Health Clinic. He has been examining the behavior of sport fans since the late 1990s and has published five articles in the area and given over 10 presentations on sport fans. He has received the WKU Department of Psychology and the College of Education and Behavioral Sciences awards for Distinguished Service. He has also published in the areas of eating disorders and male body images.

Paul M. Haridakis (Ph.D., Kent State University) is an associate professor of communication studies at Kent State University. He conducts research in media uses and effects, sports media, law, public policy, new communication technologies, and media ethics. His recent work has focused on First Amendment issues related to the regulation of content in various media such as the Internet and television.

Allison Harthcock (Ph.D., University of Missouri–Columbia) is an assistant professor in the Department of Media Arts at Butler University. Her teaching and research interests focus on the cultural implications of mediated sports and inclusive pedagogy. Her research on media narratives has appeared in the *Journal of Popular Film and Television* and her research on attack messages has appeared in *Communication Monographs* and *Southern Communication Journal*.

Barbara Hugenberg (Ph.D., Bowling Green State University) is an assistant professor of communication studies at Kent State University. She is the co–author of a forthcoming article on NASCAR fans in the *Journal of Popular Culture* and has also co–authored articles on Bristol Motor Speedway in *The Encyclopedia of American Sports Icons* (Greenwood Press) and an organizational study of NASCAR in *Horsehide, Pigskin, Oval Tracks and Apple Pie: Essays on Sports and American Culture* (McFarland). Her dissertation was an ethnographic study of Cleveland Browns' fans upon the team's return to the National Football League.

Lawrence W. Hugenberg (Ph.D., Ohio State University) is a professor of communication studies at Kent State University. He is the co-author of a forthcoming article on NASCAR fans in the *Journal of Popular Culture* and has co–authored articles on Bristol Motor Speedway in *The Encyclopedia of American Sports Icons* (Greenwood Press) and an organizational study of NASCAR in *Horsehide, Pigskin, Oval Tracks and Apple Pie: Essays on Sports and American Culture* (McFarland). His research interests include sports fan identification and motivation, media studies, parasocial relationships in sports, and sports organizations. He is the initial and current editor of the *Journal of Communication Studies* (Marquette Books).

Jason R. Lanter is a Ph.D. candidate in social psychology at Miami University. His interests include the attitudes and behaviors of sport fans, gender roles in career and family, and the role of athletics in higher education.

Katherine L. Lavelle (Ph.D., Wayne State University) is the Director of Debate and visiting assistant professor of speech communication at Augustana College.

Hyangsun Lee (doctoral candidate, Indiana University) is currently pursuing the Ph.D. degree in telecommunications with a minor in law. Her research interests are in telecommunications law and policy in comparative and transnational contexts. Her research focuses on media ownership and copyright issues. Her dissertation considers the issue of government mandated adoption of technological content protection measures for digital broadcasts.

Steven E. Martin (Ph.D., Pennsylvania State University) is an assistant professor of communication at Ripon College. His research has appeared in *Communication Teacher* and the *Journal of the Wisconsin Communication Association*, and he is a winner of the Robert G. Gunderson award for Outstanding Debut Paper, Public Address Division, at the National Communication Association.

John P. McGuire (Ph.D., University of Missouri–Columbia) is an assistant professor in the School of Journalism and Broadcasting at Oklahoma State University, Stillwater, OK.

Michael Serazio (M.A., Columbia University) is a doctoral candidate at the University of Pennsylvania's Annenberg School of Communications. He worked as a staff writer at the *Houston Press*, where he was a finalist for the Livingston Awards. His scholarly research agenda focuses on popular and consumer culture, journalism, global studies, and religion and media.

Lloyd Reynolds Sloan (Ph.D., Ohio State University) is graduate professor of psychology and NIMH Research Training Program Director at Howard University. His interest in the attractions and impacts of sports for fans led to researching sports fans at the University of Notre Dame and subsequently at Howard University. His other research interests include the causes and consequences of stereotype threats' detrimental effects on stereotyped groups' performance (including sports), ostracism and social exclusion, social and personality impacts on health, political attitude change mechanisms, time orientation impacts on behavior and social judgments of justice across cultural groups.

John S. W. Spinda (M.A., Clarion University) is a Ph.D. candidate in the School of Communication Studies at Kent State University. His research interests include uses of media, computer-mediated communication, and sports communication. He serves on the executive boards of the National Communication Association Student Section and the Eastern Communication Association Political Communication Division.

Kevin A. Stein (Ph.D., University of Missouri–Columbia) is an assistant professor of communication at Southern Utah University. His research interests involve *kategoria* (attack), *apologia* (defense), and *antapologia* (response to *apologia*). He has co–authored a book on the 2004 campaign and published numerous articles on campaign messages and acclaiming/disclaiming discourse.

Paul D. Turman (Ph.D., University of Nebraska–Lincoln) is the Director of Academic Assessment for the South Dakota Board of Regents. His research interests focus on the instructional qualities of coach messages on young athletes, as well as the role of family interaction for encouraging sport participation. His research has been published in journals such as the *Journal of Applied Communication Research*, *Communication Education*, *Small Group Research*, *Journal of Family Communication*, and the *Journal of Sport Behavior*.

Debbie Van Camp (M.S., Howard University) is a doctoral student at Howard University. Her research interests include the influences on, and consequences of, social identities, including how this relates to sport fandom and to Stereotype Threat arousal. Other key interests are the development of group identity, in particular racial identity which is the focus of her dissertation, reasons for attending HBCUs (Historically Black Colleges and Universities), and African-Americans' attitudes towards homosexuals.

Daniel L. Wann (Ph.D., University of Kansas) is a professor of psychology at Murray State University, a member of the Executive Board of Directors for the National Alliance for Youth Sports, a member of the faculty for the Academy for Youth Sport Administrators, and a member of the Editorial and Advisory Board for the NCAA Scholarly Colloquium on College Sports. He has been studying the psychology of sport fans and spectators since the mid–1980s, with a particular interest in fan identification, spectator violence, and the actions of parents as spectators at youth sporting events. He has published two books: *Sport Psychology* (Prentice-Hall) and *Sport Fans: The Psychology and Social Impact of Spectators* (Routledge), and more than 100 referred journal articles, and has given several dozen conference presentations on the topic of sport fans and parental involvement in sport. He currently serves as director of the Sport Fandom Special Interest Group for the Association for Applied Sport Psychology.

Rebecca B. Watts (Ph.D., Texas A&M University) is assistant professor of communication studies at Stetson University. Her interest in the online Florida Gator Nation came through daily exposure to it through her husband, a University of Florida graduate. She is the author of *Contemporary Southern Identity: Community through Controversy* and is presently writing a rhetorical analysis of college football coaches who have made public statements opposing the Confederate flag.

Lawrence A. Wenner (Ph.D., University of Iowa) is the Von der Ahe Professor of Communication and Ethics in the College of Communication and Fine Arts and the School of Film and Television at Loyola Marymount University in Los Angeles. He is the former editor of the *Journal of Sport and Social Issues* and his books on sport and communication include *MediaSport* (Routledge) and *Media, Sports, and Society* (Sage).

His current book, with Steven Jackson, entitled *Sport, Beer, and Gender in Promotional Culture*, explores how mixing beer and masculinity are integral to contemporary commodified sport.

Brian Wilson is a doctoral student in the Department of Telecommunications at Indiana University, Bloomington. His interests include information processing of mediated content and political communication.

Index